SOUNDS OF REFORM

SOUNDS of REFORM

PROGRESSIVISM AND MUSIC IN CHICAGO, 1873–1935

DEREK VAILLANT

THE UNIVERSITY OF NORTH CAROLINA PRESS

CHAPEL HILL AND LONDON

© 2003 The University of North Carolina Press
All rights reserved
Manufactured in the United States of America

Designed by Kaelin Chappell
Set in Caslon 540
by Keystone Typesetting, Inc.

The paper in this book meets the guidelines for
permanence and durability of
the Committee on Production Guidelines for
Book Longevity of the Council on Library Resources.

Library of Congress Cataloging-in-Publication Data
Vaillant, Derek.
Sounds of reform : progressivism and music in Chicago,
1873–1935 / Derek Vaillant.
p. cm.
Includes bibliographical references (p.   ) and index.
ISBN 0-8078-2807-6 (cloth: alk. paper)
ISBN 0-8078-5481-6 (pbk.: alk. paper)
1. Music—Political aspects—Illinois—Chicago.
2. Progressivism (United States politics) 3. Chicago
(Ill.)—Politics and government—To 1950. I. Title.
ML3917.U6V35 2003
781.5′99′0977311—dc21
2003006859

CLOTH 07 06 05 04 03   5 4 3 2 1
PAPER 07 06 05 04 03   5 4 3 2 1

*For
my parents
and for
Sarah*

CONTENTS

.

MAPS AND ILLUSTRATIONS

ACKNOWLEDGMENTS

The book that you are holding reflects the contributions of many generous individuals and institutions. Mentors, colleagues, friends, and family members as well as the professional staffs of public and private archival repositories and libraries gave assistance in large and small ways to the production of this book. It is a pleasure to thank some of those who shone their beacons and illuminated the way.

The ideas and preliminary research for this book derived from my dissertation, which was written under the auspices of the University of Chicago's Social Science Division and the Department of History. One could not ask for a more inspiring setting in which to take flight as a historian. The spirit of challenge, the commitment, and the talents of my committee—George Chauncey, chair; Kathleen Neils Conzen; and Philip Bohlman—tremendously enriched the thesis. George Chauncey deserves particular recognition for believing in this project and for rendering his intellectual acuity and judgment. He sets a shining example as a scholar, mentor, and supportive friend. Kathy Conzen introduced me both to the fascinating intricacies of urban history and to Philip Bohlman of the University of Chicago's Department of Music. Phil graciously answered the call of a neophyte seeking guidance in the complexities of an outside field, and he became a major contributing force as the dissertation morphed into a book, serving as an engaged reader and selfless friend.

Like so many students of Chicago history, I have benefited hugely from the life's work of those who tend the nation's research collections. I am indebted to the archivists, librarians, and scholars who keep history so vibrantly alive. I especially wish to thank Archibald Motley and Linda Evans of the Chicago Historical Society, Julia

Bachrach of the Chicago Park District, Tab Lewis of the National Archives, Daniel Meyer and the staff of the University of Chicago's Regenstein Library Special Collections, Michael Henry at the Library of American Broadcasting, Pat Bakunas at the University of Illinois at Chicago, and the Interlibrary Loan Office at the Hatcher Library at the University of Michigan. Karl Longstreth provided invaluable assistance with the maps. For almost two years, I worked at Chicago's Newberry Library—an absolute jewel of an institution. I wish to thank James R. Grossman, Ann Keating, Jan Reiff, Carol Summerfield, Elliott Gorn, Karen Sawislak, Robin Bachin, and the many others who made that experience so rewarding.

I wish to thank colleagues who have read and commented on either all or part of the manuscript and helped to strengthen it through their suggestions. They include Frank Couvares and Kathryn Oberdeck (readers for the University of North Carolina Press), Susan J. Douglas, George Lipsitz, Burton Perretti, Regina Morantz-Sanchez, David Scobey, Susan Smulyan, Roy Rosenzweig, Robert W. Snyder, and the anonymous readers who reviewed a manuscript that I submitted to *American Quarterly*. Chapter 7 appeared in a substantive form previously as "Sounds of Whiteness: Local Radio, Racial Formation, and Public Culture in Chicago, 1921–1935" in *American Quarterly* 54, no. 1 (2002). I wish to thank Lucy Maddox and the journal for permission to reprint the work.

At different stages various endowed and unendowed sources supported my research and writing, including the University of Chicago's Social Science Research Fund, the Mellon Predissertation and Dissertation-Year Fund, and the Annette K. Baxter Grant of the American Studies Association. At the University of Michigan, Ann Arbor, financial and logistical support came from the Howard C. Marsh Fund of the Department of Communication Studies, the Faculty Assistance Fund, the Office of the Vice President for Research, and the College of Literature, Science, and the Arts.

My friends and colleagues in communication studies at the University of Michigan have been wonderfully supportive. Thanks go especially to the indefatigable Susan J. Douglas and to intrepid Chairman Michael Traugott. I also want to thank Rowell Huesmann, Richard Allen, Russ Neuman, Kristen Harrison, Nick Valentino, Tony Collings, Travis Dixon, Catherine Squires, Nojin Kwak, and Michael Yan. Research assistants Shawan Wade, Daniel Krauth, and Emily Chivers Yochim offered invaluable help in the final stages of the book.

My deep appreciation also goes to my wonderful editor at UNC Press, Sian Hunter, and her colleague David Hines. Sian's tact, professionalism, and humor helped make this book better.

Special *abrazos* go to colleagues and friends who have encouraged and inspired me along the way, including Laurie Green, Jonathan and Susan Keyes, Anne Wolverton, Geoff Klingsporn, Gabi Arredondo, Russell Lewis, Mary Jane Jacob, T. R. Durham, Penny von Eschen, Kevin Gaines, Sara Blair, and Jonathan Freedman. Pratt Bennet, Mark and Anna Perlberg, Rachel Richardson and David Lyons, Dolly Setton, Sophie Grillet and Bipin Patel, Liz Anderson and Dave Jacobi, and Andrea Kambara helped keep the big picture in view. Bill Abelson poured on the milk of wonder in the form of musical infusions from Seattle. Karen Lange and Stuart Gagnon unfailingly brightened my frequent research visits to Washington, D.C.

In rough waters as well as in calmer seas, my family offered invaluable support. I am grateful to my parents, Janet and Henry Vaillant, for their sacrifices and for the passion for learning that they embody. My affection and thanks also go to Marian and Andy Wrobel; Eliza Vaillant; Joanna V. Settle; Norman, Julia, Peter, and Matthew Kennedy; and Margaret Schumann. Devin, Ty, and Jane Vaillant bring music to their father's ears every day. Finally, for singing "beyond the genius of the sea," for her love, counsel, patience, and editorial eye, and for bearing too many burdens, I acknowledge, but can never adequately thank, Sarah Hering Kennedy.

INTRODUCTION

LISTENING TO MUSICAL PROGRESSIVISM

In Chicago in 1905 Jane Addams and Eleanor Smith, head of the Hull House Music School, collaborated on a song celebrating the work of the Near West Side social settlement. "A House Stands on a Busy Street" listed the activities available to the immigrant and ethnic laborers and families who visited Hull House. One verse described the special role of music at the settlement:

> Some hours they sit 'neath music's spell,
> and when the air is rife
> With all the magic of sweet sound,
> It heals the pang of life.
> Some hours they dream of civic pride
> Of cities that shall be,
> Within whose streets each citizen,
> Shall live life worthily.[1]

The words written by Addams traced a reform arc connecting "music's spell" and "the magic of sweet sound" to a "dream of civic pride / Of cities that shall be." Equating exposure to music with renewal and civic transformation, the verse expressed the ambitious design of music outreach at Hull House. The dream of harmony transcended the use of music for education or entertainment. It aspired to musically bind the diverse urban population together in hopes of creating a city in which each citizen could "live life worthily." Musical outreach efforts at Hull House marked part of an unheralded, but highly influential reform movement that transformed the cultural politics of music.

Addams's and Smith's efforts to produce sounds of reform illustrate a campaign of musical activism between approximately 1873 and 1935 that I call musical progressivism. The term describes a range of efforts by activists to claim secular music as a reform tool.[2] Musical progressives aspired to promote social and cultural linkages and "American" ideals in order to invigorate public culture and promote civic engagement. Musical progressives focused their energies on public space as a propitious realm of democratic encounter, particularly among ethnic and immigrant laborers. They instituted public programs and musical activities that blended aesthetic idealism with pragmatic awareness of the power and cultural authority inhering in the music of Chicago's industrial neighborhoods.[3] The resulting dynamic of partnership as well as struggle between reformers and musical publics elevated the status of music as a democratizing force in American society. By claiming that music did more than ennoble or entertain, that it improved civic engagement, and (equally important) by acting on their beliefs on a massive scale, musical progressives changed the meaning of music in everyday life.

The ideals and activities of musical progressives attracted my attention because they do not fit neatly within the "reform" tradition most familiar to nineteenth-century historians. Discussions of music and social reform commonly invoke the so-called cultured generation of postbellum romantics and professional music critics.[4] These activists championed European classical music as the perfect accompaniment to American democratic progress. From the pages of major urban newspapers, music journals, and periodicals, including the *Atlantic*, the *Century*, *Harper's Weekly*, and *Scribner's*, they extolled the moral and social benefits awaiting Americans who refined their tastes and embraced cultivated music. Thrilled at the prospect of sowing Euroclassical ideals in the United States, the cultured generation paid little heed to the folk/vernacular or popular commercial musics of North America. They downplayed, denigrated, or simply ignored the civic benefits that these forms might confer on a multiethnic nation. The cultured generation helped to "sacralize" cultivated concert music in the United States while strengthening the Eurocentric flavor that permeated America's leading musical institutions. It took many decades for indigenous and vernacular American musics from native American song to folk music to blues to effectively counter the "reform" assumptions that marginalized them and to receive scholarly recognition as critical embodiments of America's democratic culture.[5]

Musical progressivism represented a movement whose outlook and tactics were discernibly different from those of the cultured generation. Nor is it correct to label them sacralizers. While many of its adherents, both male and female, came from bourgeois backgrounds and appreciated European classical music's role in promoting social refinement and uplift, musical progressives were neither library-bound aesthetes nor dogmatic standard-bearers of cultivated music. Their democratic social preoccupations and urban orientation set them apart from their peers. Their ranks included social workers, politicians, minor municipal officials, and philanthropically minded citizens, the majority of whom lacked formal musical training. They shared a desire to expand public services and to tap into the musical energy flowing through the industrial neighborhoods of Chicago. Their desire to implement change required that they venture out into the public city to connect with the immigrant, ethnic, and laboring population.

Musical progressives displayed a distinctive aesthetic pragmatism and social perspective that distinguished them from the cultured generation and the influential generation of male and female patrons and amateur musical societies who collectively supported the development of a cultivated musical infrastructure in the United States.[6] Some musical progressives equated music reform with a stern regimen of Euroclassical forms and styles, but the vast majority did not. Instead, musical progressives engaged the social power of music inherent in the everyday lives of Chicago's industrial population. They believed that civic engagement came in many musical flavors. Beethoven performed by a professional orchestra, an immigrant student chorus singing European folk songs, or a military brass band punching out a popular standard on a Sunday afternoon all offered exciting opportunities to bind the urban population more tightly together. Activists therefore promoted an eclectic range of music at free

popular concerts in parks and settlement houses. They urged poor
urban residents to enroll in subsidized music lessons at park field
houses, to join settlement music clubs, and to attend municipal
dances and community sings in the name of metropolitan unity.

This book interrelates the shifting status of music in urban life
with the extraordinary social and cultural processes transforming
America during the Progressive Era. It seeks to correct a problematic
disjuncture between the extensive literatures of American music history and the cultural history of progressivism. The disjuncture compromises our historical understanding of how cultural practices and
political tendencies form and reform one another. I argue that music
served as a medium for the tendencies of the Progressive Era; these
tendencies in turn redefined the centrality of music in expressing
individual, group, and civic aspirations. From this perspective, the
history of musical progressivism engages broader arguments about
nineteenth- and early-twentieth-century musical performance and
social power, popular culture and democratic expression, and processes of communication, identity formation, and acculturation. To
demonstrate these connections, I use case studies of music in public
to track civic outreach and reform efforts at major nineteenth-century
music festivals, in large and small urban parks, at the Hull House
settlement, at community sings on the municipal pier, in the city's
commercial and municipal dance halls, and even, by the 1920s and
early 1930s, on the city's radio waves.[7]

The book's historical framework draws on the extensive secondary literature on urban reform in the United States. It follows the
theoretical trend that views terms such as "progressive" and "progressivism" as vexed yet indispensable markers for a complex set of
ideals and actions whose intended and unintended consequences
affected the lives of all Americans and the structure of democratic
society.[8] The book also stresses the improvisational character of progressivism, especially in matters of cultural outreach. It studies the
words and actions of activists and the clients of reform in dynamic
relationship with the history of music in everyday life and with the
changing urban social and cultural character of Chicago.[9]

Given the attention devoted to culture by historians of progressivism, it is odd to find music so overlooked. One finds occasional
mention of progressive music reformers, usually the activists at Hull
House. But these actors and programs and the significance of their
activities are most often buried in accounts of the minutiae of social
work and cultural uplift. Though it raises distinctive aesthetic and

social questions, music education and performance as a meaningful category of analysis is lumped together with book clubs, art history lectures, and ceramics classes as yet another example of settlement cultural programs. The disregard for music in the history of progressivism is particularly regrettable in light of what Daniel Rodgers has written: "That the core values of a society should be written in its street designs and public buildings, its shelters and its cityscapes, was a conviction deep in progressive culture on both sides of the Atlantic."[10] Until now, the music shaping the progressive reform landscape and the battles waged for its control among different constituencies have not received systematic attention.[11]

This book forges a connection between musical progressivism and discourses of democratic freedom and self-fulfillment linked to the rise of urban commercial music forms. Studies of commercial American music in this period implicitly or explicitly credit the inherent genius of musicians and musical forms (ragtime, blues, jazz), audiences, and/or the marketplace with connecting self- and group realization and consumer desire in ways that enlarged the expressive possibilities of democratic life. By embracing commercial popular culture, the argument goes, different segments of the population weakened patriarchal and elite claims to culture as a form of bourgeois cultivation. Despite its exploitative aspects, commercial amusement culture proffered a model of self-fulfillment that consumers tailored to suit a variety of needs, including democratic satisfactions and empowerment of a kind for consumer publics.[12]

This book argues that musical progressivism helped fuse popular musical appetites and democratic rights. The resulting connection proved central to twentieth-century debates over consumerism, social change, and struggles to define the parameters of civic life. Musical progressivism did not alone effect the convergence of these complex ideas and processes, but it sparked a sustained and influential new public discussion about music, multicultural populations, reform, and civic engagement. Part of the influence of musical progressivism came from its engagement with efforts of immigrant, ethnic, migrant, and laboring populations to produce a cultural politics of civics on their own terms. Rather than casting musical progressives as obstructionists to the rise of commercial musical culture and its links to expressive freedom and Americanism, it is better to see these activists as innovative forerunners of the consumerist ideology of musical expression as a democratic civic act.

It is not surprising that music attracted reform interest in the late nineteenth century. Tied to culture, history, and self- and group expression, music represented an indispensable resource for urban adaptation. Musical publics had long coalesced in order to shape social and cultural space, constitute individual and group identity, and declare their values and civic aspirations in visible and audible ways. Reformers also noted that music influenced (not always positively in their view) the tenor of recreation in public space, and they discerned the ways in which urban residents used it to help negotiate the parameters of individual, group, and "American" identity.[13]

Reformers intuited that music linked populations in a web of relationships constituting what Thomas Bender once identified as "public culture."[14] Music represented an example of the contested "cultural and categorical dimensions of power" operating outside the traditional frame of electoral politics, but which nevertheless expressed civic concerns. In other words, music in public generated democratic debates at the point of performance and audience reception. One can also think of the struggle over control of the discourse and application of musical progressivism by considering Nancy Fraser's model of "counter publics" vying for authority within the constraints of the bourgeois public sphere imagined by Jürgen Habermas.[15]

Because they wished to transform everyday music into a domain of civic reform, musical progressives conferred a new level of attention to the myriad sounds of industrial neighborhoods. While some musical progressives regarded the city as a tabula rasa on which to affix a reform apparatus, the more astute, and often more successful, reformers developed their methods by paying careful attention to the ritualized aspects of neighborhood music. Activists often borrowed from local immigrant, ethnic, and plebeian music practices, taking ideas and retooling them into what they hoped would be appealing instruments of citywide reform. Channels of negotiation opened as a result, ones that complemented the work of reform as a democratic enterprise.[16]

But the idealistic sheen of musical progressivism could not mask the cultural biases and blind spots of its white, bourgeois practitioners. The technique of "borrowing" from local practices also led to instances of containment of popular forms of expression. Reform versions of neighborhood musical activity competed with or sought to quell musical recreation that ran counter to reform ideas of what made good musical citizens. Activists moved swiftly to single out specific musical forms, such as ragtime and jazz, and their audiences for censure if they challenged conventional expectations of self-control, women's place, sexual mores, and youth behavior, or if they appeared to encourage interracial social mixing. By impinging on vital subcultures, reformers risked destroying the very examples of alternative democratic sounds that they purported to value. And, like many of their contemporaries, musical progressives believed racial segregation to be a necessary practice. At various moments activists consciously excluded minority groups from full participation in re-form activities. But despite its flaws and missteps, musical progressiv-ism broadly expanded public musical services, especially for the poor. It pushed the concept of music as a civic good to a new plateau and created tangible institutions to bolster musical education and the democratic public culture of the city.

Like the broader movement for which it is named, musical pro-gressivism emerged amid the national concerns of post–Civil War American society.[17] Progressive activists feared that rugged individ-ualism had run amok in the unregulated economic climate of "Gilded Age" America. They expressed concern over the effects of exploit-ative corporate consolidation and mass industrial production. Pre-senting modern society not as a field of isolated individuals, but as a web of interconnected lives and human needs, reformers challenged the power of business trusts, critiqued corrupt bossism in city politics, and demanded that municipal service standards be raised. Progres-sivism stimulated remarkable changes in the urban municipal in-frastructure from social services, health care, and legal protections to recreational outreach and scientific regimens.

Because it self-consciously promoted the domesticating ideals of music associated with listening and performing in the private sphere of the home as a public good, musical progressivism engaged chang-ing gender roles pertaining to women's presence in urban public space.[18] In the decades following the Civil War, shifts in industrial production and accelerated population migration from country to city drew young female wage earners into the city and challenged gender and sexual roles.[19] Urbanization and commercial growth prompted the development of public and semiprivate establishments where women were welcome, such as department stores, libraries, pleasure gardens, theaters, skating rinks, and restaurants.[20] These institutions catered to women as consumers, first, and as ladies, second. A hetero-social commercial nightlife culture also sprang up, drawing young men and women to cabarets and dance halls. The revolution in market-based leisure and recreation sparked a moral "crisis" surrounding commercial culture that drove reform activity at the turn of the century.[21] Amid these many changes, musical outreach sought to include women in public events while striving to constitute a facade of respectability so important to progressive activists.

Chicago offers an excellent site in which to examine the rise of musical progressivism in conjunction with the history of urbanism and American music. The industrial giant's development into the nation's production and distribution entrepôt and a hub for east- and westbound commercial rail traffic shaped the social and cultural character of the city and the politics of civic music that emerged in the late nineteenth century. By 1890, Chicago had grown to well over a million residents, and a remarkable 78 percent of the population claimed "foreign stock," meaning having at least one parent born outside the United States.[22] For thousands of newcomers, music celebrated key facets of individual and group identity. Residents brought traditions of cultivated and vernacular music with them. Transplanted uses of old forms as well as new forms and contexts for producing and evaluating musical expression helped urban residents orient themselves in their new surroundings and structured the civic texture of music in everyday life.

This book interweaves several bodies of scholarship that contextualize neighborhood and metropolitan musical practices in different ways. Historical musicologists have supplied essential background on America's emergence as a musical nation by tracing the development of a cultivated musical canon, the rise of formal institutions, including symphonies, and the emergence of specific genres and types of music.[23] Others have charted the history of a specific genre or musical form, such as blues, ragtime, Tin Pan Alley, or jazz.[24] Ethnomusicology emphasizes the importance of the ritual function of everyday musical forms, including the effects that space and geography have on musical meaning. In addition, this book considers audience reception issues by comparing and contrasting specific performance venues and local dynamics to recover the ways that reform impacted the multilayered musical lives of ordinary citizens.[25]

Finally, this book builds on the framework that historians and cultural studies investigators have developed to address music's power to structure group and individual identity. Such studies are especially useful for what they reveal about the processes that create a sense of boundedness within a musical public and about how sub-cultures form in relationship to a single genre of music.[26] Musical progressives often espoused an idealized view of an American musical nation that groups within the metropolis often contested. Struggle over cultural power is central to the focus of this book relative to the impact of music reform in a multiethnic and multicultural nation.

Because this book emphasizes musical progressivism as a dynamic movement in which power shifted between reformers and ordinary folk, it often mines "official" sources for "unofficial" insights into the responses to musical progressivism. The research incorporates archival and manuscript materials collected from federal, state, local, and private collections. It draws on records of local civic groups and municipal bodies and officials, such as the Chicago Parks Commissions and the Civic Music Association; private social agencies; archives of musical institutions and schools; papers and publications of local and national music critics and teachers; contemporary newspaper accounts, periodicals, musical trade journals, and popular fiction; oral and written testimonies of band leaders and musicians; and unpublished documents and papers of independent and network radio stations, listeners, and federal regulators. It also draws on the trove of material gathered by investigators of the "Chicago School" of sociology, including Robert Park, Ernest W. Burgess, Paul Cressey, and numerous graduate student investigators. Finally, this study would not exist were it not for the extraordinary array of excellent secondary historical sources that provide invaluable insights into the everyday lives of residents in Chicago's industrial neighborhoods.

ONE

PRELUDES OF REFORM
THE CHICAGO JUBILEE,
THOMAS "SUMMER NIGHTS" CONCERTS,
AND THE 1893 WORLD'S COLUMBIAN EXPOSITION

During the first week of June 1873, tens of thousands of residents, out-of-town visitors, and dignitaries jammed the two-block-long Michigan Southern and Rock Island Railway depot to attend the largest music festival in Chicago history. The Chicago Jubilee celebrated the resurgence of a city reduced to rubble following the Great Fire of October 8–9, 1871.[1] The blaze had devastated the central business district, causing almost three hundred deaths, destroying a staggering 18,000 buildings, and leaving one-third of the stricken metropolitan population temporarily homeless. In eighteen remarkable months, however, a mammoth effort of laborers and tradesmen, builders and manufacturers, and politicians and investors had transformed a burnt shell into a city more vibrant than its predecessor.[2] Residents thus had good reason to cheer the "Great Rebuilding" and to reflect on a shared civic accomplishment, while looking optimistically toward the future. Jubilee organizers selected Patrick Sarsfield Gilmore, the most popular bandleader in the country and famous for his "monster concerts," to present three musical spectaculars to accompany the festivities celebrating the "New Chicago."[3]

The Jubilee is a virtually forgotten event in Chicago history, but a significant beginning point from which to chart the development of the nineteenth-century civic reform ideals that culminated in musical progressivism. Though not a musical milestone in a formal sense, the Jubilee showcased music's power to communicate the civic aspirations of the rebuilt city and its population. The festival called on residents to gather as a musical body and to play a participatory role in defining metropolitan and national purpose.

Buried within the campaign touting the "New Chicago," a conflict simmered over the role of music at the Jubilee. The controversy revealed an important struggle waged at various levels of postbellum society to control outlets of democratic expression and public culture. The dispute pitted the Jubilee's Committee of Arrangements, dominated by the local business and political elite, against George Upton, music critic and editor for the *Chicago Tribune* and president of the Apollo Club, a prestigious men's choral society.[4] Each side represented a distinct position concerning music's place in democratic society. The committee embraced Gilmore's popular aesthetic and his proven record at appealing to the masses. Upton, the aesthete and voice of the cultured generation in Chicago, challenged organizers to exercise their civic duty by assembling a high-quality European classical music festival that would confirm the civilized greatness of the city and its people. More than a difference of musical taste, the split over musical arrangements exposed deep social anxieties as the swiftly growing city confronted its social and cultural heterogeneity and the need for a civic discourse capable of unifying the population as a whole.

Beginning with the Jubilee, this chapter explores three major nineteenth-century musical festivals that exemplified civic reform tendencies in Chicago. Taken together the festivals serve as instructive preludes to the musical progressive project that arose in the late nineteenth century. While very different in scope and organization, the Jubilee, Theodore Thomas's "summer nights" concerts of the late 1870s and 1880s, and the music of the 1893 World's Columbian Exposition provoked a set of questions about urban identity, popular tastes and traditions, and the musical possibilities of creating a common bond among the diverse urban population. Each festival in its own way produced a civic model from musical material that revealed struggles among various publics angling to claim music's putative reforming properties and to control democratic public expression. This chapter also introduces the reader to some of the music makers of Chicago's immigrant, ethnic, and industrial neighborhoods, whose habits, local institutions, and outlooks on music in the public arena discernibly impacted the tenor of major Chicago music festivals and exerted a sizable impact on later experiments in musical progressivism.[5]

NOTES FROM THE EMBERS
The Ghosts of Unheard Concerts Past

Long after the flames were extinguished, and the city of Chicago rebuilt, George Upton remained haunted by the casualties of the Great Fire. "I remember that the announcements of the season which was to be and never was, included among other numbers, Schubert's Quartet in D Minor, Schumann's First and Fourth symphonies, Beethoven's Third ('Eroica') and Fifth, and concertos by Rubinstein, Mendelssohn, Beethoven, Litolff, Weber, Chopin and Liszt," Upton wrote in his memoirs.[6] On the evening that the terrible blaze erupted, New York conductor Theodore Thomas and his celebrated symphony orchestra were scheduled to perform at the gala unveiling of the renovated Crosby Opera House, one of Chicago's finest concert halls. That afternoon, Upton and other bystanders watched helplessly as flames devoured the building before Thomas and his orchestra could play a single note.[7] Though benefactors soon rebuilt the opera house and Thomas resumed his occasional visits to Chicago, the irretrievable "loss" of such performances lingered in Upton's mind. The Great Fire and the rebuilding heightened Upton's wish for a serious classical music festival in Chicago, preferably one in which Thomas would triumphantly vanquish the ghosts of unheard concerts past and demonstrate the city's refined civic sensibilities.[8]

Upton's preoccupation with the losses of the Great Fire reflected the fact that Chicago devotees of classical music endured long waits between visits from outstanding symphony orchestras such as Thomas's. On the eve of the Jubilee, residents who wished to hear technically accomplished symphonic music or opera had limited options beyond the sporadic visits of outside touring groups from eastern cities or from abroad.[9] Despite its booming agriculture, industrial, and market economy, Chicago had an unimpressive cultural infrastructure (no permanent symphony or major opera company). This fact placed it on a lower tier relative to the metropolitan centers of the

East Coast, such as Boston or New York.[10] The 1873 Jubilee offered a unique opportunity for the midwestern city to do more than show off the McCormick Reaper Works, the Union Stockyards, the Hyde Park Hotel, and the new Calumet Harbor. A high-quality musical festival could enable the "New Chicago" to vanquish any doubts that its cultural vitality and civic character matched its economy.[11]

Upton had strong evidence for favoring Thomas to lead the Jubilee. In the months prior to the Jubilee the conductor had presided over triumphant classical music festivals in New York and Cincinnati, Chicago's arch rival to the southeast.[12] In praise of these events, Upton wrote: "The New York and the Cincinnati festivals, both of which owe their success to Mr. Thomas, are the first well-considered and legitimate steps towards elevating the musical standard in this country by popularizing the works of the best composers." Other critics compared Thomas's performances favorably to the much-publicized people's favorite, Patrick Gilmore.[13] Thomas's supporters included the music critic of the German-language *Illinois Staats-Zeitung*, who admired his unwavering dedication to craft. In praise of a Thomas concert in Chicago, the critic noted: "Thomas was practically the only director who did not permit himself to be impressed by the fashionable people who are always late, and who could be depended upon to give at 8 o'clock the sign to begin, unperturbed by no matter how many silk gowns there were rustling on the staircase."[14] Encapsulating Thomas's redoubtable approach to his art, George Upton wrote: "[H]e has been as true as steel to the cause of music."[15] The "cause of music" meant nothing less to Upton than a commitment to developing European cultivated music in the city to uplift and enrich the masses.

If Upton and other cultivated music supporters hoped to find an ally on the Jubilee's Committee of Arrangements, they might have looked to committeeman Chauncey Marvin Cady, late of the music publishing concern of Root and Cady.[16] Though his firm catered to the popular demands of the sheet-music industry, Cady had served as conductor of the short-lived, but influential Chicago Musical Union, a choral and orchestral group, and might have lent a sympathetic ear to calls for a "serious" music festival in Chicago. But businessmen and politicians dominated the body, including Joseph F. Bonfield, a prominent attorney with ties to municipal government, R. S. Thompson, a state senator, and businessmen William P. Gray and Michael Doyle. The majority evidently favored guaranteed crowds and proven for-

mulas. With his unquestioned ability to please huge crowds, and his
national prominence as a showman, Patrick Gilmore won the invitation over Thomas to lead the Jubilee.[17]

PATRICK GILMORE
The Civics of Aural Extremity

Irish-born, charismatic, and unflappable, Gilmore embodied a populist sensibility that enamored him to his audiences and suited the
organizers of the Jubilee. A century before "arena rock" entered the
American popular lexicon, Gilmore built a national reputation using
showmanship and enormous quantities of vocalists, instrumentalists,
including percussion, and tympanum-blasting decibels (Gilmore was
fond of cannons) to produce memorable aural extravaganzas. In June
1869 his National Peace Jubilee and Music Festival rumbled through
Boston's St. James Park to widespread acclaim. Three years later, the
World Peace Jubilee rocked Boston's Back Bay and cemented Gilmore's reputation for musical spectaculars.[18] The concert programs
typified the era's eclectic popular tastes, emphasizing choral music,
familiar operatic airs, as well as German lieder, Russian folk song, and
American popular song.[19] Gilmore capped the two Boston jubilees
with showstopping renditions of the "Anvil Chorus" from Giuseppe
Verdi's *Il Trovatore*. As the orchestra began the piece, "[o]ne hundred
firemen wearing helmets and carrying long-handled blacksmith's
hammers at 'right shoulder shift' like muskets marched to the stage
in two files of fifty. . . . Reaching the specially made anvils, the
firemen faced the audience, lifted their hammers to the proper position, and at the right moment began to pound the anvils."[20] Crowds
loved the combination of stirring choral music sung by thousands of
voices and the bombast and pyrotechnics that sent the energy level at
the concerts skittering into the stratosphere.

    In order to amass the thousands of participants that he envi-
sioned for the Boston jubilees, Gilmore zealously recruited professional and amateur performers to create a heterogeneous ensemble of
talents. He wooed internationally prominent singers and virtuoso
instrumentalists to the festivals as the main attraction. He also can-
vassed the preeminent cultivated musical institutions in Boston, including the Handel and Haydn Society, and convinced many to perform. Gilmore rounded out his roster by including local and regional

choral groups, semiprofessional and amateur singing societies, and rough-and-ready town and village military bands. With this wide-net approach, Gilmore promised jubilee audiences a 10,000-voice chorus and 1,000-piece orchestra.[21]

The democratic ethos of the "monster concerts" captured the imagination of audiences by inviting them to become part of the civic pageantry. Thousands of men, women, and children, from Boston Brahmins to day laborers, crowded together inside the coliseums specially built for the two jubilees. The scale and organization blurred the lines between professional and amateur musician, performer and spectator, producer and consumer, and ultimately artist and citizen. These events typified the social heterogeneity of urban public culture associated with the antebellum period, but, in a twist, the events drew on chorale music and the European classical music repertoire to bring the masses together.

Some professional music critics, such as John S. Dwight, founder of *Dwight's Journal of Music*, and another spokesman of the "cultured generation" of critics, found Gilmore's paeans to democracy aesthetically objectionable. The Boston-born Yankee took a dim view of the civics of aural extremity. He attacked the artistic compromises that it represented. At the conclusion of the World's Peace Jubilee, Dwight wrote sardonically: "The great, usurping, tyrannizing, noisy and pretentious thing is over, and there is a general feeling of relief, as if a heavy, brooding nightmare had been lifted from us."[22] George Upton, who attended both events, wryly likened them to "[v]olcanic eruptions, cyclones, and earthquakes—very grand and impressive, but not of any benefit to the surrounding country."[23] But the seismic force of Gilmore's oeuvre altered the landscape of American music and democratic public culture in impressive ways, as even Dwight grudgingly acknowledged. Of the impact of the 1872 concerts, the critic noted: "Whether the Festival, considered musically, was good or not, it musically did good. It has given a new impulse, a new consciousness of strength, a new taste of the joy of unity of effort, a new love of cooperation, and a deeper sense of the divine significance of music than they ever had."[24] Dwight, Upton, Gilmore, and Thomas all had overt designs on the musical masses. Each believed in the power of music to constitute a public good, whether measured socially, culturally, or aesthetically. Gilmore's Boston jubilees captured the ebullient hopes of the postbellum nation and brought the city together in a democratic and festive manner. The Boston concerts left many questions unresolved, however, about music's role in nation building or in consolidating a community among populations facing new challenges in the urban industrial age.

STAGING GREATNESS
The Chicago Jubilee

Chicago's jubilee reflected the impatient quality of a city yearning for greatness—it preceded the city's actual fiftieth birthday by a decade—but not altogether comfortable with its civic identity. Brazenly appropriating Boston's model of a jubilee celebration, the Chicago organizers eschewed originality for what they hoped would be a guaranteed publicity hit catapulting the city into national prominence. But Chicago did not commit itself to a civic celebration that took jubilee principles to heart. At the National and World Peace Jubilees, participants celebrated the end of the Civil and the Franco-Prussian Wars and rallied around the "Divine art of music."[25] The 1872 World Peace Jubilee stressed music's transcendent power on an international scale by drawing on a variety of musical traditions associated with vernacular musics of Ireland and Russia. Reviewers agreed that perhaps the most striking moments of the 1872 festival occurred when 150 African American members of the famed Jubilee Singers from Nashville performed "Turn Back Pharaoh's Army," "Swing Low, Sweet Chariot," and "Roll, Jordan, Roll." These spirituals encapsulated the resonant theme of the jubilee as a turn toward an emancipated, more peaceful and just society.[26]

The Chicago festival presented a curiously mixed message about what the city stood for, who its builders and citizens were, and where its ambitions lay. Consistent with booster rhetoric during the rebuilding period after the Great Fire, the Jubilee boldly presented a civic face in which class and cultural differences and tensions were subordinated to unity of purpose. As Karen Sawislak has shown, however, the strain of rebuilding the city under intense time pressures and national scrutiny stirred class and cultural resentments that roiled the surface narrative of a selfless cooperative project of placing Chicago back on its feet.[27] A hesitancy among organizers to share authority and credit in the rebuilding enterprise may help to explain the conspicuous absence of the city's many immigrant, ethnic, and working-men's singing groups from the performance roster at the Jubilee.

Likewise, although almost 4,000 African Americans resided in Chicago, organizers kept this group inaudible and out of sight as well.

Drained of the symbolic power that celebrating Chicago's multiethnic and multiracial population might have afforded the Jubilee—such as its association with the Old Testament theme of freeing enslaved persons every fifty years—the festival became a tepid, homogeneous publicity mechanism for Chicago's rebuilt economic engine. Tightly controlled by its elite committee, the event celebrated a kind of ersatz democratic unity that used popular music and Patrick Gilmore to construct a mass audience, but one that lacked the symbolic potency and democratic practices that had defined Gilmore's work in the past. Hard questions about the role of Chicago's multiethnic and multiracial laboring citizens in influencing and participating in a formal, civic celebration were largely deferred.[28]

Despite a steep one-dollar admission price, unseasonably warm temperatures, and inadequate ventilation in the hall, an estimated 20,000 spectators streamed through the doors of the Exposition Building to hear the opening concert until "[t]he Great Depot [was] packed almost to suffocation." Hundreds more loitered outside, trying to listen through the open windows. What they heard to celebrate the "New Chicago" bore a suspicious resemblance to the Boston jubilee concerts in miniature, from the mix of European classical and popular national airs to the "Anvil Chorus" finale. A few original touches appeared, such as a dedicatory ode, the "New Chicago Hymn of Praise," which included the stanza:

> O city bend before His throne!
> In joyful notes your Sovereign own!
> Let grateful fervor move the throng!
> In thy new temples swell the song!

The words may have been new, but Gilmore recycled the melody from the popular hymn "Old Hundred" that he had performed at the National Peace Jubilee. Spectators reportedly enjoyed themselves immensely despite the heat and overcrowding. They reserved their heartiest cheers for the "red-shirted firemen, sledges, [and] anvils" of Gilmore's signature big finish.[29]

While unquestionably entertaining, the Chicago Jubilee failed to match Boston's volume and populist brio or the Euroclassical musical refinement of the New York and Cincinnati festivals. "The Chicago Jubilee will take its place in numbers and noise at least with the great

The Interstate Industrial Exposition Building, Chicago.
From George Upton, ed., *Theodore Thomas: A Musical
Autobiography*, vol. 2 (Chicago: A. C. McClurg, 1905).

musical festivals of the country," the *Chicago Tribune* noted, mixing
hopefulness and sardonicism. But the opening gala matinee and evening concert on June 5 managed only 160 instrumentalists and 750
singers, a meager lineup by Gilmore's standards. Plans for Chicago
had come together too hastily to muster the musical armies of previous extravaganzas. Limited rehearsals, acoustical problems in the
vast railway terminal, and overflow crowds created issues that adversely affected the quality of the concerts. Those performances that
were audible above the hubbub, critics noted, were often ragged and
uneven.[30]

Beyond these shortfalls, the question of whether Chicago's leaders had used the Jubilee occasion appropriately as an instrument of
civic moral uplift remained controversial. In the midst of the Jubilee
week, the *Tribune* published a tirade against event organizers and the
public who seemed to revel in the lackluster quality of the festival.
Perhaps written by George Upton himself, the piece skewered the
Committee of Arrangements and lambasted ordinary citizens for
their shared culpability in the mediocre festival: "The Chicago Jubilee is the biggest kind of musical sell, and Pat Gilmore's slam-bang
dins its strident clamor into the unresisting ears of the biggest crowd

ever collected on a similar occasion; and what does Chicago care about art and all that sort of foolishness as long as she makes the loudest clatter and draws the biggest mob? The Chicagoans themselves don't pretend that it is anything else. They laugh out of the corners of their mouths and look wise whenever you say 'jubilee' to them."[31] Content to sup on Boston's reheated musical leftovers, the writer continued, Chicago had squandered the opportunity to make a compelling artistic and civic statement with its jubilee. With the eyes of the nation on it, the city had stumbled badly. Marked by cynicism, apathy, and a concern for "clatter," the Jubilee confirmed the worst stereotypes about midwestern provincialism and tarnished the accomplishment of the Great Rebuilding.

Chicago's competitor cities crowed over the inert Jubilee as proof that, despite its claims, Chicago remained a cultural backwater. The *New York World* disparaged the booster talk and modest results of the Jubilee as thoroughly "Chicagoish." The paper also poked fun at Chicago's rivalry with Cincinnati. According to the *World*, the announcement of Chicago's plans for a jubilee had given the impression that Chicago "[i]ntended to 'see' Porkopolis and 'raise her one' with a genuine festival which should do for music—pure and artistic music— in the Northwest what the Cincinnati Festival has undoubtedly done for music more to the South of us. Any anticipations of this nature were rapidly and ruthlessly defeated by the announcement that Gilmore was to conduct the proceedings and that the program was to be modeled after that of the Boston Jubilee."[32] The *World* likened the Jubilee's musical results to "a program as would be gotten up in the parlor of a village residence." Then, twisting the knife a bit further, and alluding to the fact that Chicago had no symphony orchestra to call its own, the writer added: "Given plenty of time and Theodore Thomas, and Chicago could have rivaled Cincinnati."[33]

Even as it derided Jubilee spectators as a "mob," the *Cincinnati Gazette* leveled most of the blame on the Committee of Arrangements. "The Jubilee would do discredit to Chicago if it were in any fair sense a public affair," one writer pointed out. "As it is, it illustrates the questionable shrewdness of its managers, who number not more than half a dozen. It will doubtless move Chicago to an effort to retrieve the character these few men have caused her to lose."[34] Because of the actions of a feckless few who had hijacked the Jubilee for their own purposes, the civic musical possibilities of the "New Chicago" remained, at least for the moment, unfulfilled.

The tendency among critics either to defend the shoddy Jubilee as a treat for the "masses" or to attack it for failing to aesthetically uplift the public ignored the complex ways that cultivated music, civic engagement, and group pride shaped the lives of many residents of the city's industrial neighborhoods. The assumption that equated plebeian status with underdeveloped musical knowledge or aesthetic appreciation, or assumed outright hostility toward "art and all that sort of foolishness" on the part of the masses, confirmed the self-serving biases of cultured-generation critics like George Upton. Tending toward oversimplification and caricature, such criticisms of public taste buttressed ideologies of refinement and hierarchical class status present in American culture at the time of the 1873 Jubilee.[35]

The disappointment of those wishing to see cultivated Euro-classical music promoted as a civic standard reflected the struggle among various interests to take charge of urban public culture. What contemporary critics were slow, or perhaps unwilling, to grasp was that while the disproportionately poor, immigrant, and ethnic "mob" was commonly described as an obstacle to the development of cultivated music as a component of civic life, elites also acted to appropriate neighborhood-based perspectives on uplift, cultivation, and regulation of public musical behavior into the idealized domain of self-consciously "civic" ritual. Although excluded from direct participation in the 1873 Jubilee, the same laborers who had helped rebuild the city, along with tens of thousands of others who inhabited Chicago's streets and public spaces, had clear perspectives on the question of music and democratic public culture. They mounted efforts of their own to promote group identity and to enrich civic identification via music at the neighborhood level. These ordinary citizens refuted the right of business, political, and aesthetic elites to dictate the preferred shape of urban music and public culture. Their actions played an important role in shaping the future imagining and realization of civic music as a reform project in the late nineteenth century.

SOUNDS OF OURSELVES
Neighborhood Music and Civic Participation

In the years following the Jubilee, music in Chicago's industrial neighborhoods helped to define the democratic possibilities and characteristics of music in public in important ways. While the "New Chicago" enjoyed a leap forward in economic vitality, changes in the social and cultural composition of the urban population were contributing to processes of identity formation that transformed the public culture of the city. The following pages briefly sketch these patterns to introduce some of the conceptual distinctions that the urban populace made about themselves, their neighbors, and their status as Chicagoans through the modality of music. Just as dramatic events like the Jubilee attempted to do, these everyday processes produced small opportunities to influence music's status in what might be called the civic imagination. Local music makers and social leaders anticipated many of the musical progressive reform tendencies that would emerge later on, and they contributed to the sense that neighborhood music and recreational activity should be the focus of musical progressivism.

To speak generally of "neighborhood" music in late-nineteenth-century Chicago denotes activities in areas that had a high correlation between residential settlement, occupation, and ethnic identification. However, neighborhood music practices also demonstrate the way that everyday musical rituals created a realm of civic participation connecting the neighborhood to the greater city. Certain types of neighborhood music production, namely performances of and support for cultivated European classical music, reflected a fluid dynamic between local and metropolitan horizons and between self-consciously ethnic particularism and more universal civic projects. In retrospect, neighborhood music raised critical questions about the relationship between localized, semiprivate musical practices and the large-scale formal staging of Chicago's civic ideals.

Western and eastern Europeans comprised the principal waves of immigration to Chicago in the latter half of the nineteenth century. Immigrant Protestants, Catholics, and Jews from Germany came in two waves during the 1850s and the 1880s.[36] Bohemians arrived both prior to and after the Civil War, and Catholics and Jews from Poland came to Chicago in significant numbers in the final decades of the century.[37] The settlement patterns of Chicago's northern and western European immigrants produced a fairly decentralized geography of trades and professions. By contrast, unskilled and semiskilled immigrants and migrants arriving in large numbers after the Civil War most commonly clustered in proximity to the shops, plants, and factories in which they worked. In the 1880s and afterward, many eastern European Jews, Italians, and Greeks settled along the north and south branches of the Chicago River in the so-called River Wards. Here they worked in the needle trades and other light industrial occupations. Significant numbers of Polish and Slavic immigrants found jobs in the meatpacking industry and moved into a residential area adjoining the stockyards and processing plants on the Southwest Side, referred to by some as "Back of the Yards." To the far southeast of the metropolitan area in the industrial zone of Lake Calumet and Southeast Chicago, various eastern European populations joined Bohemians, and later Mexicans and African Americans, in finding work in heavy industries, such as steel.[38]

The quotidian musics of Chicago's industrial neighborhoods influenced the construction of a musical civic sensibility that shaped the atmosphere of public space. While different neighborhoods displayed distinctive cultural attributes, the presence of music served a common role as an ingredient of communication networks. Music sounded in virtually every setting in which social contact regularly occurred, from parks and vacant lots to storefronts and street corners, from commercial and private clubs, parish halls, church basements, schools, and settlements to rented halls, boarding-house common rooms, apartments, and private dwellings. Street vendors, jobbers, and itinerant musicians sent vocal and instrumental melodies coursing through streets and alleyways. Melodies and lyrics in multiple languages traveled orally borne in the heads of residents and visitors who sang and taught them to others. The medium of printed sheet music, and later the phonograph and radio, further accelerated the circulation patterns of music in the neighborhoods and beyond.

Neighborhood music was typically of, and for, specific ethnocultural groups, whether the venue was a saint's festival or an ethnic holiday, a singing society engagement, a fraternal or benevolent association fundraiser, or a political or local union rally.[39] Although commemorative events, metropolitan festivals, and parades brought laborers into the downtown streets, concert halls, and exhibition centers on special occasions, the primary venues of everyday musical life, other than forest preserves and picnic groves on the urban periphery, were located in Chicago's industrial neighborhoods. For many urban residents, studying music, gaining competence with an instrument, joining singing societies, or supporting local musical organizations and clubs represented key aspects of group interconnection. In such everyday contexts, musical production and consumption bound

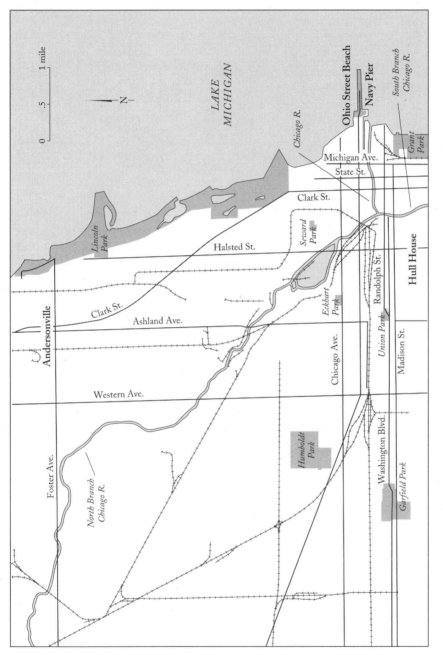

LAKE MICHIGAN

Chicago R.

Ohio Street Beach

Navy Pier

South Branch Chicago R.

Michigan Ave.

State St.

Grant Park

Clark St.

Lincoln Park

Halsted St.

Seward Park

Hull House

Eckhart Park

Randolph St.

Union Park

Clark St.

Ashland Ave.

Chicago Ave.

Madison St.

Andersonville

Western Ave.

Humboldt Park

Washington Blvd.

Garfield Park

Foster Ave.

North Branch Chicago R.

N

0   .5   1 mile

Chicago in the Era of Musical Progressivism, ca. 1920: North Side

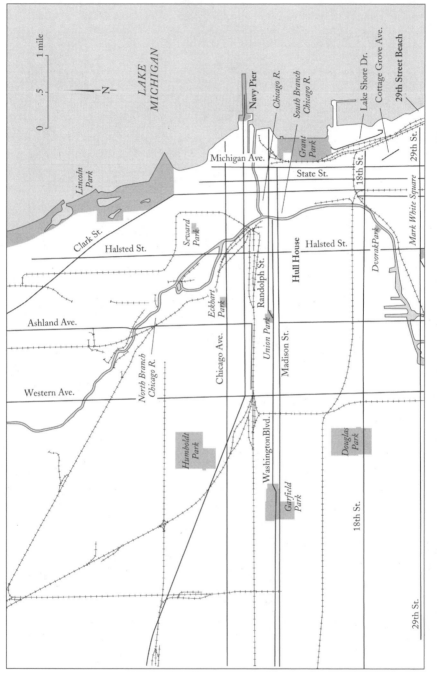

Chicago in the Era of Musical Progressivism, ca. 1920: West Side and Downtown

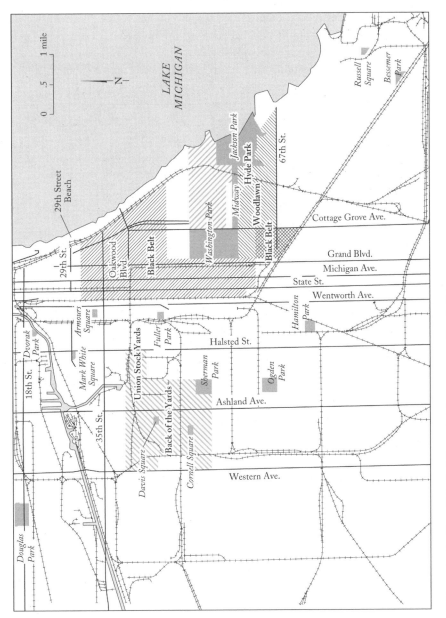

LAKE MICHIGAN

1 mile
.5
0

—N—

29th Street Beach

Jackson Park

Midway
Hyde Park
Woodlawn

67th St.

Black Belt

Cottage Grove Ave.

Oakwood Blvd.

Washington Park

Black Belt

Grand Blvd.

29th St.

Michigan Ave.

State St.

Wentworth Ave.

18th St.

Dvorak Park

Hamilton Park

Halsted St.

Armour Square

Mark White Square

Union Stock Yards

Fuller Park

Sherman Park

35th St.

Back of the Yards

Ogden Park

Ashland Ave.

Davis Square

Cornell Square

Western Ave.

Douglas Park

Russell Square

Bessemer Park

Chicago in the Era of Musical Progressivism, ca. 1920: South Side the urban citizenry into face-to-face neighborhood collectives with spokes radiating out to the city, the nation, and beyond.[40]

Neighborhood music accomplished more than encouraging community affiliation or establishing group boundaries. In singing society events, festivals, and Sunday afternoon concerts, industrial neighborhood residents drew on transplanted and hybridized traditions to produce musical events that sketched a local and civic horizon.[41] At times, the power of music transcended localized geographic constraints to contribute to a given group's status in civic affairs. The Janus-faced quality of late-nineteenth-century neighborhood musical production looked backward to the power of a local and particular public, often ethnic in character, while also gazing forward to court the regard of metropolitan Chicago.

A brief survey of activities and institutions that produced European classical music in Chicago's German, Bohemian (later Czech), and Polish neighborhoods shows that the local attention paid to music in processes of identity formation was remarkably consistent across ethnic and national divides.[42] Members of local immigrant, ethnic, and laboring populations marshaled the power of music to solidify community allegiance while often striving to secure civic prominence through music. Such efforts reflect the power that local music activated in propagating group status claims at the neighborhood level. Far from having been a marginalized activity, neighborhood music contributed to the nature of Chicago's public culture. It complemented, but also sometimes challenged, elite assumptions about music's power to express Chicago's civic identity.

SINGING FROM THE SAME SONGBOOK
Choral Groups and Singing Societies

Amateur singing and choral societies thrived in Chicago in the nineteenth century and shaped the neighborhood and metropolitan attributes of music as a civic force. Beginning with Chicago's early settlers and continuing with the arrival of immigrant and migrant groups, amateur singing and choral societies offered an important recreational outlet that expressed a democratic musical sensibility.[43] As the largest foreign-stock group in Chicago in the 1870s and 1880s, Germans supported an especially vibrant culture of such groups.[44] Approximately sixty *Männerchöre*, or men's choral groups, flourished in Chicago between 1872 and 1885. Though immigrant and ethnic Germans ran the majority of these, Bohemian and Scandinavian groups also existed.[45] The most prestigious Bohemian group, the Lyra Singing Society, established in 1870, enjoyed an international reputation. The Polish Singers' Alliance appeared in 1889, and dedicated itself to promoting music by Polish composers, sponsoring choral groups, and supporting the virtues of European classical music.[46]

In addition to their recreational and aesthetic project, singing societies and choral groups often embodied a spirit of group realization. As the Czech-language *Svornost* newspaper noted, singing societies, such as the Lyra, helped immigrant and ethnic Bohemians construct a bulwark of tradition in their new surroundings: "The singing societies are of all our national societies probably the foremost defenders and upholders of our nationalism in this strange land. Their only purpose and function is the maintenance of the Bohemian song in its original form so dear to the Bohemian soul, so sweet and cheerful in jolly or troubled times. Their fruits have access to the hearts of all. They are for young and old, for rich and poor, entertaining and encouraging."[47] The paper did not need to spell out the importance of such "maintenance" to readers facing assimilation pressures at work and in public settings. When the Polish-language *Zgoda* newspaper exhorted its "brothers" to join men's choirs as a form of ethnic community service, it conjured up the multifaceted role of music in consolidating a fraternal bond among "Poles" of various backgrounds. The appeal recognized music as a quasi-political medium with which Poles could express values and customs that they wished to validate publicly via the delivery system of the singing society.[48]

Interethnic competition for civic status also shaped the call for support of singing societies within the industrial neighborhoods of Chicago. As one editorialist wrote in *Zgoda*: "I particularly urge that you, young folks, who know of no way to spend your leisure evening, spending them uselessly is of no benefit to you or to anyone else. Persons should sacrifice at least one evening during the week for culture, by participating in singing and familiarizing themselves with the Polish language and songs." "Elders criticize the Polish singers for their poor singing and praise the German and Swedish choirs as an example to follow," the rebuke continued. "If everyone would understand their duties toward their nationality and would spend this one evening for singing, then our choirs would be above all other national choirs, and we would not then have to be ashamed of our ignorance in this art."[49] The extent to which such stern words convinced young Poles to alter their recreation habits is less clear, but it suggests the theme of sacrifice and civic duty that some Poles attached to singing and choral societies. While youths might be tempted to squander a "leisure evening" in idle pursuits, the musical construction of a distinctively Polish public profile mattered to local elites.

The mistrust among community leaders and conservative elders toward competing forms of public recreation, particularly those attracting younger people, shaped a related message encouraging youths to join singing societies and choral groups as a way of staying out of (cultural) trouble. Encouraging local music habits would bind participants into relationships that would keep them closer to home and in contact with supervisory ethnic institutions. As one editorialist noted in a Czech-language newspaper: "We are complaining of the lack of wholesome amusements. The people say there is no place where our young men and women pass their leisure time and that's why they amuse themselves with drinking, parties, card games, etc. . . . We do not intend to enumerate societies and clubs where young people can find anything they want in decent amusement. We will point out to our young people only the singing clubs. In the sixth ward there is the Club Lumir, conducted by Mr. Kounovsky. Can there be for Bohemian youth any better entertainment than a Bohemian song?"[50] For many participants, however, appeals to duty are less likely to have influenced participation in singing societies than the chance to sing, to socialize, and, often, to drink together in festive, homosocial rituals.[51] Combining a traditional affinity with European classical music and the gregarious social energy of plebeian recreation, many singing societies of the 1870s and 1880s forcefully countered tendencies toward the sacralization of European classical music in which class standing, formal surroundings, and musical taste grew more rigidly aligned. Some singing societies were overtly active in class-based social action, as when a number of German singing societies began appearing at public events in the 1870s rallying workers behind socialist political activity.[52]

Though the majority of Chicago's singing and choral societies contented themselves with their amateur status in serving the entertainment needs of their members and neighborhood supporters, others attained wider renown by performing in larger concert halls and at intermetropolitan galas sponsored by national associations.[53] Festivals such as the Twenty-second Grand Festival of the North American Singing Societies, or *Nordamerikanischer Sängerbund*, held in Chicago from June 18 to June 22, 1881, offered a counterexample to the 1873 Jubilee. Rather than an elite-conjured claim to Chicago's veritable civic identity, the festival put ethnically identified singing societies on center stage. Held in the same Exposition Building where Gilmore had performed, the Grand Festival featured seventeen of Chicago's men's singing societies along with groups from Milwaukee; Cincinnati; Bloomington, Illinois; and Fort Wayne, Indiana. The seven concerts featured a men's chorus, mixed chorus, and large orchestra, under the direction of Austrian-born conductor Hans Balatka, who had extensive musical ties to Chicago and neighboring Milwaukee.[54] The Grand Festival also featured the internationally renowned prima donna, Minna Peschka-Leutner of Leipzig, who had appeared at London's Crystal Palace and the 1872 Boston World Peace Jubilee.[55]

The event underscored the complexity of signification of European classical music throughout the Midwest.[56] In the manner of the New York and Cincinnati festivals of the early 1870s, the program emphasized German composers. Major works included Max Bruch's *Odysseus* and "Salamis, or Battle Hymn of the Greeks"; August Reissmann's "Death of Drusus"; selections from Richard Wagner's *Lohengrin*; and Ludwig van Beethoven's Ninth Symphony.[57] Over fifty societies, many of them German, performed, along with societies of other cultural and national backgrounds. But as one news report observed, the 1881 festival ought not be reduced to a "German" event since only an estimated 10 percent of the crowd appeared to be German.[58] The entertainment value of the festival coupled with the pan-ethnic popularity of the singing societies made these downtown concerts a symbolically "civic" as well as a proudly "German" and musically accomplished event that underscored the intricacies of Chicago's musical landscape.

Thousands of spectators of different backgrounds attended and expressed enthusiasm for European classical music. Far from an arid exercise in aesthetic contemplation by a select minority, the Grand Festival filled the Exposition Building with high-quality music while invigorating the city's nightlife, filling the downtown with celebrants to such an extent that newspapers reported that "[s]aloons and streets [were] crowded with happy singing members of the societies until after midnight."[59] The major "Sängerfests" demonstrated the variety

of local and regional musical publics eager to celebrate civic spiritedness in their own way. The singing society offered a counterexample
to elite claims on Chicago's public culture and taste of a kind demonstrated at the Jubilee.

"THE MUSIC WAS VERY FINE . . . AND THE BEER VERY GOOD"
Turner Concerts

The Sunday afternoon concert marked another neighborhood musical institution that shaped the heterogeneous character of music in
public and affected Chicago's civic musical culture as well. These
events were commonly sponsored by the German *Turnverein* or the
Bohemian and Polish *Sokol*. These gymnastic and social clubs an-
chored a significant portion of neighborhood ethnic life.[60] The Turners, as they were known, presented Sunday concerts that defined
music's place in everyday life in meaningful ways for the development of musical recreation both inside and outside the German enclave. Bandmaster Christoph Romanus inaugurated the first Sunday
series at Turner Hall, leading the Philharmonic Society in programs
of European classical music selected for their promise of entertaining
audiences in a relaxed setting. Though the majority of the audience
were German speakers, other groups were attending the concerts in
significant numbers by the 1870s.[61]

The combination of accomplished European classical music and
a relaxed social setting attracted devotees of the European masters as
well as other groups, including citizens resisting Sabbatarian restrictions on Sunday amusements and women seeking diverting yet "respectable" public forms of heterosocial recreation. Turner concerts
and allied concert events at the city's numerous commercial beer
gardens where string as well as brass ensembles performed helped to
popularize a Bohemian form of public recreation in the Midwest
where men, women, and sometimes children gathered. These multiethnic and cross-class events encouraged boundary crossings and
public social exchange among the broader population. In a letter to
her mother in the spring of 1873, Frances Roberts, a young Yankee
office worker, glowingly described the pleasures of the Sunday concerts at the Aurora Turner Hall. "[T]he music was very fine," she
wrote, "and the beer very good." Roberts mentioned only one minor

drawback to the atmosphere. "When I got home, I seemed to have been soaked in tobacco smoke, and had to hang my clothes in the wind all day next day." The need to rid her clothing of such an odor suggests Roberts's self-consciousness about the telltale signs of her Sunday excursion. She even confessed to her mother that the events would undoubtedly strike some respectable Yankees as "wicked." Nevertheless, Roberts informed her mother that she planned to return to the hall again.[62]

Chicago's German-language press provides a fascinating perspective on the cultural politics of Sunday Turner concerts. Most audience members enjoyed the Bohemian character of the events and, as Frances Roberts did, made adjustments to compensate for any discomforts, such as the smoky atmosphere. But the sentiments of at least one spectator, identifying himself as "A Music and Family Friend," called on the German readers of the *Illinois Staats-Zeitung* to reform the Sunday concerts: "The terrible tobacco smoke which filled the Turner Hall from A to Z, was sufficient to so permeate our clothes that even today they still smell. Such a smoke drives any lady and gentleman away from the concert. Is it not possible for the Germans to abstain a few hours from smoking for the sake of the ladies? No wonder so few ladies attend these concerts. The German public does not only want good music but also a decent recreation place—a recreation place where one listens to good music more *en famille* than *en canaille*, where one gladly brings one's wife and daughter. As the concerts are conducted now, they certainly will not last."[63] The writer's repeated use of the definite article—"the Germans" and "the German public"—addressed an imagined community of concerned readers with a shared stake in the good reputation of the events.[64] Not only did smokers poison the atmosphere for "any lady and gentleman," but the insensitivity of heavy smokers reflected poorly on the civic display of "German" musical culture at the hall and its claim to being a "decent recreation place."

Seeding the letter with French phrases established the Continental status of "A Music and Family Friend" and asserted his authority over less-worldly concert patrons and readers. Attacking the male privilege of smoking in public, the writer suggested that sophisticated German music lovers stood to benefit from the lessons of Victorian domestication. The appeal on joint behalf of "music," "ladies," and music *en famille* (that is, in the family circle) asserted differences transcending "Germans" and non-Germans. It implied the risks of censure from those outside the German enclave, who might equate smoking at a concert with *la canaille* (meaning the riffraff). Gender and bourgeois conventionality informed the writer's perspective in lobbying for reform even as his ultimate critique focused on German behavior as it shaped standards within the group and publicized those standards in the city at large.[65]

A retrospective in the *Staats-Zeitung* occasioned by the twenty-fifth anniversary of the Sunday concerts expressed the deep sense of pride that the musical events kindled among ethnically identified Germans. Supporters gloried in the concerts' success at popularizing European classical music and cultivated German composers for a broad audience. Turner concerts supplied music that celebrated transplanted rituals of Germanness while instilling those cultural values and traditions into metropolitan life. The Turner concerts served to Germanize Chicagoans while Americanizing Germanness. To some, the music also signified a particular kind of cultural power rooted in nationalist claims of superiority: "During the first few years while the performances were still inferior, and the English and Irish American who mingled with the concert audiences had not yet learned from the Germans how to behave in concert halls, disturbances were by no means rare. The appointed committee for order succeeded, however, in putting reason and respect into the noisy dullards. Later . . . as a better understanding of good music gradually developed in the public, greater devotion and attention resulted."[66] The writer's account of German music's conquest of midwestern audiences blended notes of condescending chauvinism with genuine concern to uplift the masses via European classical music. The pedagogical sentiment connecting enlightened minority activity to the betterment of the general public resembled the uplift aspirations of the "cultured generation," who were also seeking to reform the aesthetic sensibilities of American music audiences.

The story of the Turner concerts' legacy of uplifting the general public, while enshrining German music at the apex of civic definitions of quality music, reflected the important role that neighborhood music activists occupied in constituting local to metropolitan forms of public culture. It also hinted at the undercurrent of struggle among immigrant, ethnic, and laboring populations jockeying for status and cultural authority. The *Staats-Zeitung*'s smug tone of superiority in describing German neighborhood music's improving effects on noisy

English and Irish American "dullards" revealed the pressures that accompanied the development of neighborhood musical standards. Where the reforming group perceived the democratic triumph of a worthy musical form or a social behavior deservedly vanquishing an inferior one, we can also perceive the machinations of power squelching behaviors and music deemed unsuitable as worthy sounds of the city.

Singing societies and Turner concerts demonstrated the powerful influences of neighborhood music institutions in specifying the democratic character of civic musical events. The history of both institutions showed how specific ethnic commitments to entertainment and group socialization coexisted with self-conscious efforts to favorably situate a given group in the public eye (or ear). Struggles over music demonstrated the high expectations that industrial neighborhood residents had for the impact of their activities on standards of public cultural expression and display. As the rest of this chapter will show, local efforts to solidify group affiliation spread to the broader metropolitan stage, where various groups competed to define the democratic traits of musical expression and culture in public.

TUNING A CITY
The Thomas "Summer Nights" Concerts

Beginning in the late 1870s and continuing throughout the 1880s, a major summer concert series brought Chicago residents from different economic, social, and cultural backgrounds into a new geographical and cultural alignment that heightened excitement about music as an agent of civic transformation. In 1877 at the urging of George B. Carpenter, a leading Chicago music promoter, famed New York symphonic conductor Theodore Thomas agreed to present a series of classical summer concerts in the Exposition Building.[67] At twenty-five to fifty cents a ticket, the "summer nights" concerts were far cheaper than the dollar admission charged to witness the Jubilee, and the standard of musicianship promised to be far higher. The Thomas concerts attracted thousands of spectators hailing from both Chicago's finest lakefront neighborhoods and its most humble industrial areas. The public spectacle of musically driven democratic mixing kindled lively discussion about music's mass educative and entertainment functions, particularly music's power to impact class and gender roles, as well as its power to unify spectators of all backgrounds.

Though he once spoke of himself as "a teacher as well as an entertainer," Theodore Thomas came to Chicago in 1877 following a disastrous attempt at balancing these roles as music director of the nation's Centennial Exposition in Philadelphia.[68] Narrowly selected over his Jubilee nemesis, Patrick Gilmore, to direct music at the 1876 exposition, Thomas encountered difficult conditions at the site. Lack of adequate financial backing from Centennial organizers required charging steep ticket fees for the Thomas concerts and forced the removal of the concerts to a venue several miles from the center of the exposition. Complicating matters further, Thomas ordered that no alcohol be served at his concerts, and he instituted a rule that audiences remain seated while the orchestra performed. These restrictions alienated visitors, who expected to find the casual, convivial atmosphere of summer concert gardens, and not the reverent atmosphere of a fancy urban concert hall. In steamy Philadelphia, crowds vastly preferred the free entertainment that Patrick Gilmore's popular military band provided in Fairmont Park, where liquid refreshments were plentiful. Humiliated and buried under a landslide of debt due to poor attendance, Thomas came to Chicago a bit bruised and in need of professional redemption.[69]

It is not known to what extent Thomas's bad experience at the Centennial directly affected the form and execution of the Chicago summer concerts, but they bore little resemblance to the experiments in sacralization at Philadelphia.[70] Thomas set an informal tone for the Chicago summer concerts, following the historical model of European pleasure gardens and his engagements in New York's Central Park. Pleasure garden concerts emphasized relaxation and melded entertainment with gentle uplift. While the quality of the musicianship at such concerts was often very high, organizers historically understood the distinction between works appropriate for summer concerts and those suited to more formal, indoor listening environments. But while European pleasure gardens traditionally catered to an urban public comprised largely of the bourgeoisie, the Chicago concerts were meant to appeal to a mass audience. Thomas had succeeded in New York's Central Park with such an approach. He appeared ready to engage the masses of Chicago with symphonic music in a way that they had never been engaged before.[71]

The Exposition Building where the concerts were to be held lacked the physical comforts of the halls in which Thomas and his orchestra customarily performed. Plush interior appointments, guaranteed seating, and strict rules of audience comportment (such as silence and not standing up or moving about) were absent at the "summer nights" concerts. With its unfinished interior, rough wooden chairs, and proximity to the noisy rail yards, the building would never be mistaken for a temple to Apollo's art. It was, Thomas recalled, "the last place in the world in which one would have expected orchestral concerts to succeed."[72] Rose Fay Thomas, wife of the conductor, recalled that "there were no fixed or even reserved seats in any part of the building, and people sat where they pleased, or moved the chairs into little groups to suit themselves." The only physical barrier dividing the thousands of spectators who attended the performances was a small rail separating holders of twenty-five- and fifty-cent tickets.[73] Beyond the railing, throngs listened casually to the orchestra while seated at tables drinking lemonade or beer and consuming such advertised delicacies as ham or beef-tongue sandwiches.[74]

The inaugural summer season faced challenges beyond the fact that a series of popular classical music concerts for the masses had never been attempted in Chicago. Whereas a natural disaster had interfered with Thomas's plans for reopening the Crosby Opera House in 1871, the conductor and his orchestra confronted a different kind of conflagration in July 1877. "The city was in a disturbed condition," recalled George Upton with uncharacteristic understatement, alluding to the national railroad strike that paralyzed Chicago and much of the nation's transportation system. Labor stoppages and riots erupted in the rail yards and spilled into industrial neighborhoods of the South Side. Officials declared a state of emergency in the city, while the members of Chicago's industrial elite avoided unnecessary public appearances. Thomas and the orchestra soldiered ahead, trying to ignore the distracting presence of several military companies on alert at the back end of the building, ready to scramble to protect the adjoining rail yards should trouble erupt.[75]

Despite the spartan character of the Exposition Building and the disruptions of the "strike excitement," the first season ended on a hopeful note. Thomas drew respectable crowds, with broad support from the wealthy patrons of Chicago's cultivated concert halls, habitués of the turner halls, and common laborers from the industrial neighborhoods of the Near North and West Sides. As one report observed: "The comparative cheapness of the concerts and the absence of the stiff formalities of the ordinary concert-room, the freedom to wander about, chat, and smoke without offending those who simply wish to listen, are just the elements needed to make them delightful to tired workers and men fatigued with the cares of business."[76] Spectators also responded enthusiastically to a number of special promotions that season: "Composer's Night"; "Ballroom Night," in which the orchestra played dance music; "Modern Composers Night"; and "Une Nuit Française," dedicated exclusively to French composers (hardly Thomas's favorites). These popular concessions demonstrated that under the right conditions the redoubtable Thomas accommodated the public's need for entertainment. In a final conciliatory gesture to the masses, Thomas presented a "Request Night" concert in late July based on a tally of the estimated 600 to 1,000 ballots that flooded the orchestra's office each week during the summer season.[77]

"THEODORABLE THOMAS" AND THE MASSES

Whatever lingering doubts remained from the 1873 Jubilee that Chicago residents could never appreciate the refining sounds of European classical music seemed washed away. Sponsors commended Thomas's talents "in the way of pleasure and musical instruction" and begged him to return regularly.[78] Thomas agreed. "Chicago is the only city on the continent, next to New York," he declared, "where there is sufficient musical culture to enable me to give a series of fifty consecutive concerts."[79] At last the ghosts of unheard concerts past and the fumbled opportunity of the Jubilee to celebrate Chicago's superior civic qualities appeared vanquished. "By this token," wrote an ebullient George Upton, "Chicago regains her place as a musical center which she lost at the time of the Great Fire." As if to punctuate the city's redemption, the *Chicago Tribune* reprinted a dispatch from the *New York Graphic* chastising Manhattan concert audiences for "the achievement of starving out Theodorable Thomas and compelling him to lead his trained melody to the West."[80]

Between 1877 and 1890, the year Thomas took charge of the city's first permanent symphony orchestra, the conductor presented approximately 369 summer performances.[81] These events were not punitive exercises in white-gloved social discipline; they melded high technical standards with popular selections from the European classical canon. During his triumphant run, Thomas ably matched programs to the varying tastes and knowledge of the audience and brought forth distinctively different publics on different summer evenings. "On the 'composers nights,' " noted a *Chicago Herald* critic, "the learned students of music, amateur and professional, are sure to be there. With a thoughtful and studious aspect they sit and drink in the music and sometimes the beer . . . [O]n 'request' nights the audience are marked by thoughtful and intelligent persons who have caught the fever, but not reached the secondary stage from which the 'composers' night people are suffering."[82] Rather than mocking Thomas's interest in educating and uplifting the masses, the popular press embraced his efforts. The "summer nights" concerts demonstrated the deep support for cultivated music across economic and social divides as well as the entertainment value of symphonic music presented in the Bohemian manner. The concerts expanded the democratic possibilities of public culture in Chicago by balancing demands of elite critics, like George Upton, who demanded high-quality music, with general audience preferences for accessible music delivered in the relaxed mode of the neighborhood Turner concert.

A typical season from the 1880s illustrates the range of Thomas's orchestra and its ability to perform works requiring advanced technique and interpretive skill while also delivering crowd-pleasing selections in the manner of Patrick Gilmore. Evening concerts included selections from Handel, Beethoven, Bach, Cherubini, Weber, Schumann, Brahms, Berlioz, and Mozart. Thomas also led one matinee of "popular" concerts consisting of arias and overtures from popular operas as well as lighter works by Schubert, Bach, Weber, Schumann, Liszt, Rossini, Verdi, Gounod, and others. The balancing of composers and styles reflected a prevailing strategy in popular music, according to which the boundaries between "high" cultivated and "low" popular were to remain fluid and negotiable in certain settings. For a brief shining moment, it seemed, education and entertainment, popular taste and uplift were in a state of equilibrium.[83]

Among Thomas's most popular introductions was his Wagner-centered program, variations of which featured selections from *Das Rheingold, Die Walküre, Siegfried,* and *Götterdämmerung.*[84] These programs drew devoted Wagner fans, some of whom reportedly arrived clutching complete scores, which they followed assiduously during the performances. The program played on a popular fad for the com-

poser spreading across the country. Wagner enjoyed a fleeting period
of favor with mainstream music audiences for his tempestuous operas, in which bold heroines, violence, and sexual intrigues added
drama and spice to summer concert gardens.[85]

"SUMMER NIGHTS" AND DEMOCRATIC DESIRE
Charlotte Teller's The Cage

Almost two decades after the last of Thomas's "summer nights" concerts, the writer, socialist, and suffragist Charlotte Teller recaptured
the excitement of the events in her novel *The Cage* (1907). Though a
work of historical fiction, the novel contains perceptive insights into
Chicago in the 1870s as well as into the social and cultural impact of
the concerts themselves.[86] As the novel begins, Frederica, a young
American woman, is living an isolated existence on Chicago's Near
West Side. She and her father, a widower and social gospel reformer,
work to assist struggling immigrants and laborers. She has also been
taught, however, to keep her distance from the male laborers of
the neighborhood. In this respect, she represents a sympathetic caricature of the well-meaning, repressed Victorian woman coming of
age. The sheltered Frederica vaguely supports "reform" but has
not yet begun to question her privileged status or its effect on her
perspectives.

To show solidarity with discontented workers, Frederica attends
a German workers' protest rally at the neighborhood sawmill, where
she hears a singing society perform. Alec, Frederica's frustrated ad-
mirer, who is the effete son of the union-busting sawmill owner,
jealously observes her watching the display of manliness and cama-
raderie. He belittles the resolute workers. "They sing like wild beasts
anyway," he sniffs, confirming in Frederica's mind that she will have
to do better for herself in finding a compatible suitor.[87]

Frederica meets Eugene Harden, a charismatic socialist labor
organizer visiting from Germany. Their friendship develops into a
romance after he casually invites her to attend a Thomas summer
concert one evening. Arriving together at the Exposition Building,
Frederica is surprised when Eugene escorts her past the rows of
chairs near the orchestra toward the tables in the back: "Before this
when she had come to a concert it had been in the afternoon, and she
had always gone into the first rows of the twenty-five-cent seats and

had not even looked around at the people sitting at the tables; they had belonged, in her mind, to a world so far outside her own and her father's. To-night she found herself in the very midst of that world."[88] Teller captures Frederica's illicit thrill at leaving the familiar spaces of the hall behind and transgressing the protocols of her background that they symbolize. At the back of the hall, among immigrant and ethnic laborers, Eugene gives Frederica her first taste of a Bohemian public sensibility. Seated amid the population she has literally turned her back on in the past, Teller's heroine discovers a fresh perspective on the public world that she thought she knew, and she begins to question her own personal biases.

Wagner's "Ride of the Valkyries" diverts Frederica's attention from Eugene, and she listens transfixed by the music and the fable of a powerful war woman—a Valkyrie—carrying a dead man to restore him back to life. "The end came and it was as though she had been thrust back and down just before she had reached the summit. Her nostrils were tense, and she did not relax, even though she sat with her hands folded in her lap, a most unusual attitude of quiescence for her."[89] Teller links the music to the erotic subtext of Frederica's personal "ride" across the boundaries of class, culture, and Victorian respectability. With Eugene and Wagner as her co-tutors/seducers, she glimpses an escape route from the confines of her cloistered everyday life. The power of music is not limitless, however, and she masters it by retaining the external signs of bourgeois equipoise, with her hands remaining primly "folded in her lap."

Frederica's boundary-crossing aural experience and her struggle to reconcile private passions and middle-class codes of gendered respectability in public are a dramatic device as well as an accurate indicator of the kinds of tensions and democratic desires circulating at the Thomas concerts. Frederica understands the rules that bourgeois elites apply to make public musical spaces respectable, but she also subverts them.[90] Like Frances Roberts, seeking new sensations at the Aurora Turner Hall concert, Frederica crosses the symbolic divide that separates her Yankee social cohort from the immigrant and ethnic patrons of the beer garden. In the process she discovers the power of music to redefine the meaning of democratic public culture.

Surviving commentaries that describe the crowds at the "summer nights" concerts support Teller's imagined account of the interpersonal and cross-class dynamics of the concerts. As Teller noted,

gender issues influenced behavior at large public concerts and raised
specific dilemmas for women in the company of men, as well as
without them. As one journalist observed of the Thomas audience:
"On the 'popular nights' the young persons who think that Theodore
Thomas is 'just too lovely for anything' throng the building and clap
their little hands. . . . [S]ometimes three of the dear girls come together to a matinee without any male escort at all, and then one can
tell at a glance that they love music for its own sake and not for the
sake of spending an evening in the company of men."[91] The critic's
patronizing indulgence of the idea that "dear girls" might actually
know a thing or two about classical music reflects an example of
gender-bound thinking. Its rather paradoxical assurance that the unaccompanied women at the concert truly do "love music for its own
sake" points to deeper apprehensions about the lure of music in
public for young women and the specter of unregulated female sexuality. While clearly within the range of "respectable" public amusements, the "summer nights" series foreshadowed a moral dilemma
for supporters of democratized public culture: how to respond to the
increasingly common phenomenon of respectable women without
men in public?[92]

SOUND CONSEQUENCES
The Problem of "Democratic Spite"

The Thomas concerts marked a wonderful triumph for aesthetes
who equated refined music with moral uplift and democratic enrichment. But the interaction of the heterogeneous audience participating in the civic ritual illuminated conflicts dividing the city. The
concerts stirred worries among elite critics about the reliability of
codes to differentiate groups in the urban social hierarchy. While the
support of the concerts by the masses expanded the aesthetic and
democratic possibilities of urban public culture, some observers worried about inappropriate familiarity among concert patrons of different social classes. As one reviewer wrote of the scene at the Exposition Building: "Society meets and chats between the parts. It
uses the nooks around the Michigan Avenue window for a sort of 5
o'clock tea . . . The democracy across the railing ate ice cream or
drank Milwaukee beer. It brought its girl, and occasionally its girls.
They had much more fun than society. They pulled all the aris-

tocratic bonnets to pieces and vowed that among the fashionable dresses, 'not one was fit to be seen.' This was democratic spite."[93] The observer humorously described a showdown between subgroups of the audience who would rarely find themselves in such close proximity. Some readers may have wondered about the implications of such familiarity and whether "democratic spite" might carry over to other settings where the socially prominent patrons of the Thomas concerts and the men and women who worked in their factories, shops, office buildings, and homes interacted under a set of quite different rules.

The liberties of association taken at the concerts extended beyond verbal expressions of "democratic spite" to boundary crossings and temporary role reversals involving elite patrons, too. George Upton noted that "the space outside the bower," where the less well-to-do enjoyed the music, "was invaded by even the most fashionable folks, and the swell girls who had been accustomed to raise their eyebrows in amazed contempt if they saw an acquaintance in this cheaper precinct suddenly found that their favorite youths were running away from them . . . and that the best thing to do was to join the rest of the party at the tables outside the barrier."[94] Upton's description of the collapse of social order and hierarchy probably set readers chuckling. But the spectacle of wealthy, cultivated citizens abdicating their privileged spaces in order to "join the rest of the party" expressed an inverted form of "democratic spite" in which one generation challenged the conservative conventions of its predecessors. Efforts to promote civility via the universalizing powers attributed to cultivated music had produced rather unexpected challenges to the very assumptions of civility. Flirtatious high jinks at the concerts aside, the question of the social effects of such democratic forms of public musical recreation touched on serious and sensitive issues concerning the future of the democratic social order and the place of music as an authoritative mechanism to manage it.

LOVE AND THEFT
Claiming the Audience of Reform

The enthusiastic adoption of the summer garden/Turner concert model by crowds flocking to hear Thomas raised the interesting question of whether civic elites had appropriated the gregarious German neighborhood model, or if the model had in fact overtaken the Yankee establishment. For Upton, two impulses were warring within the Exposition Building. "Nearly 4,000 people were present," wrote the critic, describing one of Thomas's concerts in 1886: "[T]he people . . . seemed to have caught the Bohemian tinge that characterizes the German prototype of these concerts. They gathered in groups to gossip and chat; loafed about the tables, eating ices and drinking lemonades, and in every way comported themselves like persons who understand that one is only half-human who forgets the animal."[95] Having noted the pleasurable aspects of the German prototype, Upton chided the "Teutonic element" for its overfondness for the sensual world of cafés and beer gardens at the implied expense of a singular focus on the music. Though he never suggested closing the beer garden at the Exposition Building, Upton believed that the mass appeal of the "Bohemian tinge" undermined the aesthetic operation of musical uplift, which required discipline and self-abnegation. Bohemian concert practices incorporated music, talk, food, drink, and amusement into a compelling recreational package. Musical aesthetes preferred to place music on a pedestal and regard it with contemplative seriousness. The tension between entertainment and more severe forms of education and uplift would recur in the era of musical progressivism as well.

Reports in the German-language press hailed Thomas's accomplishments but expressed ambivalence toward the masses of new concert patrons. The *Arbeiter Zeitung* found something mildly unnerving about plebeian (and non-German) audiences commingling with elite listeners educated in the subtleties of European cultivated music. One review in the *Arbeiter Zeitung* had a proprietary tone: "An audience of more than 3,000 persons listened with great interest to yesterday's concert of the exquisite Thomas Orchestra at the Expo Building. The request for compositions by Wagner, Beethoven, and Liszt deserve special mention. But we are inclined to believe, that it was not the majority of this audience who appreciated such classical music, but a comparatively few who have the necessary musical education and understanding."[96] As if to reassure readers concerned about the (over)popularization of German music among the mass of citizens, the review pointed out that popular enthusiasms ought not to be mistaken for appreciation and "understanding." Ironically, the idea of Wagner or Beethoven as popular artists would likely go unremarked if speaking of an ethnic event, but such a possibility among the non-German masses raised concern. The mass embrace of music formerly understood as a treasure of locally produced German culture represented outsider love becoming theft and threatened to leave its original custodians and boosters behind.

Talk of minor social transgressions and inversions accompanying the music presented a sharper edge in the context of rampant class antagonism. During the era of the "summer nights" concerts, dozens of strikes and violent labor disputes split Chicago's population. From the 1877 railroad strike to the 1886 Haymarket massacre, thousands of Chicago workers clashed with their employers during the years in which Thomas entertained the public at the Exposition Building. Music critics, fulfilling their role, emphasized the aesthetic quality of Thomas's performances and the civic marvel of such diverse and peaceable audiences. But the conflict between capital and labor added a palpable edge to the reportage of civic musical engagement. The image of a city of tea drinkers and "Milwaukee beer" aficionados gathered together to enjoy concert music suggested an appealing illustration of civic harmony. At the same time, however, eruptions of "democratic spite" and critical feedback launched toward "society" by "the democracy across the railing" suggested the potential liabilities of such public gatherings for elites or other targets of mass disapproval. Who intended to reform whom remained a persistent question that would find continued elaboration in the emergence of musical progressivism.

DEMOCRATIC GHOSTS AND THE THOMAS LEGACY

Scholars implicate Theodore Thomas as an exemplar of the elitist, sacralizing impulse in nineteenth-century American music. Again and again, Thomas strove to institute stricter rules governing audience behavior at indoor classical concerts. In Europe as in the United States, rules governing such performances would grow increasingly strict and audiences would become increasingly stratified as musicians and concert organizations professionalized themselves. What is easy to overlook, however, is that as late as 1890 Thomas enjoyed in some circles a reputation as an educator and as an entertainer, who had popularized the European classical canon in such a way as to enlarge the sphere of democratic public culture. Tens of thousands of spectators at the "summer nights" concerts attested to his widespread popularity and his willingness to satisfy popular preferences. Despite his priggish temperament, Thomas's art enfolded the masses. Neither the eager young women at matinee performances nor the thousands of beer-quaffing spectators "outside the bower" could possibly have regarded the conductor as merely an autocratic disciplinarian. "Thomas knows his public well," noted a writer for the *Chicago Daily News*. "He knows that speaking generally, the public wants to be amused in the summer rather than educated." The writer grouped Thomas with Patrick Gilmore in this regard, and he drew a sharp line between Thomas and "poor Seidl," whose desire to " 'educate' merely, is receiving a rather negative encouragement from empty benches."[97] The pairing of Thomas and Gilmore seems at first odd, as does the distinction between Thomas and Anton Seidl, the New York Philharmonic conductor who promoted Wagner to mass audiences at Coney Island's "respectable" resort of Brighton Beach. But these groupings suggest that popular taste, civic reform, European classical music, and Theodore Thomas were compatible elements of Chicago's musical landscape through the 1880s.[98]

In his posthumously published autobiography, Thomas dismissed the Chicago summer concerts as necessary evils in a career that was singularly devoted to the most challenging forms of symphonic music. He downplayed the remarkable feat of consolidating a mass audience for cultivated European music in Chicago. According to Thomas, "The Summer Night Concerts had done valuable service by awakening a general love of music, but it was chiefly music of a lighter character, with symphonies administered in very small doses." Although he had enlarged the aesthetic range and participatory base of civic music in Chicago by refuting the assumption that popular audiences could not respond to European classical music, Thomas failed to register the accomplishment. "Wagner to some extent interested the people," mused Thomas, but "he had also accustomed them to strong doses of excitement, and contrast, and everything without these tonic properties was regarded with indifference." With bitter irony, Thomas complained that the principal effect of his summer concerts was to create false expectations among audiences who "found much fault with my [subsequent] programs, which they thought were too severe."[99] Out of an apparent desire to be remembered as the uncompromising champion of the cultivated classical music tradition in America, Thomas fashioned a self-report on the Chicago summer programs that obscured their impact on the democratic civics of music.

Despite Thomas's deserved reputation as a rigid sacralizer, the "summer nights" concert era reveals an underappreciated side to the conductor's career linked to the advancement of a democratic discourse of musical civics in Chicago. For more than a decade, tens of thousands of listeners obtained direct access to high-quality symphonic music in a public setting characterized by remarkable socioeconomic and cultural heterogeneity. Score-reading Wagner fans, Turner concert veterans, and male and female patrons drinking and flirting "outside the bower" came together at these concerts and formed a musical public that reflected new possibilities for urban recreation. The concerts also demonstrated the influence of neighborhood music on creating wider receptivity to European classical music in the civic realm. As such, the concerts suggested a multiplicity of claims on music as an instrument of self-fashioning and democratic reform. Neither the masses nor the sacralizers had hegemony in the Exhibition Building. The issue of defining and promoting musical recreation for the public good would resurface again in 1893 when the largest music festival of the century began in Chicago.

THE BEST-LAID PLANS
The World's Columbian Exposition, 1893

From May to October 1893, millions of people converged on Chicago to visit the World's Columbian Exposition in Jackson Park, a 500-acre preserve south of downtown.[100] Known simply as the "fair," the international event honored the 400th anniversary of Christopher Columbus's arrival in the Americas. It also celebrated Chicago's role in a drama of industrial prosperity and power that had existed chiefly as a boast at the time of the Jubilee. At the center of the fair, at the so-called White City, which was a cluster of monumental Beaux Arts–style buildings, scores of exhibits touted the historical, political, economic, scientific, technological, and cultural achievements of the United States, the Americas, and Europe. To the west along the Midway Plaisance, visitors traversed acres of diverting commercial amusements, such as cafés and entertaining exhibits, including the world's first Ferris wheel. Historians have contrasted the White City and the Midway to show the tension between pedagogical uplift and cathartic plebeian recreation at the fair. Studies stress the themes of progress, democracy, and celebratory consumerism that the fair promised to be the nation's entitlements in the future. Scholars have critiqued a prevailing elitist culture of "imperial abundance,"[101] marked by the Eurocentric vision of the White City, the virtual exclusion of African Americans at the fair, and the voyeuristic display of non-Western cultures on the Midway. Others emphasize the countervailing energy of joyful plebeian crowds on the Midway. Some also point to the Midway's contributions to new sounds of American accomplishment, such as Scott Joplin's unpublicized piano performances that helped to promote ragtime music to a new audience.[102]

There is also a well-established narrative and critique of music's place at the fair that conforms in large measure to the interpretive model of the White City/Midway geographies of power and cultural hierarchy. At the White City, a view of European classical music at the apex of Western civilization prevailed, with other forms falling beneath it. On the Midway and in adjoining parks, visitors reveled in popular vernacular music from military band concerts by John Philip Sousa to folk music, to ragtime, and to non-Western musics.[103]

Struggles over music and democratic expression at the fair linked the 1893 event to prior public debates among different constituencies, stretching as far back as the 1873 Jubilee, over the use of major festival occasions to declare civic and cultural principles. In its hierarchical organization, the fair revealed the tremendous power still vested in elites to dictate the frame of music in civic life. Nonetheless, fair audiences and a profusion of musical producers demonstrated tremendous power in producing alternative representations of the democratic musical character of the nation. Music created multiple spheres of face-to-face democratic social interaction and engagement, but these left some uncertainty about the future direction of civic reform in an era of musical abundance in which multiple, overlapping sounds and publics appeared to be the desired form of democratic expression.

Theodore Thomas headed the music bureau charged with planning and coordinating concert performances at the fair. Enjoying newfound job security as the recently appointed permanent conductor of the Chicago Orchestra, and with generous financial resources at his disposal, Thomas set about providing high-quality symphonic music to audiences in a controlled and deferential formal concert setting. In a fateful decision, he attempted to reengineer the musi-

World's Columbian Exposition "Chicago Day" poster.
Chicago Historical Society, ICHi-14835.

cal civic landscape whose inclusive and democratic contours he had
helped to sustain through his many years conducting summer concerts in Chicago. He steered a course away from the cheering crowds
of the "summer nights" concerts toward a vision of uncompromising
aesthetic perfection that had eluded him throughout his career.

A "FULL ILLUSTRATION OF MUSIC"
Thomas and the Music Bureau

Unlike its Jubilee or "summer nights" predecessors that assembled a
mass audience under one roof, the fair's organization codified distinctions among publics, genres, and performance locations in a manner
that eroded the possibility of cohesion across lines of difference. It
relied on a hierarchical system of genre classification that scattered
performances and audiences across the entire reach of the fair. Just as
exhibits at the White City ordered and ranked the world's technologies, industries, peoples, and cultures, the fair attempted to order and
rank its musics in isolation.[104]

   Theodore Thomas served as principal architect of the hierarchical and partitioned arrangements at the fair. He coordinated a master
plan with the help of William Tomlins, choral director and director
of the Apollo Musical Club, and George Wilson, secretary of the
music bureau, who also edited Boston's *Music Herald*.[105] The bureau
pledged "to make a complete showing to the world of musical progress in this country in all grades and departments, from the lowest to
the highest, [and] to bring before the people of the United States a
full illustration of music in its highest forms as exemplified by the
most enlightened nations of the world."[106] In addition to concert
performances, the fair included a series of musical congresses devoted to orchestral and vocal music, music history and theory, so-
called songs of the people, organ and church music, music in art and
literature, criticism, and opera, and music's links to science, education, and everyday life. The bureau extended dozens of invitations to
international composers and ensembles, including the nation's most
distinguished music societies, such as New York's Oratorio Society,
Boston's Handel and Haydn Society, Philadelphia's Orpheus Club,
and Chicago's own Apollo Club, as well as leading instrumental organizations, such as the New York Philharmonic and the Boston and St.
Louis Symphony Orchestras.[107]

The musical center of the universe in the Thomas plan was the Court of Honor Music Hall at the White City, where he would conduct a special Exposition Orchestra that included key personnel selected from his orchestra.[108] With architectural quotations from classical antiquity, the design of the Music Hall—like the White City more generally—lent a solemn majesty to the concerts inside. A supplemental ticket fee was required to hear a Thomas concert (on top of the fifty-cent admission price of the fair). Resurrecting the model attempted in Philadelphia in 1876, Thomas insisted on formal rules of concert spectatorship, from a sacral hush once a performance began to the practice of closing the hall to latecomers.[109] As one guidebook explained, the Music Hall was "to be used by musical talent and connoisseurs of the art rather than by the mass of people who will visit Jackson Park," referring to the outdoor bandstand to the immediate south where popular, military band concerts by Sousa and others were planned.[110] The pattern of organization left no doubt that sacralization and specialization were intended to replace the democratic eclecticism that had won popular support at the "summer nights" concerts.

David Guion's analysis of the official compendium of music bureau programs reveals the narrow interpretation Thomas and his staff applied to their "full illustration of music in its highest forms." Under the category of "Symphony concerts" the bureau emphasized the works of Wagner, Schubert, Brahms, Beethoven, and Schumann, while excluding northern and eastern European composers. Thomas's "popular programs" category comprised of short works, dances, and overtures performed by the Exposition Orchestra eschewed beloved Italian composers, such as Verdi and Rossini, and stuck to a narrow band of Europeans and the occasional American artist.[111] Gender bias compounded the exclusionary Eurocentric and hierarchical perspective of the music bureau, leaving disappointed women composers excluded from extensive formal exposure at the White City outside the Women's Building. The Exposition Orchestra performed seven orchestral works by women, and more than fifty small-scale works composed or arranged by women appeared on programs over the course of the fair. The first national convention of women's amateur music clubs at the fair could not offset the fact that female composers were relegated to the musical margins.[112]

National music days were the result of the organizational logic that included permanent pavilions at the White City promoting the history and accomplishments of such nations as Germany, Austria, Great Britain, and Norway.[113] Fair organizers and sponsors ran special theme days on which musical performances celebrated the traditions of Chicago's principal national groups. On June 15, 1893, "German Day" presented the music of over two dozen German-language singing societies.[114] Antonín Dvořák visited Chicago for "Czech Day" and conducted a program that included his Eighth Symphony, as well as three pieces from his second series of Slavonic Dances and the overture to Bohemian composer Bedřich Smetana's "Ma Vlast" ("My Country").[115] Likewise, "Polish Day" and "Russian Day" featured various demonstrations of cultural solidarity at the White City's Fine Arts Building that included Polish and Russian composers.[116]

FROM "THEODORABLE" TO THEODEPLORABLE
Sacralization and Its Discontents

When the fair officially opened to the public on May 1, the Exposition Orchestra drew respectably well. But attendance then dipped precipitously, even though the performances were affordably priced and accessible in a way that the 1876 concerts were not. With the music bureau's budget deficit widening, squabbling broke out between Thomas, Colonel George R. Davis, the director-general of the fair, and members of the National Commission, the congressionally appointed oversight body of the fair.[117] Calls for Thomas's resignation came in two waves: first, at the opening of the Exposition, during the so-called Piano War—when Thomas defended the right of virtuoso pianist Ignazy Jan Paderewski to perform on a Steinway rather than the brand backed by western piano makers—and again in midsummer when Thomas refused to lighten concert programs to pump up sagging ticket sales.[118] With no end to the impasse in sight, and with a job to fall back on, Thomas resigned. He sardonically suggested that organizers, in George Upton's choice phrase, "treat music as an amusement, not as an art, during the remainder of the Exposition period."[119]

During his struggles to effect his musical vision at the fair, the popular press support that Thomas had once enjoyed failed him. Stung by the actions of a conductor once perceived as a friend of the masses, the *Chicago Record-Herald* disparaged Thomas as a haughty elitist whose only loyalties lay with the wealthy subscription holders of the Chicago Orchestra.[120] George Upton stood by his hero, lamely reminding others of the smattering of "working-men's concerts" presented in recent years by Thomas and the Chicago Orchestra as a sign that he remained attuned to the masses, but the general sentiment remained unfavorable.[121] Confirming that his touch with the baton outstripped his public relations abilities, Thomas published a rude response to his critics: "In the art of music almost everything that is written for the daily press is rendered of no value on account of either the prejudices or the ignorance of the writers."[122] On that note, whatever vestiges there were of "Theodorable," the triumphant promoter of good music and democratic public culture in Chicago, disintegrated, leaving an elitist caricature behind, who might as easily have been referred to as Theodeplorable Thomas.

MUSICAL PUBLICS ON THE MIDWAY

At the end of June, between rounds of Thomas's feud with fair officials, the Midway Plaisance, a mile-long strip about six hundred feet wide, opened with enthusiastic support from fair organizers.[123] Brass bands, strolling musicians, piano players, and other entertainers delighted crowds in cafés, beer gardens, and ethnic exhibits, such as the Hungarian café, where Paul Olah's Gypsy Band performed.[124] Music accompanied performances and demonstrations connected with commercialized non-Western cultural installations, combining a blend of voyeuristic fantasy and quasi-ethnological interest. Customers heard songs and witnessed dance performances on the "Streets of Cairo," and at the Dahomey, Chinese, Turkish, and Javanese Villages.[125] The combination of these attractions, warm weather, and the decision to open the fair consistently on Sunday to serve a sizable population of laborers previously excluded due to schedule conflicts boosted attendance considerably.[126]

In August, with Thomas out of the picture, organizers gutted the remaining classical concert schedule and shifted the focus to open-air concerts by John Philip Sousa's New Marine Band. Sousa delivered festive, energetic, crowd-pleasing music. Unlike Thomas's self-consciously severe tutorials in the cultivated musical canon, Sousa entertained in a familiar, informal, and accessible style that appealed to the senses of thousands sweeping in by rail to celebrate "Iowa Day," "Michigan Day," and "Wisconsin Day." According to Neil Har-

John Philip Sousa. Library of Congress.

ris, Sousa appealed to the crowds at the fair because he provided the sound of a "culture of reassurance" via the masculine vigor and directness of a 4/4 beat and plenty of brass. In a nation unsure of how to reconcile the politics of taste and musical aesthetics with its own emergent democratic tradition, Harris continues, Sousa sloughed off any hint of the effeminate or brooding tendencies attached to the refined sounds of classical concert music.[127]

Harris's argument raises important questions about the specifics of the extraordinary evaporation of popular support for European classical music in Chicago. If gender anxiety made Sousa appealing to the masses, how are we to explain the turn against the manly singing societies or the Turner concerts, where men drank and smoked to the accompaniment of classical composers? It seems clear that Thomas had no interest in attempting to sustain the democratic civic model with any form of music other than uncompromising classical music. The disciplinary regimen of the White City had little to offer the patrons of garrulous Turner concerts who had felt reasonably at ease in the beer garden during the "summer nights" years. Did sacralizers simply drive off the public that Thomas had created during the late 1870s and the 1880s? Alternatively, did the much publicized battle between Thomas and Sousa distract attention from the more important work of music expressing and enlarging democratic public culture that transpired on the Midway?

MULTIPLE PUBLICS
Music on the Midway

The plethora of musical activity on the Midway does not fit neatly into the formulation of a sacralized, classical mode embodied by Thomas versus the popular, brass band mode identified with Sousa. Other forces actively shaped the sounds and meanings of music on the Midway that reconnect to the neighborhood music practices discussed earlier in this chapter. In addition to its carnivalesque qualities, the Midway sustained serious countersacralized and counterimperial music programming on the part of Chicago's inhabitants. Here a range of immigrant and ethnic neighborhood musics manifested alternative representations of civic music and Americanism operating outside the debate over classical uplift and vernacular populism. Exhibits sponsored by different ethnic and national groups of the city used music as part of a strategic intraethnic self-promotion and public display against the backdrop of the fair.

Though able to claim a building on the grounds of the White City, German-speakers used the Midway as a second stage on which to promote practices, customs, and traditions to outsiders associated with less formal, but no less significant, aspects of what it meant to self-identify as German *and* American at the fair. Months before the official opening of the fair, participants spoke excitedly of the financial support from German financial institutions in Chicago and Berlin that would be used to construct a "German Village" on the Midway incorporating elements of a hamlet, a medieval city, and a traditional concert garden. This installation was destined "to become the general rendezvous for Germans and German-Americans," where the *Illinois Staats-Zeitung* promised "one can feel at home." Like the Turner concerts or a neighborly North Side beer garden, the exhibit would create a haven of Germanness in the self-consciously American setting of the fair. The German village offered a distinctive opportunity to integrate German culture past and present. "[Visitors] will be able to hear genuine German sounds and words, without a mixture of the so-called Pennsylvania Dutch," promised one description of the plan. "Music from German military bands, in brilliant uniforms, will fascinate them. . . . [T]o speak German freely and sing German songs will be their delight and privilege."[128] Amid the commercial amusements and diversions of the Midway, active processes of identity formation via music attempted to enfold visitors into a transnational celebration of Germanness.

The German Village promoted and mediated German and American group identity, but with a pronounced German accent: "Anglo-Americans will observe this spectacle, but they will not be able to enjoy that sweet pleasure the Germans are favored with, because the latter's heart strings are tied to their homeland." The image of proprietary racialism, perhaps to counter the American boosterism of the fair, drew attention to the importance of sharing a distinctive tradition and fostering group identity. At the same time, the exhibit attempted to claim civic relevance and space for German culture as a valued component of American culture. The German Village promised to perform public relations work among non-German visitors, namely, to "teach that the German is not so bad as is generally supposed. It will be a living demonstration of the fact that German songs, German entertainments, and German joviality and geniality are valuable treasures of the German people, of which it need not be ashamed."[129] Striking the notes of nationalist pride so as to counter what may have been the residual criticism of German unification, the German Village used music to celebrate lives that were unapologetically both German and American.

"AFTER THE FAIR"
The Ascent of Musical Progressivism

In the midst of the Columbian Exposition, a parody of Charles K. Harris's waltz hit "After the Ball" (1893) appeared. Originally performed on a downtown minstrel stage, "After the Fair" was circulated widely in the form of sheet music and via Sousa's repeated performances of the waltz at the fair itself.[130] The lyrics contrasted the fair's sensational culture of abundance with amusing speculations about the colossal letdown awaiting Americans once the fair closed. With couplets such as "I'd rather live in Brooklyn (somebody'd know me there) / Than to live in Chicago, after the Fair" and references to "empty houses, run up with sticks and glue," the parody hinted at the artificiality and bombast of the fair as well as the anxious undercurrents of a complex and contradictory nation with divided peoples and cultures. What lessons, if any, the song seemed to ask, had the fair provided the nation and its people?

The aesthetic pretensions of the fair had failed to generate a model of civic musical cohesion other than via a market model on the Midway in which consumers picked and chose among multiple recreational options. In sharp contrast, the Jubilee was a Chicago-centered event. The selection of popular bandleader Patrick S. Gilmore promoted a view of civic celebration as a popular enterprise: full-throated, gregarious, yet aesthetically unadventurous. Civic celebration and uplift did not mix in this case, nor were subgroups of the population substantively engaged in shaping the sensibilities of the event. Several years later, the Thomas "summer nights" concerts translated support for European classical music coming from neighborhood immigrant and ethnic musical quarters into a mainstream civic phenomenon. The concerts promoted a people's music that melded education and entertainment for a cultured and democratic city. At the Columbian Exposition, however, Theodore Thomas refused any compromises and retreated from the aesthetic negotiation and democratic engagement that the previous concerts had represented. The public that had once connected with the conductor refused to recognize the tune he now played and rejected his overtures of aesthetic reform and social discipline.

The Jubilee and Thomas "summer nights" concerts exhibited a reform sensibility that connected civic involvement with shared experiences designed to transcend most barriers of class and cultural difference. The hierarchical musical ordering of the 1893 fair stressed aesthetic and social particularism that fragmented the civic model into a multiplicity of musical genres, sites, and audience publics. The glut of space and resources at the fair produced a messy vitality that attested to the diversity of cultures and community voices in metropolitan Chicago, but which offered no clear understanding of how to knit these into a broadly beneficial reform sensibility.

The collapse of the music bureau under Thomas produced a Hobson's choice between sacralized or popular music that left no official space for alternative models as a facet of group identity and civic belonging. The fair encouraged a retreat into a symbolic American mansion of many musical rooms in which citizens self-segregated rather than engaging their multiplicity in an explicit way. The military marches of Sousa may have reassured anxious Chicagoans by consolidating them into a mass audience, but its democratic meanings paled in comparison to the potential of a democratic musical sphere in which the cultural histories of the city's many peoples might be linked as part of a unified civic sensibility. As the Midway musics suggested, chaotic surfaces could conceal the efforts of neighborhood and ethnically identified publics to create musical room for themselves in urban public space. The resilience of these musical producers amid the clash of sacralizers and commercial populists suggested a hopeful future direction for civic musical reform, which a new generation of activists stood poised to explore.

The failure of the 1893 fair to produce a coherent model of civic musical engagement did not discourage others from pursuing their dreams of civic harmony. In the city of Chicago, removed from the headlines and bustle of the fair, musical progressives were at work. They included educators, social activists, municipal officials, private citizens, and entrepreneurs busily engaged in generating new ideas about music as a democratizing instrument. They were the inheritors of almost a century of efforts to incorporate democratic ideals, music, and civic engagement into recreational activity. In contrast to the aesthetic rigidity of Thomas or the commercial pandering of Sousa, these reformers sought to balance education, entertainment, and uplift anew. They willingly eschewed hierarchy and sacralized dictums to fulfill their musical outreach plans. Their efforts, as described in the chapters that follow, promoted fresh thinking to address the issues of inclusion, aesthetics, and democratic processes of identity formation stirred by the Jubilee, the Thomas "summer nights" concerts, and the fair.

TWO

BATTLE FOR THE BATON
CEREMONIAL PARKS AND THE LANDSCAPE OF MUSICAL REFORM, 1869–1904

On a crisp evening in early September 1902, several thousand residents of Chicago's West Side gathered for a ritual of musical progressivism—a free outdoor concert at the Garfield Park bandstand. The concourse and walkways surrounding the bandstand teemed with young shop clerks, seamstresses, mechanics, salesmen, and salesgirls out for an evening of music and dancing. Older spectators and families sat on long benches or under the trees preparing themselves for a pleasant evening's entertainment. Up on the bandstand, uniformed members of the Second Regiment Band fiddled with their valves and adjusted their instruments in preparation for the performance. At last, with a signal from the conductor, the first selection of the program of lively marches and popular songs burst forth from the bandstand.[1]

In a few moments, however, the bucolic scene of musical Americana took a nightmarish turn.[2] "The evening was cool," recalled one witness, "and many of the spectators to warm up began jigging and dancing when the Second Regiment Band struck up an unusually tuneful air." "This seemed to be the signal for the slugging and bouncing," continued another report. As the band played on, un-aware perhaps of the trouble just below them, plainclothes po-lice in the employ of the West Chicago Park Commissioners (WPC) surged into the crowd and began clubbing dancers and spectators. Panic-stricken spectators bolted in every direction pursued by baton-wielding cops. According to eyewitnesses and news reports, one dancer, Locke Wilbur, "was seized by the collar, dragged and kicked to the stone stairs leading to the stand, thrown down and brutally hit in the face." Clarence E. White, another dancer, "was beaten and trampled upon until he became unconscious." With horrifying speed, the scene of civic life at its best had degenerated into chaos and ugly violence.[3]

Headlines reporting police officers clubbing the heads of music lovers were not the kind of critical notices park commissioners proba-bly expected from the penultimate concert of a very successful sea-son. Crowds estimated at 10,000 spectators per concert had attended events in the district that summer. The public support vindicated the decision made six years earlier by the WPC to invest the princely sum of $37,000 to erect the Garfield Park bandstand as a shrine to the music in the park system. Built of Georgian marble, the elegant oc-tagonal structure could accommodate an orchestra numbering as many as 100 instruments. Its striking appointments included Sara-cenic motifs invoking the exoticism of the Middle East, an iron roof sheathed in copper, railing panels with intricate mosaics made of colored glass, and electric lighting for the performers.[4] The fracas at the base of the elegant bandstand seemed utterly out of character with the ideal of social harmony and civility that park sponsors had sought to instill for over thirty summers of concerts at Garfield and other parks across the city.[5]

The history of music making in Chicago's ceremonial parks sug-gests that weekend concerts around the bandstand were hardly the genteel affairs that one might assume. Though violent incidents of this kind appear to have been uncommon, the 1902 Garfield Park disturbance revealed a lengthy history of struggle for control of music in the parks. The root issues extended as far back as a quarter century when these massive public green spaces were established and a con-cert regimen was instituted within them.[6] The disturbance illus-trated the intensity of what one Chicago music editor referred to as the "long-debated question" of the people's right to musical self-determination in public settings. Music had complex, at times con-

Crowd at Douglas Park concert, ca. 1900. Chicago Park
District Special Collections.

flicting associations with bourgeois uplift and popular forms of commercialized public recreation, such as dancing. With its supposed
powers of influence over the moral behavior of men and women, the
character of music struck progressive reformers and ordinary citizens
alike as an essential civic concern, or even, on occasion, something
worth fighting over.[7]

This chapter analyzes the rise of music as a reform tool in Chicago's major parks of the late nineteenth century. While leading studies of Progressive Era parks mention music in passing, virtually none
treat it analytically, either in the context of the reform "landscape"
that urban parks constituted spatially and discursively or as a contested public activity in which residents spiritedly engaged progressive outreach.[8] The history of the development and implementation
of these concerts and their change over time reveals a fascinating and
important manifestation of progressive outreach and cultural politics.
Music made a distinctive contribution to the reform environment
envisioned by progressive park planners, landscapers, and municipal
officials. Music added an important aural dimension to the landscape
of the senses in Chicago's large, ceremonial parks that included ornamental plantings, picturesque vistas, wide lawns, leafy glades, and
tranquil ponds and lagoons.[9] Free summer concerts in the park ex-

pressed the romantic idealism accompanying the creation of the city's three major park districts. The programs blended entertainment, uplift, and a disciplining undertone that reflected activists' desires to engineer the civic welfare via music.[10]

The history of music in urban parks also offers a fresh perspective on the complex reception given by ordinary folk to progressive cultural outreach. As late-nineteenth-century neighborhood music practices migrated into Chicago's public park spaces, they created a fascinating interplay in which citizens and municipal officials competed to shape the character and function of urban public culture. The musical publics that coalesced around these concerts successfully enlarged the definition of music in civic life, often in ways that circumvented reform preferences.

"NO PLACE FOR SOCIAL DISTINCTIONS"
The Garfield Park Incident in Context

In the days following the September 1902 disturbance at the Garfield Park bandstand, news reports provided a chilling account of the attack by the supposed defenders of park tranquility. "Clubs Choke Mirth. Dancing at a park concert is vigorously repressed . . . Citizens badly beaten," declared one headline. The report noted that "[t]he officers making the assaults showed no stars to indicate their authority."[11] The *Chicago Tribune* confirmed that several plainclothes West Park police officers were being investigated for "throwing several young men down a flight of stone steps from the walk surrounding the bandstand."[12] No report contained clear information of what specific action had spurred the officers to strike at the moment that they did other than the observation that officers charged into the crowd at the beginning of a particularly danceable march.

Eyewitnesses described how a uniformed park police captain stood by as his undercover cops lit into the dancing crowd. He allegedly made no attempt to stop the violence, though in their pursuit of suspected troublemakers his officers caused one woman to faint, injured several citizens, and tore the clothes and broke the cane of another bystander. "From several persons it has been learned that similar brutality has been given the public during previous [WPC] concerts," reported one source, though no details were provided. In a letter to the *Chicago News*, a citizen sarcastically advised concert patrons to beware the "royal bouncer," adding: "Don't go to the band concerts in Garfield Park and try to dance to stirring music unless you want to be slugged by the park policemen."[13]

Captain T. H. Nolan of the wpc police department defended his men's actions as necessary to protect the refined character of the concerts. "The people attending the band concerts have been seriously annoyed this summer by a number of young hoodlums who have mingled with the crowd on the walk above the bandstand," he explained. "They have insulted women and we have made a determined effort to get rid of them." Nolan added that "it was necessary to have men in plainclothes at the concerts to be on the lookout for thieves and pickpockets and other general nuisances."[14] The unapologetic defense of the covert surveillance of concert patrons and the rough handling of dancers suggested that the officers had been waiting for the slightest provocation to assert their authority, if not over suspected "young hoodlums" or "thieves and pickpockets," then over a broad range of "general nuisances," including, it appeared, enthusiastic young dancers themselves.

Public anger over the behavior of Nolan's men grew in part from perceptions that the park police and commissioners had too much arbitrary power within their vast jurisdiction. Both the West and South Park districts maintained independent police forces to patrol hundreds of acres of parklands and miles of adjoining boulevards. Dubbed "sparrows" for their gray uniforms (and perhaps for their ubiquity), the park police had the authority to intercede in virtually all matters taking place on park property. Extensive regulations prohibited many activities common to other public areas of the city. Stringent ordinances and arrest statistics kept by the park police suggest that, at the time of the Garfield Park disruption, the ceremonial parks were among the quietest, most conscientiously policed if not the "safest" acres in the city.[15]

The lengths to which the wpc police appeared willing to go to keep the parks quiet and orderly struck many citizens as excessive. Prior to the incident in September, tensions between concert patrons, particularly young workingmen and -women, and officials had been mounting due to differences of opinion over appropriate codes of behavior in the parks. A crackdown earlier in the summer on flirtations between the sexes suggested that relations between young patrons and the police were deteriorating. In July, a judge fined a number of park users ten dollars for infractions that included "mashing," that is, making passes at young women, and for openly kissing in the park. The judge publicly chided young women of the West Side for flirting with handkerchiefs, which constituted an infraction of park rules and was punishable by a fine. These and other police actions reflected an uneasy dynamic between the keepers of public order and the young men and women who wished to enjoy themselves on public park property in their own way.[16]

In the aftermath of the Garfield Park melee, one citizen argued in a letter to a local newspaper that more was at stake than a case of police brutality or a case of a few misbehaving individuals inciting policemen. The struggle pitting revelers against park cops reflected larger cleavages between the WPC's idealized conceptions of public recreational space, concert audiences, appropriate rites of expressive culture, and the needs of hardworking (and occasionally hard-living) citizens seeking relief from the stresses of industrial discipline: "The park belongs to the people—not to the park commissioners or the park police. It is not a mere showplace, where people formally attired may walk primly up and down the gravel paths under the watchful eye of the police. It is a public pleasure ground, open to every citizen whether he superintends a Sunday school or runs a crap game. It is no place for social distinctions; still less is it a theater for the autocratic operations of park policemen."[17] In retrospect, the complaint about "social distinctions" and "autocratic operations" can be seen to have expressed a frustration among some park users about the bourgeois conventions sown (literally) into the ceremonial park landscape by its nineteenth-century planners and still resolutely cultivated by its twentieth-century custodians. The writer implied that park-user dissatisfaction could be attributed to the inability of a current generation of park officials to reconcile themselves to the lives and diversity of contemporary users.

Dissatisfaction with the responsiveness of park officials to public needs reflected the significance of these green spaces in the civic imagination of many Chicago residents. Prior to the establishment of the major park districts, a variety of so-called parks had dotted Chicago's landscape. These ranged from areas designated by city ordinance to undeveloped federal, state, and municipal lands (often adjoining public schools), to cinder-strewn vacant lots, to privately owned picnic groves and beer gardens, and to commercial amusement grounds operated by individuals and organizations under various arrangements. While such spaces displayed public features of a

Bandstand and adjacent grounds in Garfield Park, ca.
1900. Chicago Park District Special Collections.

kind, they represented a limited conception of service to the public
broadly defined. The parties who controlled the public, semipublic,
and private commercial spaces in the city freely practiced discrimina-
tory practices on the basis of race, class, ethnicity, and gender.[18]

By contrast, the major park districts of Chicago were founded
amid a national wave of progressive reform committed to invigorating
the democratic character of urban public space, adjusting public recreational habits, and improving the health and moral character of
urbanites. In 1869 the landmark Park Acts established Chicago's independent Board of Commissioners of Lincoln Park (LPC), South
Park Commissioners (SPC), and West Chicago Park Commissioners to
oversee hundreds of acres of parkland expressly for "public use."[19] In
theory, any Chicago resident could expect to be welcome in the ceremonial parks subject to rules and protections applying to all. To
progressive idealists, these new green spaces constituted a common
ground, literally and figuratively, designed to accommodate the varied needs of urban users of all social classes wishing to relax, play,
listen, or dance. Nonetheless, class, cultural, and racial biases among
planners, park officials, and park users would compromise the realization of this vision at different times and in different ways.[20] In the
struggle to perfect the civic promise of public parks, open-air concert

music served as a medium in which park officials and users developed and contested urban public culture and democratic expression.[21]

AURAL ARCADIAS
Music and Nineteenth-Century Park Design

Frederick Law Olmsted and Calvert Vaux, the famed landscape architects of New York City's Central Park, included music as a design element in their plan for Chicago's South Park district. Music accompanied the assemblage of trees, shrubs, water, buildings, and human activities that collectively constituted a reform relationship between the individual and the landscape. Speaking of his most famous work in New York City, Olmsted wrote: "The effect of good music on [Central Park] is to aid the mind in freeing itself from the irritating effect of the modern conditions."[22] In their plan for the spc, the two designers envisioned "weekly band concerts played on an island in the Jackson Park lagoon" sending melodies wafting across the lake to listeners grouped on the shore or bobbing in rowboats. Not surprisingly, the plan for the West Park district, designed and built by an Olmsted protégé, William Le Baron Jenney, also incorporated musical pavilions and bandstands.[23]

As S. Frederick Starr has suggested, bandstands garnered attention in nineteenth-century design and social reform circles as icons of a romanticized ideal of communal interaction. Though commonly associated with vernacular structures on the town green, bandstand design attracted the talents of the notable American designer and architect Richard Morris Hunt. Andrew Jackson Downing, whose *A Treatise on the Theory and Practice of Landscape Gardening* (1844) established many tenets of urban park design in the United States, emphasized the rejuvenating purity of the rustic gazebo, whose picturesque lines and thatched roof made it a forerunner of bandstand designs in many of Chicago's parks. By 1900 the shift from Gothic Revivalism toward the monumentality of the "City Beautiful Movement" would also leave an imprint on the built environment of park music reform, evidenced in such grandiose structures as the Garfield Park bandstand.[24]

Building bandstands, pavilions, and music courts, and hiring bands to perform in them, reflected only the most obvious steps in implementing park music reform. The goal of "freeing" the mind via music, as Olmsted put it, required additional measures to quell competing musics, noises, or distractions associated with unrefined urban spaces or persons that might interrupt the contemplative processes of the musical park landscape.[25] In 1881 the South Park Commissioners published the injunction that "without the permission of the Superintendent, no one shall play at any games . . . or shall play a musical instrument" on park property. The SPC also banned music accompanying parading, drilling, performing, or exhibitions of any kind. Violators could be fined the princely sum of twenty-four dollars per offense.[26] The West Chicago Park Commissioners listed unauthorized playing of a musical instrument under the category of "Misdemeanors." Likewise, the Lincoln Park Commissioners specified that "[n]o person shall play upon any musical instrument or thing."[27] In attempting to create a kind of aural cordon sanitaire around the parks, these restrictions reflected Victorian biases against activities associated with plebeian or disorderly recreation. The park commissioners did not tolerate the presence of musical activity accompanying political campaigning and labor, ethnic, or religious rallies and parades. Any such activities challenged the authority of park commissioners to direct public attention to the uplifting recreational pastime of listening to "appropriate" sounds of park concert music.[28]

Official apprehensions about spontaneous or calculated eruptions of competing music or noise extended to concern about human disruptions of the reform landscape of the senses. So seriously did ceremonial parks take their commitment to aesthetic representations of order and regimentation that they prohibited anyone appearing in a park with a physical ailment or deformity. To be sure, beggars and panhandlers might be seen as nuisances, but such marginal populations could be aurally disruptive, too. Likewise, the unpredictable or inappropriate cries, laughter, or other noises made by the infirm or the mentally ill were problematic in an aural arcadia. Park "noise" prohibitions emphasized the premium on self-presentation and bodily control attached to the aural reform regimen. Oddities such as appearing in public dressed in the attire of the opposite gender were also banned. These policies may not have been consistently enforced, but they suggest the mutual reinforcement of reform programs to instill proper conventions of musical taste and response, to promote proper physical dress and display, to encourage self-conscious mastery of the body, and to control what might be misused as potential sites of resistance to, or subversion of, the codes of restraint that characterized the recreational reform culture of the ceremonial park.[29]

PUTTING ON AIRS
Early Park Concerts

Before many of the ceremonial parks were fully landscaped, audiences began flocking to hear park-sponsored concerts. In the South, West, and Lincoln Parks, philanthropists helped to defray costs of the first concerts, but as time passed, the three districts soon established regular budgets for concerts, augmented by contributions from individuals, groups, and such interested parties as local rail and streetcar companies.[30] In 1873 the South Park Commissioners instituted summer concerts at a temporary music stand at the "Park Retreat" in Jackson Park. Over in the "West Division" soon to be named Washington Park, the SPC presented additional band concerts before erecting a permanent ornamental bandstand in the spring of 1875.[31] By the mid-1870s, crowds in the thousands attended concerts at Lincoln Park, Jackson and Washington Parks, and Douglas, Garfield, and Humboldt Parks in the West Park district.[32]

Significantly, despite the emphasis on aural discipline within the ceremonial park landscape and on respectability generally, park concerts did not uniformly emphasize the cultivated European classical music canon. Nor were park officials deeply invested in creating a kind of alfresco equivalent to the sacralized indoor concert hall where conductors demanded silent obedience from audiences. In keeping with the genteel informality of European pleasure gardens in which entertainment and uplift coexisted, concerts in the parks presented entertaining and widely accessible music programs.[33] The concerts featured orchestras and military brass bands, the two most common large musical ensembles of the day. These units featured brass, woodwinds, and occasionally strings, and performed popular material for listening and dancing. Park audiences heard accessible selections from classical European composers (Wagner, Meyerbeer, Gounod), familiar operatic airs (Rossini, Verdi), popular American songs, and marches, as well as polkas, waltzes, and two-steps.[34]

Though musical selections were light, park officials carefully limited performers to an established pool of prominent Chicago bandleaders. In the early 1870s, Hans Balatka, whose cultivated ties to the Oratorio Society, the Germania Männerchor, and the Philharmonic Society made him a local rival to Theodore Thomas, conducted weekly summer concerts in Lincoln and Washington Parks, where he drew "immense crowds of visitors both on carriage and on foot."[35] Balatka's presence in the parks suggests the artistic expectations that park commissioners and audiences had during the initial years of ceremonial park concerts.

On the North Side in the 1870s, Johnny Hand, another gifted conductor, began an extended tenure in Lincoln Park that would last thirty years.[36] Though not in the same technical league as Balatka or Thomas, Hand's charisma made him both a favorite of park audiences and the darling of Chicago's leading families, at whose parties and functions he regularly appeared. Bertha Honoré Palmer, doyenne of Chicago society and wife to the real estate mogul Potter Palmer, would describe the dapper Hand as "one of the institutions of Chicago." His private engagements included the weddings of General Philip Sheridan, industrial magnate George M. Pullman, and the Palmers themselves.[37]

Pretensions to creating an aural arcadia aside, the nature of concerts performed outdoors before hundreds or even thousands of spectators challenged musicians as well as the reformers who were eager to control the tenor of the events. The placement of bandstands among groves of trees produced a romantic visual and aural effect for park visitors, but it tested the skill and patience of performers. During the 1874 season in Lincoln Park, noting that his summer orchestra numbered twenty-two men, including several string players, Hans Balatka requested that the Commissioners of Lincoln Park support more men. "In order to increase the effectiveness of the orchestra," he explained, "it is very desirable to double some of those parts, which carry the melody, as to make them better heard at a greater distance." Wind gusts, chattering spectators, the whinnies and snorts of horses, creaking carriage frames, and the background movement of bodies and vehicles added a chaotic counterpoint to concert performances.[38] Though he could not reasonably impose codes of silence or stillness on his audiences, Balatka could demand more firepower. "Should the attendance, especially of carriages, be very large," Balatka warned, "the number of the orchestra should be increased to 30 at least."[39]

The conductor's demands for more volume reflected a simple desire to be heard clearly, but it also communicated a truism of open-air concerts: the desire for control by a conductor competed with the power of the audience to shape the tenor of the outdoor gathering. The limitations imposed on park sounds and behaviors could not stop spectators from adding spontaneous embellishments to the reform event. Racing off noisily in one's carriage in the midst of a tedious piece, talking loudly during quiet musical passages, and even dancing giddily off to the side suggest some of the possible ways in which patrons expressed themselves and could inject aspects of themselves into the civic spectacle.

At the outdoor concerts, spectators transformed the seats, lawns, and walkways surrounding bandstands into 360-degree performance arenas where multiple social minidramas might be staged within view of others.[40] Band concerts created a distinctive and highly inter-active aural and social space that included seated, standing, and danc-ing listeners, as well as knots of observers talking on the periphery, rubbernecking at the crowd, or merely passing through the park. Though many spectators arrived in carriages, riders were encouraged to descend from their private vehicles in order to mingle with their fellow citizens near the bandstand.[41]

The informal seating and spatial arrangements of park concerts, the opportunity for social mixing, a general tolerance for background noise and talk, and the circulation of spectators during the perfor-mance contrasted sharply with trends in the management of indoor concerts, particularly for cultivated symphony orchestras. Theodore Thomas respected the European pleasure garden model during the "summer nights" concerts of the 1870s and 1880s. But Thomas and others preferred silent and attentive audiences, who remained seated throughout the entirety of a performance in regimented rows, tiers, and boxes of seats facing a stage.[42] Open-air park concerts in the 1870s and 1880s conformed neither to the exuberant informality of a laborer's Sunday picnic nor to the exacting codes of audience be-havior in cultivated concert halls. Instead, they supported a hybrid form of musical recreation akin to the "summer nights" concerts, whose intentional uplift features would prove to be surprisingly ame-nable to the varied aesthetic and social needs of participants.

"IT WILL NOT BE MUCH USED BY THE CITIZENS"
Geographies of Privilege in the South Parks

Despite the potential of free park concerts to link citizens in a shared ritual of refined public recreation, evidence suggests that not all resi-dents were equipped to enjoy the early concerts presented in Wash-ington and Jackson Parks. The sheer distance separating the South Parks from Chicago's industrial wards, the prosperous residential neighborhoods that sprang up adjacent to the ceremonial parks, and a

lack of affordable or convenient public transportation limited the
initial participation of significant numbers of laborers in the South
Parks.[43] "In regard to the district about your site," Olmsted and Vaux
had written to SPC officials in March 1871, "the advantage which will
come with the park for securing domestic comfort can hardly fail to
soon establish a special reputation for the neighborhood and give
assurance of permanence to its character as a superior residence quarter. . . . [I]t will be in the center of a really populous and wealthy district."[44] The report continued: "Under these circumstances, it may be
thought that the park to be formed upon it *will not be much used by the
citizens of Chicago*, except as a distant suburban excursion ground. . . .
It is then a question how far it should be treated purely as a local
park."[45] The creation of the South Park district sprang both from an
idealistic progressive rationale about the power of parks to reform the
urban population and a rare chance to build a fantasy landscape on
the urban periphery. The first few decades of the district's existence
suggest that to a greater extent than at Lincoln or the West Parks,
suburban homogeneity rather than urban heterogeneity characterized the user profile of the South Parks. Civic musical outreach remained a luxury afforded to leisured residents, who made up, most
conspicuously, a prosperous local population residing along fashionable boulevards laid out by park planners.[46]

　　Although concert attendance in the South Park district increased
steadily throughout the 1870s, surviving accounts of audience composition suggest that the events attracted a selective constituency
with access to private transportation or a willingness and ability to pay
the high costs of public transportation. The boulevard network developed and managed as part of the park system provided a conduit for
local carriage owners, who descended on the parks via Grand Boulevard, such that the route was "often crowded for a space of two miles
with carriages averaging three abreast."[47] Most laborers would not
have had access to, or the funds to hire, a team to travel to the parks
very often, and streetcar surcharges applied for the long trip.[48]

　　South Park officials acknowledged that if their ceremonial park
concerts were going to serve a wide swath of the population and fulfill
their democratic mandate, the public access problem between the
city center and the South Parks would have to be addressed. Noting
the imbalance between carriage and foot traffic in Washington Park,
the SPC surmised that "the latter attendance would probably be much
more numerous if the fare by street cars from the city were reduced to

five cents instead of fifteen, the present charge."[49] In 1876 the spc
made a modest gesture to address the deficiency by commissioning
three phaetons to ferry passengers from the intersection of Oakwood
and Drexel Boulevards (a few miles north of the parks) down Drexel
and Grand Boulevards to Jackson Park for twenty cents for a round
trip. By the early 1880s, the phaetons were collecting over 20,000 fares
during the summer season.[50] Nevertheless, the rides were still expensive, and the route did not extend sufficiently northward to serve Chicago's industrial neighborhoods. As one commentator noted, the boulevards near the South Parks remained conduits of privilege where
"the richly attired ladies and stylish looking gentleman reigned supreme, and the common people did not block the way."[51]

    Challenged with the observation that the phaeton service cost
too much for most laborers who might want access to the parks,
the spc responded defensively. "As soon as the steady patronage of
the phaetons is such as to justify it the passenger rate will be reduced," the commissioners declared in 1880.[52] But the spc rejoinder
to charges of elitism relied on specious reasoning. As long as the
routes of the phaetons remained confined to the upscale boulevard neighborhoods, the demand would be unlikely to increase dramatically, since many, if not most, citizens in these areas had access
to private carriages. It took continued residential development, metropolitan expansion, and the special circumstance of the World's
Columbian Exposition to extend the Cottage Grove surface line to
make the South Parks readily accessible to the downtown area and to
open them up to more frequent use by Chicago laborers.[53]

"THE ÉCLAT OF THE SCENE"
The Musical Crowd in Lincoln Park

In contrast to the relatively remote South and West Parks, Lincoln
Park, which ran along the Chicago lakefront north of downtown, had
a deserved reputation for serving the recreational needs of the laboring classes in addition to those of the mobile carriage set. Various rail
and streetcar lines made a weekend trip to hear a band a reasonable
proposition for residents in industrial as well as more outlying areas.[54]
"Its somewhat less area [relative to Washington and Jackson Parks] is
offset by its greater proximity," explained Everett Chamberlin in
1874, "and as yet it is of more *public* benefit by far than either of the

other large parks."[55] Combining beaches, lawns, paths, leafy glades, and regular summer band concerts, the former Lakefront Park fulfilled its democratic function as a "daily resort of all classes."

After the Civil War, Lincoln Park regularly hosted festive musical gatherings in the summertime.[56] By the early 1870s, the LPC presented concerts on Saturdays and Sundays in the summer. Weekend activity transformed the adjacent Lake Shore Drive into a massive tangle of carriage and foot traffic. "This drive is, as might be expected, largely resorted to," wrote one observer, "especially on Saturdays when music by a band of thirty pieces, under distinguished leadership, contributes to its pleasurable and refining influence, and on Sundays, when boats and music on the water add to the *éclat* of the scene." With a robust heterogeneity that the South Parks of the 1870s and 1880s appeared to lack, Lincoln Park resounded with the sounds of music and the bustling presence of citizens from various backgrounds sharing one of the most beautiful areas of the city.[57]

Lincoln Park's concert culture bore the discernible imprint of the classical music-loving residents of the Near North Side, particularly Chicago's Germans, who perceived Lincoln Park concerts as a natural extension of neighborhood musical life and social activity.[58] In the spring of 1875, when Sabbatarian controversies caused the North Side Railroad Company to refuse to underwrite Sunday concerts in Lincoln Park, the *Illinois Staats-Zeitung* appealed to its loyal readers for help. As it often did in matters of ethnic pride, the paper appealed to enlightened self-interest and civic duty in urging readers to fund the expansion of German music in this public setting. "If all our prosperous Germans take an interest—and we entertain no doubts on that score—if the owners of summer gardens and refreshment places on the upper part of the city who derive considerable profit from the park concerts do their fair share, it would be a simple matter to raise the required sum."[59] With financial help from locals, the weekend concerts flourished, so much so that park commissioners had to post additional "Keep off the grass" signs in both English and German.[60]

The success of popular concerts in Lincoln Park in the 1870s and 1880s stirred apprehensions about inappropriate social mixing and the civic consequences of musical progressivism gone too far, apprehensions that were similar to those circulating in connection with the Thomas "summer nights" concerts downtown. Public concerts symbolized attempts to use musical recreation to promote civic pride and refined recreation, but the heterogeneous gatherings chafed at elite sensibilities. In an 1887 item in the *Chicago Tribune* offering an explanation as to "[w]hy the Lincoln Park concerts are not attended by fashionable people," the society columnist wrote: "The park concerts at one time bade fair to be popular with society people, but the crowds got so big that there was no comfort to be had. Why, at Lincoln Park the drive was so packed with carriages that it was impossible to move. A large force of policemen is kept there to keep a passage open, but they can't do it. After society got crowded in there once, it stopped going. South Park is so far away that it is a little better in this respect. However, society doesn't go to either very much. Outside of a ballroom it positively won't be crowded you know."[61] The writer's fascinating observation of the retreat of "society" from the public concert scene makes evident the sacralizing wave of privatization that competed with musical progressive attempts to expand the public sphere of music to include diverse audiences. The account underscored the irony of park commission efforts to bring urban citizens together in the name of the civic good. Expressing nostalgia for the time when "society people" patronized concerts in Lincoln Park captured a sense of the changing social and cultural character of the park. Laborers had always made use of Lincoln Park, but musical progressive outreach courted their participation in a reimagining of public music making as a civic enterprise open to all. The distress of "society" at such an invitation marked the shift in the power of elite interests to dictate the conditions of their public recreational experiences with quite the same confidence that they might have previously enjoyed. In sum, the first years of musical outreach in Chicago's major parks penetrated to different degrees into the urban population due to geographic variations across the major districts. What had begun to emerge, however, were self-aware musical publics, drawn together by civic music and motivated to function as agents in the democratic reform of urban public life, whatever their private credentials or status might be.

MUSICAL PUBLICS
Neighborhood Variation and Reform from Below

In the 1880s excitement about park concerts grew as a national craze for brass band music swept through Chicago. Legendary popular conductors and arrangers, such as Patrick Gilmore and a rising star named John Philip Sousa, inspired the formation of thousands of bands in villages, towns, and cities.[62] In Chicago, Lyon and Healy, one of the largest music equipment suppliers in the country, manufactured and sold band equipment, uniforms, and sheet music presenting simple arrangements of patriotic songs, popular ballads, and light-classical numbers formerly popularized by string or mixed instrument ensembles. Brass bands rapidly eclipsed concert orchestras as the dominant type of entertainment ensemble in parks and many public settings across the country. As one contemporary observed: "The gavot [sic], the waltz, the polka, and compositions reaching into the classics are now the common property of military bands." Classical symphony orchestras continued to perform occasionally at popular outdoor venues, but, as Theodore Thomas learned in 1876, and would again in 1893, popular affection for brass band music had grown explosively and given audiences wider choices for their musical entertainment.[63]

Rapid population increases and shifts in urban social relations and recreational habits among wage earners affected the changing character of park concerts by the turn of the century. During the 1870s the population of Chicago had increased from slightly less than 300,000 to over 500,000. It more than doubled between 1880 and 1890, however, and then grew an additional 50 percent in ten years to approximately 1.7 million persons by 1900. In slightly more than a generation, Chicago's population of potential ceremonial park patrons would increase by well over five-and-a-half times.

Continued improvements in public transportation serving the southern and western reaches of the city made it cheaper, easier, and faster for citizens from all walks of life to visit the ceremonial parks on a semiregular basis. The South and West Park districts became increasingly popular destinations for residents of modest means seeking relief from the summer heat and the overcrowding and noise of their industrial neighborhoods. By the 1890s, ceremonial park concerts entertained tens of thousands of spectators annually. One official study estimated that by 1900, 80 percent in attendance at Washington and Jackson Parks were "from the foreign population." Many, if not most, of these workers probably traveled by public transportation to reach the parks.[64]

The demographics of the upscale boulevard residences near Washington and Jackson Parks and the ethnic, plebeian neighborhoods near Lincoln Park shaped the respective music reform cultures

American bandleaders of the late nineteenth century.
National Music Museum, University of South Dakota,
Vermillion.

of these public spaces. In turn, the residential character of Chicago's
West Side exerted influences of its own. Although park officials were
not elected by the people, they nonetheless showed a pattern of
responsiveness to the varied needs of their neighborhood constituents.[65] At Douglas Park, about four miles west of downtown Chicago,
a student of West Park concerts found the musical selections skewed
toward "light popular airs of the day" rather than the European classical works popularized by Hans Balatka and Theodore Thomas and
still performed by Johnny Hand in Lincoln, Washington, and Jackson
Parks. "Classical selections may do well enough for certain occasions," noted the observer, "but they 'don't go' here."[66] One explanation for the character of the music came from the plebeian character
of the crowd: "Although many hundreds of the prosperous businessmen who reside in the vicinity gather in Douglas Park with their
families on these evenings, and many carriages are to be seen gathered on the drives near the stand, nevertheless the audience, in the
main, is made up of 'toilers.' "[67] Apparently many younger workers
frequented the concerts, less to listen carefully to the music than to
spend a warm evening socializing with friends or meeting members

of the opposite sex. "Brawny young mechanics and bright-eyed young shop girls, sturdy laborers and comely servant girls prevail in the throng, though many bright-looking salesmen and flirtatious young milliners, are scattered among the crowd," continued the report.[68] Despite its condescending tone, the sketch captured an important aspect of neighborhood park concerts: for all of the efforts by park officials to "reform" audiences, they also served alternative forms of recreation and social interaction.

Despite stringent rules, turn-of-the-century concerts, such as those at Douglas Park, offered appealing destinations for young people, whether they particularly cared for the music or not. For wage earners with limited entertainment budgets, it made sense that an individual or family should attend a free park concert to escape the confines of the home, apartment, or boardinghouse. Insular neighborhood events in private picnic grounds or forest preserves did not necessarily afford the anonymity that a large concert offered to young men and women wanting to spend time together, flirt, or pursue more illicit pleasures. The refined character of progressive musical outreach conferred respectable associations onto park concerts, particularly when contrasted with the uncertain character of commercial dance halls and cabarets. Concerts may well have supplied a cover for behaviors that reformers would never tolerate in association with an unregulated public recreational site.[69]

The evidence suggests that at least in some neighborhoods young concert patrons were finding a variety of ways to reform public park space in their own way. The behaviors of young patrons countered the quality of bourgeois stiffness that accompanied the ceremonial park concert model. Youths voiced their differences through mildly rebellious behaviors such as talking and laughing loudly during concerts, flirting with strangers, or dancing with abandonment on the lawn, to the consternation of seated listeners. Defying park rules, some reportedly used concerts as an opportunity to steal away from the crowd for romantic assignations in the dark recesses of the park.[70]

A scant mile away, a different mood prevailed at Garfield Park concerts. Spectators from "Washington Boulevard boarding houses [and] boarders from rival 'hasheries'" flirted on the periphery with an avidity matching the crowd at Douglas, yet any bandleader at Garfield "would feel that he had failed in his duty if he had not introduced some music of a high order in the programs." Audiences appeared far more interested in concert music as the focus of their evening out than as pleasant background accompaniment to other activities. "The immense audience gathered on the seats and on the grass within sight and hearing of the music stand are well dressed. . . . [T]he bulk of the audience is composed of clerks, male and female, salesmen and saleswomen, stenographers and cashiers, with a sprinkling of servant girls from the wealthy residences nearby."[71] This public of listeners at Garfield Park departed only marginally from the "toilers" at Douglas in their social and economic position, but they expressed a more serious devotion to European classical music than their counterparts elsewhere in the West Park district.

The fault line between spectators favoring popular standards, such as marches and hits from the American musical stage, and those preferring "music of a high order" concealed another tension dividing specific neighborhood ethnic and immigrant groups eager to see their national musical heritages on civic display. On the West Side, aficionados of German classical music asserted their tastes in the ceremonial parks with their customary air of self-confidence. Humboldt Park, north of Douglas Park, served as a public gathering point for many West Side Germans. An observer noted that band concerts consistently favored Strauss waltzes and airs from Wagner, "with maybe one or two popular pieces to give 'American' character to the entertainment." Refining sounds came in various forms, and the WPC willingly hired bandleaders whom they entrusted to appeal to local musical tastes. As in Lincoln Park, however, officials diligently enforced extramusical restrictions on ceremonial park reform space: "While in many features the scene brings to the mind a thought of Germany and the fatherland," the report on Humboldt concluded, "the observer will miss one essential viz.: 'the beer.'"[72] On numerous occasions, ceremonial park concerts adopted the taste preferences of local neighborhoods, even as control remained with park officials.

The preponderance of German music in the ceremonial park concert settings reflected the late-nineteenth-century classical canon, but it also symbolized the continued power wielded by Germans in shaping aspects of musical public culture. This fact provoked challenges from other ethnic groups seeking to use music in public to promote group pride. In the summer of 1896 the *Chicago Tribune* reported that "Poles desire folk songs at park concerts. At a meeting of representatives of the Polish Young Men's National Alliance yesterday, a committee was appointed to frame resolutions to request that Polish national airs and folk songs be played more frequently at the open air concerts. They say they are not trying to be bombastic in the display of loyalty and love to America and Poland by this action, but the airs of the various nationalities draw people to the parks, and they feel their demand is just."[73] Ethnic and immigrant groups sought the publicity and honor that musical inclusion in civic ritual settings represented. The allusion to "bombastic" display may have referred to the self-conscious shows of German musical nationalism that regularly appeared in public Chicago in the late nineteenth century. Several years later, after the Seventh Regiment Band, a forty-five-piece military band presented a special concert of Polish music at Douglas Park, the Polish-language *Dziennik Chicagoski* duly reminded readers of their responsibilities to support Polish national consciousness in the United States: "There can be more Polish festivals presented, but it is up to the public to demand them."[74] Like any other kind of civic improvement, the editorial seemed to say, special interests needed to lobby their cause for recognition and inclusion. Taking the opportunity to inject the civic musical realm with national sounds was among the gestures linked to effective democratic activity in the era of musical progressivism.

In another example of the interplay between the reform-tinged entertainment agenda of the commissioners and local audiences, officials of the WPC reported that they planned to shift the major summer concert of the week from Saturdays to Sundays. They defended the move by explaining that the WPC could best perform its public function by catering to the needs of "the population surrounding Douglas and Humboldt Parks where a greater portion of the laboring classes reside." These workers were far more likely to be able to attend a Sunday rather than a Saturday concert. Perhaps to defuse attacks from Sabbatarians on the morality of Sunday recreation, park officials also emphasized the beneficial effects that the switch would have on West Side families.[75]

Not all park concert patrons greeted the decision to defer to workers' schedules with enthusiasm. Certain community groups challenged the WPC's attentiveness to the needs of the laboring classes. The Twelfth Ward Tax Payers' Protective Association quickly passed a resolution entreating the WPC to reallocate its resources to provide smaller concerts each weekday in Douglas Park rather than a single, large event on Sunday when laborers would crowd into the park. The resolution claimed to favor increased recreational options, but the proposal came on the heels of the Saturday/Sunday switch. The likely scenario is that middle-class property owners sought to regain control over public recreational activity in what they perceived as their greater backyards. Crowds of laborers jockeying for space at Sunday concerts probably unsettled local property owners whose schedules afforded them a Saturday and a Sunday of leisure.

By requesting concerts at times most convenient for the leisured and proximate, these activists expressed a backlash against the democratization of public space that musical progressivism represented. Though the commissioners held fast to the Sunday schedule, political skirmishes like these expressed the way that public musical recreation exemplified interclass tensions in Chicago as citizens struggled for power in the civic realm. Increased patronage of park concerts by wage earners and laborers would force a reexamination of the reform-minded entertainment and uplift practices of the past, particularly as a new style of popular music challenged the aesthetic orthodoxy and social tenor that had dominated the parks during the first decades of concerts.[76]

CALLING THE TUNE
Ragtime in the Ceremonial Parks

At the turn of the century, the soaring popularity of ragtime challenged the balancing act of genteel aesthetics, popular tastes, and social needs that defined the tenor of ceremonial parks concerts.[77] As a style of song and dance music, ragtime was characterized by irregular rhythms, syncopated beats, and alternating bass lines. It arose from the postbellum blackface minstrelsy and vaudeville tradition, most directly through the so-called coon song. Originally sung in racialized dialect on the stage by grotesquely caricatured "Negroes," coon songs and their ragtime offshoots inspired a national fad for cakewalks, prances, and other dramatic dance styles. Scott Joplin, who appeared as a relative unknown on the Midway in 1893, defined the ragtime style for popular audiences and sold thousands of sheet music copies of his "Maple Leaf Rag" (1899). Touring stage companies further popularized ragtime and promoted its innovative and suggestive dances, such as the grizzly bear, the turkey trot, and the bunny hug. Unlike the smooth meter of a waltz, the uneven rhythmic accents of ragtime dances were emphasized by jerky movements of arms and legs and bodily gyrations.[78]

With its unorthodox rhythmic style and historical connection to the racially and sexually charged traditions of minstrelsy and coon songs, ragtime—and its popular emergence—unsettled many music and social critics. Though its arrival preceded the Great Migration of African Americans to Chicago in significant numbers, negative reactions to ragtime as a threat to American music, public morality, and even racial purity anticipated to a remarkable degree the racialized reception of jazz and blues that followed.[79] Some critics regarded ragtime as an aesthetic pollutant threatening to contaminate the nation's musical tradition. Others saw the dance music as dangerous because it appeared to encourage the loss of bodily control, vice, or even devil worship. "Its charm lies largely in its rhythm," wrote a typical analyst, "take the songs composed in ragtime; the syncopations that form their principal feature give rise to jerky rhythms, and these act upon the nervous system of the listener at unexpected and unnatural parts of the measure. . . . To the injudicious uses of rhythm may be attributed those sudden impulses which lead to crime."[80] Rhythmic recklessness and the explicit African American cultural quotations in the dances, however much they were caricatured, challenged the Eurocentric aesthetics and social conservatism of musical progressive outreach. With ragtime's legions of young fans transforming the urban recreational scene, the music and the dancing incarnated fears of an insidious interloper into the park reform landscape.

The issue of how to adopt ragtime into the time-honored formula of entertainment and gentle uplift at park concerts divided park officials and conductors. The typical ceremonial park concert of the 1870s and 1880s was skewed toward the lighter end of the European classical tradition. Well-known overtures and operatic arias from Wagner's *Tannhäuser* and Rossini's *William Tell* were interspersed with peppy American marches, as well as waltzes, gavottes, and quadrilles for dancing. By the 1890s, however, a number of programs embraced increasing amounts of material from the popular musical stage, including syncopated rags with titles such as "My Heart's Tonight in Texas," "Everybody Has a Whistle Like Me," and "Ma Rainbow Coon."[81] While some conductors followed the dictates of popular taste, others cleaved to the light-classical styles of earlier park concerts. The widely perceived gulf separating ragtime from other "pop-ular" musical styles challenged park officials, conductors, and au-diences to rethink the aesthetic and social tone of park concerts. The difficulty in reconciling this question would result in open conflict at one of the city's most popular ceremonial parks and alter the direction of musical progressivism.

JOHNNY HAND VERSUS THE "RAGTIME STRENGTH"

On August 24, 1898, the polarization of European classical music and American popular music struck the civic realm of park concerts with brutal force. The front page of the *Chicago Tribune* reported the out-come of a bitter musical struggle at the Lincoln Park Commission. The conflict pitted Joseph E. Dunton, a new vice president of the Board of Commissioners of Lincoln Park, against Johnny Hand, the mustachioed, éminence grise of ceremonial park concerts. Bearing the headline, "Calls for Negro Music," the *Tribune* article described a letter from Dunton to Hand ordering the conductor to cut back on European classical music and to add more ragtime to his pro-grams. Paraphrasing the letter's contents, the article stated: "[Dun-ton] said 'Siegfried' must not occur again, and intimated that 'Take Yer Clothes and Go' had several points of superiority over the *Jewel Song* from Faust." Accompanying the story, the *Tribune* published a line drawing of Commissioner Dunton next to facsimiles of two pieces of sheet music. The first sheet, captioned as "Mr. Dunton's Idea of a Hot Tune for Park Concerts," included the opening bars of "I Don't Care If Yo' Nebber Comes Back," a ragtime song by Ray-mond A. Browne and Monroe H. Rosenfeld. The second caption read "What Johnny Hand Thinks is Proper" and featured the opening bars of Wagner's overture to *Tannhäuser*. "So Wagner is defeated," lamented the *Tribune*, "Meyerbeer is doomed. Bach must go away from Lincoln Park."[82]

The *Tribune*'s provocative cover story indirectly accused pro-gressive park officials of abdicating their authority to a ragtime mob whose demands for the popular genre strained the founding ideals of refinement as a component of civic musical service. Until now, Lin-coln Park officials had successfully avoided controversies over pro-gram aesthetics at concerts. But the volatile, racialized genre of rag-time drew fire to the LPC for its apparent endorsement of ragtime over

Johnny Hand. Photograph by *Chicago Daily News*;
Chicago Historical Society, DN-0006474.

European classical music. In an ironic twist, a park commissioner, the
very custodian of refined recreational sensibility, stood accused of con-
taminating the aural landscape of Lincoln Park with "Negro music."

By impugning Commissioner Dunton as a champion of "Negro
music" (and perhaps of Negroes themselves) and Johnny Hand as a
Wagner disciplinarian à la Theodore Thomas, the *Tribune* helped to
polarize discussion of music's place in the parks. The use of symbols
of "low" ragtime versus "high" European classical music suggested

that the eclectic reform sound of past park concerts had fallen prey to the politicization of musical appetites. By the *Tribune*'s reckoning, the LPC's endorsement of ragtime recklessly undermined the kind of enlightened aesthetic stewardship that Hand and others had previously provided through their classically tinged popular concerts. It also suggested a growing rift within park audiences over the appropriate sound and style of public musical culture.

Hand's fall from grace represented a humbling reversal for the once-powerful symbol of concert music as an entertaining and uplifting feature of Chicago's parks. Since the early 1870s, he had been conducting summer concerts at Lincoln and other ceremonial parks after the European pleasure-garden model. When military band conductors in the parks began adding ragtime material in large quantities during the 1890s, Hand kept to his old formula. His programs incorporated pieces by the local, popular composer Reginald De Koven and Sousa marches, but they avoided the coon song altogether.[83] Hand had brushed off earlier requests from park officials to modernize his programs, but, under direct pressure from Dunton, he relented. Swallowing his pride, he reluctantly "made a tour of vaudeville theaters and roof gardens" to assemble a new program brimming with ragtime material.[84]

Hand's protestations represented a minority voice among park concert conductors and many ceremonial park officials. One month before the *Tribune* story on Dunton's intervention broke, the WPC instructed its bandleaders to deemphasize light-classical music and to increase the proportion of ragtime songs in parks concerts. The WPC had long accepted ragtime, but the directed nature of the endorsement ran counter to their operating procedures in the past that gave freer rein to individual conductors. One prominent booster of the WPC ragtime plan was Charles Tyson Yerkes, the unscrupulous Chicago transit magnate. Yerkes contributed $1,000 to enable the WPC to extend the concerts through September. Beyond making a public show of his appreciation of popular music, Yerkes stood to reap a potential return on his investment as a result of increased streetcar traffic to the West Parks on concert days.[85] Whatever the underlying motivation of these shifts may have been, the WPC appeared to have abandoned even the tacit assumption of musical aesthetic uplift in its parks. Whether the same would hold true for Lincoln Park hinged on a series of events in the coming years.[86]

SETTLING THE "LONG-DEBATED QUESTION"
The 1901 Chicago American *Concert Contest*

In the years after the ragtime policy announcement by the WPC and LPC, public support for park concert music surpassed attendance levels of the 1880s and 1890s. The summer of 1901 marked a particularly active season of musical offerings in the ceremonial parks and a fateful one for the evolving reform character of ceremonial park concerts. Chicagoans could attend a concert somewhere in the three major park districts any day of the week, except on Mondays, throughout the entire months of July and August. Brass bands provided the bulk of the entertainment, with the exception of a string band of about a dozen instruments performing cultivated European classical music on Tuesday evenings at the German Building in Jackson Park. Along with the park boards, the street railway and Union Traction systems provided financial assistance for the concerts.[87] Johnny Hand continued to perform in Lincoln Park and in the South Park district, though he now presented a remarkably elastic program stretching from parts of Gounod's *Faust* to Gene Jefferson and Leo Friedman's smash musical theater hit, "Coon! Coon! Coon!"[88]

In August 1901 the *Chicago American*, a cheeky Hearst affiliate, weighed in on the sensitive issue of ragtime versus European classical music. It announced a people's music contest in which readers would be able to take charge of programming at Lincoln Park so that "just the music *you* like best will be played."[89] For an entire week, the *American* printed tear-sheet ballots to enable readers to submit votes for their twelve "favorite tunes" to be performed at a series of special concerts featuring none other than Johnny Hand's band. The paper boasted that at last "the long-debated question of what is the most popular kind of music in Chicago will be settled by a vote of the people."[90] The *American* framed the "long-standing debate" over popular music as an urgent civic matter that demanded democratic processes of resolution. The contest confirmed that if the subject of musical choice and taste had not been so before, it was now inextricably bound in the public mind to conflicts over democratic expression in Chicago's public spaces.

Commissioner Dunton had since left the district, but the LPC's interest in supporting such a people's contest suggests that park officials wanted to assert the identity of the parks as people's concert halls, or at least to make their programming decisions reasonably accurate representations of public taste. The *American*'s music editor stressed that democratic musical service could only proceed once the public's true opinion on an appropriate civic music standard for Lincoln Park had been measured even by so imprecise an instrument as a write-in contest. "A year ago, ragtime would have won [the contest] without a doubt," he reflected. "Like many other good songs, however, syncopated music has been popular for so long a time that its enthusiastic devotees are tiring of it. . . . The class of melody which will win is, therefore, in the deepest kind of doubt. The fight between the supporters of the different classes is spirited."[91] The *American* described the issue of music in the parks in polarized terms that further indicated the divisive impact of the sacralization of classical music and the rise of the commercial music industry on attempts to construct a unitary civic musical taste. According to the *American*, Chicago residents were reducible to exactly two musical publics: the "lovers of the masters" and the "ragtime strength," with each faction allegedly determined to see its group identity validated in Lincoln Park.[92]

As the days passed, the *American* supplied a blow-by-blow account of balloting to heighten expectation of the outcome. It seemed that "for every written request for the 'anvil chorus from *Il Trovatore*'" came "demands for 'Goo-Goo Eyes'" by ragtime aficionados. In the end, voting tipped in favor of popular ragtime rather than classical selections. The people appeared to have validated the new direction of park musical outreach: to eschew uplift and refinement for popular commercial tastes.[93]

On August 18, the day of the first of three popular concerts at which Johnny Hand was to perform, the *Chicago Tribune* published a story ripping the outcome of the people's concerts. Titled "'Ragtime Out of Date,' Says Hand," the story quoted the conductor declaring confidently that "I think the park board is convinced that the people want good music and not coon songs all the time." Hand implied that the park board must regain its bearings and forge ahead with a progressive agenda of musical uplift blended with entertainment. Whether the public knew it or not, declared Hand, "ragtime is out of date in Chicago." But the brashness of the statement did not make it true. Audiences remained enamored of ragtime and were further emboldened to demand it in their ceremonial parks.[94]

RESUSCITATING UPLIFT IN LINCOLN PARK

In a remarkable turn the following spring, the LPC embarked on a new concert outreach project to bring what it called "good" music back to Lincoln Park. But instead of reinstating the light-classical repertoire popularized by Johnny Hand, the commissioners announced that they intended to discontinue brass band concerts entirely in favor of performances by thirty-five members of the Theodore Thomas Orchestra (minus Theodore Thomas), the most accomplished cultivated symphony in the city. Though vaudeville and ragtime would still appear on some concert programs, the commissioners declared their intention of "improv[ing] the taste of those who frequent the playground" by bringing serious classical music performances to the people. "Ragtime has been the favorite among them," one commissioner said of audiences in recent years, "and there is some doubt about the manner in which the Thomas programs will be received." The explicit acknowledgment that they acted in the interest of reform and not in response to the mass fervor for dance music suggested a move to restore the uplift focus of musical progressivism temporarily overwhelmed by the "ragtime strength."[95]

City newspapers generally expressed support of the commissioners' decision to reassert their governing authority over music in Lincoln Park. The effort of the LPC "to uplift popular taste and to make these concerts attractive for those who enjoy not only the surroundings the music happens to be in but the music itself" struck the *Tribune* as a wise corrective to past policy.[96] Other commentators agreed, though at least one indignant columnist blasted the return to Euroclassical sounds. "A good brass band patterned after Sousa's is worth a hundred symphony orchestras on a summer night in the open air," he fumed.[97]

Much of the positive commentary about the new LPC concert season focused on the benefits that exposure to the Thomas Orchestra would have on citizens otherwise unable to afford access to symphonic music. "Chicago will have the Thomas orchestra free for the first time," reported the *Chicago Journal* approvingly.[98] Another report emphasized the liberating effects of hearing fine symphonic music in an outdoor park setting: "It seems eminently fitting that good music should be heard out of doors, for roofs, opera chairs, and kid gloves frequently act as a barrier to one's enjoyment of a concert." Bringing the orchestra out of the sacralized environs of the formal concert hall into public space embodied the democratic ideals behind this act of musical progressivism.[99]

Watching the latest reform maneuver in Lincoln Park from across town, the West Chicago Park Commissioners reiterated their position concerning the compatibility of popular taste and public duty. "The people want light music these hot days," Parks Superintendent William J. Cooke told the press. "The money to pay for the music is coming from the people, so it is only fair that they should be suited. If we find that they want the classics we shall change the arrangement."[100] Cooke hastened to reassure the public that there would be no changes in the popular programs for the 1902 season or attempts to inject unwanted levels of uplift into the programs without strong evidence of support from patrons.[101] What Cooke did not say, however, was if park officials intended to indulge the liberated audience behaviors associated with the proliferating ragtime subculture in commercial dance halls and cabarets. Although the WPC chose not to take musical progressivism in the same direction as the LPC, they continued to expect that order and social decorum would prevail on park property as it traditionally had.

Responding to Cooke's statements disavowing musical uplift on the West Side, one paper predicted "very vigorous protests before many days elapse" by classical music lovers of the West Side.[102] Another accused the WPC of promoting morally dubious content in the public sphere of the parks. "Bands Must Play Ragtime," boomed one headline. The article in the *Chicago Inter-Ocean* went on to say: "Wagner, Handel, Lizt [*sic*], and even John Philip Sousa, will be barred when bandmasters choose their composers for concerts in the West Parks this summer. The relative merits of classical and 'ragtime' music were too much for the commissioners. Superintendent William J. Cooke quickly decided that 'My Zulu Babe' and others of the type were more suited to the popular ear than the compositions of the old masters. 'The Mobile Prance' from the pen of Mr. Brown of uncertain fame, is one of the numbers for tonight's concert."[103] Similar in tone to the *Tribune* attack on Commissioner Dunton in 1898, the news story presented Cooke as a ragtime patsy or even as slightly depraved, when, in fact, modern light opera and popular airs routinely appeared alongside ragtime at public concerts. The suggestive allusion to the "uncertain fame" of the composer Charles Brown sounded concern about the civic embrace of the unspeakable racial and sexual indecencies some associated with ragtime culture. While Cooke plugged the notion of the people's parks, the predicament he and other park commissioners faced remained daunting. Musical progressivism stressed outreach efforts melding entertainment and education, but the practices often exacerbated tensions between bourgeois sensibilities and modern plebeian demands for municipal responsiveness to tastes and needs at variance with reformers' own.

"NO DEMAND FOR 'CATCH' MUSIC"
Reclaiming Concert History

Efforts to define the role of music as an embodiment of civic culture produced pitched struggles in late-nineteenth- and early-twentieth-century urbanizing Chicago. The "long-standing debate" concerning music contributed to the tensions that boiled over at the Garfield Park bandstand in early September 1902. Park officials frequently succeeded in integrating their musical progressive vision of providing uplifting entertainment in harmony with the changing social and cultural dynamics of the metropolis. Nevertheless, the Victorian constraints of the park reform landscape and evolving forms of musical recreation, particularly the advent of ragtime, tested the spirit of partnership between audiences and park officials and produced conflicts.

The park-centered struggle between "lovers of the masters" and the "ragtime strength" eased somewhat by the 1910s, even as the polarized distinctions between "low" popular music and "high" cultivated European music promulgated at the World's Columbian Exposition fractured opinion about music's place in the public sphere.[104] In other urban settings, musical progressives would continue to grapple with the social and aesthetic balance of outreach programs. In July 1906 the South Park Commissioners presented a special thirty-year anniversary program. A. F. Weldon's Second Regiment reprised a complete program performed in the park by Hans Balatka in 1876. As the *Chicago Tribune* hastened to point out, "The souvenir programs to be given out today will be likenesses of the programs given out in '76, and show that at that date no demand for 'catch' music was acknowledged by the bandleader. Therefore no ragtime selections will be played today." The program consisted principally of overtures and waltzes, including works by Johann Strauss and Felix Mendelssohn.[105]

West Park Police, 1914. Chicago Park District Special
Collections.

In its irrepressible swipe at ragtime fans, who had so successfully
stretched the popular parameters of ceremonial park concerts, the
Tribune missed a larger insight contained within the South Park concert program of 1876. The fallacious assertion that "no demand for
'catch' music" existed in the early history of concerts in Chicago's
ceremonial park was an attempt to erase the popular character of
early public concerts and the role that the concert public played in
shaping the sounds of reform in its parks. By 1906 the light European
compositions that Balatka favored were co-opted in a fractious debate
pitting sacralized classical music against popular commercial musical
forms. Musical progressives would struggle against these divisive
claims of the legacy of public park space as they planned new campaigns of musical outreach.

Ceremonial park concerts in the 1870s were freighted with bourgeois uplift ideals in tension with everyday social and cultural activities associated with Chicago's industrial population. From the beginning, however, park users at Lincoln Park and elsewhere fought to
transform the grandiose, but not always human-centered reform sensibility of the creators of ceremonial parks into a more inclusive,
democratic social ethos. The great paradox for park officials lay in

how to manage "success" because large concert audiences confirmed nothing if not their own power to make fresh demands on the public servants providing outlets for musical recreation.

The early history of concerts in Chicago's major parks reveals that park officials and audiences redefined the cultural politics of music as both a tool of uplift and an instrument of popular resistance. By the 1900s, however, musical progressivism had entered a new phase. The focus of civic activists and reformers shifted from the pastoral ceremonial park to the cacophonous industrial neighborhoods of Chicago's ethnic, immigrant, and laboring classes. The enterprise of engaging the masses via music moved from the urban periphery of the South and West Parks to the urban industrial core. On Chicago's Near West Side, in the dense "river wards" where tens of thousands of immigrants lived, Jane Addams, Ellen Gates Starr, and other idealistic middle-class reformers were incorporating music into social settlement work. So it happened that the neighborhoods where the majority of Chicago's laboring men and women worked, played, and made music became the next site of musical progressive activity.

THREE

I WAS IMPROVISING RIGHT FROM THE START

MUSICAL PROGRESSIVISM AT HULL HOUSE, 1889–1919

On a wintry day in 1896, Hilda Satt, a fourteen-year-old Jewish immigrant from Poland took a seat in the Hull House auditorium located in the Nineteenth Ward of Chicago's Near West Side. She did not have far to walk. Her family lived on Halsted Street, four blocks from the social settlement established by Jane Addams and Ellen Gates Starr in 1889. Until this late December afternoon, however, Satt had steadfastly avoided crossing its threshold. She was particularly nervous about making the trip in this season since "in Poland it had not been safe for Jewish children to be on the streets on Christmas." At the urging of neighborhood playmates, however, Satt buried her misgivings and, without telling her mother where she was going, attended the holiday concert presented by the Hull House Music School.[1]

Looking about her, Satt was astonished to discover a public gathering unlike any she had ever witnessed in her neighborhood:

> There were children and parents at this party from Russia, Poland, Italy, Germany, Ireland, England, and many other lands, but no one seemed to care where they had come from

or what religion they professed, or what clothes they wore, or
what they thought. As I sat there, I am sure I felt myself
being freed from a variety of century-old superstitions and
inhibitions. There seemed to be nothing to be afraid of . . .
The children of the Hull House Music School then sang
some songs that I later found out were called "Christmas
carols." I shall never forget the caressing sweetness of those
childish voices. All feelings of religious intolerance and big-
otry faded. I could not connect this beautiful party with
any hatred or superstition that existed among the people of
Poland.[2]

Since its inception, the annual Hull House Christmas concert had
attracted large audiences eager to hear seasonal carols and folk songs
performed by a chorus of neighborhood children. A typical program
might include carols drawn from English, French, German, and Bohemian traditions. "Possibly it is the spirit of Christmas," wrote
Amalie Hannig, codirector of the Hull House Music School, describing the popularity of the annual concert. "Possibly it is the influence
of music which holds together the souls of these people." Whatever
the explanation, as Hilda Satt personally discovered, the concerts
exerted a sublime force that eased the tensions of difference that she
associated with the neighborhood.[3]

Satt described an epiphany at the concert that transformed the
way that she understood herself and her relationship with the multicultural neighborhood in which she lived. "As I look back," she
wrote, "I know that I became a staunch American at this party."[4] It
was not the "spirit of Christmas" that moved the young Jewish visitor, but the power of music to constitute a common bond among a
diverse group of spectators. Satt likened the phenomenon to a rite
of civic passage in which she felt incorporated into the nation as a
"staunch American."

Until now, despite numerous academic studies of Jane Addams,
her colleagues, and the impact of Hull House on the settlement
movement, the role of music as an instrument of outreach and reform
at the settlement has remained unexplored. Uncovering the history
of music reform at Hull House reveals a critical connection between
progressive reform and the changing politics of music and democratic
culture in urban America. Obviously, one cannot extrapolate from
Satt's experience to that of others seated in the room that December

afternoon, or to the experiences of the thousands who patronized concerts, took music classes, or danced at Hull House at other times of the year, but her story hints at music's pivotal role for immigrant, ethnic, and laboring people struggling to define themselves as members of an American nation.[5] As this chapter will demonstrate, music in settlement work helped foster new relationships among diverse, even previously hostile, groups of users. Musical outreach at Hull House transformed the use of music by progressive activists. It promoted a democratic musical discourse that championed intercultural connections in a way that dramatically altered the politics of music in urban society.[6]

For scholars of the Progressive Era, the history of musical progressive reform at Hull House offers a fresh perspective on issues of settlement outreach and user agency, cultural conflict, and power in the urban United States. Settlements emerged amid a welter of late-nineteenth-century anxieties over social change in urban America. They constituted institutions in which a range of activists contemplated the vexed subject of incorporating groups perceived as outsiders—immigrants, the poor, unwed mothers, persons of color, and other minorities—into the nation. Case studies of different settlements underscore the tremendous variability of approaches, the ambivalent attitudes of many reformers toward their clients, and the unanticipated outcomes of "settlement work." Studies seeking to recover the perspectives of the clients of reform outreach further convey the complex, at times unintended legacies that social reformers left among the publics that they attempted to serve.[7]

The history of musical progressivism offers a means of engaging one of the sharpest criticisms of activist cultural outreach of the period: that efforts to promote so-called adjustment among industrial populations represented a subterfuge for imposing bourgeois pieties on culturally diverse populations.[8] Settlement workers have been lambasted as "antimodern" Victorians, as thrill seekers communing with their social inferiors, or as unwitting apologists for corporate industrial hegemony. Caricatured as saintly figures, settlement activists, especially women, have also been portrayed as feckless busybodies, self-serving narcissists, and reactionaries gaily (or grimly, as the case might be) effacing cultural values other than their own while imposing a Victorian worldview on the diverse peoples of urban industrial society.[9] Championed as a seedbed for twentieth-century pluralist thought, Hull House has also weathered revisionist claims

that it was a haven for Americanizing and racist proclivities.[10] Noting
the manner in which musical outreach attempted to engage the urban
population and to foster social and cultural exchange may not resolve
scholarly controversies, but it can enrich specific understanding of
the relative agency of users and the linkage between settlement outreach and music's changing status in urban cultural politics.

During the 1890s a community of musical activists coalesced at
Hull House. These reformers believed that wider access to high-
quality music education for the immigrant, ethnic, and working poor,
exposure to uplifting classical concert performances, and efforts to
supply visitors with affordable alternatives to commercial musical
amusements could dramatically enhance the welfare of the urban
population and promote civic engagement. Music outreach programs
ranged from instructional opportunities in classical music at the Hull
House Music School and a Sunday classical concert series to more
casual men's, women's, and children's choruses, along with folk music
and social clubs and dancing at the settlement. Collectively, these
efforts in musical progressivism inspired widespread imitation and
musical reforms across Chicago in settlements and municipal settings. The Hull House Music School spawned a national network of
community music schools dedicated to serving the poor.[11]

Reformers at Hull House attempted to provide area residents
with formal music instruction and recreation opportunities while also
encouraging visitors to incorporate aspects of neighborhood musical
activity into the domesticated and avowedly "American" milieu of
the settlement house. Certain programs at Hull House actively promoted so-called Americanization, that is, they attempted to substi-
tute a musical regimen defined implicitly or explicitly by settlement
leaders as proper or "American" for a preexisting one. Morals activists, for example, often locked horns with the purveyors of commercial musical recreation in the city, whom they considered exploiters of
youthful energy and virtue, and encouraged visitors to pursue other
avenues of settlement-based leisure. Other Hull House programs
encouraged acculturation, meaning they emphasized a give-and-take
process of exchange of cultural and musical ideas and behaviors between teachers and pupils. The success of users in making music
reform a joint enterprise defined Hull House's special significance to
the development of musical progressivism. While hardly immune
from pressuring visitors to adopt new ways, musical outreach at Hull
House fueled a robust and new democratic cultural politics for civic

music that would spread far beyond the confines of the immediate neighborhood.[12]

The musical interaction between and among users and settlement activists helped to promote a new sense of democratic civic life inclusive of the diverse urban populace. Deflecting the cultural biases of reforms that would deny them the right to be different, Hull House users frequently asserted their power as joint architects of the democratic civics that musical progressivism aspired to create. Injecting their own interests, skills, and perspectives into their experiences, visitors often appropriated the tools of musical outreach and put these resources to use in the service of their own individual or group agenda.[13]

Although Hull House music reform enabled alliances across many social and cultural divides, it must be emphasized that the opportunities and benefits were not universally available. Musical progressivism proved insufficient for the daunting task of building a public culture free of racism. While it broke from many conventions of its time, and often embraced cultural difference in innovative ways, one of the major shortfalls of musical progressivism at Hull House was that reformers posited an ideal of democratic harmony in which people of color, most notably African Americans, were excluded from participation. As a result, a sound of whiteness accompanied musical outreach at Hull House. Musical progressivism proved capable of embracing (though not without occasional ambivalence) European immigrant and ethnic populations as part of the civic reform project, but it left racial minorities to the side.

DREAMS OF HARMONY
The Education of Jane Addams

Belief in the links among music, social harmony, and the cosmos; confidence in the power of music to stir and soothe the emotions; and a shared conviction in the uplifting (or degrading) effects of music on individuals, groups, and society bound musical progressives at Hull House together.[14] Jane Addams's and Ellen Gates Starr's decision to put music to work at Hull House drew its inspiration from a reservoir of sources, some of which can be traced to their unusually thorough exposure to classical literature, philosophy, and languages as students.[15]

Ellen Gates Starr, cofounder of Hull House. Jane
Addams Collection, Swarthmore College Peace
Collection.

Both women attended Rockford Female Seminary in Illinois.
Addams studied ancient and modern languages, classical Greek and
Roman texts, and European romantic literature, including the works
of William Wordsworth, Thomas Carlyle, and John Ruskin.[16] Addams
wrote prize-winning essays on philosophical questions and won aca-

demic accolades as a debater. In her 1881 valedictory address, she invoked Plato, whose theories of aesthetic moralism informed the reform culture that she and Starr would bring to fruition years later at Hull House.[17]

While at Rockford, Addams had enrolled in the "Conservatory of Music" under Professor Daniel N. Hood, but she withdrew after only one year. According to her biographer and nephew James Linn Weber, while she enjoyed it, in the technical area of music "she had no talent whatever."[18] Nevertheless, Addams's humanistic education, as well as her upbringing as the daughter of a respected state legislator and Stephenson County landowner, instilled mannered behaviors in her that included a belief in the importance of aesthetic cultivation and an appreciation of the arts as a social good. What distinguished Addams from her contemporaries, however, is that she rejected genteel passivity for a life dedicated to actualizing the social potential of aesthetic cultivation. She did this, in part, by making high-quality musical instruction available to talented residents of the industrial neighborhoods of Chicago's Near West Side.[19]

After graduation, Addams embarked on a European grand tour—a perquisite of the privileged—lasting from August 1883 to June 1885. She steeped herself in history and culture, spending large amounts of time in England and Germany touring museums, visiting religious and historic sites, and attending plays, operas, and concerts.[20] Unsure about her future path, Addams returned briefly to the States before leaving again for Europe in December 1887. On her way to meet Ellen Gates Starr in Munich, she stopped at the stately medieval Ulm cathedral on the banks of the Danube. In her journal she marveled at the accretions of culture displayed under one roof: "The religious history carved on the choir stalls in the Ulm cathedral contained Greek philosophers as well as Hebrew prophets, and among the disciples and saints stood the discoverer of music and builder of pagan temples."[21] James Weber Linn speculates that these effigies frozen in time inspired Addams to fantasize in her journal about a "cathedral of humanity" open and inclusive enough to comfortably house the disparate peoples and cultures of the world. Whatever the chain of inspiration may have been, later on the same trip Addams made the fateful visit to Toynbee Hall in London's East End. Here she witnessed idealistic Oxford men struggling to combat the effects of poverty in that district of the city. Addams returned home inspired. In 1889, with help from friends and patrons, she

established the Hull House social settlement in an industrial neighborhood on the Near West Side populated by Sicilian, Russian Jewish, Irish, Greek, and Bohemian immigrants and their families.

THE GENEALOGY OF MUSICAL PROGRESSIVISM

The decision to offer music at Hull House as part of the settlement's
charter "to provide a center for a higher civic and social life" reflected
moral and aesthetic concerns central to women's reform work in the
United States since the Civil War.[22] Due to rapid industrial growth,
immigration, and metropolitan expansion, social reformers in Chicago and elsewhere had begun paying increased attention to the
domestic milieu, in part to insulate it from the depredations of urbanization and the marketplace. Scores of ladies' homemaker journals,
catalogs, and advice columns extolled the virtues of the home as a
rejuvenating haven. They celebrated domestic life as an ennobling
and virtuous preoccupation.[23]

Despite the constraints of a bourgeois gender discourse that artificially split the "public" sphere from the "private" sphere and nat-
uralized male and female roles in accordance with a market/home
dichotomy, female reformers nevertheless engineered many ways of
making a difference.[24] For those committed to cultural outreach, music marked a natural choice to extend the time-honored values and
activities associated with bourgeois domestic culture into the city
itself. Musical appreciation and instruction embodied object lessons
of self- and group cultivation that seemed well tailored to the project
of domesticating and uplifting, where possible, the industrial population of the city.[25]

The most crucial link between arts outreach and social change in
the minds of Addams, Starr, and others at Hull House came via the
philosophy of John Ruskin, who, along with the English poet, artist,
and socialist William Morris, captured Jane Addams's imagination at
Rockford Seminary.[26] The Arts and Crafts Movement praised the
virtues of premodern craft sensibilities and the ennobling benefits of
art, handicraft, and creative design as antidotes to the dehumanizing
effects of industrial culture on laborers. Ruskin argued that aesthetic
choices represented moral positions with far-reaching social consequences. The call to resist the debasement of workers and of the
aesthetic character of the world by industrialization resonated with a

cohort of middle-class Americans confronting the implications of modernity and seeking to improve the nature of society.[27]

As evidence of their commitment to the ideas of Ruskin and Morris, Addams and Starr founded the Chicago Arts and Crafts Society in 1897. Starr developed an explicit critique of mass commercial culture and stressed the importance of artistic expression as a prerequisite for dignity and social freedom. "The peasant immigrant's surroundings begin to be vulgar precisely at the point where he begins to buy and adorn his dwelling with the products of American manufacture," she wrote.[28] To Starr, reclaiming control of aesthetic production offered Americans a solution to the tyrannical effects of mass industrialization: "There is one hope for us all,—a new life, a freed life. He who hopes to help art survive on earth till the new life dawns, must indeed feed the hungry with good things. This must he do, but not neglect for this the more compassionate and far-reaching aim, the freeing of the art-power of the whole nation and race by enabling them to work in gladness and not in woe."[29] In the romanticized spirit of supplying aesthetic succor to the people and creating space for self-generated "art-power," Hull House hosted Arts and Crafts theme events and established its own art department, offering classes in fine arts and design.[30] Though she too, lacked formal training in music, Starr took charge of scheduling concert activity at the settlement as an extension of methods "to help art survive on earth."[31]

Jane Addams echoed Starr's assertions of the critical relationship between social life and aesthetic enrichment, and she explicitly invoked music as part of any reform regimen in the area of cultural outreach at Hull House. Wrote Addams: "The chief characteristic of art lies in freeing the individual from a sense of separation and isolation in his emotional experience, and has usually been accomplished through painting, writing and singing; but this does not make it in the least impossible that it is now being tried in terms of life itself."[32] Musical progressivism at Hull House combined elements of the genteel aesthetic tradition, the social urgency of the Arts and Crafts Movement, and a pragmatic spirit all its own. It proposed to generate a robust, emotionally replenishing community in which music would represent a lifeline binding the immigrant, ethnic, and laboring population of Chicago's Near West Side together. Innovative rather than antimodern, and brash, though it appeared to embrace the trappings of gentility, musical outreach at Hull House ambitiously gazed outward, seizing on old and new educational ideas, while experimenting with mechanisms to engage youths and adults in music across the cultural divides of the surrounding neighborhood.

BREAKING THE ICE
The First Sunday Concerts

During the first winter at Hull House, Addams and Starr instituted free Sunday afternoon concerts in an effort to recruit newcomers to the settlement community. Held in the Hull House drawing room, the first concerts emphasized European classical music and featured the performance talents of settlement music teachers and "various musicians and musical clubs of the city."[33] Between mid-November 1891 and mid-April 1892, there were twenty-two such concerts. Though the Hull House Music School was not founded until 1893, several teachers, including Eleanor Smith, who arrived at Hull House in 1890, offered singing and piano lessons to children and adults. Smith would later be named head of the music school.[34]

Knowing that the Sunday concerts competed for the attentions of weary laborers and their families with lively forms of neighborhood music entertainment, Hull House organizers carefully selected appealing programs. "It was at that time thought necessary to give very 'popular' music in order to hold the attention of the hearers, as a whole," Jane Addams later recalled.[35] While the "popular" Sunday concerts did not include the marches and waltzes that energized ceremonial park concerts, they did emphasize familiar songs and airs from well-known operas and concert works deemed accessible for a general audience. A typical program from Sunday, November 27, 1892, featured works by Mozart, including the "Overture to Don Giovanni," two arias from the same opera, and his Symphony no. 27, followed by a work by Neidlinger and a barcarole by Schubert.[36] The Sunday concert series presented occasional special features, including performances of children's songs, folk songs, or old ballads aimed squarely at the tastes of non-native-born residents.[37]

As one 1896 account described the first concerts, "the audiences were small and the proportion of curiosity-seekers rather large." Reformers persevered with the formula of light-classical programs and mixed song assortments, however, and soon the drawing room had become too small to accommodate crowds now numbering in the hundreds.[38] Evidence suggests that once large audiences grew com-

Exterior of the Hull House Music School. From Jane
Addams, *Twenty Years at Hull-House* (New York:
Macmillan, 1910).

monplace, the self-consciously popular emphasis of the programs
shifted toward a more challenging selection of material suggestive of
musical uplift. As the report explained, "[T]he [Sunday] programs
have been selected with more and more severity and the music during the last year has been almost entirely of a very high order."[39] Typical programs included cultivated singing, piano, and violin performances, as well as "an occasional string quartet." One week in 1897
visitors heard Egon Mayer, a cellist, perform "Reverie" by Dunkler
and "Majourka" [*sic*] by F. A. Kummer. Mrs. Carl Brandt performed
"Die Bekerte" [*sic*] by Max Strange and "At the Dawn" by Otto
Cantor.[40] The self-congratulatory tone and rhetoric of uplift in the
announcement suggested that expectations for music's place at the
settlement included hopes of aesthetic cultivation on a high plane.

Rather quickly, however, the tone of the Sunday gatherings appeared to shift from self-consciously casual affairs that served as
musical icebreakers for curious locals to more cultivated events in
the manner of performances at a formal concert hall. Describing the

transformation, the *Bulletin* noted with pride that "regular attendants, who come to gratify a love of music, are subjected much less often than formerly to annoyance from conversation." "Curiosity-seekers" who might have been expecting a Sunday event along the lines of a North Side Turner concert were likely to feel disappointed. No alcohol was permitted at Hull House events, and background chatter was made unwelcome as well. The eradication of conversation during concert performances paralleled the kind of disciplining agenda pursued by Theodore Thomas during his career.[41]

But the impression that Sunday concerts represented a project to make concert culture at Hull House indistinguishable from the sacralized formal concert hall proved incorrect. In 1899 the Chicago-based journal *Music* described a tense meeting at the settlement in which Jane Addams and the music staff debated the status of musical events at Hull House. The disagreement over the organization of the Sunday events concerned a classic dilemma already playing out in debates among parties connected with ceremonial park concerts. Should popular and accessible songs prevail at concerts to attract and retain the largest audience possible, or should reformers dare to promote a pedagogical, uplift approach at the risk of alienating potential reform subjects?

Eleanor Smith, now head of the Hull House Music School, defended the importance of high-quality program choices at the Sunday concerts. Rather than deferring to assumptions about popular taste, she advocated presenting challenging programs as a worthy reform end in itself. Addams, however, disagreed. Though her arguments were not specified, the report explained that Addams felt that the Sunday concerts had drifted from her intention of using them as a universal recruitment tool that promoted Hull House as a musical center. At the end of the meeting, the group agreed that both "popular" and "serious" classical compositions must coexist on Sundays. Each genre furthered, in its own way, the musical progressive objectives of reaching a broad public and promoting the uplifting power of music on both aesthetic and social planes.[42]

The disagreement between Eleanor Smith, a classically trained musician and educator, and Jane Addams, who lacked formal training in music, underscored a central tension in the ideology of musical progressivism. Professional music critics of the cultured generation, like George Upton; conductors, such as Theodore Thomas and Johnny Hand; and professional music educators, like Smith, placed

their faith in the innate properties of compositions that their technical and aesthetic training taught them to label "good" music. To
them, aesthetics, program selectivity, and technical execution were
essential traits of any musical reform exercise.

By contrast, Addams and Mary Rozet Smith, whose financial
largesse helped keep Hull House and its music school afloat, perceived music more practically as one tool among many in the arts for
engaging the spirits of the urban poor and fostering positive communal experiences. Addams had neither the qualifications nor the interest to debate the relative aesthetic, technical, or educative merits of a
Brahms sonata versus a Verdi aria. "Neither [Addams or Smith] was
musical," Eleanor Smith emphasized years later, "though they believed in the civilizing and ennobling influence of good music."[43]
Addams expected music to bow to her vision at the settlement. The
resulting struggle to balance Eleanor Smith's technical and aesthetic expectations of the music school and its associated programs
with Addams's idiosyncratic ideals of musical outreach created a pro-
ductive rather than a debilitating tension that would define Hull
House's distinctive contribution to musical progressivism in the years
to come.[44]

Since all agreed that the Sunday concerts served as an invaluable
conduit for newcomers to the settlement, the leadership agreed to
a compromise: the Sunday concerts would be lightened, and more
challenging programs would be scheduled on weekday nights. In
1900 an item in the *Bulletin* encapsulated the new formulation of
Sunday concerts: "A great effort is made to secure programs which
shall be a real education in musical taste, while at the same time they
are not so severe that they cannot be enjoyed by the average audience."[45] Shading Sunday programs back in a more popular direction (a relative shift, to be sure) enabled reformers to provide a social
setting in which visitors would feel comfortable further exploring the
community-building exercise that the settlement had to offer.[46]

It is not known to what extent the flare-up over the Sunday
concerts contributed to her feelings, but Eleanor Smith grew increasingly unhappy in her position at Hull House. Toward the end of
the summer of 1901, she informed Addams in a letter that she was
giving serious consideration to resigning.[47] Addams's response alone
survives and provides a rare glimpse of her skills as a persuader and of
her views of music and reform at Hull House. "Your letter quite hurt
my feelings in spite of its sweetness and sincerity," began Addams's

Eleanor Smith (left) and philanthropist Mary Rozet
Smith. Jane Addams Memorial Collection (JAMC neg.
418), University Library, University of Illinois at
Chicago.

reply as she hastened to reassure Smith of her valued contributions to
the settlement. "I suppose it is the punishment for my wild activity in
the early days of H. H.," Addams continued, "that people refuse to
believe me when I say that I care more for the quality of the resident's
work than for unceasing doings." Referring to Smith's musical adaptation of a work by the Yiddish poet Morris Rosenfeld, Addams
wrote: "If you had only written the 'Sweat Shop' and taught it to
the girls, it would be in my mind a complete justification for all of
the 'room' you ever took." Admonishing Smith to "stop calculating
how 'profitable' you are," Addams urged the beleaguered teacher
to reconsider her decision. The combination of charm and firmness
worked. Smith became the unsung heroine of musical progressivism
at Hull House, where she remained for another thirty years.[48]

"SOME HOURS THEY SIT 'NEATH MUSIC'S SPELL"
Eleanor Smith and the Hull House Music School

Eleanor Smith's work as head of the music school proceeded from the mandate of Jane Addams "to give a thorough musical instruction to a limited number of children," meaning the talented, but poor young musicians living on the Near West Side.[49] By reaching out to this constituency, Hull House filled a dire need. Although dozens of private music schools and academies catered to Chicago's music students, the cost of professional training typically exceeded the financial reach of most families residing in the Nineteenth Ward. Chicago's public schools offered rudimentary music classes, but the programs were uneven and chronically underfunded. Music teachers were rarely professionally trained, and the specialized classes in sight-reading, scale singing, composition, or vocal training necessary for preparing students for professional careers were not generally available.[50] Admission to the Hull House Music School guaranteed a select group of promising students professional-quality instrumental and vocal instruction, access to rehearsal rooms, and opportunities to work with serious-minded peers and collaborators.[51] Some went on to the professional ranks as performers and educators.[52] The school also provided personnel and logistical support for the many musical activities offered at the settlement, such as the Women's Chorus, the Boys' Brass Band, choral and glee clubs, and a group known simply as the Quartette.[53]

Addams and Starr believed that the music school's reform mission had to include an effort to attract and accommodate musical aspirants who were balancing work schedules with their attempts to sing or perform. "[W]e constantly see the most promising musical ability extinguished when the young people enter industries which so sap their vitality that they cannot carry on serious study in the scanty hours outside of factory work," Addams lamented.[54] Attending to the plight of young women thrust into potentially compromising circumstances by economic hardship added urgency to musical progressivism: "[A] Bohemian girl, who, in order to earn money for pressing family needs, first ruined her voice in a six month constant vaudeville engagement . . . another young girl . . . extinguished her promise . . . a third girl . . . used her fine voice for earning money at entertainments held late after her day's work, until exposure and fatigue ruined her health as well as a musician's future."[55] While the school could not overcome the stressful circumstances under which these women

worked, the opportunity of affordable or even free professional training and a symbolic music room of their own offered poor women a
glimmer of hope of beginning a legitimate career in music. Classes
and performance opportunities at Hull House served students lack-
ing either wealthy patrons or the educational credentials needed to
support themselves as music teachers. The vaudeville and cabaret
stage struck reformers as a thoroughly inappropriate place in which to
be apprenticed, especially for young women and girls, and the music
school represented an attempt to provide a preferable alternative.[56]

Eleanor Smith's imagination, spirit, and musical talent left an
indelible imprint on musical progressivism at Hull House. Her considerable responsibilities included first translating Addams's and
Starr's inchoate ideas of music's powers to effect social change into
concrete programs. Smith's technical skills, energy, and acute sen-
sitivity to the power of music of all kinds in the lives of neighborhood
residents produced a noteworthy reform ethos at Hull House. Rather
than making the settlement an instrument of aesthetic uplift and
sacralization, Smith turned Hull House into a true musical center in
which multiple musics and cultural influences interacted in ways that
promoted individual and group development and civic enrichment.

Before settling in Chicago, Smith studied music in Germany,
where she began to develop ideas about reform and music education.
While in Berlin, she struck up an acquaintance with Amalie Hannig, a
young piano teacher at the Klindworth Conservatory, who shared an
interest in musical education for children. The two sketched out a
preliminary plan for a school in which to apply their ideas.[57] Their
plan drew on the perspectives of the German composer-critic Robert
Schumann, who had written at length on the validity of systematic
musical education for children. Schumann and his followers stressed
the importance of introducing children to music in technical and ex-
periential ways. Smith and Hannig envisioned a school where broad
musical training would be emphasized, including knowledge of both
singing and piano playing. They imagined a school in which students
would be able to explore the technical discipline of music while
remaining attuned to the emotional, subjective power of art.[58]

When she first reached Chicago, Smith taught in a variety of settings before committing to full-time responsibilities at Hull House.
She worked at the progressive Francis Parker Normal School on the
North Side and helped to institute music reforms in teacher training at the University of Chicago's Education Department, which

was then run by John Dewey. Smith believed that all public school teachers needed greater formal exposure to music since they were commonly required to teach music without prior qualifications. Smith and Dewey also traded ideas about music's place in the development of younger children and about the need to use music more imaginatively in the classroom.[59] Smith's influence may even have led Dewey to incorporate music into his work at the Laboratory School at the University of Chicago between 1894 and 1904, where he hired Calvin Brainerd Cady to direct the music program. Cady attempted to incorporate music into Dewey's philosophy concerning an integrated educational experience for children, and went on to become a nationally renowned figure in music education circles.[60]

With Amalie Hannig joining her at Hull House as her assistant, Eleanor Smith built the music school into a progressive showcase.[61] In a break from standard teaching practice, students seeking piano instruction at the school were required to enroll in voice training to enrich their range of musical experiences and skills.[62] Smith emphasized singing to make music more accessible to her pupils. She added mastery in this area to the more conventional methods of rote memorization of scales, key signatures, and drills to gain command of the structural elements of music. A composer herself, Smith stimulated her young pupils by preparing original musical material for them. A spring 1897 recital at Hull House featured four different classes from the school performing a program that included songs composed or arranged by Smith herself ("Daisies Are for Dancing," "Windy Nights," "Pussy Willow's Secret"), as well as "Song of the Mermaids" by Carl Maria von Weber, "Evening Star" by Schumann, "Sleeping Beauty" by Brahms, and the first movement of Mozart's Sonata in C Major.[63]

Although a European classical aesthetic structured much of the training and repertory at the music school, Smith also taught folk songs from the homelands of the school's German, Russian, Irish, and Scotch students.[64] Smith engaged students from a variety of cultural backgrounds through the imaginative intermingling of cultivated and vernacular music styles and lyrics. She penned compositions for her students using words from *Mother Goose* to Christina Rossetti and from William Blake to William Shakespeare. In 1905, with the feminist poet and modernist Harriet Monroe as lyricist, Smith composed the music for *The Troll's Holiday*, a play in three acts set in Norway.[65]

Smith's reform approach emphasized what she described as a

Program of Labor Songs

BY THE MEMBERS OF THE
HULL-HOUSE MUSIC SCHOOL

February Fifteenth, Nineteen-Hundred-and-One

SONG OF THE SMITH . . . . *Gruenberger*

WEAVING SONG . . . . . *Irish*

SPINNING SONG . . . . *Rheinberger*

THE POST HOLE . . . . . *Russian*

OVER HERE . . . . *Irish Famine Song*

THE PAINFUL PLOW . . . . *Old English*

SPINNING SONG from the "Flying Dutchman," *Wagner*

THE SWEAT SHOP . . . . *Eleanor Smith*

Poem translated from the Yiddish of Morris Rosenfeld by J. W Linn

The roaring of the wheels has filled my ears,
  The clashing and the clamor shut me in;
Myself, my soul, in chaos disappears.
  I cannot think or feel amid the din.
Toiling and toiling and toiling—endless toil.
  For whom? For what? Why should the work be done?
I do not ask, or know. I only toil.
  I work until the day and night are one.

The clock above me ticks away the day.
  Its hands are spinning, spinning, like the wheels.
It cannot sleep or for a moment stay.
  It is a thing like me, and does not feel.
It throbs as though my heart were beating there—
  A heart? My heart? I know not what it means.
The clock ticks, and below I strive and stare,
  And so we lose the hour. We are machines.

Noon calls a truce, an ending to the sound,
  As if a battle had one moment stayed—
A bloody field! The dead lie all around ;
  Their wounds cry out until I grow afraid.
It comes—the signal! See, the dead men rise,
  They fight again, amid the roar they fight,
Blindly, and knowing not for whom, or why.
  They fight, they fall, they sink into the night.

HOLLISTER BROTHERS, PRINTERS, CHICAGO

"Program of Labor Songs by the Members of the Hull-House Music School" (1901). Chicago Historical Society, ICHi-35631.

"catholicity of taste" as the key to good musicianship and good citizenship. "We made friends whenever possible with the parents of our pupils," Smith recalled, "[and] endeavored to connect the musical experiences of our pupils in every way possible with the racial background of the family." Rather than imposing a top-down musical regimen, Smith remained receptive to suggestions from students. "In some cases the pupils introduced us to the songs," she recalled. "I first heard in this way the 'Volga Boat Song,' since grown so familiar to all Americans, though sometimes in a form which robs it of local color and charm."[66] Smith's remark demonstrated that cultural information flowed in various directions at Hull House. She also acknowledged the risks that the reform appropriation and Americanization of European folk songs posed to the vitality of cultural difference, displaying a level of self-awareness that distinguished her career as a musical progressive.

To supplement her menial earnings, Smith published a number of instructional books and musical anthologies that provide additional information about her views on cultural difference and musical progressivism. In the 1908 introduction to her anthology *The Eleanor Smith Music Course*, she explained how teaching the music of the European world promoted democratic civic engagement:

> A cosmopolitan collection has been aimed at as being peculiarly fitted to the needs of a nation whose people are constantly being recruited from other and older civilizations. The work of distinguished foreign artists, as well as a large group of American songs, have been included, and it is believed that catholicity of taste and the advantage of a varied musical experience will result from the study of such a collection. A broader patriotism will be served by singing the national songs of other countries as well as our own national anthems, for singing the world's songs, like studying the world's history, will give knowledge and sympathy, which are the best foundations for intelligent patriotism.[67]

Smith's appeal to the relationship between musical knowledge and "intelligent patriotism" reflected the civic mission that informed her musical progressive activism. Welcoming an international horizon of multiplicity to promote unity rather than suppressing variation in the name of uniform standards of expression was the most important facet of Smith's contribution to reform outreach.

Nor did Smith's interest in promoting "the world's songs" isolate her from the everyday concerns of the residents of the Nineteenth Ward or the community of activists living at Hull House. Smith's own compositions exemplified musical progressive hopes for reimagining the link between aesthetics, politics, and the place of music in democratic life.[68] In addition to "A House Stands on a Busy Street," her paean to life at Hull House, Smith wrote songs whose subject matter addressed themes important to the daily lives of her students and other settlement visitors. "The Sweat Shop," "The Shadow Child," "The Land of the Noonday Night," "Suffrage Song," and "Prayer" invoked battles for women's suffrage and improved labor conditions while respectfully depicting the dignity and perseverance of workers struggling to improve their conditions.[69] Among the musical progressives who were active at Hull House, Smith demonstrated a particular ability to balance high aesthetic and technical standards with a generous regard for the multiple cultures joined by music on the Near West Side.

"NOT FROM THE AVENUES, BUT FROM THE ALLEYS"
William L. Tomlins, Children's Choruses, and the "Moral Forces" of Music

Shortly after the establishment of the music school, Jane Addams invited William L. Tomlins, a prominent figure in Chicago's cultivated music circles, to organize several choruses at the settlement. Unlike some musical progressives who were social activists drawn to music as a tool of outreach, Tomlins had considerable experience in the field. His credentials included over twenty years as director of the Apollo Musical Club, among the city's most prestigious men's choruses; he was an organizer of workingmen's classical music concerts in the early 1890s and choral director under Theodore Thomas at the 1893 World's Columbian Exposition.[70]

Born in London in 1844, Tomlins trained professionally as a choirmaster and organist and maintained ties with the distinguished Royal Academy of Music. He also attended the Tonic Sol-Fa College in London. It was a center of innovation in the teaching of music that promoted a simplified system of musical notation that did not require traditional sight-reading skills and enabled children or adults to sing fairly complicated melodies and arrangements in unison. While many music professionals dismissed the approach as faddist, Tomlins embraced the democratizing and mass educative possibilities of the new system and brought his enthusiasm for it with him to the United States.[71]

Tomlins arrived in America in 1870 and worked his way from Milwaukee to Chicago, where he headed the Apollo Musical Club from the mid-1870s until 1889. Tomlins strove to broaden the reach of the Apollo Club beyond a circle of wealthy patrons. He organized affordable concerts featuring the Apollo Club at the downtown Auditorium Theater and at venues in industrial neighborhoods.[72] Describing his outreach, Tomlins told an audience in 1893: "We went into factories and workshops and said 'You are our brothers; pay us ten cents to save your own self-respect and hear us sing.'" Evidently, some audiences reacted to Tomlins with skepticism. "At first the poor people looked on [the concerts] as charity and were inclined to repudiate them," he confessed, but he then added that "love and brotherhood" eventually prevailed and that subsequent workingmen's concerts garnered enthusiastic crowds.[73]

At the World's Columbian Exposition in 1893, in another challenge to Theodore Thomas's sacralized vision, Tomlins used his power as choral director to promote children's music at the White City, which reflected an alternative civic vision. In the years prior to the fair, Tomlins had won notice for successfully introducing the Tonic Sol-Fa method to children at venues such as the Apollo Music Festival of 1884, where more than 1,000 children sang.[74] With the assistance of Elizabeth Nash, Tomlins organized a youth chorus to perform at the fair. But rather than relying on experienced young voices with the prior advantage of private training, Tomlins recruited the children of poor immigrants and laborers to produce the sound of musical democracy. "These children came not from the avenues, but from the alleys," Tomlins boasted. "They were disorderly, they were a little rough, they did not know what was wanted of them." Nevertheless, Tomlins and Nash trained and rehearsed the chorus, which appeared at the dedicatory exercises of the fair in 1892, as well as during its high season, and won enthusiastic notices from critics and the public alike.[75]

Despite a tendency to speak patronizingly of his pupils, Tomlins demonstrated that he meant to include children of varied backgrounds and social stations in his musical progressive outreach. He believed that exposing children to "the moral forces of music" could inculcate virtue, a love of the classics, and good recreation habits at home. Tomlins claimed that the boys in his chorus were "carrying their singing into action" in nonmusical contexts by visiting hospitals, organizing a clothing drive, and even establishing a "little philanthropic newspaper." The connection between musical uplift and civic engagement inspired Tomlins, as did his faith, which he had no qualms about speaking of publicly: "This then is the object of our work. To purify the child nature . . . To ennoble him by contact with the highest in thought and feeling that brain and thought can produce. To have him know that his fellow is his brother, and that God is his Father, and then to send him a missionary in his own home. This is the use which we put to music, and measurably we accomplish our purpose."[76] Tomlins's Christian rhetoric set him apart from the secular humanist discourse prevalent at Hull House. Nevertheless, his work placed him squarely in the musical progressive tradition, whose zeal for musical outreach drew on democratic social concerns, and made him receptive to Addams's invitation to continue his musical social outreach at Hull House.

Tomlins's celebrity attracted philanthropic support to Hull House's music program and lent credibility to the outreach going on there. With an endowment supplied by Harlow N. Higinbotham, the president of the Exposition Company, which oversaw the 1893 fair, Tomlins and Nash organized a series of Hull House children's concerts in May 1895 and June 1897.[77] The second concert featured 200 youth singers, who performed before a standing-room-only crowd. "The attention of the audience was held until the very last," reported the *Bulletin*, "when all joined with the children in singing 'America.'"[78] Over a decade before Israel Zangwill's play *The Melting Pot* explored experiences of immigrant transformation using characters with ties to a settlement music school in New York City, the fundamental work of musical progressive reform was under way in Chicago.

"APPARENTLY THE WORKERS ARE
NOT YET READY TO SING"
Activism and Ambivalence

With the exception of the adult choruses he helped establish at Hull House, Tomlins's successes at working with immigrant and laboring children did not translate as readily to the adult inhabitants of Chicago's industrial neighborhoods. In the spring of 1895, Addams, Higinbotham, and Tomlins attempted a different form of musical outreach to the workers of Chicago by issuing a public call for ballads from the people. The *Chicago Record* published details of a contest seeking the best of the "people's songs" in verse form for musical arrangement by the Hull House music staff. The paper claimed that Tomlins had "a desire to teach something besides the lays of Scotland, the ballads of Germany and the rollicking crooning songs of the South" at Hull House.[79]

In a variation on the spirit with which Tomlins had once bluntly called on industrial workers to "save your own self-respect" by listening to the Apollo Club, Thomas asserted that "the labor movement will not attain a full and peaceful development without an orderly and musical expression of its hopes." Acting as self-appointed musical consultant to the workers of Chicago, Tomlins criticized industrial culture's negative effects on the aesthetic quality of music in the city. Though he lacked firsthand experience with hard manual labor, Tomlins addressed Chicago workers by invoking the connective tissue of masculinity despite the fact that thousands of women worked in industrial occupations, too. "In these days of abundant machinery and the minute divisions of labor," Tomlins observed, "workmen are in danger of losing their individuality and consciousness of manhood. In this connection, song music should be welcomed as tending to restore the sense of human development and companionship."[80] Tomlins invoked the recuperative power of singing equated with the virile culture of the German *Singverein* and the Apollo Club, which continued the form that remained a lively form of entertainment in neighborhood music circles.

Although the popular-song contest ostensibly celebrated working people and invited their authoritative input in producing new songs about laboring experience, Tomlins's public statements betrayed hints of his problematic attitude toward organized labor. Alluding to recent incidents of bloody labor turbulence, he addressed Chicago workers: "There is good authority for the statement that in labor assemblies and kindred gatherings the distinctive labor songs are too often only those which are born out of bitterness of past strife such as Homestead and Pullman." Without acknowledging the exploitative conditions and authoritarian oppression that generated these songs of outrage, Tomlins attacked the "doggerel of their word expressions" and suggested that such songs were both ineffective tools of mobilization and aesthetically impoverished.[81]

It is not known to what extent Tomlins's challenge or the promise of cash prizes in the amounts of $100, $50, and $25 for the top three compositions motivated would-be lyricists. Jane Addams reported that Hull House was deluged with submissions, apparently enough to fill several barrels. But the efforts of the neighborhood disappointed Addams, who remarked with what seemed to be forced levity that "[a]pparently the workers are not yet ready to sing."[82] Clearly, the volume of submissions showed that workers were ready and eager to sing, but not, it appeared, in the manner that music reformers desired. Though delivered in good humor, Addams's dismissive remark showed that reform sometimes turned a deaf ear to the sounds of the masses. Residual uneasiness about aesthetic issues and broader reservations among activists, like Tomlins, about encountering workers on their own terms muted the potential of certain programs. The popular-song contest exposed reluctance among musical progressives at Hull House to cede true authority to visitors, whether they were music students, Sunday concert patrons, or workers invited to submit "Hull House songs."[83]

As it turned out, the reform call for a new generation of worker songs would be answered resoundingly, though not perhaps in the form that Tomlins or Addams imagined. In 1911 the works of Joe Hill first appeared along with those of other contributors in the *Little Red Songbook*, published by the International Workers of the World. Released in multiple editions, the songbook inspired laborers associated with the IWW and a generation of workers who followed.[84] For the time being at Hull House, the burden fell to Eleanor Smith to compose, arrange, and eventually publish the *Hull-House Songs*, written about, rather than by, the residents of the Nineteenth Ward.

EFFACING THE MUSIC
Countering Local Music Culture

Eleanor Smith's appeal to a "catholicity of taste" notwithstanding, part of the music reform mission at Hull House freely embraced principles of Americanization that strove to alter the cultural outlook of settlement visitors. As Addams famously wrote: "In the deep tones of the memorial organ erected at Hull House . . . we realize that music is perhaps the most potent agent for making the universal appeal and inducing men to forget their differences."[85] The manifestations of this ideal included attempts to reduce cultural "differences" on occa-

sions where activists perceived them to be impediments to democratic civics. In attempting to reconstruct selected elements of Old
World music and folk practices within the settlement's civic reform
culture, activists redefined the public meaning of cultural difference.
The settlement officially celebrated cross-cultural musical relationships, but the celebration proceeded within a field of power relations
in which reformers reserved a privileged position in directing the
process of "forgetting" and remembering difference.[86]

Musical education at Hull House attempted to recover aesthetic
embodiments of premodern life in the lives of the pupils while
also providing them with tools to shape modern, independent lives.
"From the first lessons they are taught to compose and to reduce
to order the musical suggestions which may come to them," wrote
Addams, "and in this wise the school has sometimes been able to
recover the songs of the immigrants through their children."[87] Pledg-
ing assistance in exchange for control, Addams noted that "[w]e have
conscientiously provided careful musical instruction that at least a
few young people might understand those old usages of art; that they
might master its trade secrets, for after all it is only through a careful
technique that artistic ability can express itself and be preserved."[88]
Technical training interested Addams primarily as a tool for salvaging
the submerged musical traditions of an immigrant and ethnic population perceived as lost in a valueless modern industrial culture.

Presenting music as integral to the recovery of immigrant and
ethnic cultural memory underscored the problematic assumptions
of progressive activists toward lives they did not adequately understand. Addams's notion of recovering lost identity and fostering immigrant enthusiasms for folk music only worked if one assumed
immigrant and ethnic area residents to be unanchored from self-
generated cultural forms of expression. Addams recognized that the
linear, one-track model of immigrant to acculturated "American"
scanted the complexity of identity. She disavowed the suggestion
that her project could be construed as that of simply annihilating
difference. Selective resuscitation might be a more apt formulation of
the enterprise. As Addams explained the mission: "One thing seemed
clear in regard to entertaining immigrants, to preserve and keep whatever of value their past life contained and to bring them in contact with
a better type of American."[89]

At times in speaking of music's role in cultural recuperation, the
tone of polite condescension could not mask outright ignorance.

Speaking of Hull House's offer to local German American music groups to use settlement rooms for practicing, Jane Addams took credit for "reviving their almost forgotten enthusiasms" for traditional folk songs.[90] The power of music to hasten the forgetting/reviving of one's past appealed to Addams, whose interpretation of German-American patronage stressed the role of Hull House as a catalyst of user identity formation and did not take user agency very seriously.[91] Addams presented musical progressivism as an exercise in acculturation that supported a degree of difference and visitor autonomy—but in the service of reform-sanctioned outcomes.

Concern over the plight of the cultural "trade secrets" of urban immigrants and their children resounded in the thought of Addams's reform colleague John Dewey, who fixed his gaze on the troubled passage from ethnic to American. "Indeed, wise observers in both New York and Chicago have recently sounded a note of alarm," he wrote in 1902. "They have called attention to the fact that in some respects the children are too rapidly, I will not say Americanized, but too rapidly de-nationalized. They lose the positive and conservative value of their own native traditions, their own native music, art, and literature. They do not get complete initiation into the customs of their new country, and so are frequently left floating and unstable between the two. They even learn to despise the dress, bearing, habits, language, and beliefs of their parents—many of which have more substance and worth than the superficial putting-on of the newly adopted habits."[92] Dewey's astute recognition of the pressure that urban industrial life and consumer culture brought to bear on new arrivals and the subsequent native-born generation illustrated the impulse of musical progressives to concentrate on the nexus of cultural tradition and change that music in everyday life represented. At the same time, the universalized plight ascribed to the marginal generation of immigrant and ethnic youth failed to register the complex musical spaces of neighborhood and civic expression shaped by residents themselves.

As Chicago's musical history reveals, German immigrant and ethnic associations, to give an example of just one national population, helped to shape the civic landscape of the nineteenth century in which "German," "American," and "German American" identifications flowed across divides of geography and time. Addams's comments about the German music club are surprising given that Eleanor Smith made it clear how directly European influences and their ethnic embodiments in Chicago collectively shaped her thinking about how to teach music to children. Surely no such "forgotten enthusiasms" could exist among musicians using Hull House for group meetings and practices when ethnic German music traditions remained robust in Chicago in the 1890s! Addams's sidestepping of this preexisting and still vital German American musical culture suggests that musical progressive perspectives on difference tended to narrow when activists wished to demonstrate their control and influence over users.

Whether or not it intended to do so, Addams's description of the cultural mechanics of musical progressivism implied a problematic erasure of preexisting immigrant and ethnic musical practices in the name of recuperating those selfsame authentic and "real" traditions. Even as settlement discourse celebrated the musical traditions of various immigrant groups, and Eleanor Smith engineered substantive cross-cultural communication, Addams's commentary subtly reclaimed a proprietary right of reformers to decide the manner in which such traditions should be enshrined within the idealized civic life of Chicago.

Another example of the ways in which settlement reform attempted to control and define musical "difference" by selectively acknowledging the powerful presence of Chicago's multiethnic population emerges in the case of the so-called Italian Orchestra. The independent orchestra performed under the direction of Maestro Guiseppe Vecchione, former first flute of the San Carlo Theater of Naples. Hull House provided a practice and performance venue for this group of itinerant musicians who were in the process of reinventing themselves as an "orchestra." As one reviewer noted: "The majority of the members of the orchestra are composed of young Italian musicians who have never before played in an orchestra, but in streets, saloons, and at parties. The fact that now, through the admirable efforts of Maestro Vecchione, they are able to play very creditably, in full orchestra, classic Italian and German music, cannot fail to spur them on to higher aspirations in their profession."[93] The reviewer made an implicit contrast between amateur music as an immigrant preoccupation and social activity and the standards of professional musicianship associated with an orchestra. The Italian Orchestra was precisely the kind of work-in-progress that interested Hull House reformers and fit well with the values ingrained in musical progressivism. Staging such a concert at Hull House provided a living object lesson in musical performance as a sign of self-improvement and reinvention. The process included the change from amateur to professional, from vernacular music of the neighborhood to cultivated music of the metropolis, and, most notably, from immigrant to American. If settlement users could dedicate themselves to their musical training, their singing group, or their choral society at Hull House, they too could expect to see a transformation in their status as musical "Americans."

Like any enterprise based on philanthropic support and good will rather than on making a profit, musical progressivism had to justify its accomplishments—in particular, as mediator of the boundaries separating non-native-born immigrants and ethnic populations from fully acculturated Americans. A German American folk revival did not constitute a threat to reform if Hull House could take credit for catalyzing and controlling it. Instructing the Italian Orchestra how to sound professional and American demonstrated Hull House's contributions to fostering allegiance among users to mainstream values and purposes. But displays of difference outside the settlement's comfort zone of authoritative engagement with local populations represented something altogether different. They challenged the power of reformers to control the cultural staging of democratic life via music.

"WE ARE ONLY BEGINNING TO UNDERSTAND WHAT MIGHT BE DONE"
Learning from the Marketplace of Recreation

After 1900, musical progressivism at Hull House began to garner increased national attention and emulation among a widening circle of music educators and social activists. "What Plato says of good or bad dances and songs—namely, that they have the same effect on a man as bad company—applies equally to music," declared the notable critic Frederick Niecks in a 1902 article on the subject of music, democracy, and society in *Music*. "Noble music induces and strengthens nobleness, vulgar music, vulgarity. . . . This being so, it is clearly the duty of parents, of guardians, of teachers, and last, but not least of all, the State, to make the utmost use of this powerful instrument."[94] Though not affiliated with the "State" in any formal sense, Hull House had made remarkable progress in convincing reform-minded activists that musical outreach could strengthen the foundation of democratic society.

Among the growing ranks of social workers desiring to communicate with populations in which many spoke little or no English, music represented an ideal medium. "The music settlement has a center of attraction which is definite and alluring," wrote Richard Watson Gilder in the social welfare journal *Charities*. "It supplies a demand which does not have to be explained or urged upon those who wish to be taught music."[95] By 1905 a survey of eighteen Chicago settlements reported that 50 percent boasted musical concerts and entertainment and/or some form of music classes. The report also noted the uplift tenor of many of the settlement music offerings: "[T]he people now listen to and enjoy music which it would not have been possible to give at first."[96]

Concerns about the increased commercial domination of public recreation added urgency to discussions of adapting musical progressive outreach to more directly compete with the marketplace for youth leisure time. The aesthetic emphasis of musical uplift championed by Eleanor Smith seemed outmoded relative to the crowd-pleasing sounds of Tin Pan Alley and the streets. "The appreciation of music by all sorts and conditions of people is too patent to admit of question," wrote reformer Alfred Lincoln Seligman. "From personal observation it can be stated that no social function among the poor can be carried through so successfully as with the aid of music *in some form*, be it a pathetic ballad, a jingling ragtime, or an inspiration made of sterner musical stuff."[97] Prim gatherings in settlement drawing rooms had little chance of attracting youth compared to the exciting world of beery neighborhood club dances, minimally supervised public dance halls, and risqué cabarets. The rise of the urban commercial music industry drove innovation at many settlements, including Hull House, to widen the scope of musical progressive activity, in part by appropriating selected features of the marketplace itself.

During the 1900s and 1910s, outreach at Hull House underwent a tactical shift from focusing chiefly on educating the talented few to attracting as many young inhabitants of the Nineteenth Ward as possible. While the music school maintained its high demands for its pupils, the broader settlement increased music club activity, added dances, and hastened to introduce other musical activities.[98] "We are only beginning to understand what might be done through the festival, the street procession, the band of marching musicians, orchestral music in public squares or parks, with the magic power they all possess to formulate the sense of companionship and solidarity," wrote Addams, describing the reorientation toward a broader audience.[99] Just as ceremonial park concerts amended their concert programs to include ragtime, Hull House moved toward a self-conscious cultural rapprochement with its neighbors. Ragtime never sounded within the walls of the music school during regular hours, but the Euroclassical and folk music aesthetics that Eleanor Smith favored had begun to embrace a more popular orientation in the interest of establishing credibility with a broader pool of potential users.

In 1907 the settlement constructed a Boys' Club Building that could accommodate the recreational interests of 500 boys. The facility included space for musical activities designed to make the widest social impact possible on boys and young men between the ages of twelve and twenty; choruses, group classes for participants of all levels of musical talent, and dances were organized.[100] Among the popular innovations was the Hull House Boys' Band, whose membership ranged from sixty to seventy players. The unit could "play creditably both classical music and the standard band music of the day," meaning that the band performed popular song styles and arrangements not emphasized by the music school.[101] The band represented an important physical and symbolic extension of Hull House musical outreach beyond the walls of the settlement. Its members performed in a uniform of blue trousers and a red coat at the settlement as well as in neighborhood halls and theaters, public parks, and other municipal settings.

Addams's personal orientation toward commercial music culture distinguished her from many bourgeois critics of public recreation who concentrated their energies on disparaging and seeking to suppress its aesthetic forms. Where some morals reformers saw licentiousness on display in public, Addams saw healthy and self-affirming impulses gone astray. Addams forcefully differentiated between the economic circumstances compelling workers to frequent the five-cent theaters and vaudeville houses and workers' desire to seek humanizing diversion from long days of numbing labor. While Addams hated the ragtime featured at cabarets and dance halls, which was to her mind "a vulgar type of music," she stressed the great importance of providing recreational alternatives to energetic youth. Addams attacked the hollowing out of vernacular expressive public culture and blamed the morally suspect condition of commercial public culture in large measure on the failings of the state and the marketplace: "The classical city provided for play with careful solicitude, building the theater as it built the marketplace and the temple. . . . Only in the modern industrial city have men concluded that it is no longer necessary for the municipality to provide for the insatiable desire for play." Comparing Chicago to Restoration London, Addams added: "Since the soldiers of Cromwell shut up the people's playhouses and destroyed their pleasure fields, the Anglo-Saxon city has turned over the provision for public recreation to the most evil-minded and the most unscrupulous members of the community."[102] Adams accused industrial and commercial forces of exploiting "starved imaginations" with minimal consideration or regard for the resulting impoverished civic culture. To combat the situation, Addams held up the example of the noncommercial and chaperoned dances at Hull House, where two dozen groups could regularly hold their own events rather than seek out rented or commercial halls. Through such outreach, Hull House combatted the siren call of commercial amusement culture. The strategy would broaden and spread in the decades to come.[103]

WHERE HAVE YOU GONE, DAVID QUIXANO?

In 1908, with Theodore Roosevelt, Jane Addams, and other progressive activists cheering him on, the playwright Israel Zangwill debuted a work celebrating the crucible of democracy that was transforming immigrants into Americans. "I do not know when I have seen a play that stirred me as much," gushed Roosevelt. Addams called Zangwill's work "a great service to America."[104] In addition to introducing the nation to a resilient metaphor, *The Melting Pot* incorporated themes of musical progressive reform, however crudely, into its message. In the dramatic final act, David Quixano, a young immigrant fiddler and fledgling composer, premieres his symphonic tribute to his new homeland at a Lower East Side settlement music school. The ritual performance of immigrant music by the settlement music school symbolizes the power of music to fire new civic forms of unity and American solidarity. Not merely a literary device, the presence of music in the acclaimed drama indicated the national level at which musical progressive ideas circulated by the early twentieth century.[105]

Hull House never produced a David Quixano of its own to sing the praises of its pioneering efforts in musical progressivism. Nor did it quite serve as the Americanizing musical crucible of Zangwill's imaginings. In more complicated and subtle ways, Hull House generated a legacy of musicians who found ways to appropriate reform resources for their personal and professional development. To do so, Hull House did not exclusively venerate cultivated music. It encouraged music clubs to form around immigrant and ethnic user interests as well as to embrace the idealized American forms to which many activists subscribed. Extant evidence suggests that the disciplining function of musical outreach at the settlement did not necessarily lead neighborhood users to value Euroclassical expression over alternative styles or sensibilities. Immigrants studying within the music school and participating in the less formal music clubs and group activities found ways to appropriate settlement resources to serve their unique needs as musicians and as musical citizens on their own terms.

When West Side resident Art Hodes, a Russian-Jewish immigrant, recalled the Hull House Music School, he remembered his mother's saying that "it was a place where you could get the best teaching possible for the least price." He also pinpointed the beginning of his artistic development and his affinity for blues and jazz to his experiences of playing cultivated music at a Saturday dancing class at Hull House.[106] Between 1916 and 1920, the teenaged Hodes studied piano and voice with Eleanor Smith and her sister Gertrude.[107] The training that Hodes received laid a technical foundation from which he launched a professional career playing blues and jazz. Ironically, the forms that Hodes favored derived from African Americans—the one group excluded from participation in the training that settlement music afforded.[108]

While a student at the music school, Hodes began to fashion an alter ego for himself as a jazz improviser, exploring the spaces between the written notes of the sheet music set before him. He diligently absorbed what the Smiths could teach him, while he also cultivated his skills and sensibilities as a jazz musician. On Saturday afternoons at Hull House, his instructors put his talents to work. "I had become good enough to play for the dancers," the pianist recalled, referring to a youth dance group known as the Marionettes, "and they asked me to play for them while they were practicing." Keeping time at dancing class afforded Hodes practical training in the European traditions favored in the bourgeois drawing room. The experience supplied him with insight into the relationship between

the moving bodies dancing in the room and the rhythms accompanying their dances.[109]

These extra workouts also gave Hodes a chance to expand his
own development as a blues and jazz player. Ragtime and jazz may
not have been part of the Hull House canon, but Hodes nevertheless
found ways to connect his training and his interests. He used the
Saturday dance class to stretch beyond the boundaries of the pieces
and the circumscribed social setting in which he studied: "I was
improvising right from the start. When I was playing for dancers at
Hull House, I was beginning to find things to do besides the written
note and to follow it."[110] Hodes took the skills he had acquired at
Hull House and began playing at taxi-dance joints, cabarets, and
small jazz clubs on Madison Street rather than pursuing a career as a
classical musician.[111] But in all of his recollections of Hull House,
Hodes never suggested that his teachers reprimanded him for his
flights of improvisation. The climate of artistic freedom instilled by
Eleanor Smith and others at the music school complemented rather
than suppressed the young Hodes's negotiation of the aesthetic
boundaries of Euroclassical, blues, and jazz music. "What it did for
me musically," recalled Hodes of his time at Hull House, "I can never
over-appreciate."[112]

Benny Goodman's parents, also Russian-Jewish immigrants living on the West Side, steered their young prodigy to Hull House.
Like thousands of poor families in Chicago, the Goodmans soaked up
free entertainment whenever and wherever they could. "The first
music I ever heard, as I recall it now, was in Douglas Park in Chicago," Benny Goodman recalled. "We went to the concerts for two
reasons. In the first place, Pop genuinely liked music and enjoyed
listening to the band. In the second place it didn't cost anything,
either for him or for us—and when there are ten or eleven in the
family and not much money coming in (his weekly income, in a good
week, was rarely more than twenty dollars), that was an important
item."[113]

Hull House's musical resources provided Goodman with an important platform for his own development as a swing performer. Art
Hodes recalled the day that the young clarinetist joined the Hull
House Boys Band to which Hodes also belonged: "The first jam
session I ever had with a kid [at Hull House] was with Benny Goodman. And the band master brought Benny in one day, and he looked
at me and says, do you mind if he plays along with you?"[114] Goodman

described the group at the time that he joined it as "the standard Dixieland band of cornet, trombone, clarinet, tuba and drums." Performing all over the West Side, and using the resources of the West Park field houses for his own jazz combo, Goodman and other musicians drew on a range of musical progressive settings and opportunities to gain the skills and exposure necessary for launching meaningful music careers.[115]

Hodes, Goodman, and James C. Petrillo, the trumpet-playing son of an immigrant sewer digger who studied at Hull House before going on to run the American Federation of Musicians for many years, are among the better-known figures who crossed the Hull House threshold.[116] These storied figures were joined by scores of other youths and adults benefiting from musical progressive outreach. The ability of the Hull House music school to make professional training affordable and to attempt to incorporate a range of cultural traditions of music into its reform mission created an important space of social exchange and debate concerning the meanings of identities expressed and redefined through music.

As Hilda Satt noted, musical progressivism enabled ordinary Chicago residents to make or listen to music in ways that helped them to redefine their own lives and make contributions to public life. By acknowledging music's power to transform identity and civic life, musical progressivism at Hull House brought together a diverse community of individuals who found expression, social contact, and a variety of resources with which to explore the interplay of art and civic engagement. Acknowledging the richness of neighborhood musical practices, Hull House promoted social and cultural crossings, samplings, and improvisations among users—and among teachers as well. Despite the occasional patronizing commentary, and despite the seeming contradiction between the aim of overcoming "differences" and the goal of strategically "preserving" musical heritage, musical outreach at Hull House did not suppress or obliterate cultural differences. Those differences were multiplied, instead, and with them the democratic possibilities of urban public culture increased as well. Jane Addams, Eleanor Smith, William Tomlins and others may sometimes have erred in the assumptions that they made about those they sought to reach, but their work created new opportunities and lasting models for public efforts to make music an agent of cultural politics and democratic social change.

Coinciding with the impact of musical progressivism at Hull

House was the rise of the "playground movement," which called for greater municipal support of youth recreation; combined, these developments dramatically expanded public music reform. Beginning in the 1900s, reform legislation directed Chicago's major park commissions to begin a second wave of parks construction. A new generation of field house parks built in Chicago's working neighborhoods brought the ideas of musical progressivism to a vastly expanded audience. Park officials drew directly on the model established at Hull House and hired music coordinators from among the ranks of settlement workers. The translation of musical progressivism from Hull House to dozens of neighborhood parks promised dramatic opportunities in music reform, as well as new challenges to promoting the idealized spirit of reform for the people of Chicago. Among the daunting tasks confronting musical progressivism and its practitioners as it moved into a new phase was that of reconciling the civic promise of musical outreach with what W. E. B. Du Bois had named the central challenge of the new century, the "problem of the color line."

FOUR

COME OVER HERE AND LISTEN TO THE MUSIC

MUNICIPAL POWER AND LOCAL AUTHORITY IN THE FIELD HOUSE PARKS, 1903–1919

On May 13, 1905, Henry G. Foreman, former two-term Cook County board president and current president of the board of Chicago's South Park Commissioners (SPC), stood jubilantly before an audience of several thousand residents of the Southwest Side. He had come to dedicate Davis Square, a new eight-and-a-quarter-acre field house park, located at the intersection of Forty-fifth Street and Marshfield Avenue, not far from the Union Stockyards. Joining him was Mary McDowell, a leading progressive activist and head resident of the nearby University of Chicago Social Settlement. Entertainment at the dedication included musical performances and an exhibition by members of the Polish and Bohemian Turners, neighborhood social and athletic organizations, who entertained the throng as they "executed maneuvers with wands and dumbbells."[1] The dedication represented a highlight of a major campaign to redefine the nature of public park service and the scope of musical outreach in Chicago.

Advocates of neighborhood park expansion, such as Foreman and McDowell, and neighborhood leaders had long pointed to the sprawling "Back of the Yards" neighborhood to illustrate the unequal distribution of parkland in the city. Not a single public park served an area whose population totaled 100,000 and whose family income averaged less than $500 per year. In the entire South Park district, an estimated 50 percent of the population lived beyond easy walking distance to a park. A family wanting to reach Washington Park, located about two miles to the southeast of the neighborhood, would have had to rely on public transportation, an inconvenience that deterred many poor residents from regularly making the trip. The opening of Davis Square represented part of a broad campaign to bring public park resources to Chicago's poorest and most underserved areas.[2]

In his dedicatory address, Foreman extended a munificent invitation from the park commission to the neighborhood. "When you people who live in this part of Chicago come home tired at night," he declared, "or when you have a holiday, or when you are tempted to do something wrong, come over here and listen to the music."[3] His exhortation might easily be dismissed as empty rhetoric. Among Chicago's musical-progressive activists, however, using Apollo's art to rejuvenate worn bodies and numbed minds, to promote public spiritedness, to reform recreation, and even to curb criminal impulses, was not idle wordplay, but a technique already widely practiced in ceremonial parks and at Hull House and other major settlement houses. Foreman and the major park commissions planned to expand music reforms pioneered at Hull House into the field houses as part of a municipal commitment to musical progressivism.[4]

This chapter analyzes the spread of musical outreach into the new field house parks of Chicago's West and South Sides during the first two decades of the twentieth century.[5] I examine the rationale for building the neighborhood parks to more directly serve the recreational needs of the public broadly construed, and I look at the complementary musical programs and activities introduced there. I also analyze the behavior of park users who patronized these new public spaces and incorporated musical resources into their everyday lives. While tensions sometimes strained relations between officials and visitors, field house services catalyzed the expansion of a civic musical culture in which immigrant, ethnic, and laboring citizens used municipal services to redefine democratic public culture. This chapter will show the unintended consequences of the triumphant expansion of musical progressivism. Even as musical progressivism strengthened civic bonds among a highly diverse group of park users in the field houses, the process relied on the widespread exclusion of African Americans, and a pattern of racial bias undermined the democratic viability of the movement. It exposed a tacit reform culture of whiteness whose exclusions boded ill for the future of the city and its public culture.[6]

FANFARE FOR THE COMMON PEOPLE
The Rise of the Field House Park

The burst of neighborhood park construction in Chicago during the 1900s and early 1910s constituted a veritable "playground movement." Throughout the United States, municipalities constructed hundreds of public playgrounds and recreation centers to provide healthful activities for boys, girls, and adults. Park designers and operators drew on knowledge about human and group behavior derived from the precedent of settlement work and the findings of the emerging disciplines of the social sciences. Neighborhood park creation emphasized the responsibility of society to serve individual and group needs for the betterment of the nation as a whole. In 1907 Chicago hosted the first convention of the Playground Association of America. President Theodore Roosevelt used the occasion to praise "the magnificent system that Chicago has erected in its South Park section, one of the most notable civic achievements in any American city."[7]

Some historians have charged exponents of the playground movement of using "reform parks" to promote an ideology dedicated to stripping ethnic, immigrant, and laboring people of their identities in favor of a bourgeois set of Americanized aspirations, values, and recreational practices.[8] While xenophobia and elite bias against plebeian sensibilities are discernible themes in park reform history, the resounding popularity of neighborhood parks reveals a more complicated set of aspirations and needs entwining citizens and park officials. Most of the evidence of everyday encounters does not support the thesis that playground operatives sought or, more importantly, generally attained significant social control of park users. Reformers had complex, sometimes contradictory ideas about music and reform that necessitated a process of trial and error and required, above all, assistance from local residents. In turn, users were far too adept at using municipal public space for their own purposes to be consistently

Plan of Park no. 1 (later Eckhart Park), 1912.
Chicago Park District Special Collections.

duped by a progressive cabal. Outreach via the field houses signified a critical development in musical progressivism that incorporated tens of thousands of everyday users in a democratic negotiation of power, culture, and civic participation.

One of the key political moments that precipitated the construction of a new generation of parks in Chicago occurred in November 1899 when the Chicago City Council adopted a resolution to create an investigation into the troubled state of park service in the city.[9] Sponsoring groups complained that few of Chicago's workers had easy access to existing parks. The council created a Special Park Commission (SPKC) comprised of nine aldermen, representatives from the three major park commissions, and a number of private citizens. Their investigation produced the landmark 1902 "Report on Sites and Needs," which called for major initiatives to democratize the park system as a resource for all citizens.

The commission found that despite a greater than five-and-a-half-fold increase in the population of Chicago between 1870 and 1900, and despite chronic residential overcrowding on the predominantly working-class Near West Side, virtually no new park construction had occurred in the three major districts since the heyday of the 1869 Park Acts due to restrictions in the enabling legislation.[10] In 1880 Chicago's park system had ranked as the second largest in the United States, surpassed only by Philadelphia's. But the annexation of surrounding towns and massive population growth had almost knocked Chicago out of the top ten.[11] The SPKC reported that as a result of increased population density in the "river wards" of the Near West Side and the stockyards of the South Side, including the "Armour Avenue District . . . commonly called the 'Black Belt,'" approximately one-third of city residents lived a mile or more from the nearest ceremonial park.[12] Some reformers blamed the situation on complacent park commissioners. The commissioners fingered the state legislature for constraining their ability to expand. "Wage earners are most in need of park service," agreed one park commissioner. "The welfare of these people—physical, moral, mental—is the great municipal problem of the day. It will become more and more acute as our population increases." Reformers demanded new state legislation to free the major park districts to act. They adopted the slogan "Take the park to the people, if they cannot come to the park."[13]

On the eve of the release of the SPKC report, the Illinois state legislature rumbled into action. On May 10, 1901, lawmakers authorized the major park commissions to build in their districts new parks of no more than ten acres. Then on May 14, 1903, the legislature removed the size limits as well as the rule that parks be "contiguous to existing parks or boulevards," giving still greater flexibility to the commissions in site selection.[14] Illinois ultimately appropriated $500,000 for each of the major park districts to support neighborhood park construction, and local voters enthusiastically passed a referendum to make the changes.[15]

In 1904 the South Park Commissioners announced that plans

had been finalized to build a dozen "small parks" landscaped by the Olmsted Brothers firm with architectural design by Daniel H. Burnham and Company at an estimated cost of $80,000–$90,000 per park. The parks featured field house recreation centers with outdoor and indoor athletic facilities, such as playing fields, gymnasiums, swimming pools, and showers. The field houses also included refectories, reading and club rooms, and assembly halls.[16] The West Chicago Park Commissioners (WPC) built eight neighborhood parks of their own using a similar field house design. By 1908 seventeen new parks were operational across the South Park system, including one in the Armour Avenue area that was proximate to, but clearly outside, the boundary defining the African American Black Belt.[17]

Following the view that civic reform needed to compete with extant recreation in industrial areas, the invitation to "come over and listen to the music" was meant to induce neighbors to defect from street and commercial amusements to the field houses. The new parks sought to create an alternative community setting—a unified civic beachhead on a shore characterized by heterogeneity and difference—supervised by a paternalistic municipal authority. Applying lessons learned in ceremonial park concert settings, officials listened to the streets in hopes of enticing a loyal group of followers. Reformers would have to present music in forms and contexts that would attract and retain locals, while maintaining ultimate authority over the reform mission.

As a leading publicist of the new park initiative, Foreman had spent the past few years making numerous speeches to citizens explaining the need for park expansion and outlining the philosophies of service that the field house parks were designed to implement. The argument contained a tacit admission that thirty years after their grand inception, many of Chicago's ceremonial parks had not fulfilled their vaunted civic tasks.[18] Despite metropolitan expansion and gradual improvements in public transportation, ceremonial parks remained underutilized by Chicago laborers. Geographically, socially, and culturally, ceremonial parks still stood a world apart from the recreational needs and interests of a sizable and growing portion of the population.[19] Though tens of thousands of immigrant and ethnic laborers patronized ceremonial parks on weekends at the height of the summer, city parks were neither sufficiently plentiful nor accessible to make a difference in the everyday lives of most residents. A petition by German Turners on the West Side had spurred Douglas

Park officials to open a swimming pool and outdoor gym in 1896, but ceremonial parks typically emphasized contemplative or "passive" recreation over more active modes of physical recreation.[20]

Invoking a buzzword of the progressive lexicon, Foreman declared that in the industrial neighborhoods of Chicago "[t]here is a crying necessity for *useful* as well as ornamental parks." He added: "The masses need, for recreation, more than a plot of grass with some flowers, a few trees, and a little running water."[21] A desire to create human-centered play spaces for the people challenged the aesthetic emphasis of the ceremonial park era. Explaining the shift in ideology, a journalist wrote: "A decade or two ago the only thought was to preserve 'bits of nature' at the outer edges of a city for those who had the leisure and the means to enjoy them. The new spirit demands the preservation of the bits of human nature, the teeming millions of them whose only ideas of outdoors is a narrow strip of cobbles underfoot and a thin streak of sky overheard—even at a sacrifice of trees and shrubs and grass."[22] Though this account oversimplified the complex aesthetic and uplift strategies of Chicago's ceremonial park reform landscape, it captured the rebellious spirit of new park construction dedicated to serving the recreational needs of park populations.

Plans to build field houses to cater to the local needs of the laboring masses evidently displeased some park commissioners, who considered it the responsibility of visitors to conform to park protocols rather than the reverse. Controversies over popular music programs in the ceremonial parks and eruptions such as the 1902 Garfield Park riot had exposed a rift between citizens and certain park officials concerning the democratic spirit of public recreation. Reformer Charles Zeublin noted that despite high demand for field house parks "[t]here is, however, a steady conflict to obtain them, for the old-fashioned ideas of park commissioners continually urge garden parks instead of playgrounds."[23]

Advocates noted that several decades of unprecedented immigration and industrial growth had altered the geography and social and cultural composition of the city. These changes coupled with the rise of commercial amusement culture on a vast scale required a new recreational reform landscape that offered more than the rarefied atmosphere of ceremonial parks of the past. Activists contended that the hallmarks of large parks, such as abundant flowering shrubs, well-tended gardens, and gracious walkways struck many potential users as cloying, inhibiting, or downright dull. In order to be viable reform spaces, neighborhood parks must be more than ornaments. They must be appealing and "useful," but in a manner that maintained the authority of park officials to shape the tenor of recreation conducted in them.[24]

The turn to a kind of deferential localism in park outreach rejected the metropolitan gigantism of ceremonial park service. It reflected a desire among activists for a more intimate scale of reform as an antidote to the social fragmentation associated with the awesome, even frightening growth of the city. As one Chicago editorialist put it: "Many close observers believe that one of the weakest spots of our great modern cities is the lack of any method of bringing public spirit to a focus locally. The city of a million or more inhabitants is so huge that the mass of the people are lost in it. The vast majority have no hope of impressing themselves individually on the conduct of its greater affairs, and they have no opportunity to develop public spirit in neighborhood interests. . . . Perhaps the distribution of the small parks will prove to correspond well with the real local grouping of the population."[25] The hope of building "public spirit" from the neighborhood outward inspired field house park reformers like Foreman. "Above all," he promised, distancing the new vision from its predecessor culture associated with the elite excesses of ceremonial parks, neighborhood parks "will belong to the masses. The people will not be *trespassers* there."[26] As Foreman's remark acknowledged, the didactic quality of the ceremonial park reform landscape had not adequately balanced the recreational preferences of many users with the ideals of civic reform.

Foreman took pains to portray himself as a friend of the industrial masses. Indeed, there remained substantial reason for park personnel to worry that *they* might be the ones perceived as trespassers once the parks opened in the neighborhoods.[27] Trends in ceremonial parks adjacent to industrial neighborhoods had shown the powerful impact that local sentiments and tastes had on the nature of concerts and recreational routines. Based on cases of resistance to top-down regulation of user behaviors, neighborhood park reformers could not be certain that bourgeois preferences would be warmly welcomed at the local level. Neighborhood leaders had determinedly lobbied park officials to bring field houses to their constituents, but this did not imply an abrogation of power or cultural authority once the centers opened.[28]

Besides the promise to "take the park to the people," reform interest in respecting the "real local grouping" of Chicago's population, understood in geographic as well as social and cultural terms, marked a radically new reform perspective. It may have derived from officials' frustration at accommodating the myriad demands of cere- monial park audiences, though there is no direct evidence of this view. More likely, it represented a genuine desire to ensure that the ethnic, immigrant, and laboring population had city parks to call their own and that municipal resources would be fairly placed at their disposal. The field house park rationale promised to give the people greater power to shape the democratic character of public space with minimal interference from reform-minded officials.

As it happened, however, by partially basing the validity of dem- ocratic field house park service on respecting normative social group- ings, reformers inadvertently placed themselves in a double-bind when it came to the substantive class, cultural, and racial animosities prevalent in many Chicago neighborhoods. Defending local author- ity to shape field house park culture, reformers sidestepped some of the most daunting issues impeding the flowering of democratic public culture. Park officials demonstrated quiescent and sometimes complicit attitudes toward local patterns of racial injustice. By send- ing a message, however unintended, that such "real" differences would be tolerated in the field houses, officials violated the demo- cratic promises made to the citizenry when these public spaces were created.

DOMESTICATING THE SOUNDS OF REFORM

When they visited the new parks, area residents entered a noticeably different reform landscape from the ceremonial parks.[29] Limited to plots of about ten acres, park designers highlighted domesticity and intimacy over the pomp and intimidating scale of the ceremonial parks. Following the lead of settlement houses, the field houses of- fered programs for children as well as adults. In addition to athletic facilities, each park offered youth and adult classes in instrumental and vocal music using rooms akin to the interiors of a middle-class residence. While women played a primary role in music education and supervision at Hull House, field house parks favored male per- sonnel as musical supervisors. In this respect the field houses bor- rowed techniques from settlement ideology that prized a model of domestic protectiveness, albeit emanating from a paternal, rather than maternal, locus of authority.[30]

Anticipating a domestic discourse of neighborhood park reform, field house boosters praised the new public centers as "family clubhouses for the masses."[31] "Let the field house be the symbol of a civic home of the citizens," enthused Mary McDowell.[32] Simon N. Patten, a leading national figure in progressive issues, predicted that the parks would redefine the boundary between "public" and "private" life to the enrichment of both: "Parks should be the outer, public home of the people, contrasting with the inner, private home. Museums have a place in them, and books, resting places, eating places and in full measure, amusement establishments. Their perfect force will be utilized when people are made natural by restoring nature there, and adding social, educational, and entertainment functions."[33] As musical progressives had already discovered, music could offer particularly salutary features for those wishing to make the city more homelike, whether for educational or for recreational purposes.

Edward B. DeGroot, general director of field houses and playgrounds for the South Park Commissioners, praised the transforming power of music in children's lives. He suggested that field house music administered in intimate indoor settings would expose impressionable young minds to aesthetically beautiful music. It would teach children to listen, sit still, and channel their energies into an uplifting and lifelong pursuit. Moreover, children made wonderful ambassadors of reform outside the walls of the field house: "Dirt upon the hands and faces of the children of the street rubs off when it comes in contact with the bathing facilities of the park. Likewise art and beauty 'rub off' in contact with young folks in the park and is [sic] no doubt carried to the homes in expressions of home improvement."[34] Under park supervisors' care, children could be "cleansed" of street contagion and exposed to the rejuvenating balm of healthy recreation and musical uplift. Transformed, they would rub off their new selves on their families and communities.

Park officials hoped to "rub on" formulations of popular music culture different from those that catered to Chicago youths elsewhere in the city. In 1913 Eckhart, Stanford, and Dvorak Parks presented fifty-three indoor concert events alone.[35] At Dvorak Park, officials hired an orchestra and chorus director to work directly with children in the neighborhood. In the words of John F. Smulski, West Park president, these musical instructors "taught the children all kinds of games, songs . . . and such pastimes as their interests directed and their little minds could comprehend."[36] Smulski's tone smacked

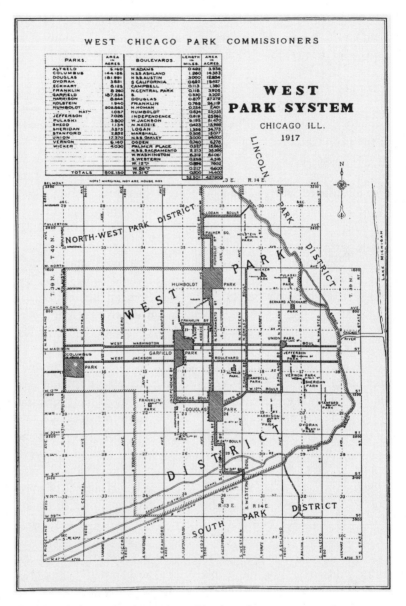

West Park System, showing parks and boulevards, 1917.
Chicago Park District Special Collections.

predictably of the paternalism that often characterized social out-reach in the Progressive Era. Filling "little minds" with music repre-sented an exploitative activity when a commercial cabaret or dance hall operator was involved—but not when musical progressives called the tune.

Reformers self-consciously co-opted developments in the mar-ket and embraced technologies, such as the phonograph, to pro-mote musical reforms. The WPC presented phonograph "concerts" in many of the field houses beginning in 1910. In the years to come, phonograph labels such as Columbia and Victor sold to field house music supervisors records that were endorsed by their "educational departments" and designed for specific use in park physical educa-tion classes and music clubs. Following the innovative example of Eleanor Smith at Hull House, the labels also teamed with field house park music directors to promote suitable folk music sounds for musi-cal progressivism.[37]

Expanding on the settlement model, the SPC and WPC field houses turned themselves over to local sponsors of community events. The WPC leased pianos for public use in every field house park in the system. The instruments became the centerpieces of club gather-ings, socials, and dances and were described as virtually "in constant use by the public."[38] Local organizations took advantage of the con-venient, free rooms and assembly halls for dances, concerts, and other social events. Patrons were required to meet directly with the staff in order to use the facilities. Frequent users got to know park employ-ees personally, and such ritual forms of contact strengthened the familial dynamic of the field house, with its patriarchal supervisors overseeing an extended "family" of clubhouse users. While limited to some degree by the controlling authority of the supervisors, neigh-borhood residents nevertheless succeeded in shaping the field house social and cultural environment as best they could to meet their individual needs.[39]

"THE STANDARD . . . IS UNIMPEACHABLE"
Band Concerts at the Field House Parks

Outdoor summer concerts remained an important part of musical progressivism and drew tens of thousands of visitors to field house parks annually. Instead of grandiose bandstands, however, park officials constructed modest outdoor music courts and pavilions. By the end of 1904, the SPC reported fourteen music courts in operation.[40] Many of the same brass bands and military orchestras who performed at the ceremonial parks began appearing at the smaller music courts, saving locals a lengthy trip to the large parks. J. Frank Foster, superintendent of the SPC since 1891, personally investigated the bands to hire and ranked his favorites accordingly for consideration by the other commissioners.[41] In 1905 Foster oversaw 116 concert performances for the SPC featuring popular military bands, such as A. F. Weldon's Second Regiment Band, the Pullman Band, Johnny Hand's Band, the First Cavalry Band of the Illinois National Guard, and Forrest's Seventh Regiment Band, each of which performed free about once a week during the summer at the various neighborhood parks.[42] South Park concerts proved hugely popular and averaged 4,000 to 5,000 listeners per performance at the field house parks.[43]

While J. F. Foster relied on his personal tastes to choose bands for the SPC, his compatriots in the West Parks appeared to cater more overtly to the tastes of the home crowd. By 1908 enthusiastic reports described "very good attendance" at field house concerts on the West Side. "It is hoped that these park concerts may be increased," wrote the WPC, "as it is a well-known fact that there is nothing in life that has such a wonderful influence." Like the SPC, the WPC routinely hired stalwart military bands with citywide, even national reputations and touring experience, such as the Second Regimental Band, the Pullman Band, Ellis Brooks's Band, and Bredfield's Band and Orchestra to entertain in the parks. The roster of choice also embraced local, ethnic favorites, such as the Pilsen Band, Tony Konopasek, and Emil Kopp's Band. Such groups were a familiar presence in industrial neighborhoods because they regularly appeared at ethnic parades, national festivals, picnic grove concerts, and semiprivate local occasions.[44]

The practice of favoring groups whose leadership and personnel reflected the local cultural composition of the West Side's multiethnic communities reflected the negotiated aspect of musical progressivism. Many of these bands combined popular American songs and marches alongside material favored by their ethnic supporters. These groups used their performances to celebrate metropolitan/American and neighborhood/ethnic identifications in ways that stimulated audiences and made field house music culture relevant as a site of civic engagement, in which local and municipal authority collectively responded to the desires of a musical public.

While musical groups enjoyed some leeway in selecting their programs, concerns about audience behaviors kept park officials on guard against the potential dangers of mixing large crowds of workers and lively concert bands. Incorporating popular musical styles and sounds into neighborhood concerts risked encouraging the wrong kind of social dynamic and potentially unleashing rebellious energies. WPC officials stressed the importance of vigilance in future programming, as was evident in one report: "It is of the greatest importance that the musical selection should be of the very best."[45] The commissioners only considered bands whose popular material would draw crowds while not transgressing the musical boundaries of bourgeois respectability.[46] In deference to the domesticated tenor of the neighborhood parks, only entertainment deemed appropriate for women, children, and family groups appeared. Ragtime songs with ribald themes or popular songs featuring lyrics associated with sex, drinking prowess, and other aspects of plebeian amusement culture were risky propositions at field house concerts. Despite the challenge of managing audiences numbering in the tens of thousands, the WPC made discriminating musical choices and monitored crowds in order to be able to assure the public that "the standard of morality and discipline required and maintained [at concerts] is unimpeachable."[47]

Concerns about commercial recreation, youth, and morality strengthened ties between field house park officials and local ethnic elites. The community leaders tied to churches, parochial schools, and ethnic organizations who lobbied park officials for field houses in their neighborhoods served as guardians of bourgeois morality within their local spheres of authority as well. The runaway popularity of commercial amusements, such as cabarets, dance halls, and cheap musical theaters, sapped the authority of local ethnic elites no less than that of the self-appointed progressive regulators of Chicago's public music culture. Evidence suggests that many locals supported reform musical outreach as a disciplining activity and clean recreational pastime that could strengthen rather than erode their ethnocentric power.

Political subtexts informed alliances between park officials and local authorities, too, as when ethnic leaders sided with reformers against other immigrant or ethnic populations in the neighborhood. Following the dedication of Eckhart Park on the West Side, the German-language *Abendpost* reported the response of one cleric: "Pastor Evers expresses his thanks to all, who have in such distin-

guished manner interested themselves, that the new park should be
created, but stressed upon the necessity, of protecting same against
the dance hall evils and the wedding celebrations which are held in
neighborhood saloons, and have a bad influence upon the respectable
citizens. It is not uncommon that Polish weddings held in such localities are celebrated for three days and nights. The results are generally fights and orgies; therefore they should be prohibited near the
park."[48] Inflammatory attacks on one ethnic group in the pages of
another's foreign-language newspaper and struggles for turf and resources were commonplace. But the emergence of field house parks
as civic spaces within neighborhoods made them of vital interest
in battles waged inside and outside park borders. The progressive
image of "clubhouses of the masses" did not adequately represent
the contested political and cultural issues that neighborhood music
makers and leaders attached to reform discourse, some of which had a
prehistory dating to the nineteenth century. Tensions between Germans and Poles underscored burning questions about the commonalities and differences of neighborhood musical publics and the viability of promoting civic unification via recreation.

Determined to attract visitors to field houses on Sundays when
laborers commonly took their day off, South Park officials instituted
a regimen of musical activities in field houses aimed at what they
understood as the recreational needs of local families.[49] But their
desire to offer a competing alternative to Sunday beer blasts at commercial picnic grounds put field house officials at risk of offending
neighborhood clerics, some of whom had previously pressured park
officials to recognize that even progressive reform should observe a
day of rest.[50] To ensure local support, SPC officials consulted with
clerics, teachers, and "leading citizens of the neighborhood" to build
a supportive coalition before establishing a weekly musical program
known as "A Pleasant Sunday Afternoon." Local youth and adults
studying music in the field house performed at these events, and the
casual, family tone demonstrated a remarkable resemblance to traditional Sunday musical gatherings, affording merriment and ethnocultural shows of solidarity among Germans, Bohemians, Poles, and
other linguistically, nationally, or culturally identified groups, minus
the inflammable element of alcohol.

Behind its facade of blandness, "A Pleasant Sunday Afternoon"
marked one of the more pointed efforts of field house park operators
to co-opt certain habits and folkways of the neighborhoods for the

purpose of uplift. What made the events "pleasant" to reformers, but perhaps less so to others, was the strict prohibition of alcohol on a day where moderate to heavy drinking accompanied plebeian leisure activity in many industrial neighborhoods.[51] To the average exhausted worker, the cathartic potential of an afternoon of amateur performances of waltzes and arias at the local field house had its good points, but so too did a day devoted to garrulous fellowship and gaiety in which singing, dancing, playing, and drinking might well be featured. Though hardly as exalting as Turner concerts, the combination of music and social attractions conveniently and affordably presented just down the street "met with immediate favor" among locals, according to officials, and garnered large audiences. The concerts in the parks performed an added promotional function, as they did at Hull House, by introducing children and their families to a new, more progressive environment. An official at Ogden Park noted that the Sunday afternoon concerts were "the beginning of social movements which have brought the use of the assembly hall and club rooms in this park up to within thirty per cent of the possibilities."[52] Outreach did not simply accommodate itself to preexisting sounds or rhythms of neighborhood recreational activity. Instead, reformers skillfully managed those rhythms and routines by incorporating what they saw as uplifting activities into the field houses, while offering alternatives to plebeian entertainments not seen as consonant with the bourgeois mores of the movement.

IN THE FOOTSTEPS OF THE COMPETITION
Field House Dances

Community dancing in the field houses stirred tremendous enthusiasm among local users while offering a remarkable example of musical progressivism's reform tactic of imitative alteration. Beginning in the late 1900s, field houses challenged commercial entrepreneurs for the favor of tens of thousands of young participants in the massive prewar dance "craze." Following the example of Hull House and other settlements, field house parks provided an alternative indoor dance outlet. When young men and women from the neighborhood learned that they could hold dances in the field houses free of charge, community enthusiasm for the parks increased still further.[53]

Historically, reformers viewed dancing in commercial halls as a direct threat to youthful virtue, but their specific responses to the popularity of the phenomenon varied. Beginning in the 1890s, Hull House had offered space for club dances at the settlement as an alternative to unsupervised dances in a rented hall where costs were typically recouped through the selling of alcoholic beverages.[54] A pragmatic spirit toward recreational preferences among men and women in the Nineteenth Ward guided the policy that grew more inclusive of popular musical activity as time went by. In 1909 Louise Dekoven Bowen, an influential Hull House recreation reformer, declared: "If we are to have dance halls the municipally conducted dance hall is the thing."[55] Two years later, the Vice Commission of Chicago echoed the call for the city to provide "properly policed and supervised" municipal dance alternatives to commercial halls.[56] The *Chicago Record-Herald* hammered the point that, due to its broad appeal to the city's youth, the "dance hall must be purified and elevated. It must be divorced from the saloon, the dive, the white slave traffic."[57]

The field house dance strategy built on settlement precedent by attempting to co-opt the appealing aspects of commercial and ethnocentric recreational culture in the surrounding neighborhoods. Rather than condemning commercial dancing, supervisors invited the "craze" into the domestic setting of the field houses where it could be more easily regulated.[58] For young adults craving recreational opportunities outside the fraternal/benevolent association or church hall event, the field house offered an option with a mildly "American" flavor that aimed to operate within the bounds of cross-cultural definitions of social propriety. Neighborhood dancers found many opportunities in the field houses, but those opportunities came with a firm set of rules and regulations meant to support the bourgeois dictates of park reform ideology.

Although they were bare-bones operations, WPC field houses provided respectable neighborhood dancing schools for women ages sixteen and over and men ages eighteen and over. They were an affordable alternative to private dancing schools and a respectable alternative to the "dancing academies" of questionable repute operating out of low-rent storefronts and walk-ups on the West Side. At the field houses, interested parties paid a modest fee to enroll in small classes for tutoring "in the waltz, two step, one step, fox trot, position and general social behavior." The "new dances," as ragtime steps were sometimes called, were neither taught nor encouraged on the dance floor. Classes were sex-segregated, and pupils were encouraged to patronize field house dances to meet partners and to put their training into practice.

Dances consumed large quantities of space, and the demand for affordable locations in industrial neighborhoods at which to hold social gatherings in the 1900s and 1910s was so great that field house parks grew extraordinarily popular with neighborhood youths and young adults. In 1908 social dances comprised more than 60 percent of the activity in the assembly halls of the SPC. Just during the month of October in 1911, neighborhood groups sponsored 103 dances in South Park field houses.[59] In 1909 the WPC launched its field house dance program. By 1911 the WPC hosted 272 dances in field houses during the year. The following year, that number increased to 297. By 1913, over 300 dances were held in the West Parks.[60] These numbers continued to rise until World War I, when various wartime restrictions temporarily cooled the dance craze in Chicago.

Given their cautious nature, the field house dances could hardly match the bright-lights allure of commercial dancing with its hot rhythms and modern steps, alcohol, and the thrill of illicit sexual contact, perhaps across ethnic and class lines. Nevertheless, these events made a dramatic impact on West and South Side neighborhood recreation options and garnered national attention. In 1911 the WPC reported that in Parks no. 1 and no. 2 "serious endeavor has been made to counteract the bad effect of the cheap dance halls in their vicinity," adding that "[t]his is proving to be one of the most vital influences of our small park social work."[61] A study conducted by the Russell Sage Foundation concluded that the establishment of field houses in Chicago lowered delinquency rates in surrounding areas.[62] Victor Von Borosini, a Hull House resident, reported that in Bohemian and Polish neighborhoods "several dance halls back of saloons have had to be closed because their business has declined" in favor of field house dances.[63] "The South Park system is offering to the people a clean, attractive, well-lighted hall which may be used for any neighborhood purpose where the best influences prevail," crowed Everett Mero, an admiring reformer. "They [the park dances] have already done much to lessen the use of the surrounding dance halls, and it is hoped that they will soon be able to close many of them," he concluded.[64] In 1912 the SPC reaffirmed the Russell Sage Foundation report, claiming that "the number of dance halls and poolrooms diminished when reform parks were created in their neighborhoods."[65]

Dance at Small Park no. 3 (later Dvorak Park), ca. 1911.
Chicago Park District Special Collections.

The field house dance phenomenon exploded the idea that progressive reformers were unreceptive to public recreational needs, and it showed that musical progressivism significantly helped legitimate a "respectable" brand of youth dancing.

Prior to World War I, young dancers seeking to take advantage of the field house park programs had two options at neighborhood centers on the West Side. The WPC permitted so-called private dances in which neighborhood clubs and organizations sponsored events with no direct involvement from the supervisors. The sponsor decided who could attend. The only official park oversight consisted of a police officer on duty. The commissioners required that sponsors finance their own events (music, refreshments, decorations, and so forth) without the sale of alcohol and without charging admission at the door. These constraints reserved a considerable degree of power for the WPC to refuse applicants unable to demonstrate the financial solvency or legitimate organizational structure to put on a dance. At Eckhart Park, various neighborhood groups and organizations, including Chapter 10 of the Juvenile Protective League, held social dances on the second Saturday of the month beginning in 1911.[66]

The second type of West Park dances were the so-called open dances "to which anyone and everyone was invited."[67] At these events, Superintendent of Recreation T. J. Smergalski recalled, neighborhood residents "assumed no direct responsibility for the conduct of the dance." Field house officials underwrote, organized, and ran these community dances. The parks supplied musical entertainment (piano only); wardrobe help, since park dances required proper attire; chaperones; and the customary police officer. These dances attracted diverse crowds, including dancers who might not have belonged to the more exclusive groups throwing private dances in the field houses. Park officials reported that the "heterogeneous" character of the open dances required greater vigilance because the nature of the crowd tended to lead to a greater incidence of problematic dancing or other rebellious crowd behaviors.[68]

Attempts to sneak new sounds and dance steps into the field houses at private and community dances of the late 1910s and early 1920s kept park staff on their toes. Although outdoor concerts had featured ragtime airs for some time, park officials believed that the intimate social ritual of couples dancing required different musical and aesthetic standards. Before approving an application for a dance, supervisors consulted with would-be sponsors about musical selection and dance styles to ensure compliance with park standards of good taste. During the 1910s, the field houses did their utmost to maintain a ban on "ragtime music or any other music with suggestive titles or words, or with any form of improper dancing." By the early 1920s, the atmosphere at field house dances had changed considerably. Formerly, according to Smergalski, overseeing dances required minimal worry "since only the waltz and two-steps were in vogue" and "the attendant evils of the moderns styles of dancing did not have to be watched and directed." But the emergence of faster, syncopated dance music, new dance steps, and the rebellious fashion styles and attitudes that the jazz age inspired forced the park districts to rethink how to respond to the latest music styles.[69]

To compensate for trends in so-called tough dancing, WPC field house rules expressly prohibited physical movements linked with the popular dance styles in vogue in Chicago during the 1920s.[70] The inventory of forbidden moves included "close dancing," in which the faces and bodies of couples touched; "improper position," in which dancers failed to maintain an erect posture, or waved their arms, or produced "a distorted position of the body"; and "objectionable dancing," in which "freak, unnecessary or indecent movements" occurred, such as "suggestive wiggling, frequent low dipping, [or] extreme swaying." Dancers had their own standards, however, and "some unpleasant occurrences have accompanied some of our dances," Superintendent Smergalski conceded, alluding to popular ragtime dances such as the turkey trot and grizzly bear. "We have, however," he said, "tried to meet the problem by constructive rather than repressive measures."[71] Struggles between supervisors and dancers over acceptable modes of expression shaped the dynamic of field house events, yet neighborhood youths and adults were undaunted by the conservatism of park officials. They packed the field house dance floors, thus testifying to the success of musical progressivism's positive outreach ideals of "constructive rather than repressive measures" and commitment to civic engagement as a joint enterprise with local users.

By the time West Side jazz clarinetist Benny Goodman reached high school, he and his friends and fans had discovered the utility of park dances: "There was a big room on the second floor where the kids used to have their dances, because they could get the places from the city for practically nothing, and pay off the band for a few dollars apiece."[72] Goodman and others used field house dances to promote their acts even if the settings proved less slinky and exciting than a cabaret or dance hall.[73] Despite the extraordinary numbers of dancers using park facilities—it was estimated that in 1923 almost 100,000 citizens attended 478 dances in the West Park—many young people eschewed the staid respectability of the field houses and headed for neighborhood commercial halls and cabarets where alcohol was available to underage patrons and where lax or absent floor monitors permitted more liberal dancing and physical contact.

SELF-GOVERNMENT AND SELF-CONTROL
South Park Dances

Over in the South Park district, park dance rules conformed to the conservative niceties associated with bourgeois social dancing of the period. The SPC welcomed private dances with closed invitation lists. Sponsors had to submit formal applications to the supervisors and supply music, doorkeepers, wardrobe attendants, a floor manager, and other "necessary aid." Serving alcohol was not allowed. Advertising the dance outside the circle of invitees was prohibited in order to lessen the chance of gate crashing. In marked contrast to commercial dancing environments where teens and adults mingled freely, youths under age sixteen could only dance with "dignified and responsible chaperones" at SPC events, and curfews before eleven o'clock were enforced. All dancers were reminded that "suggestive or improper dancing [would] not be tolerated." Asserting their paternalist privilege, South Park officials declared that the "field house director will be the ultimate authority as to what is improper."[74]

Unlike the West Parks, however, the South Parks do not appear to have sponsored open dances for the neighborhood to offset the privatization of public space that invitation-only field houses dances represented. The SPC claimed that any group could sponsor a dance. It defended its strict policies by pointing to their beneficial effect, evidenced by the "self-control and self-government on the part of the groups, whether of a cultured and refined, or 'rough and ready' people."[75] Park officials boasted that dance applications came from "all grades of society, from shop and factory girls to the cultured fraternity groups from the universities."[76] Herein lay the carefully qualified democratic claim of the South Park field house system that distinguished it from the West. Yes, "all grades" could expect access in turn, but no expectation existed that "all grades" should be unleashed on any single dance floor at the same time.

The differing approaches of the West and South Parks reflected the substantive differences among musical progressives over whether melding heterogeneous neighbors into civic wholes via concerts made sense. The intimate nature of social dancing appeared to stir a hesitancy not seen in discussion of outdoor concert culture and democratization. Both the WPC and the SPC allowed for dances that supported preexisting and stable neighborhood social units. But the effect of such dance policies reflected a bias that undermined the radical democratic potential of the field house. Organizations of mixed ethnic groups, such as shop and factory girls in a singing class or club, could freely sponsor dances and participate in rituals of affiliation as "whites." Likewise, West Park open dances mixed strangers together on the dance floor. As one official explained the delicate matter, "*Natural groups*, representing various strata in society, are given the halls in rotation for dances of their particular groups."[77] African American clubs held dances, too, along with college boys and ethnic social clubs and guilds, but these were regulated by park officials (if not by sponsors themselves) as exclusively segregated affairs.

Whereas outdoor concerts catered to all regardless of race, the domestic sanctum of the field house dance primed social anxieties apparently connected to race, gender, and sexuality. Bourgeois codes of men's and women's place, a tacit culture privileging multiethnic whiteness, and deference to the Jim Crow color line by park officials ended up circumscribing the field house dance floor in significant ways. By not allowing open dances in field houses, South Park supervisors prohibited potential forms of interpersonal contact that might have democratized park and neighborhood space in positive ways. While the WPC made gestures toward democratic social mixing via open dances, South Park supervisors showed little interest in challenging what they evidently perceived as permissible forms of social and race-based hierarchies. In doing so, they abdicated a potentially powerful platform from which to challenge social and cultural biases in a controlled public reform setting. Despite democratic claims to the contrary, the rules of the dance in the South Parks in particular suggest that many park officials perceived race as a boundary that not even musical progressivism should transgress in its efforts to develop civic engagement and public culture in Chicago.

As the next chapter describes, the problem of race extended far beyond the dance floors of the field house parks. As it did the nation, the issue of racial segregation influenced musical progressivism and undermined the integrity of musical outreach during World War I. The war in Europe redoubled interest in musical progressivism as a means of constructing a unified home front, but America's entry into the war diverted the principles of reform and civic engagement in directions that distorted and compromised many of musical progressivism's most important civic ideals. Compounding these difficulties, the movement of southern African Americans into Chicago revealed the difficulties of incorporating racial minorities into the work of musical progressivism, particularly in field house parks. After the summer of 1919, these public spaces would become the center of controversy over revelations concerning the complicity of many park officials and local residents in exacerbating interracial tensions that culminated in a major race riot.

FIVE

MUSIC OF THE PEOPLE
IS MUSIC OF THE WORLD

THE CIVIC MUSIC ASSOCIATION AND
THE RACIAL CHALLENGES OF WORLD WAR I
AND ITS AFTERMATH, 1912-1919

By 1913 field house recreation centers had convincingly demonstrated their strengths to reformers and industrial residents alike as
popular recreation spaces and instruments of civic musical outreach.
Flush with victory at the initial success of the campaign to "take the
park to the people," Edward B. DeGroot, who had once marveled at
how "art and beauty" rubbed off on children in the South Park district, challenged his colleagues to reflect on what needed to be done
next. He prefaced his idea with a reminder of what neighborhood
parks did not represent: "Parks are not for the people when the
design calls for a scheme of filling them with monuments on the one
hand and 'keep off the grass' signs on the other."[1] But DeGroot
hastened to add; the new democratic park regimen did not relieve the
need for continued efforts in aesthetic reform. "The artistic argument breaks down when we say 'This park must be very beautiful.
We will have nothing in it but beautiful things,'" he continued. "So
we build a bandstand costing a quarter of a million dollars, and then
hire a forty dollar band to play the worst kind of music. Where in that
case is the artistic argument supported?"[2] Referring to the title of a

best-selling commercial ballad, DeGroot quipped: "The song of the park should not be, 'Drink to me only with thine eyes.' It should be, 'Embrace me in thy youth. Adore me forever.' "[3] DeGroot did not endorse a return to the suffocating formal park culture of the past, which he termed a strategy of "Fence in the dead ones and fence out the live ones." He did worry that in their struggles to musically engage new publics at the neighborhood level, particularly youths, activists had gone too far in appeasing popular tastes. DeGroot called for new initiatives that could harmonize aesthetic concerns integral to past park history with the democratic spirit currently alive in the neighborhood parks.

This chapter analyzes the effort to respond to DeGroot's call to refine programs of musical outreach in the field houses. It assesses the impact of a new era that challenged musical progressivism and its commitments to accommodating cultural and social difference. During the 1910s, musical progressivism gained greater public exposure than ever before while facing challenges that significantly altered the tenor of its activities. The social and cultural crisis that gripped Chicago when war erupted in Europe in 1914 and the struggles over the social and cultural dimensions of war-preparedness added urgency to musical progressive outreach, even as war hysteria threatened to overtake the movement. Issues of race that had long gone suppressed within the ideals and practices of musical progressives erupted during this period as well. As this chapter demonstrates, the combination of war, deferred attention to race problems in the field houses, and the divisive civil unrest that culminated in the Chicago race riot of 1919 exposed the limited horizons and contradictory claims of musical progressivism as an inclusive and democratic movement.

The chapter focuses on the history of the Civic Music Association (CMA), an organization that combined aspirations for uplift and culture-building with a strong, municipal focus. Beginning in the early 1910s, this private, member-supported organization began using the field houses to promote musical excellence, democratic communication, and public culture. The group boasted an array of influential citizens on its roster who wished to promote cultivated European music in the city while bringing free music to the masses. Among their interests, they hoped to counter the elitist, privatized turn in European classical music and its confinement to fancy concert settings. They decried the state of educational and artistic resources in industrial neighborhoods and stressed the redemptive features of cultivated music in civic life.

THE CIVIC MUSIC ASSOCIATION
Redefining the "Music of the People"

During the summer of 1913, Frances M. Brundage, superintendent of the CMA contacted the commissioners of the major park districts with offers to present classical Sunday concerts paid for by the organization.[4] Seizing an opportunity to expand the range of park music events beyond popular military bands without straining their budgets, the commissioners heartily agreed. The West Chicago Park Commissioners stressed the civic benefits of having high-quality classical music available to all Chicago residents: "These concerts will prove of especial interest and benefit to the general public patronizing their respective parks."[5]

By late April 1915 the CMA had successfully presented dozens of concerts and recitals in the field house parks of the Lincoln, South, and West Park systems featuring classically trained performers and averaging audiences of 500 spectators. The organization ambitiously pledged to fight against the sacralizing tendency to divorce European classical music from the lives of ordinary folk. The CMA wanted nothing less than to redefine the meanings of "American" music in the process. As its first annual report explained:

> The Civic Music Association is organized to promote city music—music "of the people, by the people, for the people" of Chicago. Music "of Chicago people" is the music of the world, for all nations dwell within our midst, bringing with them a wealth of musical tradition, understanding and creative talent that, properly encouraged, become a priceless contribution to our civic life. We may not understand German, Bohemian, Russian, Italian or Norwegian, but we do understand the language of Bach, Beethoven, Dvořák, Tschaikowsky, Verdi and Grieg, and these foreign-born citizens of ours speak this same language and long to hear it in their daily lives. . . . One has only to witness the enthusiasm

of a park audience on a Sunday afternoon to realize that the "music of the people" is cosmopolitan, the best music of all nations and of all ages.[6]

In the service of a new project, the CMA appropriated the tone of populist demands that had accompanied the *Chicago American*'s Lincoln Park concert contest over a decade before.[7] But now the "language of Bach" offered the preferred method of linking the city across the divides of cultural difference.

Calls for a high aesthetic standard for Chicago music might have sounded at first like a recapitulation of the cultured-generation language of George Upton. What had changed, however, was the CMA's adoption of musical progressive discourse to argue its case. Here the "language of Bach" represented but one of multiple possible tongues contributed by Chicago's ethnic groups to the production of the universal language of classical music. The vision extolled the aesthetic transcendence of the European tradition, but one that marked a civic unity cobbled together from the cosmopolitan differences of Chicago's greater population. Despite this apparent synthesis of the cultivated tradition and urban cultural heterogeneity, the CMA presented a Eurocentric and racialized model of civic cosmopolitanism. The invisibility of non-Europeans and (by implication) nonwhites in the democratic sphere of musical progressivism deflected, yet again, the question of how African American participation could contribute to civic musical vitality or indeed whether African Americans were welcome to participate.

The CMA leadership included aesthetic activists and culture builders as well as familiar names in the pantheon of municipal progressives. The organization's advisory council included the presidents of the major park commissions, the Playground Association, to which Edward B. DeGroot belonged, the Chicago Association of Commerce, Mayor Carter Harrison, and Ella Flagg Young, superintendent of Chicago Public Schools. Representatives from the Chicago Women's Club, the Amateur Musical Club, the Junior League, the Lake View Musical Society, and Sinai Congregation all lent their support as well. The council also included Charles Hutchinson, a South Park commissioner and millionaire whose philanthropic largesse ranged from the Chicago Athenaeum and the Art Institute of Chicago to Hull House.[8]

Using an approach remarkably similar to the Special Park Commission of years before, the CMA described Chicago as a city in a state of cultural crisis due to incompatibilities between its musical sites and needs. "To thousands of music-loving citizens," the association argued in its annual report, "the Michigan Avenue concerts are impossible; the price of admission may be prohibitive, the long car ride too taxing, the home duties too exacting, to permit of the pleasure." The CMA further observed that "[n]owhere in Chicago are there better concert halls than those of the small playground parks. Scattered as they are throughout the city, they provide ideal centers for 'community music,' eliminating difficulties of distance and carfare. Music 'for the people' must be for ALL the people—the same music impartially distributed to all localities."[9] Given public backing and financial support, the CMA stood poised to liberate the metropolitan sounds presently trapped within Michigan Avenue's cultivated concert halls and to bring them to wage earners in their own backyards. Had Henry G. Foreman had a hand in things, the CMA's motto might well have been "Come over here and listen to the classical music."

Leading figures in classical music also stood behind the CMA, among them Frederick W. Stock, who sat on the organization's advisory council.[10] Since the death of Theodore Thomas in 1905, Stock had directed the Chicago Symphony Orchestra (CSO), guiding the orchestra forward as an artistic entity while also seeking ways of increasing its relevance within the public life of the city. Though Thomas's protégé, Stock had his own ideas about the CSO's responsibilities to serve the general public. He lobbied the trustees to cast a wider net and commit resources to reaching citizens who could not afford a subscription to the symphony. In cooperation with the CMA, Stock championed so-called Popular Concerts at low cost for workers.[11] In 1920, he created the Civic Music Student Orchestra, later the Civic Orchestra, a training ground for young aspiring professional musicians from industrial areas. Alluding to the Zangwill play, the *Chicago Herald and Examiner* championed the orchestra as "the latest melting pot to be set boiling. . . . [O]f all kinds of ancestry, they [the children] are all alike in their flamboyant enthusiasm and their unbounded patriotism."[12] Hoping to counter perceptions of the CSO as an elitist institution, Stock endeavored to again make symphonic music a part of the everyday musical life of Chicago in ways not seen since the "summer nights" concert series of the late 1870s and the 1880s.

Despite an institutional pedigree that connected it to Chicago elites, the CMA had a democratic frame of reference that linked it to fresh trends in musical progressivism. Area newspapers voiced enthusiasm for the CMA's call for a new wave of musical reform that combined an interest in aesthetic excellence with a spirit of democratic inclusiveness. "The Association does not bewail the baseness of musical Chicago," noted William L. Chenery in the *Chicago Evening Post*. "It does not cry aloud as a voice in the wilderness. It has not exclaimed in brazen tones, 'make ready, for we will improve you.' In fact, its manners are extremely good."[13] The CMA avoided the unctuous tones some associated with moral reform organizations and critics of popular musical amusements. In short, it appeared that the CMA had repackaged musical uplift as a wiser, less condescending, and more "cooperative" force for change.

During the 1914–15 season, with minor financial assistance from the park commissioners as well as from its members, the CMA coordinated forty "artists' concerts," featuring 746 performers, including choral singers, at the field house parks. Over 20,000 spectators turned out for the free concerts.[14] The response from neighborhood visitors overwhelmed even park officials, who gave glowing reactions to the CMA. "Never before have I seen here such an intelligent assembly of both young and old," wrote Eckhart Park director T. J. Smergalski. "I attribute all of this to the high grade of your entertainments which filled a need which the regular entertainments did not supply." Emily Harris, a director at Mark White Square in the South Park district agreed. "I wish you could hear the things which the neighborhood are saying about it," she wrote, referring to a concert by renowned pianist Fannie Bloomfield Zeisler. "One girl told me how her old mother cried about it, she was so happy, and she said that she did not think that there was music like that in this world."[15] Performers also spoke favorably of neighborhood audiences, including several who commented on how impressed they were by the appreciation and musical knowledge that audiences displayed at the concerts.[16]

Adapting aspects of the Hull House Music School model, CMA-affiliated music teachers came to field house parks and offered hundreds of lessons, helped locals establish music clubs, and instructed singers and instrumentalists in various facets of cultivated musical study and performance. Singing groups affiliated with various parks gave concerts that sometimes also included outside soloists or professional ensembles. The American Symphony Orchestra performed at the CMA's first spring festival on May 23, 1915, and offered a program that included the Prelude to Wagner's *Die Meistersinger*, followed by "Folk Songs from Many Nations," including America, Poland, Germany, Russia, Ireland, France, Denmark, Japan, Bohemia, and Norway. These selections reflected the inclusive spirit that Eleanor Smith had made a priority at the Hull House Music School. Finally, as if Israel Zangwill himself were sitting in the back of the room, the event concluded with a performance of "America" in which the audience was invited to rise and sing with the chorus.[17] CMA musical outreach dramatically bolstered instructional activity at field houses and supported high-quality technical training not widely available in most neighborhoods.[18]

MUSICAL SELF-DETERMINATION AT DVORAK PARK

Since the nineteenth century, Chicago's industrial neighborhoods had sustained immigrant and ethnic music, including European classical forms. In different field house settings, the "language of Bach" or Beethoven or Dvořák translated differently depending on local cultural and social conditions. Located several blocks south of Eighteenth Street, the chief artery of the neighborhood known as Pilsen, Park no. 3 served a large population of ethnic and immigrant Bohemians and Czech-speakers.[19] During the 1900s, area residents had established controls over music and other services in order to direct processes of immigrant and ethnic acculturation.[20]

During the 1910s, Park no. 3 served large numbers of Poles, Lithuanians, Yugoslavs, Italians, and Germans, but Bohemian residents exerted a particularly forceful presence in the institutional life of the field house. Bohemian authority extended to park staffing and to some event coordination prior to the arrival of CMA teachers. The park had a Bohemian supervisor ("Mr. Kodl"), which suggested the premium officials paid to establishing clear links between neighborhood constituencies and field house staff. Adolf Ernst, a Bohemian professional musician, served as park music director. Ernst organized a children's orchestra, membership in which required at least two years of musical classes in the field house. The Czech-language newspaper *Denní Hlasatel* praised Ernst's hiring and urged locals to patronize his classes.[21]

In 1912 the WPC took the unusual step of dedicating Park no. 3 not to a distinguished American, but to the celebrated Bohemian composer Antonín Dvořák. The choice recognized an exceptionally accomplished and talented musician and honored the cultural heritage of many area residents. Naming a park after an outspoken advocate of the power of folk music to build national character and group identity supported, at least symbolically, the value of Chicago's multiethnic population in shaping the civic sphere that reformers recognized as an important part of musical outreach.[22]

Notices culled from Czech-language newspapers certify the importance that Dvorak Park had as a community institution even when its music programs appeared to compete with, as much as to complement, offerings by ethnic institutions in the area. The *Denní Hlasatel* reported regularly on the Bohemian Workingmen's Singing Society, which had operated a community hall and music school in Pilsen prior to the construction of the field house park. The paper also reported on the Cesky Dum, or Bohemian House, a cultural center where singing lessons were offered in 1913.[23] With the arrival of group music offerings at Dvorak, the paper added notices for field house classes and events in the park without comment or critique, as if to acknowledge that the new recreation center was a veritable part of the neighborhood, rather than an outside interloper.

Scrutinizing coverage in the *Denní Hlasatel* provides clues about the ways in which the Czech-language press comprehended musical progressivism, and about the role of the field house parks in mediating the boundaries of ethnic and "American" identity. As boosters for local business and Bohemian neighborhood life, including ethnic musical institutions such as the Bohemian Workingmen's Singing Society, the editors acknowledged the utility of the field house park in cultivating both a sense of ethnic distinctiveness and a responsible brand of what supervisors might term "park culture."[24] A typical notice ran as follows: "All Bohemian servant girls are advised that instructions in the English language and singing in Dvorak Park, on May and Twentieth Streets, will begin tomorrow, Sunday, November 29th." The announcement added that singing classes for girls fourteen to sixteen years of age would be "conducted by the music and vocal teacher, Mr. Adolf Ernst." These lessons, the newspaper mentioned, were free of charge. The special park classes for servants, as well as the participation of Mr. Ernst, made them newsworthy as a local event. The notice given to the classes also reflected the extent to which this particular park was inscribed within the cultural geography of Bohemian American respectability.[25]

The editors of the *Denní Hlasatel* did not appear to view Dvorak Park as an Americanizing threat to ethnic self-determination; rather, they saw it as a provider of beneficial opportunities that supplemented existing neighborhood services. Living in single-sex rooming houses, or in the private homes where they worked, domestic servants clearly could not afford, as a more prosperous Bohemian family might, to hire Mr. Ernst, or a similarly qualified instructor, for private lessons.[26] Learning English and studying music at Dvorak Park gave young immigrant women a chance to socialize, share in the joy of music making, and divert their minds from the drudgery of domestic labor while in a safe and respectable public setting near home. By providing notification of the classes, the *Denní Hlasatel* certified the field house park as a suitable place of diversion for young, single Bohemian women. In conjunction with the field house park ideals of paternal oversight, the paper exerted a supervisory function of its own over the gendered codes of female respectability structuring Bohemian middle-class culture and neighborhood values found in field house cultural uplift.

Interestingly, the behavior of these young women once they got to Dvorak Park suggests that they were not as pliant and subservient as their employers or even the editors of the *Denní Hlasatel* might assume. They displayed self-assurance in requesting expanded park services when they needed them. "One day when [the servant women] heard the children's chorus practicing they asked Mr. Kodl if they couldn't sing, too, and he asked me to direct them," recalled Albie Sladek, a CMA music teacher working at Dvorak. "Soon we had regular chorus practice every Sunday, always using the Bohemian songs, because the girls had not yet learned English. However, by spring we had learned every verse of 'America' well enough to sing it at a concert, and the girls and their friends were very proud. It is surprising to hear the improvement in the quality of their voices; they were really beautiful when they gave their last concert in the spring."[27] In this anecdote, Sladek used a progressive frame to describe a story of technical improvement as well as of a cultural migration of sorts from the singers' exclusive knowledge of Czech-language material to an ability to perform the iconic "America."

Even if one discounts the context in which the story was conveyed (an official CMA publication), the anecdote confirms the point that these young women derived multiple benefits as Bohemians and as Americans from their experience. Though they came from the disproportionately female and poor ranks of the immigrant service economy, they seized opportunities for self-improvement and recreation at the parks. They reaped the pleasure that came not only from technical improvements in singing and in learning English a bit better, but also from asserting their rights as citizens to public resources. In short, musical outreach produced a microcosm of civic engagement in the lives of some the neighborhood's least politically empowered individuals.

Concerts at Dvorak Park reflected the multidirectional flow of power and cultural influence that typified musical progressive outreach. The program for a 1916 concert featured a multiethnic roster of music by Grieg, Karel Kovarovic, Kodl, Karel Kukla, and Dvořák. Kovarovic, Kodl, and Kukla were lesser-known composers who would have been unlikely candidates to appear on a CSO program at Orchestra Hall. However, the localism predominating at the field house parks permitted park users and officials to build partnerships across ethnic and municipal institutional barriers. The fact that concert notes appeared in both English and Czech gives an indication of the extent to which Dvorak Park had succeeded in becoming a clubhouse for the neighboring Bohemian population. The involvement of the CMA at the park added to the significance of the field house as a public space in which new definitions of a musical Americanism, with ethnic differences attached to it, could be forged.[28]

"WHO AM I?"
Elusive Reform Subjects

Not all of the CMA's outreach produced such enthusiasm among local users. The CMA's sponsorship of children's singing groups at various other field houses raised questions about musical progressivism's tactics to win the favor of urban industrial youth. "The first work was often to wash their faces and then to get them to sing softly," declared one CMA representative, suggesting the gulf separating teachers from students and the condescension that easily colored such outreach work. Among their duties, CMA teachers recruited youths to prepare for and perform at a city music festival to show off the work of the organization. "At first we sang only Bohemian songs, the lovely old folk songs that children and their parents all knew. Afterwards it was not hard to get them to learn some English songs, so that now they sing both equally well," Albie Sladek recalled. At Dvorak Park, Sladek and others assembled a children's group, the servant girls' chorus discussed above, and hundreds of other singers, who eventually performed in the festival before audiences estimated at 6,500. "We were so proud that one of the two songs to be encored at the Festival was our little Bohemian song, 'Who am I?,'" she wrote enthusiastically.[29] The metamorphosis of Bohemian children who spoke no English into Bohemian American performers singing in English and Czech on stage underscores the calculated benefits of musical progressive outreach. By putting on stage "American" children of a distinctly eastern European ethnicity, the CMA evidently meant to celebrate them as model assimilationists, yet there is no way of gauging the extent to which the children thought of themselves as assimilated.

In other cases, the CMA's presence in the field houses seemed intended to undermine the autonomy of singing among neighborhood residents. In 1915 a CMA teacher approached the Deutsche Frauen Volkslieder Verein, a German-language women's folk singing group, and encouraged it to reorganize as a CMA group at Mark White Square in the South Park system. The singers had been together for several years and frequently provided music for various social gatherings, including religious holidays, birthdays, anniversaries, and club meetings. The teacher, Marie Ruef Hofer, who also had ties to the Chicago Commons settlement, described her pupils' reaction: "The invitation to take part in the Civic Music Association and become a chorus, found a group of women, old and young matrons, eager for the opportunity to *really* sing."[30] Despite the group's evident successes in the neighborhood, Hofer briskly set about disciplining the singers to perform at a higher technical standard for audiences at park and citywide festivals.

In this case, outreach in the name of technical excellence and aesthetic self-mastery grew entangled with the politics of culture and musical civic transformation. In order to fulfill their technical mission to educate their students, CMA teachers sometimes required participants to shuck their preexisting ethnic musical and social rituals. "It was hard to break away from the social 'Kaffee' and concentrate on music," Hofer wrote. "We had sung Christmas carols for the joy of it, now we must work for technical betterment. We compromised and gave the carols in a Nativity Play. . . . From mere native song ability we hope to bridge into something of musicianship and building of

parts and sureness of work."[31] The denigration of "mere native song
ability" challenged the informal routes of ethnic folk transmission,
implying that producing music of merit and importance required
technical precision and outside validation rather than local organi-
cism. Music education via the CMA necessarily altered the manner in
which participants understood themselves, the meaning of music in
their own lives, and their relationship to the putatively universal
"language of Bach."

The CMA reached out to Chicago residents using a civic ideal
based on a multiethnic collective of European classical music lovers:
"All nations dwell within our midst, bringing with them a wealth of
musical tradition, understanding, and creative talent that, properly
encouraged, become a priceless contribution to our civic life."[32] While
that was an inspiring formulation of music's place in binding the city
together, the triumphalist tone of the CMA-orchestrated events accompanied a problematic erasure of the music of urban neighborhoods
that did not fall neatly into the category of a "wealth of musical
tradition." The recurring celebratory narrative of white ethnic transformation into a superior "American" self suppressed a competing
narrative of self-directed musical acculturation. The questions of
democratic self-discovery, such as "Who am I?," offered no single or
predictable answer. In many ways, reform subjects remained present,
but at a remove from containment or control by CMA activists.

Patterns of resistance dogged CMA field house activities and suggest the presence of countering authority at the neighborhood level.
In a few instances, some immigrant and ethnic children and parents
attempted to avoid the zealous CMA teachers when they came calling
at the field houses. "The cooperation of parents was fair," an Armour
Square teacher admitted ruefully. Her efforts to create a girls' chorus
generated no more than twenty participants—a low turnout. "On the
whole, while somewhat hard in the beginning, the work was a pleasure to them, and I think resulted in profit to the girls who attended,"
the teacher concluded doubtfully.[33]

Concerned about anemic participation levels at Seward Park,
Anna McPherson tried a different approach. "I began visiting homes
in order to encourage the attendance, and it certainly worked won-
ders," she reported. "Most of these little children lived in dingy
basements or in third or fourth floor rooms, always in the rear, and [in]
such squalor!" Her willingness to flush children from their homes and
march them to the field houses for instruction yielded eighty-two

children for a concert. But the tactic suggested that the CMA's desire to stage its musical progressive accomplishments for the admiration of the city sometimes led to manipulations and stagecraft rather than authentic youth engagement. Among her recruits, McPherson singled out "a band of twenty Italian boys, who sang with more zest than purity of tone, it is true, but who had the real spirit after all." McPherson's unorthodox system of collecting reform subjects indicates that CMA activists may have overreached in attempting to convincingly quantify their successes one singing "American" at a time.[34]

As these ambiguous reports suggest, there were notable differences between the CMA's approach to musical progressivism emphasizing converts with an almost missionary zeal and the claims made to Dvorak Park as a Bohemian community center. The Hull House and field house method of listening to the streets, consulting with neighbors, and hiring local authorities contrasted starkly with the CMA's well-intentioned, but decidedly top-down approach of bringing in outside experts to whip the locals into shape as musical citizens. Participation rates at concerts and in classes generally buttress the argument that there was community support for the CMA, especially in the case of the series featuring well-regarded concert artists brought in to perform in the parks. Musical progressives had bigger concerns after 1914, however, than differences of opinion over methods to promote democratic community formation. Like a storm lashing Lake Michigan in autumn, international events transpiring halfway around the world would strike the city with unusual force, challenging the framework of democratic public culture that musical progressives were striving to build.

WORLD WAR I AND ISSUES OF CULTURAL DISSONANCE

The outbreak of World War I in late summer 1914 created a set of political and cultural conditions in Chicago that challenged the spirit and implementation of musical outreach. The war in Europe drove longstanding animosities and tensions among Chicago's immigrant, ethnic, and laboring population to the surface. Although the conflict stimulated the American economy, labor organizations such as the American Federation of Labor (AFL) and the International Workers of the World (IWW) split bitterly over the conflict. The IWW and the Socialist Party argued for United States neutrality, while Samuel

Gompers of the AFL lobbied for intervention. Neighbors found themselves on opposite sides of the conflict. Opportunistic newspaper
editors exacerbated social and cultural divisions by inflaming nativist
sentiments, championing "one hundred percent Americanism" as a
solution to the nation's divided condition.[35]

America's formal policy of neutrality did little to prevent Chicago's immigrant and ethnic population from choosing sides in the
war and publicizing their positions to those who would listen. In
Chicago's industrial neighborhoods, music mobilized publics into
various patriotic and ethnocultural units bound by their concerns
about the plight of their homelands in the conflict. In more formal
civic showplaces, such as the ceremonial parks and the municipal
navy pier, citizens gathered for speeches, festivals, parades, public
concerts, and rallies that addressed emotional issues of cultural difference and national loyalty.

Ethnic Poles rallied support at the neighborhood level often
through concerts and benefits. Supporters of the fight against Germany and the Central Powers patronized singing contests, dances,
and concerts to raise money to support the beleaguered Polish army.
The Union of Polish Musicians contributed its fee toward relief in
a benefit orchestral event in the nearby town of Lake. Bookstores
in Polish neighborhoods also sold sheet music of patriotic Polish-
language songs and marches arranged for military bands and pianists,
including the battle cry of "Free Poland."[36] Although such gestures
cemented group solidarity and constructed a spirit of defiance to the
powerful enemy abroad, the home-front climate also threatened the
fragile web of civic connections that linked Chicago's multiethnic
population together.

Chicago Germans faced a uniquely challenging predicament as a
result of their widespread support of the German imperial effort and
the strong opposition to Germany's actions among other Chicagoans.
When Germany went to war, thousands of German citizens paraded
in Chicago to express support for Kaiser Wilhelm. They fought to
sway popular opinion by demonstrating against United States economic assistance to the Triple Entente between 1914 and 1917 and
by scolding President Woodrow Wilson for his alleged Anglocentric
biases.[37]

Well before the United States entered the war, anti-German sentiment began percolating with increasing insistence through the En-
glish- and foreign-language press. Public displays of German nation-

alism, which had been ignored or lampooned in the past, faced harsher assessment. For the relatives and compatriots of the embattled peoples under German attack, expressions of support for Kaiser Wilhelm provoked passions and produced bitter attacks in Polish and Czech-language newspapers. Interethnic tension spilled over into street fights and playground brawls pitting German partisans against Chicago's Slavs, Serbs, and others. In 1914 in neighboring Gary, Indiana, city officials temporarily banned parades and demonstrations of any kind due to concerns about rioting.[38]

The mounting anti-German backlash focused negative attention on institutions identified with Germans and German culture in Chicago, including area bands and orchestras. Loyalties among multiethnic personnel divided area music groups, most notably the Chicago Symphony Orchestra. During a concert in August 1914, the CSO performed a program of patriotic airs carefully chosen to represent both sides in the conflict, including Tchaikovsky's *1812 Overture*, "Die Wacht am Rhein," and "La Marseillaise." At the performance, feuding allegedly broke out among German, French, and Russian loyalists in the orchestra, some of whom, it was said, went so far as to disrupt the concert with deliberately misplayed notes. The *Chicago Tribune* reported that CSO members made a truce, but the incident suggested the extent of the political crisis even for multiethnic cultural institutions operating in the supposedly transcendent realm of cultivated classical music.[39]

A few months later, the CSO again found itself under public scrutiny after members of the orchestra performed at a high-profile birthday party in honor of Kaiser Wilhelm. The *Chicago Tribune* reported the celebration tersely with no editorial comment. But *Die Abendpost*, a leading area German-language newspaper, cackled with delight over the program that featured such highlights as Carl Maria von Weber's "Jubilee Overture" and Johann Strauss the elder's "Radetzky March," a tribute to the famed Austrian field marshal and defender of the Hapsburg Empire. At the conclusion of the program, the audience sang Max Schneckenburger's lyrics to "Die Wacht am Rhein," a song that stirred memories of past German military engagements and symbolized the pride of many German Americans.[40]

After the United States officially declared war on Germany on April 6, 1917, the CSO's prominence and historical association with Germans and German culture made it an irresistible target for patriotic zealots. Along with many of the nation's symphony orchestras, the CSO faced pressure from organizations such as the American Legion, which demanded federal legislation to require loyalty oaths among the non-native-born.[41] In late December 1917, the CSO's executive committee met to discuss a letter from the state council of defense that called for the national anthem to be played at all performances in Orchestra Hall. Less than ten days later, the committee met a second time: "The question under consideration was the alien membership of the Orchestra and the possibility of its publication in the newspapers."[42] The CSO dispatched officers to try to calm city editors and kill the story, but they could not stop the inquiries into the naturalization status of several members, including conductor Frederick Stock. Despite its efforts to placate its opponents, such as purchasing war bonds, encouraging its personnel to take loyalty oaths, performing the national anthem as instructed, and even limiting the performance of German music, the CSO could not stop the backlash. Four members of the orchestra, including Stock, resigned in 1918 for fear of destroying the CSO and facing certain deportation proceedings. The proud edifice of Chicago's European classical music tradition and the symbol of the sounds that had once served as the heralds of democratic public culture at the time of the "summer nights" concerts succumbed to waves of nativist attack as an antidemocratic and even subversive institution.[43]

"MUSICAL AMERICANISM" AND THE CMA

After 1914, the issue of war-preparedness, and desires to rally public support should the United States enter the conflict, drew fresh attention to musical progressivism in Chicago. By 1917 the movement found itself suddenly in vogue. Settlement music historian Robert A. Woods recalled that the "entrance of the United States into the war raised what was a slowly growing intellectual interest [in settlement music programs] into something like a real craving." Some converts called for a new culture of discipline at home to prepare the nation for challenges that lay ahead. "This war is going to teach us Americans many useful lessons in the art of organized living . . . music is paramount," wrote Harvard University professor W. R. Spalding. But the nature of the craving and the imperative to relate music reform to the crisis in Europe raised questions for musical progressive outreach as it had existed to this point. In more peaceful times, musical progres-

sives had envisioned a civil musical sphere inclusive of, yet ultimately transcending, ethnic difference. But political pressure rapidly
swept aside the pluralism and negotiated quality of past music reform
projects.[44]

CMA personnel active in the field house parks, settlements, and
elsewhere discovered the field of musical reform suddenly more
crowded, as a variety of activists stepped forward with ideas to effect
patriotism via music. "Musical Americanism" became a rallying cry
among representatives of various political persuasions eager to control public discourse over the appropriate direction in which to steer
the nation's cultural identity.[45] Different constituencies competed to
claim music for what they saw as patriotic ends. The nation's composers; progressive educators, who supported acculturation of the
foreign-born via music; antilabor businessmen, who wanted to pacify
a restless work force through "American" musical entertainment; and
German and other ethnic leaders, who cannily appropriated the discourse of "Americanism" to manipulate public opinion, all devoted
energy to making music an instrument of their ambition.[46]

The idealistic tone of the CMA's outreach, equating "Chicago's
music" with the "music of the world," took a back seat to metropolitan campaigns to unite Chicago's fractious ethnic population and
to produce a hegemonic "American" perspective on the war and U.S.
policy. Beginning in 1916, the CMA began sponsoring dozens of patriotic "community sings" for all ages at field house and ceremonial
parks, settlements, and in other public spaces, such as Chicago's municipal navy pier. Financial and logistical support came from various
bodies, including the park commissions, the state of Illinois's War
Recreation Committee, and the National Recreation Association.[47]

The patriotic community sing underscored the irony of the historical pattern of creative thievery of forms of neighborhood music
making by municipal reformers. This sort of event drew on a tradition
of public expression linked to the German and ethnic singing societies of the late nineteenth century, but with the addition of the
modern technological enhancement of lantern slides to help participants with lyrics.[48] Highlighting the need for such musical demonstrations among patriotic Americans to rival those of the enemy, Professor Spalding explained that "foreign nations through centuries of
devotion to music in the home have far more of this [singing] instinct
in their blood." The need to sing America's way to victory implied
that the quaint presentation of Bohemian children and servant girls

performing "Who Am I?" at CMA festivals had no place on the nation's musical stage. With a war on the horizon, public displays of leisurely acculturation seemed a luxury that the nation could not afford. The community sing represented a desire to produce a univocal and un-ambiguous message of America First patriotic solidarity.[49]

Redefining civic musical reform as a kind of war readiness ex-ercise, the CMA revised its aims. Promoting the "universal language" of music and imparting technical training of a high caliber had taken on a new flavor. "Community singing means the gathering of people in groups, large or small to join in singing, without previous training, songs which are generally known and loved by all. Such singing is the one and only means of expression which is common to all Americans sprung from different races. . . . We of America desire nothing so much as a means of showing our loyalty to the country of our birth or adoption, to show that we are Americans, and nothing can so stir our mighty melting pot and mingle its many peoples as to give them this opportunity to sing."[50] Patriotic and assimilationist rhetoric, includ-ing the trope of the "melting pot," signaled a turning away from the musical cosmopolitanism that animated the CMA's founding credo. The CMA would promote "songs which are generally known and loved by all"—but rather than cultivated melodies by the European mas-ters, they would be ones drawn directly from the American popular songbook.

Statements made by the CMA indicated that a revolutionary turn was upon civic music reform in general: "The war has brought to the Civic Music Association its biggest opportunity and its greatest justi-fication. In times of peace our work is to help make good citizens. In times of war our work is to help make good citizens AND GOOD SOL-DIERS" stated one flyer.[51] The CSO's ill-advised support of the birth-day bash for the kaiser had demonstrated the power of the European classical tradition to stir German patriotic passions, but the search for a musical style to unite support for the American cause evidently required different aesthetic and cultural considerations. In 1917 the CMA sponsored Friday night summer sings with orchestra and piano at field houses in Jackson Park, Washington Park, and several South Parks. A reported 1,500 to 5,000 participants and observers attended each event. The sings also continued at Lincoln Park on the North Side and expanded into the West Parks. At these venues, so-called Four Minute Men representing the Committee on Public Informa-tion delivered patriotic speeches during intermissions of the band concerts.[52]

Perhaps out of a reflexive sense of civic duty, or perhaps for fear of drawing fire for promoting German musical culture, the CMA stressed its utilitarian rather than its aesthetic contributions to Chicago's civic life. The CMA revised its claim that European classical music represented a universal language transcending cultural differences by substituting homegrown American music. "Our foreign-born citizens are naturally musical," one CMA publication noted, "and if given opportunity to sing American songs will be helped and encouraged in the process of Americanization."[53] The CMA's utter repudiation of European classical music as a gesture of civic responsibility and patriotism lasted for the duration of the war.

GOOD-BYE BACH AND GOOD MORNING MR. ZIP, ZIP, ZIP
Community Singing in Chicago

The shift in the CMA's musical mission and horizon of activism had consequences for the way that musical outreach elicited participants at community sings. The popular American songs featured at community sings invoked both martial and lyrical themes, which provided a gendered tutorial for audiences gathered to publicly enshrine the values of the American nation. "Public opinion [during World War I] was against all those elements of community life that were destructive to the young manhood of America," recalled reform activist Jessie Binford.[54] With a war to fight, community singing avoided a preoccupation with technical excellence or aesthetic nuances that might under the circumstances appear frivolous, self-indulgent, and even effeminate. Community sing organizers favored easy-to-sing and tuneful airs. Not surprisingly, patriotic songs from other American military conflicts commonly appeared on the program. The "Battle Hymn of the Republic" and other Civil War–era standards—such as "Battle Cry of Freedom," "Tenting on the Old Camp Ground," and "Tramp, Tramp, Tramp"—invoked the heroism and pluck of the victorious Union army. Tin Pan Alley songwriters and military and naval music directors also provided rousing airs that filled lungs, pleased big crowds, and enfolded singers in the martial spirit of musical Americanism. The community sings celebrated America's doughboys with "It's a Long Way to Tipperary"; "Over There"; "K-K-K-Katy," about a stammering soldier named Jimmy "off to France the foe to meet"; and "Good Morning Mr. Zip, Zip, Zip," a song describing a new recruit's encounter with an overzealous military barber.[55]

Sheet music cover for Geoffrey O'Hara's "K-K-K-Katy."
Historic American Sheet Music digital exhibit, Duke
University Rare Book, Manuscript, and Special
Collections Library.

Inspired by the slogan "A singing army is a fighting army," the songbook of community sings for enlisted men and civilians alike symbolically invoked specific gender roles for America's men, women, and children.[56] Singing produced virile soldiers, while teaching noncombatants the values for which the nation stood: home, family, and hearth. Sentimental ballads, such as "Love's Old Sweet Song," "Keep the Home Fires Burning," and "My Bonnie" sounded notes of nostalgia and wistfulness at community sings to accompany the fighting men on their way. With themes that addressed the virtuous females tending the domestic sphere, and the males entrusted to protect the family while older brothers, fathers, and uncles fought, such songs consolidated a distinctive American emotional vocabulary that folded immigrant, ethnic, and laboring participants into the midst of a patriotic, middle-class affective culture.[57]

"OH DARKIES! HOW MY HEART GROWS WEARY"
The Racialized Nostalgia of Home Front Mobilization

But the civic solidarity that the war-era songs attempted to foster symbolically excluded a significant segment of Chicago's growing population from equal participation in the singing American community. Between 1910 and 1920, the number of African Americans in Chicago grew by 248 percent as rural southerners left home in droves as part of the Great Migration. Many factors contributed to this demographic shift, including grim economic, social, and political conditions in the South, the lure of northern industrial jobs and urban lifestyles, and a general hunger for a better life. Despite labor shortages attributable to the interruption of European immigration by the war, the large-scale arrival of African Americans in Chicago created competition for jobs, housing, and other resources that fed racial prejudices.[58]

On a symbolic level, community sings created a highly problematic niche for African Americans in the participatory universe of singers. Community singing included a preponderance of songs linked to the culture of slavery and the minstrel era, and many were actually sung in Negro dialect. Songs such as "Old Folks at Home," "Liz-a Jane," and "Carry Me Back to Old Virginny" mobilized a popular nostalgia that included demeaning racial imagery and themes of white paternalism. However unreflectively audiences may have re-

garded these invocations of race, they established the public character of the community sings in ways that denigrated African American
culture and participatory rights to civic engagement. Songs composed
by African Americans were not included at these events, leaving
negative stereotypes by default as the sole musical representation of
African Americans as parties to the American nation.[59]

As scholars of blackface minstrelsy in the nineteenth century
have argued, ethnic, immigrant, and laboring audiences cleaved to
such racist representations of African American life as part of a collective fantasy of whiteness that eased the tensions of assimilation to
bourgeois mores and established the cultural basis of herrenvolk democracy.[60] In a later era, one confronting new questions about national unity and cultural difference, community sings helped to in-
scribe the racial boundaries of civic life and American patriotism. The
events included a racial component that taught participants, however
circuitously, that white Americanism could bind them together across
class and cultural divides. In segregated divisions and barracks, African Americans were as prepared as white soldiers to fight and die for
their country. But they were taught that they had no place on the
patriotic stage except as minstrel characters, fated to "sing along" to
melodies and lyrics that reinforced their historically subordinated
status, while indirectly mocking their aspirations to fight for equality,
democracy, and freedom.

Patriotism provided cover for various attacks on outsiders and
dissidents for the duration of World War I, and the climate of anxiety
throughout this time undermined the efforts of musical progressive
activists. As a result of the war, the progressive ideals of settlement music schools and field houses that encouraged neighborhood musical activity and favored input from locals had degenerated
into constrained or even reactionary modes of musical Americanism,
which were predicated on mass displays of patriotism derived from an
American songbook tinged with racist undertones. Several years before the war, Hull House's Eleanor Smith had championed "intelligent patriotism" based on the respect and empathy that came from
"singing the world's songs." Instead, the war elicited a xenophobic
fervor that swept aside the commitments of civic musical outreach as
a democratic project.[61]

After the war, the CMA gradually returned to engaging Chicago
youth via music using cultivated European and multiethnic folk music. The organization shifted its focus to Frederick Stock's interest in

developing a private youth orchestra comprised of talented students provided with the best technical and aesthetic training possible. The CMA continued to sponsor community sings, but it never regained its prewar ambitions of a radical musical transformation of the city. Though the organization remained a significant contributor to musical outreach in the city, it did so more tentatively, insulated from Chicago's evolving public musical culture.

Nor did the end of the war relieve the race problems embedded within community singing and urban public culture more deeply. African American youth participated in CMA events along with other cultural groups after 1918, but an examination of CMA programs in the 1920s reveals that white Americanism remained a salient feature of community singing. African Americans continued to face a mixed message via a musical reform canon that treated dialect songs written by white composers as cultural equivalents to "authentic" folk compositions from various European and American ethnic groups. It seemed that in this case, African American cultural authenticity could only come from a white man's pen, which perpetuated an unfortunate set of symbols and sounds of whiteness at the community sings.[62]

THE STRANGE CAREER OF RACE
IN THE FIELD HOUSE PARKS

The problem of the color line wove itself through the history of musical progressivism from the movement's nineteenth-century festival antecedents to field house park initiatives. Even as field house construction democratized public recreation services, and established localism as a progressive tenet, race remained a critical fissure in the promise of delivering quality facilities to underserved African American populations. In 1899 investigators of the Special Park Commission made specific mention of the inadequate park facilities available to residents of the African American "Black Belt." But the South Park Commissioners discounted the concern and inexplicably bypassed the area for field house park construction. As a result, the SPC furthered the structural inequalities contributing to racism in the city. Existing field houses on the South Side became the flashpoint of neighborhood skirmishes over public space and resources, pitting white ethnic youths and adults against African Americans seeking

Crowd at Harrison Park concert (WPC), 1919. Chicago
Park District Special Collections.

recreational outlets beyond the Black Belt. With the African American population continuing to expand in the 1910s, racial tensions in
field house parks and patterns of intimidation in areas bordering the
parks grew until pent-up frustrations erupted in a citywide race riot in
July 1919.

In the aftermath of the riot, many South Park officials insisted
that they had no inkling of the troubled state of race relations in the
field houses. Closer inspection by the Chicago Commission on Race
Relations (CCRR) in 1920 uncovered the facts. Investigators found
systematic patterns of race segregation and discrimination against
African Americans in the parks. Neighborhood field house parks had
a history of turf wars among various ethnic groups, but particularly
between whites and African Americans dating to the establishment
of the field house park system.

In 1909 J. F. Foster, the venerable superintendent of the South
Park Commissioners, returned from a gala tour of major European
parks in the distinguished company of Daniel H. Burnham and Frederick Law Olmsted Jr. "It may not be possible to reproduce here the
magnificent avenues and plantations of Versailles, or the soft luxu-
riance of the vegetation of England," Foster wrote, but he added that

Chicago's field houses stood without peer in one important respect: "While the baths, gymnasiums, etc., in the ancient Greek cities were for the use only of freemen, those in the South Division parks are freely at the service of the poorest men, women and children, as well as of those who have had superior advantages of a private nature. All may, and do, use the baths, gymnasiums, playgrounds, swimming pools, reading-rooms, assembly halls and club rooms."[63] According to Foster, field houses fulfilled a uniquely democratic ideal in American culture by using municipal resources to serve the entire population regardless of private station.

In retrospect, Foster's casual use of the word "freemen" to denote the class of men with rights of full citizenship in ancient Greece had an unintended irony, given the history of race in Chicago. At the time of Foster's comments, African Americans had long been "freemen" in name in Chicago, but not always in custom in urban public space. The Illinois constitution had once barred African Americans from admission to the state, but after the Civil War the legislature supported African American residency and suffrage. Between 1874 and 1897, laws and amendments prohibiting segregation in schools and other public places were passed.[64] A degree of race mixing occurred in many occupational settings, from domestic service to meatpacking and steel work, and African Americans and whites shared thoroughfares, streetcars, and some public facilities. But the prevailing social codes of the Progressive Era extended a color line separating African Americans from whites in most social settings. Miscegenation between light- and dark-skinned populations ranked as one of the great public taboos of America's slavery-era culture, and racial anxieties remained palpable as society produced laws and everyday practices to register the postemancipation cultural status of whites and African Americans.[65]

THE CULTURAL GEOGRAPHY OF SEGREGATION ON THE SOUTH SIDE

"All may, and do," use the field houses, argued Foster, but it was commonplace for African Americans and whites to inhabit separate recreational spheres, even if they shared the same park. In Chicago as in other northern industrial cities, African Americans waged what St. Clair Drake and Horace Cayton once described as a perpetual "struggle for living space." Prior to 1900 African Americans lived in enclaves scattered across the West and Near North Sides. Prejudicial treatment forced them to settle in residential precincts that most whites tended to avoid, such as those adjacent to the city's red-light districts. Landlords used various tactics to deny African Americans leases and regularly charged them more than other immigrant and ethnic groups for the same standard of housing.[66]

About 1910 the scattered settlement pattern changed, as a housing shortage and increased discrimination funneled over three-quarters of Chicago's African American population into the Black Belt, a thin corridor about three miles in length and about two-and-a-half miles at its widest point, stretching south from the downtown business district. Within its boundaries, a city within a city developed with its own shopping emporiums, restaurants, banks, funeral parlors, clinics and hospitals, and insurance companies. Musical theaters, cabarets, and saloons popped up along State and Thirty-fifth Streets. "The Stroll" attracted a multiracial group of pleasure-seekers, including whites, drawn to integrated recreational settings, known most widely for drinking and dancing to African American jazz music, which had welled up from New Orleans and the South.[67]

One effect of residential segregation meant that African Americans were cut off from access to jobs and were often embroiled in boundary disputes with hostile white neighbors wishing to limit further expansion of the Black Belt. To the east lay the upscale white residential areas of Kenwood and Hyde Park adjoining Lake Michigan. To the west, across the tracks of the Illinois Central railroad lines and Wentworth Avenue, resided significant numbers of Irish laborers. These white neighbors expressed various objections to African Americans living nearby, most notably in their attacks on the Black Belt for its nightlife culture, seen by them to be a popular haven for crime and interracial prostitution.[68]

Residents in Woodlawn and Hyde Park sponsored so-called protective neighborhood associations to defend their communities from unwanted outsiders. Activists used neighborhood policing, while others turned to racial covenants on leases and deeds to maintain to the extent possible a cordon sanitaire around the Black Belt.[69] Rather than attempting to relieve the tensions associated with overcrowding, neighboring white residents tried to build higher walls to protect themselves. In the midst of the prewar dance craze, reform-minded

African American leaders attempted to organize a model dance hall for Black Belt youth akin to those offered in the park field houses, but a white citizen's organization from a neighboring area blocked the project, claiming that it would bring moral ruin to the community.[70]

Along the western and northern boundaries of the Black Belt, poor whites expressed their strenuous objections to African American competition for jobs, affordable housing, and public resources in other ways. Neighborhood gangs transformed public commuter lines, streets, and area parks into tense racial proving grounds in which intimidation and violence served as plebeian echoes of protective associations, racial covenants, and high real estate prices. African American migrants took jobs in the stockyards, factories, and domestic service; but, unlike immigrant groups and native-born whites who could settle closer to where they were employed, thousands of African Americans were forced to live inside the Black Belt and then commute to and from work through hostile territory. Their rides carried them on tense, crowded streetcars through lonely stretches of the city where virtually no African Americans lived or were safe to visit for long.

The South Park Commissioners made virtually no public mention of race issues in its district, but in 1908 the Special Park Commission made another plea to redress the racial imbalance in park recreation facilities. The commission described "friction between white and colored children" and noted "falling off attendance of the latter." "If there is any race problem connected with the playgrounds," the commission averred, "it seems to us advisable, for the welfare of the colored children who are to be our fellow-citizens, to give them a playground to themselves, or at least one which they would feel as free to use as the white children use other grounds."[71] But neither the SPC nor city officials would commit public funds to building an equivalent field house park in an African American neighborhood.

By the 1910s, violent incidents between African American and white children were reportedly "epidemic" in the playgrounds and parks of Chicago's South Side. Race tensions even transformed ceremonial Jackson and Washington Parks into notorious sites of interracial clashes. Though only 10 percent of regular park visitors were African American, some whites complained bitterly about "Booker T. Washington Park." Though not tabulated by race, published statistics of the SPC reveal that park police arrested hundreds of offenders charged with disorderly conduct, fighting, and other infractions. It is not known, however, how the courts treated cases of interracial fighting, or what steps, if any, the SPC took to lesson racial tension.[72]

Having ruled out the idea of building more field house parks, South Park officials had little to offer to solve the population pressure in the Black Belt; nor did they have the jurisdictional authority or inclination to weigh in on the turbulent changes affecting previously all-white neighborhoods. In 1914 the Woodlawn Ministerial Association, a white clerical organization, urged the SPC to oppose the construction of a saloon at Sixty-seventh Street and Stony Island Avenue, two blocks south of Jackson Park. The ministers also protested the installation of a roadhouse at the corner of Sixtieth and Cottage Grove directly across the street from Washington Park: "We believe that the surrounding of our great parks by these liquor road houses is a detriment not alone to the parks as real estate, and thus an infringement on the right of the people in their possession, but also degrading of the parks themselves as safe attractive playgrounds for the children of our community." Despite this credible appeal to the interests of the SPC given its reform history, park officials refused to get involved. In a letter, the SPC explained that "in as much as the commissioners were neutral on such matters, no action would be taken."[73] South Park officials knew their legal authority ended at the park gates. But their neutral perspective on the liquor issue extended to inaction on far more important ethical and civic questions. To what extent were park officials still engineers of reform, using their green spaces to further democratic public culture? Moreover, how far were officials prepared to go to ensure that all citizens be able to visit and use public field houses without threats to their safety?

A WALK IN THE PARK
Racial Violence and Localism

Before Black Belt residents could reach the nearest SPC field house, they had to cross the no-man's zone separating African American and white neighborhoods.[74] Visitors who wandered out of their neighborhoods risked run-ins with gangs who controlled streets, pool and billiard parlors, corner stores, dance halls, athletic fields, and parks and playgrounds. Some gangs, such as the predominantly Irish "Ragan's Colts," organized themselves as "athletic clubs" as a front for their many extralegal activities, such as racketeering.[75] In 1918 the African American poet Langston Hughes discovered the boundary quite by accident: "Over beyond Wentworth," where he "was set upon and beaten by a group of white boys, who said they didn't allow niggers in that neighborhood."[76] Hughes's rough handling inducted him into a street culture whose ethnic and racial geographies and informal local policing strategies shaped the city's public institutions, including the field house parks and the blocks surrounding them.

Investigators for the CCRR found that between 1913 and 1919 African American children risked constant threat of physical assault by white youths or even adults when they visited Chicago parks to take a music lesson or attend a concert or dance.[77] The beleaguered principal of the Raymond School, which served a predominantly African American student body on the periphery of the Stock Yards district, described the "gang spirit" and the climate of fear polluting the city's public institutions. "There seems to be an inherited antagonism. Wentworth Avenue is the gang line. They seem to feel that to trespass on either side of that line is grounds for trouble. While colored pupils who come to the school for manual training are not troubled in the school, they have to be escorted over the line, not because of trouble from members of the school, but groups of boys outside the school. To give another illustration, we took a little kindergarten group over to the park. One little six-year-old girl was struck in the face by a man. A policeman chased but failed to catch him. The condition is a tradition. It is handed down."[78] Even a police presence could not deter such patterns of violence directed against children on a routine trip to the park.

Many African American children who wished to take advantage of field house offerings were explicitly advised by parents, teachers, and even park personnel to stay away. According to one investigator, "A Negro playground director said that if Negro boys attended band concerts in that park [Armour Square], white gangs would wait for them outside the park, and the Negroes were slugged." Incidents of serious fighting inside field houses or on park property were relatively rare since one or two park policemen were always present and would preserve order, or at least drive the combatants out of the park. Gangs therefore preferred to move in and out of the field houses, waiting to exact their vengeance on "trespassers" in the anonymity of surrounding streets and blocks, where it was easier to ambush a victim with impunity and escape.[79]

When a group of sixty student singers from the predominantly African American Colman School, traveled to a concert program in an unspecified spc field house park, they braved a gauntlet of hostile locals:

> On the way over a group of foreign women called out insult-
> ing remarks to the [white] teachers, but no one paid any
> attention. After the program the group started marching out
> of the park and were met at the gate with a shower of stones.
> The teacher told the children to run for their lives, and they
> all had to scatter and hide in the bushes in the park or run
> toward home if they could . . . Since that time we have never
> accepted an invitation to sing outside our own neighbor-
> hood. Invitations have come from time to time, but the chil-
> dren all come with excuses. All of them, children and parents
> throughout the neighborhood, are afraid but you can't get
> anyone to come out and say it.[80]

Repeated disasters at field house events undoubtedly chilled enthusiasm for the kinds of cross-cultural outreach favored by musical
progressives. The mere fact that African American singing groups
needed "invitations" to cross the threshold of field houses outside
their neighborhoods underscores the ingrained racial inequalities
structuring these spaces.

In its investigation after the 1919 race riot, the ccrr concluded
that use patterns in the field house parks were "determined almost
entirely by the degree of antagonism in the neighborhood, and Negroes are afraid to make use of the parks where the neighborhood
sentiment is hostile." Despite having the highest relative concentration of African Americans in Chicago, the South Parks reported disproportionately low usage among that population as compared with
other park districts. On the South Side, only 3 percent of patrons at
Fuller Park were African American, 1 percent at Armour Square, and
1 percent at Hardin Square, despite significant numbers of African
Americans residing not far off.[81] By contrast, Union Park on the Near
West Side had 40 percent African American patronage, and both
Seward and Lincoln Parks on the North Side reported 15 percent
African American attendance.[82]

With remarkable bravery, African American children and families
banded together to claim a foothold at Fuller Park, at Forty-fifth

Street and Princeton on the South Side.[83] "At the band concerts and moving pictures the Negro attendance is fairly good," reported an investigator of Fuller, "and a large number of Negroes use the library, but the gymnasium and the children's playground are used very little by the Negroes, and the swimming-pool practically not at all." Outdoor band concerts offered the safety of crowds, made up of friends and families, and room to maneuver in case of trouble. Libraries were probably also supervised, with a librarian prepared to move an idling gang member along. Other spaces, such as gyms with doors that could be barred suddenly, or unmonitored playgrounds, or the unpredictable element of water, posed hazards that may have limited their use among African American visitors vulnerable to surprise attack.[84]

On July 12, 1919, less than two weeks before the Chicago race riot, concern about chronic "Ruffianism in the Parks" hit the editorial page of the African American newspaper the *Chicago Defender*. Robert S. Abbott, the newspaper's publisher, complained that "gangs of young hoodlums from the district west of Wentworth Avenue have been making it a practice of attacking our people [in parks] under cover of darkness and, so far, have been able to elude the police." The *Defender* questioned the motivation of the park police force to defend the rights of African American and white citizens to enjoy public parks equally. "The parks are public property, open to all citizens, black and white alike," Abbott declared, "and those charged with the protection of citizens who frequent such places are derelict in their duty if they do not see to it that ruffianism is put down with the strong arm of the law."[85]

A disgusted Abbott charged the SPC with blithely accepting racial harassment and failing to respond to citizen demands for action: "The attention of the park boards has been repeatedly called to this situation, and the *blame for whatever happens* under their jurisdiction rests with them alone."[86] Abbott argued that civic institutions like parks must respond to high principles of responsibility in ensuring impartial access and justice for all patrons regardless of race. Abbott's readers loved his pugnacious style in print, but the exasperated tone of the editorial conveyed widespread frustration and anger among Chicago African Americans over the pattern of public inaction on racial discrimination. It suggested that residents of the Black Belt did not intend to be passive victims should further abuse occur.

Beginning on July 27, 1919, a convergence of long- and short-term factors, including labor and race tensions, a severe housing shortage, and the return of servicemen, touched off several days of sustained violence between whites and African Americans. A tragic incident set off the rioting when Eugene Williams, an African American teen floated on a raft across the invisible line dividing segregated swimming areas at the 29th Street Beach. At least one white man on the shore began lobbing stones at Williams, one of which struck the youth. Stunned, he slipped from the raft and drowned. Witnesses alleged that a white police officer refused to arrest a suspect, igniting an interracial fracas on the beach that spread with murderous results across the South Side.[87]

When civil order had been restored, 38 people were dead, 537 were wounded, and millions of dollars were lost in property damage as a result of arson and looting. In the course of the rioting, white street gangs led murderous sallies into the Black Belt, shooting, stabbing, and beating African Americans. African Americans fought back, mounting incursions of their own, beating and killing whites in the vicinity of the stockyards. Though both sides fought aggressively, African Americans suffered a disproportionate number of fatalities and injuries.[88]

Robert Abbott's complaint in the *Defender* underscored the contamination of democratic life in Chicago by institutionalized racism. Chicago's mainstream press did little to support African American claims to equal rights; nor did it positively present the residents of the Black Belt. Chicago's leading daily newspapers revealed consistent patterns of negatively stereotyping and vilifying African Americans as criminals, and they tended to underreport violence in which the victims were African American.[89] Such biased press coverage limited public awareness and concern among whites about the injustices that African Americans faced daily and the dangerous pressures building up in public parks and field houses. Local police magistrates, often beneficiaries of ethnic patronage and the moral economy of the streets, frequently sympathized with youth gangs "protecting" their neighborhoods from outsiders, particularly African Americans. Frederic Thrasher found that judges variously refused to press charges against youths accused of violence against African Americans, put offenders on probation, or leveled nominal fines of one dollar.[90] It seemed that in matters of street justice white law enforcement officials either stood aside or, as reportedly happened in the 1919 riot, even joined the attack on African Americans themselves.[91]

DISAVOWING RACIAL REFORM
Field House Supervisors after 1919

Accused by the CCRR of fueling racial animosities on the eve of the riot by allowing racial discrimination to go unchecked in the field houses, supervisors closed ranks. The director of Armour Square declared: "I have never gone out to do any promotional work to bring them [African Americans] in because I would not choose personally to be responsible for the things that would happen outside my gates if I were responsible for bringing large groups into Armour Square. If such groups come to me for reservations I give them, but they don't come." Despite this refusal to set an example for civic unity or change, the supervisor insisted that a welcoming atmosphere prevailed within park boundaries: "They [African Americans] know absolutely that within the four walls of the park nothing is going to happen to them."[92] What the respondent conveniently ignored was any discussion of the civic responsibility of park leaders to attempt to ameliorate the hostile climate whites created for African American park patrons.

Other supervisors challenged the assertion that African Americans were disproportionately singled out for trouble in parks. One supervisor noted defensively: "I have known people coming and going who were abused, mistreated, and actually assaulted, outside the park reservations, but I don't believe our records would show very many cases—probably no more than occur where the Poles and the Irish get together, or the Bohemians and the Germans."[93] Indeed, there appears to have been a kernel of truth to this description of equal opportunity harassment at parks. Interethnic clashes between park patrons and gangs were not uncommon. Jewish residents of the West Side had raised formal complaints about repeated harassment from Poles in Douglas Park. But the pattern of systematic exclusion of African Americans that the CCRR discerned had no analogue among other ethnic or racialized populations.[94]

Another supervisor at Ogden Park admitted that he regretted that so few African Americans used the field houses for dances since he believed them to be preferable to other groups: "They are the best-behaved group that come. I never have to object to improper dancing or boisterousness, and they always leave on time. I have had to object several times to conduct at white dancing parties."[95] Perhaps the dancers left "on time" for fear of what might befall them on the way home if they stayed out too late. More to the point, such dances were segregated and held after hours and were largely irrelevant to the issue of unequal access and its reflection on the viability of the field houses as democratic public spaces.

The color line that divided urban residents and disproportionately excluded African Americans from field house experiences manifested one of the tremendous obstacles then facing musical progressivism. The divisive home front experience during the war, the anti-German backlash and attack on the CSO and the ideals of the CMA, and the patriotic demands of war transformed the fortunes of musical progressivism. The founding aspiration of the field house music programs and the CMA's early efforts to uplift citizens through affordable, professional quality music training and neighborhood-focused musical resources degenerated into crude patriotic displays. Having borrowed the settlement music idea, recreational reformers and civic officials expanded the reach of musical progressivism in dramatic fashion—but, as the troubles in the South Parks showed, often with localism producing ugly forms of discrimination that perpetuated racial inequalities.

"Take the park to the people" had been an ebullient rallying cry for the playground movement and for musical progressivism. Activists succeeded in creating a fleet of outstanding public recreation centers capable of providing musical recreation to tens of thousands of residents annually. That shining achievement could not, however, transcend the institutionalized deficiencies of field house service to African Americans or the lack of will among park supervisors, citizens, and the park leadership to pledge themselves to guaranteeing the right of minority populations to freely participate in civic musical culture. "The aim is neither to cure nor to prevent any social ills," explained the West Park board of its field houses, in a report published the year of the race riot, "but rather to serve as a vital adjunct for the normal expression of life of both young and old. The recreation centers and playgrounds are a common ground of all and for all, regardless of race, creed, or nationality, and hence in their influence are staunchly American, not so much by power of direction as by force of suggestion."[96] Such qualified statements reflected a cautiousness on the part of park officials after World War I in considering their duties as reformers or social engineers.

To call the field houses "common ground" contradicted the social fact that fear and racial unease prevailed at too many field house parks. African American boys and girls with the temerity to go to the field houses invited a hostile reception from other children, adults, and even officials. Park leaders continued to wax rhapsodic over the democratizing power of public services, but they had decisively retreated from prewar efforts to spearhead social change. The well-intentioned field house activities, dances, and concerts could not vanquish, without political willpower, the socially constructed specter of race. Indeed, as the CCRR discovered, in many cases, the "staunchly American" ideology of the field house parks legitimized public segregation by inadvertently cultivating a participatory culture and civic sound of whiteness.

Ironically, the failure of the field house parks movement to serve the urban population equitably may have helped spur the flowering of alternative recreation options for African Americans and multiracial crowds. The dance craze that drew thousands of white youths to the neighborhood park field houses in the 1900s and 1910s also transformed the character of commercial nightlife. The rise of African American jazz in the Black Belt and the presence of jazz performed by white bands elsewhere stimulated a vibrant new musical subculture in cabarets, black-and-tans, taxi-dances, and other commercial recreational settings. Here Chicago men and women embarked on various individual and group excursions across the dominant borders of class, ethnic, racial, and sexual identity.

Just as the prewar dance craze inspired the Hull House and field house dance reform campaign, developments in commercial musical amusement culture, particularly after World War I, injected new energy into musical progressivism and produced new responses among recreational reformers. As the next chapter describes, the social and cultural revolution enacted on Chicago's dance floors created a daunting challenge of mapping and regulating an unfamiliar and seemingly ungovernable nocturnal world of music, dance, and celebratory youth culture. By the 1920s, the musical progressive establishment would find itself face to face with a powerful competing project of social transformation and democratic culture building linked to the hot sounds and subcultures of jazz.

SIX

THEY WHIRL OFF THE EDGES OF A DECENT LIFE
UNMASKING DIFFERENCE AT THE DANCE, 1904-1933

In 1927 the Irish poet W. B. Yeats published "Among School Children," a poem in which an education inspector's visit to a classroom where "children learn to cipher and sing" inspires a reverie about a lost love, innocence, and experience. The poem explores civilization's quest to plumb divine mysteries and nature's canny resistance to modern instruments of reason and scientific inquiry. Yeats concluded the poem with the now-famous couplet: "O body swayed to music, O brightening glance, / How can we know the dancer from the dance?" Thousands of miles away in Chicago, where the embers of progressive reform continued to glow hotly, Yeats's teasing paradox had been driving urban recreation reformers to distraction for the past two decades.[1] Since the mid-1900s, a proliferation of halls, clubs, and cabarets, featuring hot combos and orchestras pumping out kinesthetic ragtime and jazz dance music, had been generating an uproar among Chicago's population of morals activists. The spectacle of tens of thousands of young urban residents melting into a mass of shimmying bodies on dance floors, where classes, cultures, and sometimes races intermingled, exploded bourgeois conventions of public behavior between the sexes.[2]

The dance craze inspired morals activists to embark on a city-wide investigation of commercial dancing in a variation of what might be termed "knowing the dancer from the dance." As concerned observers hastened to point out, young dancers used their public experiences for self-fashioning, but not in the manner associated with "respectable" social dancing of the nineteenth century. Contemporary dancers reveled in risqué music and dance forms; mingled casually with friends and strangers of different classes and cultures; drank, at times excessively, even when under age; and too often, by the estimates of morals reformers, engaged in intimate sexual behaviors.

Morals activists worried especially about the virtue of thousands of young female dancers. They bridled at the sexual energies openly expressed at many commercial dances and worried about the subcultures of resistance to conventional morality that the very dance itself seemed to harbor. In such public settings, participants manipulated social masks and identities with dizzying rapidity. Proliferating dance venues, styles, and publics of dancers subverted the dominant ways of seeing that bourgeois Americans used to differentiate a dancer from a dance; a gentleman from a rake; a "respectable" women from a prostitute; a girl from a sexually active woman; a "white" from a "colored;" or even a man from a woman.[3] To regulatory activists, "knowing the dancer from the dance" through systematic investigation and policing of dancing environments, forms, and publics represented a desperate attempt to restore social and moral clarity to a shadowy area of the public musical landscape.[4]

This chapter analyzes commercial dancing in Chicago during the first three decades of the twentieth century. The discussion traces developments between 1904—the approximate point that commentators discerned signs of a full-blown youth dance craze—and 1929, the final year of the "Jazz Age."[5] Case studies of the neighborhood "beer permit" dance, the cabaret, the multiracial black-and-tan cabaret, and the multiracial taxi-dance hall reveal the ways in which a generation of dancers co-opted a key embodiment of respectability—social dancing—and reconfigured it. Dancing celebrated difference and democratic expression in ways that radically extended the dream of harmony envisioned by musical progressives. Ironically, commercial dancing stimulated forms of civic engagement consistent with principles of democratic musical outreach, but to a degree that musical progressives were unprepared or unwilling to resoundingly endorse.

While various groups lobbied to improve moral aspects of public recreation, from Christian temperance and antivice groups to neighborhood protective associations, the Juvenile Protective Association (JPA) led the most dramatic civic campaign in response to the dance craze.[6] The JPA had a distinctive institutional history rooted in progressive juvenile justice work as well as musical progressive outreach. The organization ran local protective leagues dedicated to defending "innocent victims of vicious and unlawful neighborhood influences."[7]

The JPA's ties to settlement work dated to 1906 when its predecessor, the Juvenile Protective League, established a neighborhood chapter at Hull House.[8] Renamed the Juvenile Protective Association in 1909, the organization and its redoubtable chief, Jessie Binford, vowed to strike a blow to the heart of the commercial amusement industry in Chicago. The JPA used its network of local offices to promote "respectable" dance styles and musics in settlements and field house parks. One enterprising branch even sponsored park dances regularly in the early 1910s.[9] But the JPA went further than advocating alternative dance offerings or co-opting popular entertainment forms. It actively investigated the commercial dance industry and lobbied for reform of its unregulated operations.

JPA dance regulators differed from their musical progressive counterparts in that they concentrated on commercial dancing primarily to reform youth morality rather than to promote a musical vision to improve civic life. Dimly conscious of the power of music to influence social behavior (usually for the worse), these activists had no interest in, empathy for, or intention of "reforming" ragtime or jazz music when they set their sights on commercial dancing.[10] Focused on youths perceived to be at risk, activists campaigned against underage drinking and alleged moral turpitude among dancers and operators of commercial dances. JPA members took to the streets to flush moral transgressors into view, be they dancers or dance operators. To win public support, the association supplied a steady diet of pulse-pounding headlines for local newspapers, while demanding that politicians, the police, and the justice system uphold ordinances and defend conservative standards of public morality.[11]

The JPA's particular concerns about dancing are familiar to Chicago jazz historians insofar as they stemmed from deep anxieties (economic, social, and cultural) tied to the growing numbers of African Americans in the city and cultural stereotypes of the rebellious and sensual preoccupations of black people.[12] These general apprehensions support an extensive scholarship on jazz music and its associated social and cultural embodiments in which themes of race,

recreation, and identity formation are explanatory contexts for inter-
preting popular reception of the music.[13] But the musical progressive
history of outreach and debate over music as an embodiment of civic
ideals has not been adequately credited for influencing public responses to the Chicago dance craze.[14] Rather than a moral panic
reducible to racialized cultural anxieties, the "jazz uproar" of the
1920s is connected in essential respects with antecedent struggles in
Chicago's public arena over music's role in publicizing social change.
Moreover, the fact that musical publics embraced jazz represented a
serious challenge to musical progressivism's racialized framework of
civic engagement. Legions of supporters warmed to the jazz sound
and its associated rebellious lifestyle as part of an alternative personal
and public fantasy of social and democratic fulfillment that rejected
the aesthetic and moral preoccupations of musical progressivism as
practiced in the past.

SEEDS OF THE DANCE CRAZE
Social Dancing in Everyday Life

The concerns that the JPA would express beginning in the 1900s
connected to a long history of ambivalence toward dancing in American culture. Throughout the nation's history, social dancing occupied
a pervasive place in expressive culture, for purposes of play as well as
for purposes of uplift and refinement.[15] European settlers, indigenous natives, and African Americans danced at festive occasions in
villages, towns, and cities. Festivals among the Dutch of New Am-
sterdam regularly included public dancing. Aristocratic planters in
Virginia and the Carolinas danced in keeping with longstanding European customs of physical, social, and aesthetic cultivation befitting
gentlemen and ladies. By the late seventeenth century, dance masters toured the mid-Atlantic colonies, and their presence is recorded
in colonial New England by the early 1700s.[16] By 1787, writes one
historian, "social dancing had become widely accepted [in America]
both as a form of recreation and as a means of education."[17]

Social dancing also produced outspoken detractors, often clerics
or morals activists, whose concerns about dancing's social effects established a thematic precedent for events in Chicago. Ann Wagner
argues that a distinct genre of American antidance literature first
appeared in colonial New England in the seventeenth century. In-

crease Mather, a Puritan minister, wrote "An Arrow against Profane and Promiscuous Dancing," the first known antidance tract of its kind in the colonies. The Reverend John Cotton of Boston condoned dancing, since the Bible did not prohibit it, with the exception of what Cotton condemned as "lascivious dancing, and amorous gestures and wanton dalliances."[18] Conservative Protestant evangelists lumped dancing together with other leisure pastimes, such as gambling, the theater, or horse racing, as suspect pursuits that diverted energy from Christian devotion. Other critics pointed to the sumptuous costumes associated with ballroom dancing and proclaimed the dangers of self-indulgences that ran counter to notions of Protestant asceticism. Undaunted, Americans continued to dance.[19]

During the antebellum period, a range of dancing traditions accompanied European immigrants and native-born migrants pushing further into the American interior. Dance masters and teachers moved westward to industrial and market centers, such as Cleveland, Detroit, Chicago, Milwaukee, and St. Louis. These apostles of the terpsichorean art tutored the respectable populace in the steps and protocols accompanying country dances, cotillions, and quadrilles. Dance masters added a veneer of European respectability to American social dancing. Publishers produced reams of instructional and etiquette literature to support the emergence of standard practices at American dances and balls. Dance manuals instructed men and women in various steps and rituals as well as in the importance of bodily and emotional self-control while on the dance floor.[20]

Popular dances in the antebellum period borrowed European traditions linked to seventeenth-century courtly culture as well as to various forms of "peasant" dancing associated with agrarian festival culture. Both traditions emphasized group participation, whether in lines, such as the quadrille (also called the contredanse), or in circles, such as the gavotte. Communitarian dances moved participants through a sequence of steps in which they circulated among many dance partners, privileging the larger dancing unit over its individual parts. In the mid-1840s, the waltz and the polka introduced large numbers of Americans to an altogether different style of couples dancing. These faster-paced dances permitted individual couples to move unencumbered across an open floor, limited only by their energy, technical skills, and imaginations. The emphasis on the solitary dancing couple over the group symbolically liberated dancers from the group policing of previous dances and opened up possibilities for abuse that made controlling other elements of the dance experience of increased concern.[21]

BY INVITATION ONLY
Traditional Ballroom Dancing in Chicago

By the Civil War, ballroom dancing represented an important tool of self-fashioning for the urban elite of Chicago. Dance academies, such as Augustus E. Bournique's Schools for Dancing and Deportment, established in 1867, groomed Chicago's elect for their duties in society.[22] The storied ranks of Bournique's pupils included the merchant Marshall Field and the Civil War hero General Philip Sheridan. By its thirty-fifth season in 1901–1902, the academy maintained studios on the South, North, and West Sides, indicating the bourgeois character of many of Chicago's residential neighborhoods and suggesting the public demand for tutelage in the social graces associated with respectability and upward mobility.[23]

By the late nineteenth century, the privileged no longer commanded ballroom dancing as a rite of socialization. Balls constituted a popular form of recreation among many levels of urban society. They helped structure and reinforce buffers between insiders and outsiders, between the elect and parvenus, and between members of associations and guilds. While the elite may have had more frequent and lavish ballroom dancing opportunities, native-born, immigrant, and ethnic professionals, African Americans, municipal service workers, and laborers belonging to various occupational guilds participated in balls on special occasions. Invitations, dance cards, and other ephemera culled from late-nineteenth-century Chicago reveal the participatory scope of the ballroom dance culture. Major balls ranged from exclusive soirées to celebrate the World's Columbian Exposition, to annual festivities honoring Chicago firemen, to private balls to benefit charitable organizations and stalwart ethnic cultural institutions, such as the Lincoln Park Turnverein.[24]

Whether held in private mansions in posh neighborhoods or in more modest rented halls in industrial neighborhoods, formal balls in nineteenth-century Chicago created a social and recreational space at a self-conscious remove from the public world of strangers. As the popularity of the waltz, the two-step, and other couples dances supplanted group dancing, the codes of conduct for men and women at the ball grew to be of particular concern. Because couples dancing was symbolically associated with courtship and love, and could be seen as a prelude to physical intimacies, ballroom dancing proceeded under layers of regulation. At the typical ballroom dance, participants either knew one another by name or by face or were certified as reputable companions through screening mechanisms, such as private invitations.[25]

Despite the safety measures built into ballroom dancing, some turn-of-the-century morals critics worried about the effects of dance culture on youthful virtue, particularly the virtue of young women.[26] As one former dance master argued, many parents remained "blind to the awful dangers there are for young girls in the dancing academy and ballroom." Unscrupulous men sometimes bribed their way into the dance academy where "it is an easy matter to form the acquaintance of the wives and daughters of wealthy men."[27] Dancing required a kind of deference on women's part to the authority of the male partner, which some believed led to a compromised moral outlook: "At first she seems shocked at the manner in which he embraces her to teach her the latest waltz. It is her first experience in the arms of a strange man, with his limbs pressed to hers, and in her natural modesty, she shrinks from so familiar a touch . . . but she says to herself: 'This is the position every one must take who waltzes in the most approved style—church members and all—so of course it is no harm for me.'"[28] Questions of the moral underpinning of dancing grew more pronounced as the burgeoning marketplace for commercial dancing created public venues that challenged direct supervisory control of the family and the social circle over young dancers.

"THE WICKEDEST CITY IN THE WORLD"
The Moral Challenges of Commercial Dancing

Reform concerns about the direction of social dancing by 1900 stemmed from the darker side of the history of American social dancing, which was linked to commercialized vice and public entertainment for so-called sporting men.[29] Along with the conventional forms of social dancing that migrated into the Ohio Valley and Midwest in the antebellum period came various forms of commercialized sex and musical entertainment culture. In rustic frontier outposts and industrial settings where men commonly outnumbered women by a wide margin, sensual forms of female dancing for the entertainment of men occurred at brothels, saloons, theaters, and public houses. Here men of various classes drank, gambled, ogled, and enjoyed the company of dancing girls, who along with professional hostesses, provided amusement and, often, sexual favors for a price. These commercial establishments were homosocial haunts that reflected men's economic and gendered power over chorus girls, dancers, and professional sex workers, as well as over mothers, wives, and daughters, who typically remained cloistered elsewhere.[30] While some Chicago women rose to a degree of prominence as madams of brothels, such as the renowned Everleigh sisters, their economic success could not disguise the fact that from the Victorian perspective a "respectable" woman would not frequent these establishments.[31]

In Chicago prior to the Civil War, gambling, saloons and bordellos catering to river men, dock workers, and day laborers flourished in a vice district made up of shanties along the north bank of the Chicago River at Michigan Avenue known as "The Sands."[32] When law enforcement displaced the shanties, the commercial pleasure center merely relocated inland. By the 1870s, amusement zones for sporting men had taken root on the Near West and Near South Sides of Chicago. Dance halls, rowdy saloons, music halls featuring bawdy singing and dance reviews, and brothels with female prostitutes of different races catered to men of various classes, cultures, and races. Dancing and vice coexisted in red-light areas with nicknames like Little Cheyenne, the Bad Lands, Hell's Half Acre, Dead Man's Alley, and, most infamously by 1900, though it had existed in name far longer, the Levee district, which thrived on the Near West Side until 1903 before migrating to the Near South Side, where its notorious reputation continued to grow.[33]

Morals activists had long yearned to rid the city of these notorious public pleasure spaces, but a significant movement for change did not develop until the turn of the century when a wave of Christian reform/exposé literature helped stir widespread public indignation. William T. Stead's *If Christ Came to Chicago!* (1894), Samuel Paynter Wilson's *Chicago by Gaslight* (1910) and *Chicago and Its Cesspools of Infamy* (1910–15?), Robert Harland's *The Vice Bondage of a Great City* (1912), and John Dillon's *From Dance Hall to White Slavery* (1912) typified the genre. Part classic adventure-story, part pop-sociological treatise, part prurient tease, and part hellfire and damnation sermon, these journalistic works used colorful prose and first-person accounts to transport curious readers into rough-and-tumble areas of the city. Juxtaposing scenes of hedonism with melodramatic human suffering, the publications attempted to stir indignation in readers, casting a beacon on what Robert Harland called "the wickedest city in the world." Most called on the forces of righteousness and law and order to clean up the city.[34]

In *Chicago and Its Cesspools of Infamy*, Samuel Paynter Wilson, an investigator for the Douglas Neighborhood Club, characterized the commercial entertainment zone west of downtown as a dangerous thicket of musical and sensual temptations. "Night was coming on as I walked down Madison Street and south on Peoria," wrote Wilson describing his nights of dutiful reconnaissance: "Yes, there were the shanties—poor wretched hovels, every one of them. Out shone the flickering red lights, out came the discordant, rasping sound of the rented piano, out belched the shrieks of drunken harlots, mingled with the groans and curses of task-masters in a foreign tongue, attracting the attention of the hundreds of laborers, Negroes and boys, as they walked home on Peoria street from their day's work."[35] The reportage combined visceral and titillating details and anxious moralizing in response to such commercial amusement mainstays as the concert saloon and cheap music hall: "These concert halls provide a low order of music, and the liquors furnished are of the vilest description."[36] Likewise, the galleries of musical theaters in the area were "filled chiefly with boot-blacks, newsboys, and the juvenile denizens of the city, ranging in age from eight to twelve years. The orchestras are made up of amateurs and old men, and furnish a cheap class of music."[37] As the American middle class began to "step out" and participate regularly in commercial nightlife culture, studies like these sounded a cautionary note. They warned readers of street-level dangers, such as the *ballum rancum*, a dance "where all the damsels are thieves and prostitutes" and where youths were particularly susceptible to the corrupting influences of the streets.[38]

Wilson's *Chicago by Gaslight* warned especially of the inherent seductive quality and ungovernable energy of the dance itself that transcended its geographical location. While red-light districts compounded the ill effects of the dance, the author equated bodily motion with a universal loss of moral compass and control. "They who glide into the dissolute dance glide over an inclined plane," he cautioned readers, "and the dance is swifter and swifter, wilder and wilder, until, with the speed of lightning, they whirl off the edges of a decent life into a fiery future. *The gate of hell swings across the Axminster of many a fine parlor and across the dance hall of many summer resorts.*"[39] Wilson implied that the ills of the dance did not necessarily respect the bounded blocks of Chicago's red-light districts. The "respectable" private dance and vacation dance halls also harbored risks that linked them inextricably to the roughest and most dissolute of streetscapes.

For writers like Wilson, music represented an incendiary catalyst capable of producing a "fiery future" for those who dared abandon themselves to the dance. Music could manipulate emotion and impair judgment. The pleasure of dancing must not be used to rationalize improper behaviors between the sexes, whether in the private parlor or in a commercial dance hall. "We have no right to take an attitude to the sound of music," Wilson insisted, "which would be unbecoming in the absence of music."[40] Exposé/reform publications like *Chicago by Gaslight* served an important publicity function for the causes of progressive urban reformers. Despite their alarmist tone and often prurient or patronizing treatment of the street denizens they described, they legitimated a taboo subject for public discussion among educated and powerful members of Chicago society. Exposé literature rendered a form of civic education, which, however one-sided, connected an imagined community of moral readers to a set of public concerns about market-driven amusements and threats to bourgeois moral authority that musical recreation, among other features of this world, represented.[41]

MASKING THE BALL
The "Beer Permit" Dance Controversy

In the mid-1900s a citywide controversy erupted around a Chicago neighborhood recreational institution, the "beer permit" dance. The uproar marked the first in a series of skirmishes between morals activists and the generation leading social dancing in a new direction. The issues that arose signified growing public awareness of the changing constituencies and social character of public dances in Chicago's industrial neighborhoods. Journalists, morals activists, and ethnic neighborhood leaders voiced concern about a new institutional form of public dancing catering to an emerging subculture of youth wanting to socialize outside the orbit of parental and neighborhood governance. The controversy also pointed to a mounting challenge that the dance craze represented to the conceptual and geographical boundaries dividing "respectable" social dancing from its morally suspect twin, dancing and musical amusements within Chicago's red-light pleasure zones.

Like the saloon, "beer permit" dances represented a traditional staple of plebeian recreational activity and festive culture.[42] In the city's ethnic, immigrant, and laboring neighborhoods, dances accompanied festivals, weddings, patriotic commemorations, various saints' celebrations, and group and community milestones. Dozens of locally recognized organizations, including church groups, ethnic fraternal and benevolent associations, business associations, and workers' guilds presented dances and more formal balls in rented halls in order to socialize, raise funds, build constituencies, and promote their activities and status in the neighborhoods and beyond.[43] Sponsors obtained city permits for a nominal fee to offer beer for sale to quench dancers' thirsts, enliven the party, and to defray costs. City ordinances respected the custom of self-sponsored dancing and drinking events with the implicit proviso that a sponsoring neighborhood institution or club responsibly oversee the conduct of the event.[44]

"Beer permit" dances catering to underage youth were a new phenomenon that defied the expectations of tradition. Individuals ran the dances, as did some saloon keepers, who broke the law by connecting their licensed establishments to adjoining chambers temporarily transformed into illegal dance halls, often after the saloon officially closed for the evening. The parties often ran all night without limits on the size of the crowds, the ages of participants (ordinances prohibited underage drinking), or the style of music and dancing. The organizers of these breakaway dances thumbed their noses at conservative local neighborhood authorities, who traditionally oversaw club and beer permit events, and dodged (or paid off) enforcers of city restrictions designed to separate the operations of saloons and dance halls. Outcry over abuse of the right to run "beer permit" dances expanded to generalized condemnations of the dangers of commercialized youth dancing.

The "beer permit" debate grabbed the public spotlight for a number of months in 1905 and 1906 as a direct result of a series of investigations of commercialized dancing by the *Chicago Tribune* and the *Chicago Record-Herald*. Journalists found that although city ordinances required saloons to shutter at midnight on weekdays and

THE WAY THE CLOSING LAW IS OBEYED.

"The Way the Closing Law Is Obeyed." From *Chicago Daily News*, January 18, 1905.

1:00 A.M. on weekends, a bold class of entrepreneurs armed with $2.50 beer permits habitually exploited a loophole that allowed an individual or organization to conduct an all-night dance party. Under the guise of sponsoring a respectable neighborhood social function, entrepreneurs were creating instant nightclubs in storefronts and rented halls, which they packed on weekends with reputedly riotous and thirsty underage dancers.[45]

According to the investigations, the shadowy organizers of weekend "beer permit" parties donned masks of respectability to conceal their lucrative scheme from law enforcement and neighborhood and morals activists. Organizers often changed locations to stay one step ahead of the police. They relied on private mailing lists to alert area youth of upcoming events rather than publicizing them in newspapers as most dance sponsors did. Invitations sent to youth described these events as "balls" and "soirées," suggesting a whiff of respectability should parents or guardians show concern. But the impression that these dances operated by the time-honored conventions of "respectable" social dancing proved a subterfuge. Investigators found that names were rarely checked at the door and that large numbers of strangers wandered in freely off the street to join the reveling crowd inside. According to sources, hundreds of male and female dancers descended on these "beer permit" events precisely because of the absence of the restrictions of the conventional formal ball, club dance, or neighborhood festival. At these dances few rules impeded the prospect of meeting multiple members of the opposite sex and the chance to dance, drink, and fraternize well after the legal closing time of saloons and licensed dance halls.[46]

Probing beneath the clever masquerade of these "beer permit" dances, Chicago newspapers exploited the frothy combination of youth, booze, and whiffs of sexual immorality to whip up public sentiment against moral decay attributed to the new trend in commercialized youth dancing.[47] Investigators visited dozens of seemingly innocuous "beer permit" dances, "soirées," and "balls" where they reported bleary-eyed youths dancing until dawn, supine girls being hustled into taxis by men claiming to be their escorts, and other scenes thoroughly jarring to the bourgeois conventions of respectable social dancing. One news story breathlessly described young "boys and girls [who] hold wild orgies [and] dance to their doom" at the all-night Saturday dance parties that were becoming commonplace at halls on the South and West Sides. "Ends Woes at Dance" read one headline, reporting on the suicide by chloroform of a female dancer at a South Side hall. The moral panic surrounding the fraudulent "beer permit" events, where, as one writer put it, "Carousals are the Rule," drew attention to a full-blown recreational fad whose rebellious qualities stood revealed, but were imprecisely understood by morals activists.[48]

"ABOUT A DANCE YOU CAN SAY THE SAME AS ABOUT MUSHROOMS"
Rogue Dances and Challenges to Authority

The discovery of the secret network of all-night Saturday dance parties challenged conventional understanding of public comportment in which respectable women stayed away from alcohol and men in public, while men and women confined displays of passion and the body to the private shelter of the (conjugal) home. The explosive combination of underage drinking, young girls mingling in unsupervised settings with men, music, and expressive couples dancing subverted multiple conventions of bourgeois public morality, gender, and sexuality. The public expression and visible enactment of desire by young women in intimate contact with members of the opposite sex proved especially rousing news. Reports emphasizing drunkenness and physically intimate contact among youths at the dances (though no hard evidence of vice) fed concerns among activists of the risks to public morals of large numbers of unattached young girls and single women attending all-night dances in the company of large numbers of men.

To outside observers, the shenanigans at "beer permit" events, as well as at a significant number of conventional public dance halls, clashed with the model of the socially circumscribed neighborhood dance in which parties moved within a trusted social circuit approved by community leaders and governed by local customs. "One of the wildest orgies in the city was that carried on at Hoerber's Dance Hall," reported the *Chicago Record-Herald*. "Here one hundred and fifty girls from twelve to eighteen years old, with dresses hardly reaching to the knee, caroused, drank beer at the bar, and *danced with anybody and everybody*."[49] These dances mocked the screening protocols of invitation-only balls and avoided the supervisory culture that rendered municipal dances in parks acceptable destinations for "respectable" males and females. Twisting the civic reform ideal of democratic public culture, these dances permitted freedom of association, but without a self-evident guiding moral or administrative framework to police the events or to segregate participants into what morals activists would consider appropriate categories of inclusion and exclusion.

The "beer permit" dance subculture undermined the authority of neighborhood custodians of public recreation and community formation.[50] The subculture pointedly rejected Turner halls, lodges, *Sokols*, and other physical sites of "respectable" neighborhood dances and flouted their conservative social mores. Concerned ethnic leaders chided youths attending the unruly events. Appealing to the faith of its ethnic readers, one Polish-language newspaper admonished dancers to recall that "St. Francis Salezy, a man of great virtues and deep wisdom said as follows: 'About a dance you can say the same as about mushrooms; most of them are poisonous and the best of them are of very little value.' " The *Narod Polski*, another Polish-language paper, repeatedly scolded youthful dancers and abusers of the "beer per-mit" privilege, whose personal rebelliousness threatened local defini-tions of orderly behavior and risked tarnishing the public image of Poles in Chicago. "Almost every issue of Polish newspapers brings us the news of rowdyism and fighting that takes place at our balls, dances, etc., and also in our Polish saloons," lamented one editorial.[51] Another item, several years later, echoed the lament. "Polish colonies are furnishing plenty of material for the newspapers, bringing shame to us Poles," it read. "Parents, save your honor!"[52] As these writers suggested, the ills of drinking and dancing were not new, or neces-sarily confined to the youth dances, but their migration into the com-mercial arena further removed them from the oversight of families and insular neighborhood institutions. Such ill-advised displays in the public arena by Polish youth risked distorting the "true" identity of Polish Americans as respectable and responsible citizens carefully conserved by institutions such as the foreign-language press, clerics, and other ethnic neighborhood leaders.

Critical commentary in the foreign-language press lambasted commercialized dancing as symptomatic of gendered depravity spreading throughout the male population. The editors of the Polish-language *Dziennik Zwiazkowy* implicated Polish patrons of popular dances as participants in the democratic excess of unregulated social mixing. "There are clerks, property owners, magistrates, students, and even (though infrequently) the servants of knowledge, the chap-lains of literature and art. They are all there, and they all went there in pursuit of inexperienced girls, who no doubt told their mothers that they were 'going to their girlfriend's home.' "[53] Emphasizing male predatory behavior over equally irresponsible young girls, judgmental editors rarely turned the question around to explore why these rogue dances attracted such a broad spectrum of participants. The pos-sibility that the popularity of the "beer permit" dance subculture and commercial dance halls might represent a critique of the paternalistic, ethnocentric neighborhood culture did not get aired alongside the stern rebukes meted out to the immigrant and ethnic readership.[54]

Activists challenged Democratic mayor Carter Harrison II to re-spond to concerns about abuses of the "beer permit" system and to revelations about the underground commercial dance scene. Having served Chicago in the capacity of a "reform boss" since 1897, Har-rison politely listened to the pleas of moral activists, while accepting drinking, gambling, and vice in specified areas as a part of metro-

politan business-as-usual.[55] In 1903 the mayor had garnered favorable
press for his call to "close" the West Side red-light area, bounded by
Fulton, Madison, Halsted, and Morgan Streets. In truth, the action
simply led to the migration of the Levee to a more commodious area
on the Near South Side.[56] On the latest controversy, Harrison attempted to placate morals activists by insisting that good conduct
prevailed at the vast majority of "beer permit" dances. "I am con-
fident a careful examination will show that the worst abuses exist not
at dances given by regular organizations," he wrote in a public letter
to the chief of police, "but at dances given either by saloon-keepers
who own the hall or by a few young men who use these affairs simply
as a source of profit to themselves."[57] Harrison emphasized the integrity of the "beer permit" system while subtly easing concerns among
reputable neighborhood dance sponsors that the city intended to
interfere with their traditional celebrations. Harrison admitted that
there were abuses, but he made no clear pronouncement on the
linked issue of youth rebellion in commercial dancing.

The "beer permit" controversy fueled concerns among morals
activists that dancing in public represented a threat to Chicago's public recreational landscape broadly construed. More than innocent
neighborhood frolics or an escape valve for plebeian energies, the
underground commercial dance subculture exposed by the "beer
permit" investigations hinted that the boundaries distinguishing the
Levee, Chicago's red-light district, from the rest of the city's nocturnal amusement culture, appeared less secure than previously imagined.[58] Such revelations of public events masquerading as "respectable" social dances suggested to morals activists that a closer, more
systematic look would be needed to determine the nature of the
public musical landscape and to bring it under greater control.

REDEFINING RECREATION REFORM
The JPA and the Vice Commission of Chicago

On June 27, 1910, Republican mayor Fred Busse and the Chicago
City Council established a commission to formally investigate the
presence of vice in the city. Pressure for municipal action had been
mounting as a result of a series of complaints from various groups,
including the Chicago Law and Order League, a citizens' group primarily concerned with liquor law enforcement, saloon regulation, and

morals policing, and a federation of Chicago clergy seeking a response to the legal and moral transgressions associated with urban nightlife.[59] The commission was formed amid allegations of what the "beer permit" crisis had only intimated, that the sex trade had expanded beyond the visible and regulated zone of the Levee into various public spaces and settings, including commercial dance halls. The commission consisted of thirty religious leaders, educators, health officials, law enforcement personnel, and businessmen. It created ten subcommittees to explore various topics: existing conditions, alleged sites of vice activity, crime and law enforcement aspects, impacts on children, "rescue and reform" efforts, and medical and legislative features of vice management and regulation.[60]

Released in April 1911, the commission's formal report, *The Social Evil in Chicago*, revealed that commercialized prostitution constituted a $15 million business in the city and involved an estimated 5,000 full-time prostitutes. The report noted shifts in women's status as contributing factors to the alleged urban moral crisis. It blamed an explosion of women wage earners in disproportion to men, coupled with the "disintegration of the older forms of family life" (specifically, rising divorce statistics), for creating an unstable dynamic in which single women circulated freely in public space. Epitomizing the judgmental outlook of many progressive moral reform pronouncements toward the poor, the report condemned prostitutes for their professional choices, while criticizing those "respectable" wage-earning women whose economic independence permitted them to go out seeking amusements, unencumbered by husbands, or even male escorts.[61]

Among its findings the commission presented data compiled by the JPA in a massive investigation of commercialized dancing. Between November 1910 and the following March, JPA representatives had visited 328 dance halls both inside and outside the Levee.[62] Investigators estimated that on any given evening, 86,000 youths—slightly more than one in seven Chicago youths under the age of twenty—attended dance halls, 73 percent of which sold alcohol on the premises.[63] Of the halls studied, 190 featured a fully functioning saloon and slightly less than half sold alcohol freely to minors. In these halls, investigators reported commonly observing the "vilest sort of informal dancing or immoral actions."[64] Echoing sentiments expressed during the "beer permit" investigation, the commission warned of the volatile combination of dancing, music, and intoxicants available at most commercial halls, and it argued that alcohol and commercial dancing be separated to the greatest extent possible. The commission further maintained that dance halls and amusement parks, along with "saloons where music, vaudeville performance and other recreational attractions are necessary to the drink habit," were "directly tributary to the increase of victims of vice" because disreputable lodging houses were often nearby.[65]

The JPA did not ease its investigative pressure or reduce its activities with the publication of the commission report. Its agents continued to haunt commercial dance floors across Chicago. In 1912–13 the JPA made 216 visits to Chicago dance halls and established branch offices at several field house parks to more closely monitor and oversee recreational reform activities, including dances held at these locations.[66] The organization resisted the idea that dancing to ragtime tunes could be called an innocent pastime. Instead, they insisted that public dancing concealed amoral desires of young men and women. Investigators stressed the point that even club and society dances and balls bore careful watching. "At the former [club and society dances] the dangers are more subtle. The halls are cleaner and better order is preserved; drinks are higher priced, but more intoxicating; the patrons are better dressed, and there is an assumption of decency. But these halls serve as a rendezvous for immoral men and women, and crowds of young men attend with the sole idea of meeting girls for immoral purposes. . ."[67]

The vice commission report and pressure from the JPA, the press, neighborhood watchdog groups, temperance activists, religious organizations, and the Illinois state's attorney's office forced Chicago's political leaders into action. Returned to office by the voters in 1911, Mayor Harrison needed to make a dramatic gesture. Having built a career on talking tough about regulating controversial nightlife, and doing little to control it, Harrison reluctantly ordered the shuttering of the Everleigh Club, a symbol of the sporting culture of the Levee, and declared the South Side's vice district officially "closed" in 1912.[68]

The Levee closure in combination with World War I helped briefly cool the dance fever in Chicago, aided by special ordinances curbing alcohol sales in public dance halls and sumptuary taxes on the commercial amusement industry.[69] When the war ended, wrote Harvey Zorbaugh, "[t]he street [was] not the show place to the curious man from the small town that it once was." This remark did not

mean that the "wilds of North Clark Street" had been tamed by
morals reform; rather, the reputed vice and outrageous behavior associated with prewar Chicago had retreated "from the lights of the
street into back rooms."[70] Louise Dekoven Bowen, president of the
JPA, discerned an irony in the new arrangement: "In the old days,
when we had a segregated vice district, those who wanted that sort of
thing knew where to find it, and others didn't need to see it. With the
closing up of the district, conditions have changed, and prostitution
now is to be found in cabarets, dance halls and disreputable hotels."[71]
The return of servicemen to the labor force spiked renewed interest
in recreational dancing, such that reformers tabulated 445 dance
halls operating in Chicago as the 1920s began. New sounds and new
venues revealed that, unlike the kaiser, the dance craze had not been
vanquished, but merely reincarnated.[72]

"NEITHER A PROFESSIONAL NOR AN OUTCAST"
Sex, Gender, and Performance Culture in Cabarets

Demographic changes between 1914 and the end of the 1920s decisively altered the commercial music recreational landscape. Steep reductions in European immigration as a result of the war, labor shortages in industry, and economic distress in the Southeast catalyzed the
migration of African Americans from the rural South to the industrial
North (an estimated 500,000 between 1916 and 1919 alone). The
population flow doubled the number of African Americans in Chicago in a ten-year span and brought to Chicago emerging musical
forms, including jazz and blues. These musics helped rejuvenate the
commercial dance scene, and JPA activists redoubled their commitment to contain the rebellious energy of the new subcultures in the
name of the civic good and public morality.

Cabarets had existed in significant numbers outside the red-light
areas from the moment that many neighborhood saloons began expanding their operations to include regular musical entertainment
by young female singers. Cabarets constituted an entertainment
mainstay in numerous neighborhoods. They frequently appeared in
mixed commercial and residential areas and catered to a heterogeneous base of white customers. Cabarets grew noticeably more
popular following the ratification of the Nineteenth Amendment and
the establishment of federal prohibition in January 1920. Many con-

tinued to serve alcohol in defiance of state and federal laws, relying on bribes given to local enforcement officials to permit their operations to continue. Moreover, though audiences were most commonly whites-only, the cabarets' willingness to hire the vanguard of African American and white jazz performers created a new sound and sensibility in urban dance and nightlife culture.[73]

For the thousands of youths and adults who frequented them, cabarets of the 1910s and 1920s offered a novel form of public, yet intimate entertainment.[74] These businesses served a generation of men and women growing used to public drinking, dancing and listening to music, and socializing in the presence of, or with, strangers. Cabarets provided the kind of affordable gathering place that saloons had, while adding regular musical performances, dancing, and an atmosphere of sensual theatricality not typically found at dance halls. Reformers claimed that part of the danger posed by cabarets lay in their relatively inexpensive admission fees that made them competitive with city amusement parks and dance palaces in pulling in underage dollars.

Cabarets cultivated an atmosphere of intimacy between audiences and performers. Professional singers or dancers backed by small bands or combos performed directly in front of seated or dancing audience members mere yards away. The intimacy of the experience for audiences derived from the human scale of the room and the close proximity of spectators to the stage where singers and musicians sweated over their art or dancers shook their bodies. While some cabarets might have several rooms, most activity centered in a single space, a room bordered by tables and chairs with a stage at one end and an area in the middle for dancing couples or a floor show.

Cabarets inverted the sacralized ritual of concert spectatorship with silent audiences and stiff professional entertainers. Performers embraced opportunities to improvise and to transgress the invisible wall separating performer and spectator through speech or gesture. Performers frequently left the stage to continue their acts among the dancing audience or ad-libbed comments during songs in response to audience activity in front of them. Female singers roamed the aisles, touching patrons, flirting with them, even bringing them up on stage to become part of the show.[75]

The nature of cabaret culture dissolved conventional boundaries between professional and amateur entertainment and deliberately suggested that patrons—through their dress, style, and energy dis-

played on and off of the dance floor—contributed to a public spectacle for all to enjoy. Cabarets embraced bawdiness and sexual interplay between customers as part of the night's entertainment. Morals
investigators unaccustomed to strangers "performing" for one another in such ways expressed shock when "[a]n intoxicated woman
patron insisted on dancing before the other patrons, exposing herself
indecently." Racy revues and titillating vaudeville routines sometimes invited audience participation. But cabarets extended the
boundary of public display of sexuality to a new level of elaboration
in a public setting.[76]

Morals investigators from the JPA worried about role-playing in
cabarets in part because it suggested the dissolution of familiar public
and private roles for men and women. The cabaret subculture illustrated what sociologist Harvey Zorbaugh, writing in 1929, called "the
gradual letting down of all sexual conventions," such that women
who frequented cabarets inhabited multiple identity roles previously
unavailable to them. "The abolition of the segregated district has also
broken up the prostitute 'caste,'" Zorbaugh asserted. "In the days of
the Levee and red-light district the 'painted lady' was an outcast.
Now women can get into and out of prostitution easily. The cabaret
facilitates this. The prostitute of today, instead of being a woman of
professional nature, grown old in the game, is typically a young girl,
neither a professional nor an outcast."[77] Zorbaugh's broad definition
of "prostitute" condemned a wide range of expressive behaviors that
cabarets made more available and natural for women. For all that
he opposed the development, Zorbaugh discerned the implications
of the ineluctable transformation of sex in public from a regulated
trade—spatially and culturally bounded in red-light areas and the
province of visible career "professionals"—to a more fluid and diverse
activity involving a heterogeneous population of women.[78]

As Joanne Meyerowitz has argued, young female wage earners
migrating to Chicago in these years enjoyed a wider assortment of
public roles and recreational options than ever before. But this social
fact only compounded the worrisome character that JPA activists ascribed to public dance spaces in which women still invited (mis)iden-
tification as prostitutes. Complaints about the problematic passing of
women across the fraught symbolic divides of virtuous sexual absti-
nence and wanton sexual expression indicate the resistance of morals
activists to the changes that female wage earners demanded in the
personal dimensions of their public lives. Concerns about dancers

getting "into and out of prostitution easily" implied the stakes that JPA activists attached to the moral trends in commercial dancing that would grow more acute with the onset of the Jazz Age.

"EVEN THE WAITERS . . . ARE SHIMMYING"
The JPA Discovers the Sights and Sounds of Jazz

Since as far back as the JPA's contributions to the 1911 Chicago Vice Commission report, morals activists had typically ignored the music accompanying activity at "beer permit" events, dance halls, and cabarets. The JPA findings contained in *The Social Evil in Chicago* implied that dance music merely filled the spaces between drinks. That reflected the JPA's narrow focus on youth morality and its disregard for the link between aesthetic issues and civic engagement of primary interest to many musical progressives. The failure of the JPA to seriously listen to the dance craze fatally undermined the ability of dance reformers to move closer to their dancing subjects.

As the 1911 vice commission report had shown, JPA activists did not exactly "blame" music directly for the worrisome conditions found in commercial dance halls. The liquor industry and unscrupulous saloon and dance hall operators garnered chief blame. Nevertheless, reform struggles to counter ragtime and syncopated music in parks, settlements, and field houses suggested that activists tied to the JPA remained sensitive to the difference that music made. Dances in field houses, some of which JPA branch units sponsored, specifically barred dancing associated with styles popular in commercial dance halls. The pattern of past struggles showed that musical publics actively resisted the repressive dimensions of recreation and morals reform that denied them power to shape the democratic currents of popular recreation. While they did not historically foreground the power of music in their investigations, JPA morals activists nevertheless proceeded within a framework derived from musical progressivism in which music, public recreation, and moral outcomes interacted in dynamic ways.

The ongoing JPA-led investigation of cabarets took a discernible turn at the point after World War I when investigators began to increasingly encounter the sights and sounds of jazz performed by white and African American musicians. Chicago's entertainment areas generally followed the rules of Jim Crow and the guidelines of the city's white and black musicians' unions. White jazz bands dominated the cabaret culture of the North and West Sides, while African American musicians performed inside the Black Belt.[79] Louise Dekoven Bowen, a Hull House activist and an advocate of municipal dancing, led a public and print campaign on behalf of the JPA to raise public awareness about the moral dangers of cabarets, particularly those combining easy access to liquor and jazz music. In numerous public speeches and published tracts, Bowen described the horrors that jazz allegedly injected into the cabaret context and the dangers of such music to patrons. "On a small stage a band is playing jazz music" began a typical description of a West Side cabaret. "The space in the middle of the floor is crowded with youthful couples, all dancing the shimmy; boys and girls stand with their arms around each other, moving very slowly to the sensuous music; the whole atmosphere is vibrant with sensuality, even the waiters, as they bring in the liquor, are shimmying—the musicians move in rhythm to the music. . . . [I]t is an orgy of indecency and unbridled passion, and men and girls give themselves up to the sensation of the moment."[80] All present seemed under the sway of the music: "Young boys with young girls . . . old men with young girls . . . young men with thirty-five-year-old women."[81] Bowen warned the public of the ills of the cabaret as a seductive netherworld, whose existence defied virtually every aspect of the code of public behavior by which Chicago's reform-minded elite defined responsible recreation.

In ways that music prior to World War I did not, jazz—that "sensuous music," as Bowen called it—lay at the center of the JPA's anti-cabaret campaign. The music eluded specific analysis by investigators, yet Bowen argued that, in combination with alcohol, it catalyzed unseemly dances and social behaviors. "Up to about eleven P.M. generally speaking, the dances are well conducted," wrote Bowen, describing a typical cabaret. But, as the evening wore on, New Orleans–style jazz music and dancing would take over the room: "Men and women become intoxicated and dance indecently to such dances as 'Walkin' the Dog,' 'On the Puppy's Tail,' 'Shaking the Shimmy,' 'The Dip,' 'The Stationary Wiggle,' etc. . . . Couples stand very close together, the girl with her hands around the man's neck, the man with both his arms around the girl's or on her hips; their cheeks are pressed close together, their bodies touch each other; the liquor which has been consumed is like setting a match aflame; they throw aside all restraint and give themselves to unbridled license and indecency."[82]

In a tone of sheer disgust, Bowen summed up the fare that she had witnessed at a West Side cabaret performance: "On the stage a performance was taking place. A girl who gave a very indecent dance, was almost nude with the exception of a skirt so abbreviated, both top and bottom, that it could hardly be called a skirt, a jazz band furnished the music; the entire performance was lewd and vulgar."[83] The dress of the dancer, her movements, and the band backing the show compounded the injury that Bowen claimed jazz cabarets inflicted on public taste and decency.

To an extent that dance investigators had not done prior to the rise of jazz cabarets, Bowen and the JPA now impugned vocal performances. Bowen argued that many of the entertainers at cabarets were not, in her estimation, dedicated musicians or artists, in any sense of the word. By denying jazz serious consideration as an aesthetic form of any substance, Bowen and the JPA placed the music beyond the rehabilitative reach of conventional music reform. Bowen portrayed female cabaret singers as pliant instruments of amoral cabaret operators, who hired performers on the basis of their youth and attractiveness and urged them to sing "tough"—that is, bawdy—material. Echoing Bowen and the JPA's assessment that jazz in cabarets represented not so much "music" as a subterfuge for crass forms of sexual titillation, a newspaper declared: "Many of the songs sung by the entertainers are obscene; in fact when a girl applies to an agent for a position he asks her what songs she knows, and often remarks after hearing them that they are not 'tough enough' and urges her to think up something else, making it clear that he wishes to arouse the baser passions of the patrons. At one cabaret the proprietor told a girl entertainer that he would give her and the other girl entertainers rent free rooms upstairs and urged them to make 'easy money.' "[84] The apparent invitation to young women to freelance as prostitutes suggested to investigators the extent to which cabarets used the veneer of musical entertainment to engage in the underground sex trade and the purposeful denigration of women.

Risqué cabaret performances by outspoken women, suggestive dancing among patrons, and the unfamiliar cadences of jazz music convinced JPA activists that many cabarets must be fronts for commercialized vice. Previous incarnations of the dance craze had generated moral alarm when the music stopped and drunken couples had retreated into dark corners. But the multiple powers of jazz—its sensual performance culture, suggestive lyrics, and kinetic rhythms and faddish dance styles—commanded JPA attention. Echoing the complaints against renegade "beer permit" dances and prewar cabarets, where the boundaries of sexual propriety appeared to dissolve, reformers now attacked jazz music and its sensual subculture for luring "well-to-do" young people into public settings where bourgeois conventions meant little, waiters had taken to shimmying along with patrons, and the fixed boundaries between propriety and sexual immorality could seemingly be pierced by the insistent call of a saxophone.[85]

BLACK-AND-TAN CABARETS
Music and Difference

Multiracial cabarets in the Black Belt and their association with African American jazz posed a variant that challenged the framework that JPA activists envisioned should guide Chicago's public dance culture. Ironically, these exceptional cabarets grew directly out of the segregated public recreation landscape that musical progressive outreach had helped to build throughout much of the city of Chicago. These establishments embodied the power of music and commercial culture to bind social groups into new public configurations. Though hardly race-blind utopias, black-and-tan cabarets enabled African Americans, men and women of color, and a host of other kinds of patrons to create a unique public recreational environment in which standards of difference and social hierarchy expressed in terms of gender (especially female sexual passivity), race, and sexuality (specifically, heterosexual normativity), were more open to question.[86]

In certain respects, black and tans mirrored their cabaret cousins in the segregated recreational areas of the North and West Sides of Chicago. The typical black and tan accommodated fewer than 100 couples and hosted concert performances as well as floor shows of professional singers or dancers, whose entertainment and lyrics were often bawdy and designed to provoke audience reaction. What chiefly distinguished the black and tans was the presence not only of African American performers but also of multiracial audiences, among whom could be found multi- and interracial couples.[87]

Black-and-tan cabarets attracted multiracial audiences fascinated by African American jazz. The racial segregation of the music business typically limited African American jazz performers to cabarets and halls in the Black Belt, luring multiracial patrons from across the city to the South Side to witness the excitement and artistry of Joe "King" Oliver, Jelly Roll Morton, Louis Armstrong, Alberta Hunter, and Johnny and Warren "Baby" Dodds. Unlike North and West Side cabarets, where some musicians complained that audiences were more interested in the jiggly floor shows, here the skills of many of the musicians commanded attention. "No one paid especially to hear [jazz] music played, except on the South Side of Chicago, if it was a black neighborhood and a black band," recalled Art Hodes. Patrons of black and tans "were very informed about what they were coming for—to listen."[88] Youthful white jazz aficionados from Chicago-area high schools and Bohemian intellectuals affiliated with area colleges and universities made regular treks to the Black Belt to hear the music live for themselves. Many of the white spectators were North and West Side jazzmen, such as Hodes, Eddie Condon, Milton "Mezz" Mezzrow, and Benny Goodman.[89]

Besides nurturing an extraordinary music scene that drew spectators from across the city, black and tans served the entertainment needs of African Americans excluded from many commercial recreational opportunities outside the Black Belt. Black and tans sustained a uniquely diverse clientele that included social drinkers defying Prohibition; interracial couples; men seeking interracial liaisons with prostitutes; male and female homosexuals and bisexuals; gangsters; and "slummers," privileged whites who passed through the South Side on thrill-seeking, neo-imperialist concrete safaris.[90] Pulled or pushed to the black and tans, these patrons shaped an alternative to the racially segregated and conventional sexual milieu of most public leisure spaces. At black and tans, light- and dark-skinned and same sex couples could socialize and dance with little fear of censure or harassment.[91]

Unable to fathom the culture of desire on display among audience members as anything but deviant sentiments, JPA investigators again searched for clues buried in the unfamiliar strains of jazz. Fixated on the overlapping transgressions of racial and sexual norms, JPA investigators seemed blinded to the interracial cult of avid jazz fans ringing the performers. While sometimes mentioning song titles or snatches of lyrics, the dozens of surviving JPA reports from commercial dances never identify a jazz or blues artist by name, though the audiences obviously could have explained a good deal of the significance of the performances had investigators stopped to inquire.[92]

Groping for words to describe the peculiar atmosphere prevailing at the Sunset Café, one investigator noted the "jazz music which changed from loud and discordant noises to low, weird and barbaric sounds." Another characterized the sounds from the bandstand as "low and sensuous." In the dimness of the dance floor, the music inspired repetitious bodily movements that investigators described as "obscene and indecent"; perhaps because of its very obviousness, the reports did not consistently make direct causal claims between jazz music and the modes of interracial attraction and sensual movement on the dance floor.[93]

Not that every patron hung on the riffing musicians on stage with unimpeachable avidity. As JPA activists rapidly discovered, significant numbers of patrons of black and tans came to luxuriate in the atmosphere of public hedonism and interracial sensuality. A visitor to the black-and-tan Sunset Café in 1922 observed that by the time the band began to play "several of the girls were drunk and were scarcely able to move from their places when the jazz music commenced." Another observer recounted that "[t]he dancers scarcely moved their feet, but in most instances the girls' bodies were pressed tightly against the bodies of their partners and the contortions of their pelvic regions were very noticeable . . . kisses accompanied contortions."[94] The seeming erosion of conventions of public respectability and private intimacy struck a JPA observer at the Pioneer Cabaret, another South Side jazz haunt: "Five or six of the couples went through all the suggestive motions of a regular sex act. Two or three couples were really gymnastic, going through rapid motions for a while; they would then stand perfectly still for a while, close their eyes, and show evidence of extreme satisfaction."[95] A visitor to the Arabian Café took note of the self-consciously competitive aspect of these public performances of sexual desire: "When I left at 3:30, it seemed that the guests were trying to surpass each other in performing and shimmying."[96] The extension of bawdy entertainment on stage to the audience duplicated the North and West Side cabaret culture, but it nevertheless shocked investigators of the Black Belt, who were unaccustomed to such energetic sexual displays.

Investigators found that black and tans accepted and in some instances openly promoted the interracial hetero- and homosexual vice trade, provided that it was untroubled. Dark- and light-skinned African American prostitutes of various ages worked the tables, dance floors, and restrooms at many Black Belt establishments.[97] Sensual dancing between races commonly occurred at cabarets, and floor managers rarely intervened. According to one investigator, the sight of an African American man fondling a white woman below the waist as they danced produced a politely tactful comment from the floor manager. "The tall Negro floorman told the Negro man and white woman they were 'awfully close together,' but did not try to separate them."[98] However, local codes of conduct in black and tans did sometimes prohibit interracial licentiousness: "There was one instance of a colored girl about 14 years of age in the company of a drunken white man who so openly persisted in taking indecent liberties with her that a prostitute sitting near protested."[99] Whereas reformers discerned only narcissistic debauchery in such spectacles of interracial desire, celebrating patrons relished the chance to enjoy themselves. Despite the deeply problematic and exploitative features of the commercial sex trade, particularly in cases where privileged white customers sought young African American women and girls, black and tans enabled many interracial couples to fraternize publicly without harassment. Some interracial dancers happily flaunted their desire in a show of defiance in a sexually constrained and racially polarized society.

On black-and-tan cabaret stages, performers used skits and songs to tweak dominant sexual conventions through playful manipulation of hetero- and homoerotic themes and situations. Masquerades involving gender, racial, and sexual identity represented a common theme that spoke directly to the audience, as is suggested in the following account:

> A large male performer occupied the center of the floor and flourished a handful of bills, and while doing this he was watched by the girl performers, one of whom approached him and tickled him under the chin and displayed her ankle and raised her skirt in front and shook it and rotated the pelvic region of her body and held up two fingers to said male performer and said male performer then handed her two bills; that said man then violently seized said girl about the waist and that said girl wound her legs around said man and performed a stationary dance imitative of the act of sexual intercourse and pretended to faint; that said woman was then seized by the other girl performers who took her to the rear of the platform. This same performance was repeated by

> each of the other three girls; then a man performer appeared
> dressed like a woman and repeated the same performance
> above described with the said male performer.[100]

Humorous allusions to African American sexual prowess, vice, suggestive hetero- and homoerotic performances, cross-dressing epi-
sodes, jokes about mistaken identity, and gay and lesbian allusions
and situations constituted the distinctive attractions of black-and-
tan musical entertainment. Whether in parodic skits or in customer
dramas and performances on the dance floor, black and tans challenged fixed identity characteristics in ways that questioned the
dominant public representations of Chicago's multiracial and multiethnic population.[101]

Whether by explicit or implicit design, individuals often perceived by dominant society as marginal and genetically or crimi-
nally deviant formed a collectivity at the black and tans. The subter-
ranean aspect of this musical public could not diminish its symbolic
and political explosiveness in struggles to align musical recreation
and democratic identity formation. Unwelcome in the majority
of Chicago's public spaces, these seemingly atomized citizens—
multiethnic, dark- and light-skinned, male and female, homo-,
hetero-, and bisexual—amalgamated as a subculture. They shared a
common desire for spaces suited to their expressive and entertainment needs that balanced visibility and invisibility and that challenged morals activists attempting to recuperate bourgeois ideals in
public recreation settings.

In their rush to catalog affronts to public morality witnessed in
conventional and black-and-tan cabarets, reformers displayed inex-
plicable deafness to the music unfolding within them. Nor were they
prepared to engage the black and tan as an embodiment of the kind
of varied cultural assemblage that musical progressives had, at least in
theory, championed as a civic ideal. Cabarets confirmed what JPA
activists perceived as a series of democratic excesses and moral affronts in which patrons "danced with everybody and anybody," including, in the case of black and tans, members of different races, of
the same sex, or even of indeterminate races or sexes. The rejection
of fixed social norms and identifications and the defiant celebration of
eros and difference that made black and tans so exciting to patrons,
and so distressing to investigators, revealed the limits of musical

progressivism's democratic imaginings in areas of race mixing and unconventional gender and sexual expression.

"BUTCHERS AND BARBERS AND RATS FROM THE HARBORS"
Taxi-Dance Halls

Black-and-tan cabarets had raised regulators' hackles because they blithely accommodated underage drinking, indulged sexual expressiveness in public, appeared to harbor prostitution, and accepted taboo intermixtures of race, gender, and sexual variation on stage and on the dance floor. So-called taxi- or dime-a-dance halls staged a different version of these volatile intermixtures. These halls provided white female partners to nonwhite male customers, and invited the patronage of common laborers, but excluded African Americans. Their curious mirroring of musical progressivism's use of ethnicity and race made them an important case of commercial dancing's impact on the construction of an idealized civic and American public culture.

First cropping up in Chicago after World War I, "closed" or taxi-dance halls flouted the unwritten rule of racial segregation underpinning musical progressive ideology, while paradoxically reinforcing aspects of its orthodoxy.[102] Sidestepping the problem of mistaken identity of "respectable" women as prostitutes or vice versa, taxi-dances were "closed" to all women other than the Caucasian "instructors" paid to dance with and entertain male customers. Women of color did not work in the halls. Taxi-dances restored the dancing woman to the status of a "professional," though not, operators hastened to explain, as a prostitute. These halls deliberately capitalized on the segregation of public recreation and dancing through skillful and cynical manipulation of racial taboos, but in a manner whose artifice unintentionally drew attention to the instability and artificiality of the racial categories shaping everyday urban life.

Taxi-dance halls borrowed selective elements from the "respectable" dancing academy, such as the notion of professional instructors and lessons, and the commercial dance hall and cabaret, where men and women went to socialize, flirt, and meet potential partners. Taxi-dance halls operated through a continuous series of cash transactions in which men aged eighteen to fifty and from various economic and cultural backgrounds paid ten cents a dance for women's company on and, if the parties were mutually agreeable to the idea, off the dance floor. Intimate dancing styles banned from mainstream halls were often tolerated at dime-a-dance halls and a number of halls invited men of different cultural and racial backgrounds to dance freely with Caucasian hostesses. For these reasons, taxi-dance halls faced strong opposition from JPA activists and others concerned with the commodification of women's bodies and race mixing in public.[103]

One of the earliest detailed descriptions of a taxi-dance hall in Chicago appeared in a JPA report gathered on May 10, 1921, when an investigator visited the Athenian, a dance hall located on the third story of the Haymarket Burlesque Building along West Madison Street.[104] The hall operated alongside several others in an area a few miles west of the central business district adjacent to a major "furnished room district" located between Ashland Avenue and Halsted Street. In this densely populated neighborhood, single men and women lived in several square blocks of specialized single-room occupancy housing for menial wage earners and the indigent. While some halls relied on phonographs, many Madison Street dime-a-dance halls presented small ensembles and served as proving grounds for up-and-coming members of Chicago's local jazz scene throughout the 1920s and into the early 1930s.[105]

Art Hodes, who played many jazz gigs at area bars and taxi-dance halls described the tawdry, yet colorful blocks of the neighborhood as consisting of "[f]lophouses, cheap hotels, beaneries, Army and Navy stores, cheap picture shows, drunks, drunks, drunks . . . The Salvation Army Band trying to save a soul. The guy lying on the street out of his mind . . . Women to match, the bottom of the heap."[106] Smoke-filled, dusty, and redolent with the smell of alcohol and perspiration, taxi-dance halls presented a dreary contrast to the cabarets and the new "dance palaces" sprouting in Chicago. Their location bolstered reform suspicions about these halls as havens for amoral behavior, including vice.[107]

The investigator of the Athenian described entering a dingy third-floor room "about as large as the interior of a street car," in which "a player-piano furnished the music, and seven girls were present, so-called instructors."[108] The tone of the report signaled the suspicion that more than a craving for professional instruction in the niceties of the two-step or the waltz motivated the male pupils. A return visit to the relocated Athenian two years later found a bustling crowd of 125 male patrons and thirty instructors. Despite the unbalanced sex ratio, "[t]here was no trouble getting a dance with a girl if you had your ten-cent ticket." Men reportedly came to "closed" halls to ogle the dancers, pick and choose partners, listen to the bands, and mingle with the crowd, suggesting that, like cabarets, taxi-dance halls served as social centers for their patrons.[109]

In a city whose race problems had garnered national headlines during the 1919 riot, taxi-dances generated JPA attention beyond the transactional way that men and women interacted as clients and service workers. Part of the success of the Athenian reportedly came from its open-door policy with regard to men of color, who were permitted to dance with Caucasian women hired for that particular purpose.[110] "The men were a mixed lot, orientals predominating," wrote an observer. "A large part of the men were Filipinos. The girls were all Americans, the light-haired Nordics predominating."[111] For a nominal admission fee and a ten-cent dance ticket, Chinese, Filipinos, Pacific Islanders, Mexicans, and other Caucasian male customers hired young, attractive, "white" female companions for brief whirls around the dance floor.[112]

The taxi-dance format required no prior introductions or institutional affiliation to meet dance partners and likely appealed to customers of color who for a variety of reasons found themselves isolated from female social networks comprised of their own ethnic, racial, or national group.[113] Labor and occupational arrangements created conditions in which single men often lived in Chicago without families, wives, or girlfriends. Mexican laborers and wealthy Filipino men studying at area colleges, to name two such populations, had a shared interest in obtaining female companionship as well as overcoming racial segregation in commercial dance recreation. If these men were not priced out of cabarets and mainstream dance halls, their skin color barred them from participating in the mainstream musical amusement culture.[114]

"THE DIN BECOMES TERRIFIC"
Music at Taxi-Dance Halls

At first glance, the ritual of the taxi-dance appeared to brook no such subversive possibilities. Despite their shabby appearance, taxi-dances operated within carefully prescribed intervals of male-female transactions and actual dancing—the meter never stopped running. Operators kept female dancers on a short leash, not allowing them to sit and rest for any length of time in the public gathering room, or to speak to men unless a dance resulted, and they expected women to put up with rude customers or even sexual harassment in the interests of garnering profits for the hall. In one instance when a dancer slapped a customer for a crude proposition, she was chided by the manager: "He said I'd either act all right, no matter what the fellows said, or I could get out."[115]

The dances themselves conformed to strict limitations in time if not in content. Ten-cent dances ranged in approximate length from sixty to ninety seconds. The small four or eight-piece bands hired to play at taxi-dances specialized in knocking out a verse and chorus or two before pausing for a thirty- or forty-second changeover.[116] "The noise and confusion is continuous," wrote Paul Cressey, a JPA investigator, describing the typical hall. "Suddenly the music stops. The din becomes terrific. Men are running towards the girls, others are shouting for the whereabouts of their friends, and still above all is the continuous chatter of the idlers and observers." While dances ran like clockwork, what the dancers did on the floor was their own business, and the call for "clean" dancing rarely was enforced: "Some couples gallop together over the floor weaving their way in and around the slower dancers; others seek to attain aesthetic heights by a curious angular strut and a double shuffle or a stamp and a glide. Still others dance the 'Charleston,' and are granted unchallenged preemption of the center of the floor. Some couples are content with a slow, simple one-step as they move about the hall."[117] JPA investigators noted that the chaotic dancing, if not its lack of uniformity and precision, permitted intimate and sensual dancing between men and their hired partners: "These couples tend to segregate at one end of the hall where they mill about in a compressed pack of wriggling, perspiring bodies."[118] Reformers used language suggestive of animal or even rodentlike behaviors. If these dances were partially about celebrating white womanhood as pure and virtuous, the physicality of the ritual raised considerable discomfort among reformers, indirectly perhaps because of the debased status of white identity marred by colored dancing companions.

As in their assessments of North and West Side cabarets, JPA investigators portrayed musicians at taxi-dances as peripheral to the spectacle of symbolic miscegenation on the dance floor. Reports described white jazz acts struggling to compete with the din of the audience talking, flirting, and ogling other couples, with some engaged in mastering the dance steps or collecting a phone number. As one reformer described the scene: "On a platform at the end of the hall the five musicians of the orchestra wriggle, twist, and screech. But their best efforts to add pep and variety to the monotonous, 'Baby Face, You've Got the Cutest Little Baby Face' win no applause. The dancers are musically unappreciative, entirely oblivious to the orgiastic behavior on the orchestra stand." In this instance, jazz music appeared superfluous to audience behavior. It accompanied, but did not directly influence or tip the mood of the crowd into moral transgressions greater than those they appeared already willing and able to perform on or off the dance floor.[119]

   At least some working musicians stoically accepted their subordinate status at the taxi-dance relative to the energetic hostesses drumming up customer interest around the hall. At the Capitol Dancing School on Randolph and State Streets, Art Hodes recalled that his band adopted a mercenary attitude toward the audience: "We didn't bother to learn the pop tunes of the day, and we didn't play any tunes we thought weren't any good. We developed a set of deaf ears; this was one joint where the customer was never right."[120] Hot jazz tempos may have delighted the band and some dancers, but they drove other customers to fits of exasperation. "I've got to have slow music and all they give you here is fast, jazzy stuff," complained one dancer, expressing his displeasure at a band that kept dancers ricocheting around the floor.[121]

   The contemptuous attitude that Hodes and his bandmates expressed toward the majority of taxi-dancers and the approach they took suggests more than a dislike for performing in dime-a-dance settings. Concentrating on jazz rather than popular hits, Hodes played for the dime-a-dance patrons who cared about the music sufficiently to support artists like him. The fact that refusing to pander won Hodes future gigs underscores the multiple layers of activity at these nightspots and the selective portrayal of them that JPA investigators provided. Hostile, condescending, or at best indifferent to jazz music, and blind to customers who might have dropped in at a taxi-dance to hear music without paying cabaret prices, reformers missed important clues to the multiple roles that music played in the same public space. The encounter of customers of color with the meanings of whiteness and Americanness via dancing had a corollary in the encounter of listening patrons with American jazz served up by white jazz musicians. Many of the musicians, like the hostesses, were the children of immigrants producing a new definition of American culture through expressive excursions in music as well as dance.

On certain occasions, musicians seized control of the atmosphere and tempo of the dance to magically transport even the easily distracted taxi-dance crowd. At times such as these, the dingy walls of the hall would fall away, supplanted perhaps in the fantasy imaginings of the dancers with the luxurious appointments of an opulent ballroom. When the band turned to a romantic style that the crowd desired, the mood at the dance could shift dramatically, as an investigator reported: the "last offering is a slow, dreamy waltz, and seems popular with the patrons. There is a scurry for partners; laughter and conversation cease, and except for the shuffling of feet and labored measures from the orchestra, nothing disturbs the rhythmic movements of the dance . . . the saxophone croons forth its final notes, and the dance is done."[122] In certain cases, the power of music succeeded in casting a spell over the taxi-dance that rehabilitated it, albeit temporarily, in the minds of concerned outsiders.

By the mid-1920s, JPA investigators had classified taxi-dances as a lowly subgroup of dancing establishments that included cabarets, conventional dance halls, and opulent "dance palaces," such as the Aragon, the Trianon, and Rainbo Gardens, which marked the increased respectability of commercial dancing for white, bourgeois dancers.[123] In the early 1920s, under pressure from the JPA, operators of the city's largest and most popular halls formed a professional organization, the National Association of Ballroom Proprietors and Managers, to regulate their industry with supervisory assistance provided by morals activists and paid for by association members. The JPA issued certificates of approval to halls that abided by its moral codes concerning appropriate dances and other procedural rules and that supported reform initiatives such as "Correct Dance Month."[124]

Establishments that resisted JPA monitoring faced censure—and possible harassment from city officials as well. The JPA's insistence on serving as semiofficial chaperones of Chicago's commercial dance halls confounded the immigrant and ethnic operators of smaller halls, such as dime-a-dance establishments. Most dance halls and cabarets already hired "floor managers" to discourage certain kinds of dancing and to steer trouble out the door, and short-staffed businesses found the JPA's expectation that an extra monitor be put on the payroll an unreasonable burden to their livelihoods. One operator complained bitterly about "the old woman at Hull House" who arrived unbidden at his hall and interfered with business.[125]

JPA dance hall stewards developed a reputation for dispensing lectures in women's powder-rooms on subjects ranging from dance steps to underwear to the overapplication of lipstick; they even collected personal information about young dancers perceived to be morally at risk. Facing a barrage of criticism for sponsoring a Charleston contest, an exasperated operator defended dancing as a healthy way for youth to "work off this sex energy" and chastised the JPA as little more than a haven for "dirty minded voyeurs." While they could not stop the revolutionary changes in dancing and musical nightlife, the presence of investigators at public dancing establishments and a tireless publicity campaign waging war on commercial dance halls in newspapers had made a decided impact on the industry. By the mid-1920s, a number of uncooperative smaller halls had gone out of business, and the larger "dance palaces" cooperated fully with JPA suggestions for rules of conduct, conscious that their livelihood depended on getting along with these reformers.[126]

DOLLING UP
*Parodies of Whiteness, Gender, Race, and
Sex in Taxi-Dance Halls*

Urban sociologist Ernest W. Burgess and his protégé Paul Cressey, who went on to publish a book-length treatise on Chicago taxi-dancing, believed that taxi-dances offered far more to colored and Caucasian customers than female companionship.[127] These halls promised customers a fantasy payoff: the privilege of manliness and white Americanism measured through securing the attentions of attractive, youthful Caucasian women. Cressey suggested that for the racially marginalized man of color, or for the white outsider, the taxi-dance represented "a 'school' to obtain a level of ease in mainstream society."[128]

But in privileging the experience of male customers encountering white America via their female dancing companions, Cressey and his colleagues at the JPA failed to analyze female dancers with the same vigor and missed taxi-dancing's important cultural and racial work among this participatory group. In exchange for agreeing to be "not white" and relinquishing any claim to pass for "white," men of different skin hues and ethnicities could dance with "white" instructors, who bracketed their multicultural (often eastern or southern European) backgrounds under the unifying and empowering designation of "white." These women suppressed their claims to ethnic or racial difference by professionally identifying themselves as archetypal white American females of the kind popularized in Hollywood movies, fan magazines, and mass advertising. Contemporary analysts of the taxi-dance failed to examine the extent to which racial reassignments at the dance affected female dancers, too, in a way that complicated the mainstream culture's claims to the immutability of racialized dimensions of skin color and the cultural signification of whiteness as an American ideal. In short, both male and female participants at dime-a-dance halls had a cover story to tell about themselves, based on the fiction of essentialized identity that the ritual of the taxi-dance brought to a new level of visibility.[129]

Kevin Mumford has argued that because the taxi-dance catered to men of color through the commercial services of Caucasian women and excluded women of color, the institution and its female dancers colluded in the production of "sexual racism." The exploitative male desire that the taxi-dance indulged excluded women of color and treated the multicultural clientele of female dancers who worked there as undifferentiated "white" girls. Finally, female dancers expressed revulsion and racism toward their colored clients, including a desire, as one put it, to "stay white" despite the requirements of her job.[130]

But the critique that Mumford levels at taxi-dance halls underreports the social and cultural complexity of these environments, particularly the issue of female subjectivity and agency. The "sexual racism" model oversimplifies the power dynamics between employers and employees at the dance, and it mistakes the visible signifiers of the dancing environment ("white" and "black" skin) for the parodic manipulation of these supposed racial essences by the mechanics of the dance and by male and female participants.[131] Even as the taxi-dance commodified women as objects of male fantasy and desire, and fetishized their bodies as Nordic and fair-skinned, the artifice of such arrangements unintentionally opened a public space for female and male dancers to renegotiate racial and cultural conventions of identity and difference. Rather than securing institutionalized sexual racism, hegemonic male dominance and female submission, and "black" versus "white" binary thinking, taxi-dances hosted an unprecedented public performance of stylized gender and racial roles that served to undermine assumed identity essences among the dance's multiethnic participants.

Taxi-dances introduced a distinct variation on the longstanding dance reform problem of women (and now men) disappearing into the dance or passing across borders of reform-dictated "respectability," social control, and identity certitude. Unlike the gender, race, and sexual crossings common to black and tans, taxi-dances presented stylized performances of race and gender "norms" and "taboos" in which all women were American, feminine, and "white" and all men were masculine and "nonwhite."[132] Not confined to the cabaret stage, these dramas were the main event. But the temporary assignment as "white" or "nonwhite"—and the sanctioned violation of the idealized white female identity when in the arms of a "nonwhite" patron—undermined any claim these hostesses might have had to whiteness as a purified essence. By suggesting that men of color could migrate from "nonwhite" to "white" on the dance floor, these events symbolically invoked and mocked the racial power structure prevailing in American society, as did cabaret performances in the black and tans.

In making the impossible suggestion that "white" women could dance, embrace, or sleep with colored men (as hostesses were known to do) and remain "white," the taxi-dance created a parodic masquerade whose arbitrary distinctions about identity as a visible essence destabilized assumptions at the core of segregationist music recreational culture and reform discourse. The movement from ethnic female to "white" American female and ethnic male of color to "nonwhite" American male, and the subsequent staging of racial intermixture created a pageant of symbolic miscegenation that disproved, even spoofed, the very racial essences it codified as passports to American belonging. Even as taxi-dances attempted to formalize and freeze the spontaneous crossings, passings, and masquerades that characterized the black and tans, they ironically opened up possibilities for a range of subversive social and cultural representations of the fallacy of gendered and racial essentialism. Since hall rules manufactured and commodified race and gender of both males and females in polarized terms—"nonwhite" versus "white," and male versus female—and fetishized these roles still further by encouraging their symbolic violation through intimate dancing between "white" females and "nonwhite" males, taxi-dances created a complex masquerade of identity. More than symbolic miscegenation, taxi-dances transformed white American female desirability into a kind of drag performance for multicultural instructors, inadvertently drawing attention to the fallacy of such essentialized and arbitrary identity assignments, not only for the women involved, but also, by extension, for the multiethnic and Caucasian male clientele.

The managers of the halls, as well as the dancers, took pains to conform the ranks of female dancers to the physical beauty ideals saturating the nation in mass-circulation magazines, popular fiction, and Hollywood films, which promoted idealized visual and behavioral representations of sexualized, white, American women. Blondes and brunettes predominated among the pool of hostesses, and women were expected to be "slender, lithe, youthful, and vivacious." Describing the desired qualities of his staff, one hall operator explained that he tried to hire "pretty and young and well-built girls . . . that have a good reputation." Dance operators participated in a fantasy construction in that they did not want to hire "the real thing," a girl known to be sexually promiscuous; rather, they looked for employees who could play a role of desirable, yet reasonably virtuous white girlhood.[133]

Not unlike minstrel stage performers of the nineteenth century, who "blacked up" to create a mask through which to perform various racialized roles, female hostesses "dolled up" in preparation of a ritual staging of racialized desire that required a specific inventory of visible qualities including skin, hair, and clothes, as well as an attitude combining girlish enthusiasm and pluck. Paul Cressey observed the eerie way the hostesses worked to appear identical: "They wear the same style of dress, daub their faces in the same way, chew their chicle in the same manner, and, except for a few older spirits, all step about with a youthful air of confidence and enthusiasm." He regarded this aesthetic homogeneity as a sign of women's commodified status, but it may just as likely have reflected tactics of externalized homogenization to disguise the reshaping of female identities occurring beneath the mask of "white" desirability.[134]

Although the reform discourse reduced female taxi-dancers to interchangeable parts in a network of class, gender, racial, and sexual exploitation and moral collapse, the women appear to have viewed their racialization and aesthetic homogeneity as part of the parodic quality of the taxi-dance itself. Many of the dancing girls adopted pseudonyms befitting Hollywood starlets. While pseudonyms protected dancers' privacy, they also signaled a winking awareness of the coyly self-conscious staging of gender and racial ideals. Christina Stranski Americanized herself on the dance floor as "DeLoris Glenn." In an inversion of the white versus nonwhite symbolism of the dance, Alice Borden appropriated a touch of Far Eastern sexualized exoticism and color to become "Wanda Wang."[135] Creating aliases did more than protect these women from unwelcome, even dangerous advances from clients, or from the embarrassment of bumping into the wrong person on the job. The aliases reflected a self-conscious putting on of a stylized white, American femininity, whose hegemonic and racialized attributes in the dominant culture coexisted with the subversive potential of their own artifice and the camouflage they provided in more individualized negotiation with men on the dance floor.

The circumscribed racial roles that dime-a-dance halls offered male and female dancers did not necessarily conform to the self-perceptions of participants, whose lives raised provocative questions about the fixity of identity, and exposed the fallacies of conjuring a "white" versus a "nonwhite" world. Beneath the play of surfaces, hostesses maneuvered themselves into a variety of relationships with men of color that were neither strictly transactional nor strictly exploitative for either party. The identity ruses of the taxi-dance paradoxically sanctioned intercultural contact, self-examination, and growth that sometimes challenged rather than secured the institutionalization of racism and sexism in urban public recreation. Men of color might not become "white" by dancing with these hostesses, but the latter's migration from "white" to "nonwhite" by dancing with these men suggested the possibility of a significant reorientation of race in the public arena.

Even as taxi-dances manipulated the signs of Jim Crow hegemony and convinced reformers that hostesses were being exploited, female and male dancers described a range of uses and gratifications available to participants at the taxi-dance that defied reduction to power exerted through a single channel of gender or race. Working and dancing at these halls, the hostesses and their clients found opportunities to challenge and sometimes reconstitute the socially constructed nature of race and gender, to calculate and recalculate the costs and benefits of associating with, or performing as, "white" or "nonwhite" partners, and to discover commonalities and differences within the dominant identity constraints of the era.[136]

To be sure, the power to manage such interrogations within the confines of the taxi-dance varied among participants on the basis of a range of personal attributes. Wealthier, educated Filipino men could meet women at the taxi-dance and spirit them off to black and tans where the "nonwhite" versus "white" rules of the taxi-dance did not exist and the animosities from poorer patrons at the taxi-dance would not be felt. By contrast, poorer Chinese, Greek, or Mexican laborers or, for that matter, poorer and undereducated Caucasian men lacked the wherewithal to exert a range of masculine power and privilege associated with greater financial resources. These imbalances transcended racial identification even as they got reframed as a racial problem, particularly when Caucasian men complained about the success of urbane Filipino men with the dance hostesses.[137]

BEYOND "GIDDY YOUNG GIRLS"
Toeing the Color Line

The occupational masks of female whiteness shielded the complex internal processes of self-fashioning among ethnic hostesses encountering men of color in public and redefining themselves as women, "whites," and Americans. Despite what many investigators and moral critics claimed, female dancers were not reducible as a group to "giddy young girls," or helpless victims of male desire, or even virulent racists who coldly broke the hearts and emptied the wallets of their lovelorn partners. Just as their male clients of color gained enormous satisfaction from visits to the dance and the dates that sometimes resulted, female taxi-dancers found their work fulfilling on a number of levels. The pay exceeded by two to three times what other jobs offered, and many dancers enjoyed meeting a wide variety of men. Women dated their clients on occasion, but reformers concluded after a five-year study that no pattern of prostitution emerged from multiple investigations into the subject.[138]

The female residents of the furnished room districts, many of whom spent time at cabarets or worked in dance halls, inhabited what sociologist Walter Reckless termed a "new women's world," defined in part by sexual and occupational options not available a few years earlier. "She is not necessarily doomed to downfall and to the under-world, like many of her sisters who a generation earlier were penetrating the life in the downtown districts of American cities," Reckless observed. "It is through the very participation of the present-day woman in this larger and freer world of the city that sex vice is becoming feminized and refined, and is even tending to lose much of the character of vice."[139] Though Reckless, like Harvey Zorbaugh before him, questioned whether the relative emancipation of women's sexuality represented a social good, he identified what made taxi-dancing enticing for many women. Cabarets offered women a space in which to express their sexual identities more freely. Taxi-dancing offered some women a level of control over their intimate contact with men, particularly men of color, that mainstream society failed to permit.[140]

Young females raised in the patriarchal, often racist milieu of insular industrial neighborhoods could expect criticism or worse for daring to associate with men different from themselves, especially those of different classes, religions, ethnic groups, or races. But taxi-dancers enjoyed privileged access to a broad swath of the male population of Chicago, with no fear of permanent entanglements and minimal self-identification as prostitutes or fallen women. Many relished this opportunity. "When I first went out on the West Side I was very curious about the whole thing out there," reported one taxi-dancer. "Everything seemed thrilling and exciting. I felt as though I was doing something very risky and dangerous."[141] Though the occupational hazards of taxi-dancing included harassment and tedium, many dancers appreciated the freedom to spend time with men not of their immediate social orbit and to earn very competitive wages while doing so.[142]

Caucasian men and men of color purchased women's time in an act of class, gender, and racialized power, but female dancers used the rules of the game to personal advantage, too. As a young female investigator noted of the taxi-dance, "Removed from the restraint of family life, free from detection by any one who knows her actual circumstances, she is free to fashion her own world of make-believe in which she is queen for a day."[143] While economic necessity most often drove women to work in these halls, the power to put on disguises enabled women working in the halls to rethink their relationships with men, with the community, and with their own cultural commitments in a variety of ways, as exemplified by flirting with an older "sugar daddy" or by dating or sleeping with a man from a different or "inappropriate" background.

More problematically, however, as Cressey noticed, the taxi-dancer's power to "fashion her own world" often included drawing on the prevailing racial stereotypes and animosities of the era, which would occur in conversation with investigators. He found that even as female dancers defied public conventions of gender and sexual propriety, they expressed racist sentiments toward their customers. Some women who used ethnic slurs to characterize their Filipino and Chinese customers avoided dancing with them to the extent that the hall allowed, or they vowed, despite their contact with men of color on the dance floor, to "stay white." Expressing the racial gamesman-ship of the taxi-dance, employees described their Filipino clients as "fish" because they tended to have money, were generous, and were easy to reel in and exploit. Such dancers contributed to an oppressive peer pressure by belittling their coworkers who dated colored men.[144]

While scholars like Mumford extrapolate from the statements of antagonism elicited by white male investigators that there may have been a universal ambition among female dancers to keep colored men subordinated, Cressey's published investigation confounds this conclusion. Many female dancers expressed ambivalence toward or actively resisted dominant racial codes within the institutionalized dominion of the taxi-dance, as well as outside it. While complicit in the profits of racist institutional segregation, female taxi-dancers used the particular gendered, racial, and sexual status that their jobs af-forded in ways that often complicated, and sometimes challenged, existing stereotypes. Through public and private negotiations with men of color while dancing or on dates, many women created spaces with which to fight institutionalized racism and redefine themselves and their circle of social and cultural contacts, thus defying binarisms of "white" versus "colored" and "American" versus "foreign."

While some women clearly disliked certain clients because of their race, others befriended, dated, loved, slept with, and even mar-ried the men of color whom they met on the dance floor. "I thought they were movie actors or something. They were always well dressed and treated me nicely; I fell for them hard," recalled one dancer of her Filipino partners.[145] Women noted that, unlike "white" clients, the Filipinos had better manners and had more money for gifts, dance tickets, and dates to other dance halls, particularly the hot jazz spots on the South Side. While one partner might be dismissed as a meaningless "fish," another would receive free dances when the boss was looking the other way. As individuals, female dancers tendered minor and sometimes major gestures of friendship and empathy to men they favored in the crowd. Such gestures marked, however provisionally and ironically, a basis for overcoming the institutionalized racism and sexism that shaped their initial contacts. Through the prism of race female dancers who dated men of color sometimes discovered that their outsider status meant that their dates treated them in a less familiar manner than men they would ordinarily encounter closer to home. For a Caucasian woman from a poor industrial neighborhood, being treated like a "queen," whether by another Caucasian or by a man of color, made such crossings gratifying, even if an element of greed entered in as well.[146]

These alternative and oppositional practices to toeing the color line operated within the professional and social imperative to "stay white" that encouraged an occupational ethos of belittling clients of color and often consigning them to racialized categories. Hostesses noted the professional and personal risks to reputation associated with moving beyond a staged rapprochement with a man of color and electing to spend time with him outside the hall. One dancer explained defensively that "[m]ost of the white fellows won't dance with me if they learn I go out all the time with the Flips. . . . I've got to dance with some good-looking white fellows once in a while so the Filipinos will keep on dancing with me." Even as the statement underscores the way that race could be manipulated by a popular dancer, it also reveals the substantial risks that dancers took to be with men of their own choosing in defiance of social convention.[147]

THE CUSTOMER IS ALWAYS WHITE
Exercising Male Power

Men who frequented the taxi-dances used the ritual of dancing with caucasian partners to mediate the social expectations of the ethnic industrial neighborhoods in which they lived and their personal fantasies about the meaning of American freedom. In addition to the privilege that their maleness accorded them, some sought companionship with the stylized "American" dancers out of an explicit desire to distance themselves from their own neighborhood enclaves. When asked if he patronized dances sponsored by neighborhood organizations in addition to taxi-dances, one man replied emphatically: "No! I don't want to go to no Polish dances. There's too many old people there. You can't have a good time. I don't like the way they dance, some of them. They dance a lot better at these halls!"[148] The lure of the "beer permit" dance, the personal autonomy of the cabaret, and the fantasy of the dime-a-dance hall offered compelling attractions to a restless generation of young Chicagoans.

A self-identified Italian man remarked that he danced at taxi-dance halls because he hoped someday to marry an "American" girl: "I don't wanta go to old-country parties. There's an Italian dance down to Grand Avenue next Saturday; they want me to go. But I won't. I wanta go to American dances. I'm American, not Italian, and I don't wanta go where I gotta act old-country ways."[149] For these men, going to a taxi-dance implied more than a fantasy with racialized overtones. They visited taxi-dances as a relief from the pressures of ethnocentric acculturation and in hopes of creating a different self-identification. To such men, becoming "American" included finding an expressive space of pleasure unconstrained by the pressures of tradition and external modes of control.

Certain men responded to the different expectations the taxi-dance women had of them, versus those of the women within their everyday social groupings. One patron described a casual affair between himself and a dancer: "I was merely 'playing around' with the taxi-dancers; they knew it and I knew it, but nevertheless they were just what I needed. They educated me."[150] The implications of such a liaison particularly for the female within the conservative moral sphere of the neighborhood would be utterly different. At least according to this man, the taxi-dance allowed patrons and workers to create, in his words, an "open and frank" milieu in which talk of consensual premarital sexual activity could occur between partners who trusted that the other knew the rules of the game and hence neither would feel manipulated if a relationship failed.

A Mexican customer of bourgeois background admitted that he patronized the taxi-dance as a temporary reprieve from the pressures of his ambitious family: "My father has planned for me to marry a rich Mexican girl. She's a nice girl. She is in a convent school now. But I cannot be free with her like I can with these girls. . . . Anyway I like the blue eyes." Freedom came in a variety of forms at the taxi-dance:

sexual freedom, freedom to cross the color line, freedom to talk, act, or dance like an American. Regardless of which type of freedom he might enjoy there, the Mexican planned to stay respectable and "colored," at least outside the hall, by marrying the chaste Mexican girl of his father's wishes.[151]

"A YOUNG WHITE AMERICAN WHO LIKES CLEAN DANCING"
Commercial Recreation and Status Inversion

The symbolic consumption of white womanhood and the staged rites of miscegenation at the taxi-dance, however parodic, troubled many observers who objected to multiracial taxi-dancing as an example of the democratic excesses JPA moralists—and musical progressives more generally—had historically lobbied against. The owner of the Chicago Dancing Academy, a closed hall on State Street that did not welcome customers of color remarked: "Our patrons are high-class people. They won't go to the same places where these Chinks or whatever they are go. Now no really white guy is willing to go in and dance with these Chinks or Japs or whatnot. He's got to have a little nigger in him to be willing to do that."[152] The insults reflected the attitude of a competitive businessman as well as a self-conscious white male with anxieties about the destabilizing impact of a multicultural, multiracial civic recreation culture. The public possibility of status inversions benefiting men of color who danced with white women implied that white men might find themselves losing ground should they become too familiar with men of color.

The assimilation fantasy of men of color dancing with white American women rocked the confidence of some self-identified white American men. The success of taxi-dances raised the question of whether the ranks of white male power and privilege remained secure in the new commercial amusement culture. The powers of alchemy that taxi-dances advertised suggested that racial privileges were mutable. A female taxi-dancer choosing a dark-skinned male partner over a fair-skinned competitor raised the historical fear long circulated in American culture and folklore of the essentialized white race losing its male power and privilege to racial interlopers. It evoked the unspeakable prospect of white women rejecting the southern role of ravished "victims" of African American sexual advance for an active role in seeking pleasure from men of color and denying the implicit superiority of white men.[153]

Just as gangs fought for control of public space and patrolled racial boundaries in the process, gangs associated with taxi-dancing clashed violently with one another on occasion, sometimes over the women who worked there. Newspapers reported fights at dance halls between ethnic gangs, pitting Italian and Polish youths against Filipinos. Unlike the racialized turf battles that were historically a part of Chicago street culture, however, these skirmishes and the economic and cultural animosities embedded within them were attributed by observers to interpersonal dynamics on the dance floor. Referring to the basis for one fight, a Filipino explained: "They get after the Pinoys because they can get dates with some of the girls and the [whites] can't." The sight of relatively well-off men of color spiriting ethnic women off to black-and-tan cabarets or on expensive dates stirred deep class, cultural, and racial tension.[154]

The implications of the racialized economy of the dime-a-dance hall impacted different populations in different ways and revealed the racialization of cultural and gender differences dividing whites from patrons of color. Following a fight in 1926 between Filipinos and an Italian ethnic gang that produced seven disorderly conduct charges, a white combatant explained: "These damned chinks are taking all the best girls at these dancing schools . . . They go out in taxis and take them all over town. Even buy them fur coats and don't even make them come across—just chase around after them and try to get them to marry them. No American guy is going to spend his money on them unless they come across. They're spoiling the game for the American fellow that wants these girls, and that's why we're after them."[155] The symbolic loss of neighborhood girls to the free market where wealth sometimes trumped whiteness, and where marriage proposals (even if directed in jest) supplanted efforts by other patrons to make female dancers "come across" sexually, reflected the cultural entanglements and differing expectations of male dime-a-dance patrons. One man expressed his moral indignation directly to the JPA. "A friend of mine told me you and your organization are responsible for the conduct of the taxi-dance halls," he began. "Why isn't something done about young girls working in such places? In two of these joints on North Clark Street a white man cant [*sic*] even get cortious [*sic*] treatment, they cater to Spicks. I have seen one young blond girl leave the one on 443 N. Clark St. with two greasy Spicks and go to a rooming house on Chicago Ave. . . . Hoping you will do something, I remain a young white American that likes clean dancing."[156] Blaming racial interlopers for the inability of a white male to get "cortious treatment," the writer sounded a call for a renewed effort to enshrine virtue, whiteness, and patriotism in Chicago's civic recreational culture. While the JPA had long shared a belief in the general principles the man extolled, trends in urban public recreation exposed the insufficiency of these aspirations as dance subcultures fought to open the civic realm to a wider variety of voices and value systems.

By the early 1930s, morals activists had largely slaked their thirst for investigating commercial dancing in Chicago. The enterprise of "knowing the dancer from the dance" had produced extraordinary data relating to commercial dancing, but it had neither resolved Yeats's paradox nor explicated or contained the mysterious allure of the dance to Chicago youth. In the process, however, JPA investigators had successfully helped to elevate the reputation of commercial dancing as a mainstream recreational activity. Their agitation helped embolden the city to close or clean up a number of disreputable halls, some of which openly supported vice, and to prosecute criminal elements using dance halls as covers for illegal activity during Prohibition. The JPA and other morals organizations now freely conceded the point that despite commercial dancing's energetic resistance to bourgeois standards it did not always shelter or promote vice, even at the level of the dime-a-dance halls.[157]

Looking back on several Sisyphean decades of trying to control the rebellious exuberance of public dancing, Jessie Binford gave indications of having begun to accept what morals activists could and could not know about dancers at the dance. The panic of the early 1920s over interracial jazz cabarets and multiracial taxi-dances had passed into memory. Black Belt dance establishments such as the Grand Terrace, which had once worried reformers during the hot jazz era of the 1920s, seemed benign a decade later. By the early 1930s, an investigator noted perfunctorily that "the crowd was orderly and there was no mixing of the races in couples on the dance floor."[158] With white and African American swing acceptable fodder for the commercial mainstream, regulators felt little compunction to suspect the city's commercial dance halls of great crimes against public morality, provided segregation within couples prevailed.

Even the scandalous taxi-dance seemed a quaint artifact of urban Americana rather than a site of moral outrage. In 1930 America's sweetheart, Ruth Etting, notched a popular hit with a recording of "Ten Cents a Dance," a song about a female taxi-dancer written by Lorenz Hart and Richard Rodgers. What lyricist Hart mischievously called the "queer romance" of the dime-a-dance hall, with its "butchers, and barbers, and rats from the harbors," struck Jessie Binford rather differently, however. According to her, the taxi-dance had served a constituency excluded from mainstream civic recreational reform activity. "[The taxi-dance] met a real demand and provided recreational opportunities for certain men who did not know girls, for older men and for certain racial groups to whom the doors of other centers were closed."[159] Of course, Binford could afford to be somewhat charitable on the subject. In the late 1920s, the JPA had sponsored a dancing school ordinance stripping the dime-a-dance halls of their raffish aura by imposing strict standards of conduct, which may have hastened their decline. A few taxi-dances continued to operate in the early 1930s, but a public recreation study suggested that wider social acceptance of diverse and informal social gatherings of men and women in public areas made it less necessary for the ritualized meeting ground of the taxi-dance. Jim Crow segregation, however, continued to divide whites from people of color, excluding African Americans from many recreational institutions where such social mixing occurred.[160]

Between 1904 and 1933 the "beer permit" dance, the cabaret, the black and tan, and the taxi-dance collectively shattered the illusory claims of musical progressives to being able to control music as a democratic activity. These forms reflected the resistance of dancers to morally minded civic regulators. The jazz craze also demonstrated the newfound power of the commercial amusement culture and the forces of new music and youthful desire to redraw the boundaries of public social interaction, identity, and expression in American society well beyond the democratic imaginings of music reformers. Vice versus virtue, ethnic versus "American," white versus black, and male versus female were only some of the oppositions that dancing in public threw into question. The subcultures that coalesced around these dancing environments stretched the limits of acceptable forms of public culture. By the end of the Jazz Age, social dancing in commercial establishments among strangers of different backgrounds had grown increasingly routinized, even sanitized, as national commercial interests began to capitalize on the music that some investigators had perceived as destructive to the morals of American youth.[161]

Radio proved to be one of the forces driving public exposure to jazz and swing in the 1920s and 1930s. Broadcasting furthered the mass acceptance of commercial dancing and public amusements that had previously existed outside the dominant culture's frame of acceptable behavior. In the early 1920s, at many of the large commercial dance halls around the city crawling with JPA investigators, microphones began to appear on bandstands, not to amplify the performers, but to carry their music to unseen listeners throughout Chicago and the nation. The resulting radio boom drew widespread attention to a new and unclaimed public space—the invisible airwaves. The local and national possibilities of radio to express and influence civic ideals and represent Chicago to itself and others drew independent and commercial broadcasters, reform interests, and listeners into groups struggling to shape urban public culture via music radio.

SEVEN

SOUNDS OF WHITENESS
URBAN MUSICAL SUBCULTURES, RACE, AND THE
PUBLIC INTEREST ON CHICAGO AIRWAVES, 1921–1935

In Chicago during the 1920s, local radio stations, many without educational, chain, or network affiliation, shaped a vibrant on-air musical world.[1] They used music, comedy, drama, and cultural affairs programs to entertain, inform, and serve communities of ethnic, immigrant, middle-class, and working-class listeners.[2] More than a "radio imaginary" or an "imagined community," local broadcasting promoted face-to-face community life among its audiences, whether encouraging listeners to participate in programs as talent or guests, support ethnic institutions and causes, attend church, vote for local politicians, patronize local businesses, support organized labor, or even cut loose at neighborhood dance halls.[3] Broadcasting altered the nature of public culture because it linked public and private spaces into new on-air configurations that offered listeners fresh ways of mentally and physically locating themselves and others within the neighborhood, the metropolis, and the nation itself.[4] Most of all, local broadcasting resounded with music of many descriptions. It offered an exciting domain for various urban interests to shape and reform Chicago's civic life via the airwaves.

Many issues of interest to musical progressives, such as democratic expression, civic uplift, and recreational reform migrated to the local airwaves. Produced by a range of neighborhood, institutional, and commercial interests, local radio circulated a broad range of musical styles and produced musical "publics" of listeners, who used music, in part, to signal and elaborate identity both within groups organized by class, ethnicity, gender, race, or sexuality and across these socially constructed divides. Those with access to the airwaves remapped urban social and cultural geography and in so doing entered into a greater struggle for a voice within an urban public culture in which aural representations of race, ethnicity, and American identity linked and divided listeners and citizens.[5]

The early history of music radio and the struggle to shape it as a tool of reform did not involve the customary progressive activists described in prior chapters. Evidence suggests that perfunctory discussions occurred among park commissioners and Hull House and settlement leaders about radio broadcasting and civic outreach, but no known steps were taken to seek licenses or to sponsor self-produced permanent programs.[6] Jane Addams and reform activists for the Juvenile Protective Association (JPA) delivered radio addresses on various stations, and settlement music groups appeared on Chicago stations from time to time, but none of these people and institutions made a major effort to develop the medium for themselves. At least one Chicago public school, Lane Tech, held a license in the early 1920s and provided technical training to youths on the Northwest Side, and Chicago's flamboyant mayor, William H. Thompson obtained a radio license with the call letters WHT, but the station proved short-lived.[7]

Individuals and institutions representing a range of economic, social, and cultural interests used music radio to create Chicago's electronic public culture. The activist base went far beyond the newspapers (*Chicago Tribune, Chicago Daily News, Chicago American, Chicago Herald-Examiner*) and corporations (Sears Roebuck, Westinghouse) historically credited with shaping the medium. Individuals, small businesses, churches, and colleges all operated important stations beginning in the early 1920s. The significance of their efforts prior to the rise of national networks derives in part from the manner in which they used music in the service of civic and cultural aims. No less significant is the way that the cultural politics of radio influenced subsequent struggles involving powerful commercial network interests, while federal officials were seeking to rationalize the medium in the late 1920s and early 1930s.

For the diverse groups who obtained licenses, equipment, or slots on the air and for those who listened, local radio embodied obvious and less-obvious forms of power and privilege. The public nature of the airwaves—where anyone or everyone might be invisibly present and listening—conferred special status to broadcasters and listeners. The airwaves became a neighborhood as well as a metropolitan stage, and many listeners tuning in to independent stations swelled with pride at hearing music and cultural programs that acknowledged their particular languages, histories, and cultural backgrounds for both the designated group and the larger audience to hear. Self-generated broadcasts offered the possibility of a respite from the subordinate status many residents of Chicago's industrial neighborhoods experienced in other urban public settings, such as streets or parks, whether on account of language, dress, mannerism, class, or skin color.[8]

But while local music radio helped to empower many community groups and to strengthen ethnic institutions, it excluded and marginalized some potential shapers of electronic public culture, most notably African Americans. People of German, Lithuanian, Polish, and Swedish extraction and a host of others produced programs of their own in multiple languages and myriad musical styles, but African Americans were typically barred from the broadcast control room. Even as local radio brought the artistry and excitement of African American jazz and blues to the mainstream via live-remote broadcasts from black-and-tan clubs and via so-called race records, self-generated representations were relatively few. White studio bands and orchestras garnered the lion's share of local on-air broadcast opportunities.

Complicating the racialized situation further, minstrel dialect and musical entertainment featuring whites in blackface were a staple of 1920s broadcasting. These hackneyed portrayals did little to correct the skewed public perception of African Americans, whose widespread exclusion from rituals of civic community formation continued on the air. These aural representations of "blackness" produced a cultural formation—a sound of whiteness—that bound ethnic listeners together as racialized whites consuming a racialized Other. Simultaneously present within and absent from local radio, African Americans were unable to control their radio representations to the extent that others could. Their physical absence at the radio controls amplified the pattern of physical and cultural exclusion from the musical manufacture of "Americans" sponsored by musical progressives at field house park concerts, at Hull House, at community sings during World War I, and at many urban dance halls.

Chicago broadcasters took an early lead relative to the rest of the country in obtaining licenses and developing the potential of the medium. Westinghouse station KYW expressed the uplift hopes of some early broadcasters when it produced the first live concert broadcast in the city on November 11, 1921, featuring performers from the Chicago Civic Opera Company at the Auditorium Theater. Midway through the 1921–22 opera season, which KYW faithfully carried, a reporter pointed triumphantly to a tangible effect of Chicago opera broadcasts on the urban masses. He observed that "[c]rude homemade aerials are on one roof in ten along all the miles of bleak streets in the cities industrial zones."[9] Whatever the motivating factor, local interest in radio grew rapidly thereafter. One listener survey involving three local stations conducted by the federal Office of the Supervisor of Radio in Chicago over a ten-day span in November 1923 produced 263,410 pieces of mail.[10] Sales of radio parts and inexpensive radio kits also soared in the early 1920s. National publications commented on the many radio clubs springing up at public high schools across the nation, including several in Chicago.[11]

The local radio culture that bloomed in Chicago came under federal regulatory pressure by decade's end due to a combination of factors, including the uneven development of radio across the nation and the extraordinary profits that radio now represented to network interests. In response to industry concerns about license regulation, Congress established the Federal Radio Commission (FRC) in 1927, which later became the Federal Communications Commission (FCC). The FRC was a bipartisan group assigned by the government to oversee radio's development. In an effort to rationalize broadcasting, reduce congestion and static interference on the dial, and more equitably distribute licenses, the FRC issued General Order No. 40 in the fall of 1928. The order challenged the basis on which dozens of independent stations existed. Concerns associated with bandwidth overcrowding, a disproportionate clustering of stations in Chicago, and the desire to distribute "clear channel" frequencies to established commercial providers encouraged the FRC to act. The commission reassigned frequencies, cut power allotments to reduce interference, doubled up independents on the same frequency (thus curtailing the hours that stations could broadcast), and in some cases simply refused to renew licenses. New regulations forced stations to go head-to-head to defend or expand their time and power allotments with others sharing their frequencies, whether within or outside Chicago.

To survive under the new competitive regime, stations were required to demonstrate that their programs served the "public interest, convenience, or necessity."[12] Local broadcasters took to the airwaves to rally listener support, organize petition drives, and stimulate letter-writing campaigns to the FRC. Competing with well-funded and politically connected network lobbyists, officials of independent stations presented witnesses, affidavits, petitions, hundreds of letters, and other evidence to document their services to their constituents. These operators portrayed their stations as producing an electronic public culture of pluralism in which ethnic, local, and "American" themes coexisted, often citing their music programs to illustrate the point. Network representatives dismissed this ideal-type and argued for a market-driven model in which heavily capitalized, centralized producers should supply a national market with programs created for mass appeal. By 1935, when the regulatory dust had settled, 20 percent of previously operating stations across the country had shut down, and commercial networks dominated the airwaves. The model of many independent producers constituting the "American" sound of broadcasting had been replaced by a commercial network determination of that sound and the parties able to constitute it.[13]

Robert McChesney argues that the FRC failed to serve as an impartial arbiter and aided, instead, the networks at the dramatic cost of independent stations and voices. The technical imperative for closing down stations in the late 1920s in order to improve radio reception masked a larger project to prepare the nation for coast-to-coast networks by uprooting as many independent stations from the airwaves as was politically feasible. In what amounted to a fait accompli, network lobbyists and eager regulators ensured that a broad public debate about the future of this important public resource would not occur until after the networks had seized control and occupied the airwaves.[14]

But what of the local stations themselves? Who operated them, who listened, and what cultural work did they perform during the 1920s and the early 1930s? This chapter argues that local, independent radio operators—the architects of what Erik Barnouw described with mild condescension as a "Tower in Babel"—were far more significant in establishing the social and cultural identity of radio than has been previously acknowledged.[15] Moreover, their blueprint for broadcasting contained cultural features salient to understanding American life in the 1920s, particularly the role of music in the public arena as a means of expressing cultural identity and the critical role of radio in expanding debates over musical progressivism.

Using a case study approach, this chapter situates independent radio broadcasting and listening within a struggle among urban ethnic, immigrant, and middle- and working-class Americans in the 1920s to claim urban space, shape public culture, and define the contested terms of ethnic difference, racial differentiation, and Americanism. It analyzes the words and actions of independent broadcasters and their listeners, paying careful attention to their urban social and cultural milieu. It examines the tactics that broadcasters and their loyal listeners used to create and later to defend their radio world when network interests and regulators impinged on it. It also shows how the silences, exclusions, and overlapping interests of local broadcasters, network interests, and federal regulators effectively sanctioned white privilege at the expense of the city's African Americans.

In the 1920s and early 1930s, local broadcasters controlled the nature of ethnic representation on air as a means of counterbalancing the assimilating pressures of commercial advertising, Americanization campaigns, and the homogeneous fare of "chain" and early network broadcasts. Access to local radio constituted a zone of expanded white racial privilege. Western and eastern European immigrant and ethnic groups and institutions secured broadcast licenses or program access via brokered airwaves (using those stations whose owners sold slots on a per-program basis). But African Americans faced total exclusion from the Chicago airwaves, with the exception of one program, *The Negro Hour*, which was heard on station WSBC, but not until 1928.[16]

Within their negotiation of the terms of ethnic identity and Americanism, local broadcasters produced and reproduced boundaries of inclusion and exclusion that mobilized an underlying racial logic in which ethnic musical publics found affiliation as "whites" in a manner that marginalized and excluded African Americans as non-whites.[17] In the competition among stations at the end of the 1920s to win favor from the FRC, network interests appealed to the entertainment and information needs of a nation implicitly understood to be white and American. Local radio operators championed a competing model of localism, whose electronic public culture consisted of the voices and musics of dozens of different ethnic groups, also implicitly understood to be white and American, as well as ethnic. The two sides of the "debate" over the future of broadcasting were making proprietary claims to an electronic public culture that were dramatically opposed. But both sides shared an unspoken agreement that a racialized white identity should continue to serve as the basis of American broadcasting.[18]

As George Lipsitz observes, "Whiteness is everywhere in American culture, but it is very hard to see." It is no easier to hear. But over the course of the 1920s, Chicago radio produced the sound of whiteness.[19] The sound included the paradoxical presence and absence of African Americans and music of their own making. Local radio was distinguished by the virtual exclusion of African American broadcasters. The program environment included occasional live performances by African American musicians and phonograph recordings by these artists. But the vast majority of programs featured white musicians, who frequently performed facsimiles of "blackness" in the form of popular syncopated dance music, or white entertainers presenting blackface minstrel routines. Local ethnic groups often produced radio programs as part of a self-conscious project to structure a radio family or on-air community. They used combinations of folk music, concert music, and popular jazz that fostered interethnic connections and a mediated Americanism for ethnic, immigrant, and working-class listeners, while bracketing African Americans as racialized outsiders.

Studies of race and broadcasting generally focus on issues of African American representation and cultural production beginning with the network era of the 1930s and after. Several works have explored how announcers practiced "racial ventriloquy" and "passing" (whether to sound white or black) as well as the increasingly successful attempts by African Americans to control and produce their own programs and representations.[20] Shifting the focus to the 1920s offers an alternative perspective on the culture of broadcasting and race. It focuses on processes of racial formation prior to the rise of the networks by highlighting the perspectives and actions of early broadcasters and their listeners in a local historical context. It reveals the manner in which early Chicago radio produced a hegemonic racial formation—a sound of whiteness—relying on the presence *and* absence of African Americans and musical and cultural forms of expression to sustain itself.

Many social and cultural historians are already aware of local radio's role in promoting solidarity in Chicago. In her compelling study of the interwar Chicago labor force, Lizabeth Cohen argues: "Radio, probably more than any other medium, contributed to an increasingly universal working-class experience." Drawing extensively on the records of WCFL, the Chicago Federation of Labor radio station, Cohen demonstrates that by the early 1930s workers were accustomed to consuming both independent and network programs.[21] Radio, she avers, "neither enticed people away from habitual family and community circles nor undermined existing identities, as for example Polish, Catholic, and working-class."[22] Listening to local and chain broadcasts helped ethnic and immigrant radio listeners consolidate common interests across cultural divides. Radio helped to surmount ethnic parochialism and link workers in support of FDR and the Congress of Industrial Organizations (CIO). But the implications of Cohen's innovative argument about radio's powers to spur identity and class formation raises new questions about radio's representation of immigrant, ethnic, and working-class community characteristics alongside "American" ones in light of the virtual exclusion of African Americans from participation in this vital public medium.[23] New evidence reveals that while independent radio afforded immigrant, ethnic, and working-class residents new ways to declare group allegiances and mediate their differences via music, it extended the problematic sounds of whiteness accompanying musical reforms in ceremonial and field house parks, settlements, and dance halls. Racial anxieties proved integral to the cultural and political work of broadcasting in its first decade of existence and established a precedent for the way that federal regulators subsequently engaged the medium for purposes of enhancing national connectivity.

AURAL EXCURSIONS ACROSS THE COLOR LINE
Themes of Presence and Absence

Eager to woo listeners and to control costs associated with maintaining large staffs and in-house musical talent, local station operators tapped the city's bustling musical nightlife culture. Live-remote concert broadcasts, known as "pick ups," became the lifeblood of early radio and helped to fill late-night slots. By the mid-1920s, dedicated telephone lines snaked across the city from radio stations to nightclubs, hotels, and dance halls. On any given night, listeners could enjoy syncopated jazz and orchestral dance music via pick-ups from the liveliest Loop and North Side hotel ballrooms, palm courts, and West, North, and South Side music theaters and dance halls.[24] Spot advertising was uncommon, but cross-promotional opportunities abounded as stations in need of programming to fill broadcast slots cooperated with dance and concert halls seeking publicity courtesy of the hot new medium of radio. Musicians garnered wider audiences and the chance to recruit customers for future engagements. The greatest beneficiaries, however, were radio listeners of varied backgrounds who now had live access to the vibrant sounds of Chicago nightlife from the factories and businesses where they worked, the privacy of apartments and homes, or the protected conviviality of the ethnic center, clubhouse, or favored gathering place (store, tavern), where radio listening commonly occurred.[25]

Local radio remapped the symbolic geographies of class and race by bringing African American music to a wider audience. Broadcasting afforded African American jazz and blues artists a new level of exposure, bringing aspects of a culture on the margins to the attention of the mainstream.[26] In addition to chain programs from New York and other cities, listeners heard from a variety of local settings. Earl "Fatha" Hines was a radio fixture from the Grand Terrace on the South Side. WCFL carried African American acts from the Savoy. WBBM won listeners by spinning the latest jazz phonograph releases. WGN listeners heard local luminaries Dave Peyton, blues queen Albertine ("Indigo") Pickens, and soprano Ernestine Lyle. WIBO carried African American superstars such as Duke Ellington live from the Oriental Theater.[27] WMAQ carried performances from the Trianon, an interracial jazz ballroom on the South Side, and the Aragon Ballroom, catering to white youths on the North Side. WOK carried live performances from all over Chicago, including the Trianon, the Aragon, and the Woodlawn Theater, where white dance bands such as the Wayne King and Jean Goldkette orchestras performed for a white, middle-class clientele.[28]

In a substantive way, radio enlarged the possibilities of a multiethnic, multiracial public culture by popularizing the sounds of African American musicians. Radio undermined the power of morals

Dave Peyton's "Grand" Band. Photograph by Gerise;
Chicago Historical Society, ICHi-35630.

police to distort public discourse about popular music now that listeners could easily sample African American jazz for themselves.
Live broadcasts coming from jazz halls permitted listeners to arrive at
their own firsthand conclusions about the music's merit and pleasures, if not about the black bodies generating it. Along with phonograph records, radio inspired face-to-face participation by inducing
listeners to physically traverse the remapped metropolitan landscape
and attend performances for themselves.[29]

In ways that had not been possible before in real time, radio
enabled listeners to aurally "visit" parts of the city they had never
seen, or never would see, at minimal risk to their persons or reputations. Listeners could explore forbidden urban spaces and sounds
and skirt fears associated with the nocturnal city. Radio supplied aural
access to urban musical spaces without the associated costs or unpredictable prospects of an encounter with strangers that might occur at
the actual venue. Within whatever negotiations occurred around con-

trol of the set itself, radio listening provided a measure of anonymity. One listened and moved on with a twirl of a knob, without concern about any permanent record of one's participatory "presence."

Like the phonograph, but with the excitement of an immediacy never encountered before, radio brought new sounds associated with the glittery, uninhibited world of the jazz cabaret and the dance hall into the tranquil interior spaces of the domestic sphere, whether the private living room or the middle-class parlor.[30] Music radio helped to domesticate and to safely allow excursions through the symbolic and sonic "wilds" of African American music, blunting its forbidden or unseemly connotations, and sanitizing the often gritty social contexts from which the music emanated.

Such broadcasts constituted a sound of whiteness in that they afforded a privileged aural form of spectatorship for listeners who tuned in to the sounds of African American music from the Black Belt while remaining disconnected from the economic, social, and cultural relationships—many of them spatialized—within which the music mattered and signified to its makers. Even as early radio made the aesthetic and rhythmic pleasures of blues and jazz available to a broader listening public, it did so within a literal and figurative framework of uneven distribution of content and control. Radio lowered the barriers preventing ethnic white listeners from sampling forms of African American music, while reinforcing the barriers of power and privilege used to divide whites from blacks on the air and in the city at large. Even as it collapsed urban space and changed the symbolic status of African Americans as cultural producers, broadcasting disconnected aural representations of African American musical culture from a material base and deflected the issue of the absence of African American broadcasters able to speak for themselves.[31]

Although syncopated dance music—both live and recorded—filled Chicago's airwaves in the 1920s, more often than not the artists making the music were whites rather than African Americans. While stations carried remote broadcasts featuring African Americans, they routinely practiced Jim Crow within their studios, bringing in as a rule only white entertainers and music ensembles.[32] Commercial sponsors favored white over African American entertainers. The bulk of dance orchestras carried on Chicago's airwaves in the 1920s were white. Some performed syncopated dance arrangements in the "hot jazz" style of African American artists, while others employed the slower tempos and melodicism of the "sweet jazz" famously associ-

The "Weener" minstrels of WENR. Library of American
Broadcasting, University of Maryland.

ated with Paul Whiteman. Local radio popularized musical forms that
African Americans had developed, but it used white performers to
minimize risks of offending listeners. The standard practice reproduced the privileged fact of "whiteness," since the principal architects of that radio sound, many of whom profited handsomely, were of
white native-born or European-born descent.[33]

A further dimension of African American presence and absence
contributing to the sound of whiteness on local airwaves came
from blackface minstrelsy. "Blacked up" minstrel acts—white men
speaking in exaggerated dialect often with musical accompaniment—
migrated from the vaudeville stage to Chicago radio. WENR presented
the "Weener Minstrels," featuring "Chuck, Ray, Gene, and Big Bill
Childs," backed by a twenty-five-piece brass band. WGN featured the
"Pullman Porters." A print advertisement for this troupe promised
"[h]armony from the sleeper cars. . . . If you want to hear singing that's
better than good, listen to the four grinning 'yes suh' boys while they

disport themselves at 11:15." With its cosponsor, the *West Town News*, WGES offered the blackface duo of "Brown and Craig," sometimes referred to as the "Two Black Dots." WCFL presented two different minstrel teams, "Pencil and Eraser" and "Speed and Lightening."[34] WGN featured two struggling vaudevillians, Freeman Gosden and Charles Correll, who blacked up their voices in 1926 on the program *Sam 'n' Henry* before becoming a national sensation on NBC as *Amos 'n' Andy*. These stock representations bore complex codings of racial and sexual anxiety and pleasure. They amused white listeners and garnered audience share among African Americans as well. Nevertheless, their presence encoded the airwaves as a domain of white pleasure and power produced at the literal and figurative expense of racialized African Americans.[35]

ALL IN THE FAMILY
Race and On-Air Community

While self-produced representations via radio generally eluded African Americans throughout most of the 1920s, a determined group of South Side residents made an important intervention in the sound of whiteness in 1928. WSBC, owned and operated by the World Battery Corporation, had made a name for itself in Chicago during the 1920s as a brokered outlet for ethnic radio programs. The 100-watt station broadcast Bohemian, German, Italian, Lithuanian, Polish, Slovenian, and Yiddish music and cultural programming incorporating more than a half-dozen languages for listeners scattered throughout the immigrant and ethnic working-class precincts of Chicago's West and South Sides.[36]

In the autumn of 1928, several promoters of the Negro Civic League approached station owner Joseph Silverstein with a proposal for a show produced by African Americans for African Americans. Silverstein, who believed he ran the "most cosmopolitan station in the city of Chicago," agreed to appoint Jack L. Cooper as announcer of *The Negro Hour*.[37] Cooper was already an established figure in Chicago black media circles. He was a member of the National Press Syndicate and had served as drama editor of the *Chicago Defender*. Cooper supervised a staff of African American technicians, studio personnel, and talent to broadcast music, education, and civic programs. When Cooper opened the microphone and spoke on the air in the fall of 1928, it may have marked the first time Chicago radio listeners and thousands more outside of the city had ever heard an African American radio announcer, let alone an entire program produced entirely by a black studio staff. Cooper claimed that *The Negro Hour* was the first example in the nation in which African Americans programmed and controlled all facets of their self-representation.[38]

Cooper was an unapologetic paternalist who promoted the views of "the upper strata of the Negro" as precepts for Chicago's African American population. He and his supporters emphasized respectability and uplift in their efforts to instruct listeners, as well as to counter the stereotyped on-air representation of American Americans as either jazz hedonists or the kind of irresponsible buffoons and criminals depicted in minstrel shows and comedy sketches.[39] *The Negro Hour* offered representations of African American civic life, history, politics, and culture outside of, and otherwise resistant to, the hegemonic whiteness of the airwaves. Cooper used a range of music to signal not only that cultivation and aesthetic uplift mattered to Chicago's African Americans, but that they were also established features of South Side life and reflected an engagement with mainstream (that is, white) America as well as with the distinctive cultural identities and history of African Americans.

The Negro Hour presented a mix of musical programs featuring African American quartets, trios, duets, and soloists performing European art songs as well as gospel music, which was integral to African American Christian practice and cultural identity. The show drew on amateur talent, presumably unpaid, and tapped into the web of African American social clubs, societies, and church choirs active in the Black Belt. In addition to entertainment associated with the middle-class gendered virtues of the family parlor, listeners heard public affairs programs conducted by African American leaders that were devoted to issues of health, education, politics, and the law as they affected African Americans. The program performed an added civic function by directing on-air fundraising campaigns to benefit African American community institutions and organizations, such as the Provident Hospital, and by supporting the work of the South Side Community Council.[40]

Controlled by Chicago's Black Belt elite, *The Negro Hour*'s bourgeois perspective and uplift agenda invoked a respectable, domesticated model of African American cosmopolitanism at odds with the hedonism and sexual liberality associated with the culture of hot jazz promoted on other stations. In keeping with the program's orthodox, family-friendly orientation, Cooper refused to let wsbc play blues, a musical form he considered amoral. Like the progressive custodians of field house park outreach and the jpa dance reformers, *The Negro Hour* deemed blues and jazz inappropriate in polite society and in the civic realm of musical uplift. With its lyrical emphasis on sexual expressiveness (among women as well as men), drink, and violence, the blues aesthetic and its cultural politics ran counter to *The Negro Hour*'s idealized civic representation of African American life as an embodiment of middle-class stability, moral rectitude, and traditional gender roles.[41]

The decision to avoid blues may have disappointed southern African American migrants and laborers listening to wsbc for sounds that expressed and legitimated their experiences. The idealized radio family evoked by *The Negro Hour* implicitly devalued the sounds connected with everyday life for a significant portion of the city's African American population. Available evidence suggests, however, that, despite these biases, wsbc made a crucial rupture in the sound of whiteness with consequences for all of Chicago's African Americans: it gave a radio voice to a disenfranchised population. The thirst among African American listeners for self-directed representations of themselves in the public sphere and for discussion of their community concerns made wsbc hugely successful by default. The show managed to connect Chicago's African Americans across class and cultural divides by boldly countering the sounds of whiteness.

Because it focused on a group completely excluded from self-determination on air, the program's support base and sphere of influence stretched far beyond the physical and social boundaries of Chicago's African American population. Other stations garnered listeners in the hinterlands, too, but wsbc struck a fancy among African American audiences living many miles from the Black Belt. Listeners sent supportive letters from as far away as St. Louis, Baltimore, Milwaukee, and Coffeyville, Kansas. By 1935, the show had become a Chicago institution: "It would be very difficult now to find a Negro on the South Side of Chicago that doesn't know about these programs," Jack Cooper remarked, "that wouldn't be able to tell you something about them."[42]

Consolidating a racialized consciousness that invoked family and civic engagement was not limited to African Americans. Perhaps the most important contributing characteristic to the sound of whiteness on local radio came from the explicit community-building work of broadcasting in the 1920s among participating ethnic groups, who developed solidarity by using racial terms of inclusion and exclusion. J. Louis Guyon, a French-Canadian ballroom dancing instructor, dance hall operator, hotelier, and owner of West Side station WGES, used music radio to influence the character and social meanings attributed to various kinds of urban space. He operated like a radio patriarch, situated at the symbolic head of an extended multiethnic family of the air. Through a mixture of music and cultural programs, WGES produced a self-contained radio world of recognizable neighborhood spaces, institutions, and activities, binding listeners and inhabitants of Chicago's West Side. It reflected everyday social patterns and neighborhood activities, even as it subtly reshaped and reordered them in broadcast space constructing solidarity predicated on whiteness.

In 1924 Guyon began broadcasting from studios located adjacent to his capacious ballroom, Guyon's Paradise, located on Crawford Avenue in Chicago's West Town. The neighborhood surrounded Garfield Park, a major greensward, and was populated primarily by middle- and working-class German, Italian, and Irish Catholics. Guyon used phone lines to connect the ballroom studios to several Catholic churches and the nearby Guyon Hotel, where he occasionally broadcast orchestra concerts performed at midday from the hotel's palm court. The *West Town News* reported that Guyon also piped WGES programs into the 300 rooms of his hotel overlooking the park, using speakers installed in each room.[43]

Like many broadcast pioneers, Guyon reported losing money on his station throughout the 1920s, but this did not discourage him from pursuing a civic ideal via music radio from his ballroom. "I have got a ballroom that I think without question is the leading ballroom of the United States," he boasted, "and we are ambitious to serve the people and in that way obtain the good will of the people."[44] WGES provided more than a publicity vehicle for Guyon's business interests. He envisioned music radio as a tool with which to represent and reorganize leisure, commercial, and religious activity into a symbolic community circuit. Guyon described the operations of WGES as the broadcast equivalent of "a community center" for area listeners.[45]

As part of this neighborly mission, Guyon affiliated WGES with the *West Town News*, a community newspaper published by the West Side Kiwanis Club.[46] Guyon invited the newspaper to sponsor regular

Opening night at the "new" Guyon's Paradise Ballroom,
November 21, 1925. The estimated attendance was
10,500. National Archives.

entertainment segments on the air in exchange for general publicity.
The *West Town News* devoted lengthy, even fawning descriptions of
programs aired on WGES, emphasizing the community identity of the
station and the contributions of its neighborhood on-air talent pool:

> Jimmy Carroll was there with his harmonica in answer to
> many requests. . . . Vivian Sheffer was there with her sis-
> ter Genieuve [*sic*] and we are sure our listeners do not need
> our say-so to acknowledge that these two sisters though
> heard every week lost none of their charm last Thursday.
> "You're the One for Me" was sung for their father, Walter
> Sheffer, who is confined with a broken ankle. Then Vivian
> sang "Since I Found You" and "Hoosier Sweetheart" which
> were dedicated to Irene Tyrrell, who is also confined to her
> home (with scarlet fever) and of course has to have mother
> cooped up with her, so that we know that both Irene and Mrs.
> Tyrrell were sorta secretly thrilled to hear their names over
> the "Mike."[47]

If West Town represented an island community in the metropolis of
Chicago, WGES served as its hometown cheering section and as a
repository of local spirit in which broadcasters and listeners were

one and the same. In 1926, when Guyon hired twenty-four-year-old George Gubbins as station director and announcer, the *West Town News* championed the move: "Mr. Gubbins is strictly a West Towner, having been born and raised on Lawndale Avenue, just south of Garfield Park, is the son of the late Harry Gubbins and has surprised many of his friends and neighbors with the readiness in which he has adapted himself to the difficult tasks that become his duties as director in which capacity he selects the staff artists and arranges all programs."[48] Gubbins's credentials as the radio boy-next-door made him a perfect addition to what the paper liked to call the WGES "studio family."

The musical programs on WGES catered to the ethnic heterogeneity of the West Side. As late as 1930, Michael Schaut, editor of the German weekly *Der Heimatbote*, presented music and folklore aimed at the German Swabian community of Chicago.[49] Guyon also offered station time to the Servite Fathers and the Society of the Divine Word, providing music and religious talks from a neighborhood Catholic priest, as well as broadcasts of hymns and mass from Our Lady of Sorrows Church.[50] The broadcasts wove ethnic difference and religiosity together and accommodated preexisting practices and customs within a reconstituted radio world.

A variety of musical programming created cultural intersections reflective of the multifaceted lives and identities of middle- and working-class Germans, Italians, and Irish residing in areas bordering Garfield Park. WGES used music to serve the various identities adopted by its listening publics, whether as pious Catholics, lovers of Italian opera, or ardent middle-class "American" consumers of commercial dance music. Every day, radio listeners could hear the bell ringing and prayer of the Angelus at noon and six o'clock, and by midnight they could catch Guyon's house orchestra launch into its signature theme, "When I Dance with You in Paradise."[51] From Guyon's perspective, identifying and mediating among the lifestyle patterns of residents in his neighborhood, and highlighting certain connections through the medium of music, was one of broadcasting's great pleasures. "There are thousands of Catholic people in the neighborhood that I am in that patronize my ballroom, and I felt as though I owed them something in return, so I gave it to them." Merits of this altruistic claim notwithstanding, the vision of a radio world defined by multiple—and occasionally overlapping—musical publics marked a significant feature of WGES and other independent broadcasters' efforts to redefine public culture and urban identity in Chicago via radio.[52] Catholicism, neighborliness, leisure, culture, and "whiteness" represented mutually reinforcing features of this enterprise.

The dance floor of the whites-only Guyon's Paradise Ballroom served as the symbolic hearth of the WGES "studio family" home. Promoting the ballroom by radio served to accept and acknowledge ethnic difference within the listenership and metropolitan contact on the dance floor. Guyon used music radio to champion local values while burnishing his own image as a recreation reformer in the civic interest. Guyon's ballroom offered a variety of attractions to dancers, including the promise of pleasure within circumscribed limits, whiteness, and Americanness, all through interethnic participation in respectable and racially segregated dancing.

The ballroom stood as a testament to Guyon's rise from a struggling dancing instructor in a cheap storefront hall to owner of one of Chicago's most successful dance palaces. In 1909 Guyon opened the Victoria Hall Dancing Academy at the intersection of Madison and Western, a seedy commercial block of cheap saloons, lodging houses, hotels, and dingy piano bars on the West Side.[53] Guyon quickly attracted a visit from the JPA, but he placated the reformers by demonstrating that he was assiduously policing his dance floor. "This is a good well-regulated hall," reported a JPA investigator in 1912. "Men did not ask women they had not met to dance."[54]

Guyon satisfied the JPA, but he had broader ambitions of building up his business and breaking the association between public dance establishments and vice. He developed a motto for his hall, which he circulated on handbills: "No Lady will ever go home alone . . . She will be escorted."[55] Guyon's marketing pitch cleverly presented his hall as a respectable establishment where ladies and gentlemen behaved properly, even as it implied that the ballroom was a place for ladies and gentlemen to get to know each other while dancing. Guyon would proceed to make a series of moves to position himself to prosper amid the pervasive anxieties about nightlife, sex, and race in urban American culture during the years of the dance craze bracketing World War I.[56]

In the early 1910s, as JPA activists and the Vice Commission of Chicago studied commercial dancing in the city, Guyon joined the reform establishment in mounting a loud public campaign designed to differentiate "clean" ballroom dancing from popular dances such as the tango. At a public meeting in 1913, Guyon debated the merits of the popular dance with a competing dancing master, W. J. Ashton. "Ashton had many young persons with him who cheered his statements to the effect that it was the evil in Guyon's mind which caused him to see evil in the tango," reported the *Chicago Tribune*.[57] In 1921, working in association with the JPA, Guyon helped to establish the National Association of Ballroom Proprietors and Managers, a professional watchdog organization whose mission included providing for "uniform methods in dancing and the perfection of ball room dancing in general" and placing "the profession on a higher plane of respectability and morality."[58] These euphemisms expressed Guyon's and the JPA's unfavorable view of the unorthodox styles of dancing associated with African American jazz. Fenton T. Bott, a leading dance instructor in Dayton, Ohio, and president of the American National Association of Dancing Masters, echoed the view of ballroom operators like Guyon when he announced that the association hoped to appeal to composers of jazz and those who popularized its form to "improve the rhythm of the music and take the 'jazz,' or the 'jerk' out of it."[59]

In 1916, comfortably situated as a dancing instructor with a reputation for conservative tastes and moral substance, developed in part through vilifying the tango and African American jazz dancing, Guyon opened his Paradise Ballroom adjacent to Garfield Park on the West Side.[60] He marketed the hall as a haven for area residents itching to participate in the public dance craze, but preferring to do so in a controlled atmosphere of bourgeois, white respectability.[61] Guyon required appropriate dress, and patrons of color were not welcome. Guyon assembled a permanent house orchestra to perform "sweet jazz," the melodic and rhythmically tempered version of hot jazz favored by mainstream dance customers in the 1920s. Guyon's ballroom quickly became one of the most popular and lucrative operations in the city. The move into radio broadcasting from the ballroom confirmed the dance hall's local and citywide importance as a recreation reform institution as well as a shrine to civic whiteness and bourgeois respectability.

On the North Side of Chicago, the desire to create an idealized radio family also guided the operations of WIBO, a station owned by Alvin E. Nelson, president of the Nelson Brothers Bond and Mortgage Company. WIBO began operating in 1925 in Andersonville, a neighborhood several miles north of the central business district. The station served the varied needs of a community that included large numbers of Swedish ethnics, many of whom had first settled there in the last quarter of the nineteenth century. Broadcasts on WIBO helped to cement local ties and to constitute a Swedish radio community beyond the geographical confines of Andersonville. Unlike most African Americans pinioned within the Black Belt or the Union Park area due to housing discrimination, upwardly mobile European immigrant and ethnic Chicagoans were able to relocate to outlying suburban areas. Access to independent radio culturally counterbalanced this centrifugal phenomenon.

Ethnic music and Swedish-language religious services that were broadcast from local churches were especially important in maintaining ties to Andersonville for Chicago residents of Swedish heritage who were unable to attend services in person. Listeners commended the station for serving elderly shut-ins, for example, as well as those who had migrated outside of the neighborhood.[62] When WIBO reported a pending frequency reassignment to accommodate another station, they began hearing from distressed Swedish American listeners.[63] "I am very sorry to learn that your wave length is to be changed," read one letter cosigned by the Carlson and Larson families, "which will make it impossible with the receiving (five tubes) set that I have, to pick up your program." The letter bore a postmark from the Far South Side of Chicago, miles from Andersonville.[64]

Although geographically removed from the institutional center of Swedish ethnic life in Chicago, these listeners regularly gathered together to enjoy the Swedish-language music and cultural programs as part of an extended musical family. They used radio programs to maintain, and even to strengthen, ties to Andersonville, which was at least one hour away by public transportation. Another supporter wrote to share sentiments of listeners even farther afield: "I have a number of relatives and friends in O'Brien County and Cherokee County, Iowa who listen a great deal," he explained, noting that the station had a regional as well as metropolitan following.[65] Broadcasting temporarily reduced the distance separating these listeners from the ethnic world that was constituted in space among the shops, churches, and streets of Andersonville. Radio helped restructure the meanings and possibilities of ethnic membership. It mediated desires for forms and rituals of ethnic expression while acknowledging the realities of a decentered relationship with the ethnic community measured in strict terms of propinquity.[66] Swedish services and songs carried by music radio also helped mediate for listeners the Americanizing pressures to surrender their pasts and assimilate, providing a space for conserving and reworking the terms of identity.

Another example of this kind of mediation came through listener support for multilingual programs on WIBO. It reveals how local music radio shaped coexisting conceptions of what was "ethnic" and "American" by helping listeners to communicate across the generational divide of language. One listener communicated to the FRC his opinion of what made the station unlike any other in the city: "I am a young man 27 years of age of Swedish decent [sic] born in Chicago, but believe me I listen for the 'Swedish Services' every Sunday as mother does. What joy for mother there is then. It's the only time she ever listens in so to abolish WIBO never."[67] The writer expressed in written English, albeit awkwardly, what his mother could only have communicated in her native tongue. WIBO helped maintain a cultural link between a bilingual Swedish American son—poised between two worlds—and his immigrant mother. Music and cultural radio programs brought them together in a fleeting, but meaningful sense, countering the celebration of the Americanizing features of consumption that characterized many commercial stations at this time.

A stern moral message with racial overtones characterized the sound of whiteness at WPCC, the North Shore Congregational Church station. WPCC leaders took an outspokenly critical view of commercial amusement culture and the accelerating commodification of music radio on the public airwaves. They saw it as a sign of the troubling interplay of commerce and immorality. Sacred music broadcasting played a pivotal role in the charismatic ministry of Reverend J. C. O'Hair, who directed a popular Sunday night choir program of the "people's choice." Listeners contributed gospel song requests via letter or telephone. The selections were then performed by the WPCC radio singers with piano accompaniment. Radio listeners followed or sang along with their hymnals as they listened at home.[68] Reverend O'Hair likened his presence in broadcasting to a lonely pilgrim in the urban wilderness: "I am an old Presbyterian minister, but when I saw the great need in the north part of Chicago where the police sergeant told me there were fifteen hundred kept women within a mile and half of our station, I saw it was not a place for denominational wrangles and arguments. It was a place for the message of God."[69]

The church and its station operated in the heart of a furnished-room district on the North Side where many single, working women resided.[70] Such group-living arrangements had sprung up in this area around World War I to replace the nineteenth-century institution of chaperoned boardinghouses. These neighborhoods were often associated with Bohemianism, the sexual adventurism of the "New Woman," and vice. O'Hair's concerns reflected a common suspicion directed toward young, single female wage earners, which saw them not as the independent and self-determined women they typically were, but rather as "women adrift" at the mercy of sexual predators or, worse, already living as prostitutes.[71]

O'Hair equated his immediate neighborhood and the numbers of unaccompanied women on the streets with a cultural state of emergency in Chicago that radio exacerbated. O'Hair invoked the racialized constellation of liberated bodies, sex, and jazz in his attacks on large commercial broadcasters as inferior programmers and bad radio citizens. In the higher aesthetic and moral nature of his own station's programs, he saw the contrast of modern social relations with those of the Christian family he and his followers wished to construct. "Vaudeville performances, dance hall jazz, advertisements of everything from cigarettes to railroads; and during these same hours, with the exception of our broadcast . . . not one hour is devoted to the broadcast of the most important message that can be heard, and most needed message for this time of distress, for this day of lawlessness and crime, namely the Word of God and high-class religious music."[72] O'Hair portrayed his constituents as a "high-class" musical public fighting to vanquish the evils of commerce and other on-air pollutants invading the sanctified sphere of the airwaves. He lashed out at East Coast stations and networks impinging on Chicago's radio space. He chastised greedy and weak-willed local stations "who have been gradually increasing the hours of broadcasts" of lucrative chain arrangements controlled by the corporate profiteers NBC and Westinghouse rather than producing programs for the specific needs of their local communities.[73]

WPCC's listeners echoed O'Hair's representation of their musical world as distinct from that of other area stations and demanded their right to inhabit the public airwaves as a modern Christian radio family. By the hundreds they signed petitions and wrote letters to win the station favorable treatment from federal radio regulators who were concerned about too many local broadcasters in Chicago. WPCC's brand of sacred music struck supporters as being indispensable to the

cause of counteracting unhealthy musical appetites associated with
social evils in the city. "Our earnest prayer is that you will be granted
more time on the air," wrote one listener, who spoke for her family,
and then added a personal request for the Sunday gospel program. "I
wish you would sing 'Nothing Between' (on page 45 in Tabernacle
Hymns No. 3) for Mr. Fred Davies, 859 Belden Ave., and Miss
Evelyn Bryant 1200 Webster Ave. . . . I am sure the song will prove a
blessing and help to this young couple at this particular time when
they seem to have a hard time to give up the shows. They only go
once a week, but could and do have such wonderful testimony all
but for that one worldly lust."[74] WPCC listeners saw music radio as a
transfiguring tool whose powers extended beyond the receiving set
into the everyday lives of impressionable citizens who unavoidably
encountered seductive forms of urban commercial music culture,
whether on the air or in dance halls and musical theaters. Music
produced a shield capable of protecting listeners from the travails and
temptations of the outside world. WPCC used its broadcasts as spiritual
booster shots, hoping to immunize fellow Chicago residents against
on-air pathogens as well as everyday social and recreational ills.

The suggestion that commercial music, contaminated urban
space, and "worldly lust" threatened the Christian radio family
marked an extreme, but nonetheless telling dimension of the sound
of whiteness on local radio and the cultural work that it performed for
its listeners. Another letter specified this theme further: "In this
world of jazz, it is just like a little bit of Heaven to tune into your
station." To such listeners, sacred songs on the radio created a place of
grace in a veritable "world of jazz," a musical form whose popular
association with sexual license, race mixing, and crass commercialism
extended beyond the radio dial to the city streets. Misapplication of
the power of radio, the writer seemed to imply, could produce, or
already had created, a little bit of hell in Chicago. In this example, the
sound of whiteness subtly invoked a devilish Other to justify its own
righteousness. Struggles between white and dark sounds on the radio
represented to the listener a larger conflict between good and evil.
The cultural and social tensions embedded in the trope of "jazz"
music versus hymnody were yet another manifestation of the multilayered struggle involving 1920s broadcasters and listeners jockeying
for musical space, cultural authority, and social control on the air and,
by extension, in their listening communities.[75]

COMMERCIAL COMPETITION AND
THE DIFFERENCE OF LOCALISM

Even as independent music radio stations enabled forms of white ethnic Americanism to flourish, the unrelenting demand for new licenses, increased broadcast power, and more hours among stations sharing frequencies produced a space crunch on the airwaves. By February 1927, Chicago was, according to one study, "the most congested broadcast area in the world," with fifty-two stations within a fifty-mile radius of the city sharing thirty-three wavelengths. Typically, about seventeen stations were broadcasting at any one time.[76] Stations juggled hours and endured power reductions in order to minimize electrical interference among competing stations both inside and outside the city.[77] Scores of new stations broadcasting into the Chicago metropolitan area from other cities and towns made it increasingly difficult for local stations to be heard. Rising operating costs, frequency reassignments, power changes, and time shifts began to tilt the balance of power away from local independents toward well-capitalized stations with chain and network connections and an interest in commodifying the airwaves.

A widening gulf in economic, social, and cultural power divided the chain station carrying national advertising and featuring a well-known orchestra in a downtown studio from the independent station featuring a foreign-language announcer and a community band. Larger commercial stations could afford the installation and maintenance costs of multiple telephone lines from their broadcast studios to city hotels and night spots, thereby outstripping the ability of an independent to keep pace. By 1934, WMAQ, the *Chicago Daily News* station, ran evening orchestra programs from the Palais Royale, the Rainbo Gardens, the Arcadia Gardens, and the Bismarck Hotel. They also had lines to the Plaza Hotel, the Hotel Pierre, the Hotel Pennsylvania, the Oriental Gardens, and the Opera Club, each of which provided live music. The transition from jazz to swing music meant more revenues for stations carrying white popularizers of African American forms. It also marked the loss of both African American and white members of Chicago's extraordinary local music scene to New York and Los Angeles in search of brighter prospects and less segregation both on and off the air.[78] Independent stations countered deep-pocketed competitors by attempting to strengthen and refine their identities as niche programmers. They concentrated on culti-vating sustainable local audiences that were multiethnic and white.[79]

Commercial stations poured resources into technical production facilities reflecting the growing glamour surrounding radio in the Jazz Age. Some Chicago radio studios took on a dazzling allure following trends in luxury theaters, movie palaces, and concert halls. WENR, Westinghouse's "Voice of Service" station, boasted a Spanish garden studio motif, while the studio at WBCN adopted a similarly exotic atmosphere with painted wicker chairs, arbors crawling with artificial grapevines, and Japanese lanterns. The effect on visitors could be overwhelming. One radio writer for the *Chicago Post* expressed relief at the "business-like little studio" he toured in 1925 when contrasted with such excess. "It doesn't try to resemble an Italian villa, a Floren-tine garden or the Grant Park Stadium," he commented.[80] Indepen-dent broadcast outlets held the view that broadcast content and an audible presence mattered more than plush surroundings and the trappings of power.

In the minds of many commercial radio producers, however, the aural spectacle they wished to create for their listening publics began at the point of broadcast. The increasingly well-paid radio talent accustomed to performing from the stages of comfortable and daz-zling concert halls and ballrooms expected similar atmospherics in the studio. The musical public as a commodity and as a market for advertisers was coming to dominate attitudes among radio producers in all facets of their work. This development placed increased pres-sure on independents, many of whom sought to use music radio for ends other than generating profits. Such stations found their unem-bellished style of operation out of favor when federal regulators be-gan searching for stations that appeared to best exemplify the future of commercial broadcasting.[81]

In offering diverse musical programs, the independent stations' program listings during the late 1920s resembled those of their chain and network commercial competitors. Yet the presence of similar forms—opera, for example—should not be confused with the deeper meanings of the music for the independent station's listening au-dience. While they may have been unable to attract virtuoso musi-cians, or secure contracts with elite musical institutions like the Chi-cago Symphony Orchestra, independent stations sustained quality musical programming, including art music, for loyal listeners who

Cross-promotional sheet music, "Tripping Along (With You and Me)," Jerry Sullivan and Harry Hosford. Sam DeVincent Collection of Illustrated American Sheet Music, Archives Center, National Museum of American History, Smithsonian Institution.

supported these musical traditions within their own ethnic or subcultural enclaves. Stations accomplished this by pragmatically relying
on resources in the communities in which they broadcast. wpcc asked
talented members of its congregation to play piano and sing for
its Christian gospel programs. Between hymns, they solicited the
electronic congregation for contributions. By setting high standards
whenever possible, and by emphasizing local participation when they
could not, independent broadcasters fought attempts by large stations to demean their broadcasts as musically inferior and rebuffed
commercial broadcasting's attempts to colonize classical, or "high
class," music.

J. Louis Guyon knew that he could not consistently compete
financially for musical talent against large commercial stations. Instead, he used his ties in the local community to recruit Joseph Cavadore, a respected singer with the Chicago Civic Opera and the Ra-
vinia Opera, to program and star in opera performances at the station.
In exchange for full artistic control, Cavadore faced the challenge
of presenting quality music on an independent station's budget.
He relished the opportunity and the kinds of programs that resulted, saying, "We have given to the city of Chicago—this is without
boasting—I think the best operatic program they have ever had considering the size of the station."[82]

On another occasion, wges programmers used music to surprise listeners with personal and idiosyncratic programs and unusual
guests. Like many of its network competitors, wges ran educational
talks by leading municipal figures. Thus, in connection with the
"Save a Child" safety program, Municipal Boys Court judge Francis
B. Allegretti appeared on the station. Following what was likely a
standard public presentation on issues of law and order, the judge
broke character when he proceeded to sing for the audience. "The
excellent quality of his voice was heard to full advantage in the soft
and liquid tones of *Santa Lucia* which Judge Allegretti sang in Italian," gushed the *West Town News*.[83] Through such improvisatory tactics, wges and other independents countered the power and polish of
the big spenders by drawing on "friends" within their musical public
circles, giving a neighborly flavor to their programs, and emphasizing
their local identity on airwaves becoming increasingly national and
commercial in character. A performance like Allegretti's would not
have been appropriate on a major Chicago station, but, for neighbor-

hood listeners, the judge could harmonize his identity as a municipal authority and an Italian Catholic to satisfying effect.

When Congress created the FRC on February 23, 1927, the aim was to bring order to the nation's overcrowded airwaves. The commission's hearings exacerbated the simmering tensions between independent and large commercial broadcasters over the future direction of music radio. Chicago radio operators, their attorneys, and expert witnesses traveled to Washington to defend their technical advantages or to enhance their capacity (in terms of frequencies, power, hours). They sought to demonstrate that their music and related programming served the public interest. Many small stations faced the prospect that they would be terminated or would be denied power increases to remain audible above interference from new competing stations outside of Chicago. The percentage of stations allowed to broadcast at night fell by 30 percent in a five-year period, and a disproportionate number of these stations were small, undercapitalized local broadcasters. The network and chain interests in Chicago fared remarkably well, and most emerged from the regulatory hearings stronger than ever.[84]

In their zeal to clean up the airwaves for national network connectivity, FRC regulators applied the dull scythe of "public interest, convenience, or necessity" to the tangled roots of Chicago music radio without appreciating its fragile shoots and tendrils—the many musical publics supporting and built around independent radio. According to Gerald Flannery, the FRC's chairman, Eugene Sykes, formerly a justice on the Mississippi Supreme Court, "was thrown into the maelstrom without any real experience in radio."[85] Another commissioner, Orestes Caldwell, only narrowly won confirmation in the Senate because of worries that his close ties to the Radio Corporation of America (RCA) could create a conflict of interest. Overwhelmed by dozens of cases, hundreds of hours of testimony, a huge mass of data, including countless program schedules, engineers' reports, and exhibits, the FRC avoided extensive discussion of how music and the local ethnic character of a small station in Chicago might be enriching the definition of the "public interest" in a manner that a large, business-oriented aspiring network affiliate would not.[86]

In public statements concerning regulation, Chairman Sykes stressed that FRC loyalties lay with the "radio public" and that "[o]ur hope is to interfere . . . just as little as we can . . . which means the broadcasters . . . must help us."[87] But public documents revealed that FRC officials were impatient with the entrenched and combative culture of local broadcasting in Chicago. During a lengthy hearing in 1928, Ira Robinson, an FRC commissioner with no radio background, expressed frustration at the dozens and dozens of licensees in the city, remarking, "There are too many in that congested district."[88] And though he was an outspoken opponent of corporate domination of the airwaves and an advocate of educational broadcasting, Robinson expressed negative sentiments toward the city and its inhabitants. "I am anxious to know about Chicago," he said during an examination of several stations. "In fact I have been afraid to go there in recent years." Responding to this biased pronouncement, a representative of local station WQJ quipped, "We will give you safe conduct, Mr. Commissioner, if you wish to visit our city."[89]

In the late 1920s, the chambers of the FRC in Washington, D.C., were a long way from Chicago, both geographically and culturally. Joking about the city's association with crime and gangsterism or perhaps even about bad blood between regulators and local operators, Robinson expressed a veiled, but discernible aversion to some of the subjects of the hearings. Obviously, there was more to Chicago than mythic antiheroes like Al Capone. Chicago boasted thriving commercial stations such as WGN, WLS, and WMAQ. But unfamiliarity with and insufficient knowledge of the immigrant and multiethnic character of Chicago on the part of federal regulators made objective assessment of the civic contributions of other local broadcasters more difficult. It bears noting that in the following year Robinson took an aggressive position in opposing a request from WCFL, the "Voice of Labor," seeking a power increase and nighttime broadcast time in order to better serve workers who did not have access to radio during the day. The regulator defended the interests of commercial stations challenging WCFL's expansion: "Robinson reasoned that if the union could use WCFL to broadcast propaganda, the business owners should have the same rights as well."[90]

At points, investigators seemed prepared to abdicate their re-

sponsibility to act as impartial arbiters of local disputes on the basis of
arbitrary circumstances, or, worse, appeared ready to cede authority
illegally to locals connected to the network interests in Chicago. The
following exchange between regulators and William S. Hedges, the
influential radio editor of a leading Chicago newspaper that operated
a network affiliated station, illustrates the point:

> Chairman Robinson: Now in order to equitably distribute
> [licenses] we must reduce some places, must we not,
> taking into consideration radio science?
> William S. Hedges: That is your problem.
> Robinson: But you are more or less an expert, are you not?
> Hedges: I do not rate myself as such.
> Robinson: What is your line of work?
> Hedges: I am the Radio Editor of the *Chicago Daily News*.
> Chairman Caldwell: We will agree that he is an expert.[91]

Despite the appearance of a conflict of interest, the commissioners
seemed ready to rely upon an employee of a major commercial media
conglomerate to guide their determinations about stations that might
be competitors of WMAQ, the *Chicago Daily News* station. Caldwell
seemed comfortable in using Hedges (despite his protestations) as an
authoritative source on the big picture of radio in Chicago, including
"radio science." In dozens of other cases, however, the commissioners demonstrated no such willingness to trust "authorities" from
neighborhood or ethnic institutional settings.[92]

   Although the language of the 1927 Radio Act prohibited the FRC
from censoring broadcasters, the mandate to make licensing decisions on the basis of the "public interest" set the FRC on a collision
course with local ethnic producers who were using music radio for
purposes that challenged mainstream notions of "American" culture.
On occasion, musical programming itself appeared to be, in the eyes
of regulators, a salient indicator of a station's fitness to continue. At
times, the FRC expressed worries about "low class," that is, popular
Tin Pan Alley or jazz-style music on small stations, but it rubber-
stamped similar programming on larger commercial stations, provided such stations could demonstrate that, in addition to commercial dance music, they ran at least some educational programs or
European concert music.[93]

   Regulators cared a great deal about the relative financial health
of Chicago's stations. But in the case of WGES, a well-capitalized sta-

tion with an ethnic base and a local focus, the discussion concerning the station's music programs suggested a veiled unease among regulators over music radio stations catering to interests outside the mainstream marketplace. Joseph Cavadore, the opera singer who served as music director at WGES, faced a curious cross-examination when he appeared before the commission. Speaking proudly as one of a quartet of master opera singers who performed over the station's frequency, Cavadore defended the importance of cultivated music on independent radio. "We still believe we should give [listeners] the best to elevate the soul, to improve them," he argued, invoking a progressive sentiment consistent with J. Louis Guyon's philosophy of programming. Cavadore invoked works by such composers as César Franck and Charles Gounod that were used in a series of broadcasts from Our Lady of Sorrows Church, to which the FRC questioner responded, "Do you know yourself whether or not these compositions are rendered generally by the laity and by Protestant and Jewish churches as well?" When asked to explain the point of the question, the examiner continued, "I want to find out whether or not these programs are of wide public interest, if the compositions are rendered by Protestants in their churches, and by the public in operatic concerts." Cavadore, a Catholic, was forced to launch into a short lecture on the pan-denominational nature of his musical selections, and he was left to wonder why the parameters of the "public interest" should be measured by how much one conformed to or deviated from the musical appetites of Protestants, or if a Protestant performing the same composers might be more desirable in the eyes of the FRC.[94]

In response to the cultural vagaries of the FRC's concept of the public interest, one supporter of local broadcasting emphatically defended ethnic particularism in a letter: "I am the mother of four little children and can rarely hear a church service, and the Swedish service is a treat for hungry ears. Even my Greek neighbors tune in to WIBO every Sunday morning as they say they enjoy the singing." The letter could be seen as shrewdly emphasizing local radio's relevance by invoking universal and gendered themes of motherhood, family, and Christian values. It suggested that independent music radio had the power to link listeners across ethnic boundaries, as did the consumerist appeals of chain stations and networks, which the FRC perceived as meeting a definition of broad public service.[95] Music's appeal transcended the barriers of language and culture. Evidence of purposeful cross-cultural listening is difficult to extract from extant data, but the possibility of encountering other forms of music and culture was increased by the fact that brokered programming meant that many groups had to pursue ethnic programmers across the dial, chancing upon many other forms of program content in the process. Joseph Budrick, a music and furniture dealer and owner of a jewelry store, produced three different Lithuanian radio shows on stations WCFL, WHFC, and WAAF, presumably with listeners in pursuit.[96]

When challenged by the FRC, independents responded angrily to assertions that they did not fulfill a public need. "Surely it is in the public interest, necessity and convenience," wrote the station manager of WCFL, "that every reputable group shall have the opportunity to sing its song, tell its story, or proclaim its message to those who desire to hear?"[97] Listeners of WIBO produced a deluge of letters imploring the FRC to reconsider its policy of apparently favoring large commercial stations over independent music radio. One concerned patron wrote: "When there are so few stations on the air in Chicago that broadcast sacred programs and those that are worthwhile, I can't for the life of me understand why the commission must discriminate against the few that do broadcast something worthy to listen to."[98] Listeners rose to defend stations that used music and cultural programs as a means of creating affinities among listeners. What made independent music radio special was its local perspective, and listeners bristled at interference coming from outsiders in Washington.

One staunch partisan labeled an FRC directive that WIBO change its frequency as "little less than a crime." Another spoke even more candidly about what he saw happening in Washington between the government and big business. He depicted the independent commission as a pawn of the networks seeking to gain hegemony across the country: "I hope that our government has a few officials in its employ that are broadminded and not politically corrupt to see that radio station WIBO is rendering a service, and is absolutely necessary to our "City of 'I Will.'" It appeared from the standpoint of supporters of independent music radio that network interests and regulators were intent on excluding independent stations and their local followings from participating in the brave new world of the American system of broadcasting.[99]

The impression that regulators were partial to mainstream, commercial network interests and sought to relegate foreign-language and independent broadcasters to the musical margins of broadcasting raised troubling questions in the minds of many immigrant, ethnic, and working-class listeners. They had been using radio to challenge their subordinated status in urban society and assert a musical Americanism inclusive of their differences. Observing that WIBO was the only area station broadcasting in both German and Swedish, a listener inquired: "Why are clear unlimited channels assigned to Chicago given to stations broadcasting chain programs? And why do three of them happen to be newspapers?"[100] Another listener wondered why the FRC would wish to shut down independent stations and deprive music listeners of "the crumbs which fall from the rich man's table."[101] The populist critique of powerful politicians and media conglomerates seizing control of a public resource—the airwaves—resonated powerfully among local broadcasters even as it masked the exclusion of African Americans and racial minorities in its claim of a joint injury visited on the less-powerful members of the city.

Where independent 1920s music radio had created local and citywide communication links, had fostered diverse musical publics, and had promoted power and audibility in the broadcast arena for many voices, regulators discerned primarily chaos, inefficiency, and mediocrity—a tower in Babel. The airwaves were overcrowded and needed a new system of regulation. And the FRC doubted whether ethnic and subcultural interests represented by musical publics of all shapes and sizes could benefit Chicago as a whole. The conceit that commercial music radio was best equipped to provide "service" broadly conceived was a subterfuge for the commodification of the music airwaves. The removal of independent stations confirmed the worst to many: that musical publics mattered only for their varying worth to advertisers.

If the voices of protest are any indication, grassroots opposition to network control of radio in Chicago remained strong into the 1930s and beyond, despite the structural hegemony of the networks. The testimony of independent station operators and listeners surveyed here speaks eloquently to the significance of independent radio in the lives of immigrant, ethnic, and working-class Chicago residents. Music radio invigorated and sustained distinctive identities among listener publics across boundaries of space, time, and generation. It gave power to a diverse array of groups seeking control over their self-representation in the public sphere. The pleasure and pride of hearing one's group portrayed with dignity, of listening to the sounds of one's native language and sacred songs, music from a distant homeland, or simply ideas and information not heard or valued in other "public" contexts mattered as much to local listeners as the sound capable of extracting maximum economic value from the airwaves. In all of these ways, independent broadcasting served a reform function in the minds of some users conscious of tendencies in mainstream American culture to ignore or demean sectors of the population.

The story of independent radio and federal regulation at the end of the 1920s marked a crucial and contested exercise in the ongoing processes of defining and redefining music as an instrument of democratic reforms in American culture. Without economic clout, or established political institutions to securely defend their interests, many immigrant, ethnic, and working-class Chicago residents expressed their needs and desires through public display and expressive culture conducted in public urban spaces. Broadcasting opened up a new public arena to be shaped and democratized through cultural expression, and radio rapidly became an indispensable tool for urban listeners making and imagining city life in the early twentieth century.

But the hegemonic sound of whiteness that predominated on local radio in Chicago prior to the network regulation that began in the 1920s extended the racialized structural inequalities of the physical urban environment onto the invisible airwaves themselves. Even as broadcasting helped African American music reach a huge new audience via black performers and white imitators of the syncopated sounds of jazz, local broadcasting limited access to African American voices and self-produced representations. Still, radio afforded many listeners, including African Americans, room within musical publics that challenged the geographic fixity and hierarchies of music and urban social and cultural space. Radio linked Chicago residents together, albeit unequally and provisionally, to produce new cultural formations that sometimes challenged segregated social practices.

Broadcasting in the 1920s provided many immigrant, ethnic, and working-class Chicagoans a tool to reconstitute and mediate their local, metropolitan, and American selves, and to weave these selves into new configurations. African Americans, similarly poised for integration into American industrial society, found the way barred. They were denied a critical chance in which to insert their own voices and self-representation into the broadcast sphere even as the musical artistry and cultural power of African American jazz getting a wide hearing in the 1920s exposed the hypocrisy and fallacy of such barriers.

Although the regulation and removal of many independent stations drastically limited the range of uses put to music radio after the 1920s, the collective experience of fighting to be heard as far away as Washington created a new awareness about urban cultural politics, economics, and power. Stations had always competed against one another, but the regulatory struggle of the late 1920s and early 1930s revealed that "reform"-minded federal radio regulators and network interests had little regard for the neighborly world of independent radio. As they had done in the streets, parks, and public spaces of the city in the past, immigrant, migrant, ethnic, and working-class groups used the public airwaves to reframe and articulate group identity through music. At wsbc, African American broadcasters made a key contribution to asserting a voice to challenge the sounds of whiteness. Independent broadcasters recognized the power of radio as a social tool with which to make democratic use of an electronic public sphere and to empower groups in Chicago in new and significant ways. By 1935, the prospects for diverse musical publics on the airwaves may have dimmed, but the significance of musical production and consumption as a means of collective representation, consciousness, and resistance continued to influence the making of urban public culture via radio. The hegemonic sound of whiteness would face continual challenge in the coming decades as African Americans won new battles for inclusion in democratic life and began to gain greater access to the airwaves as announcers and producers.

The conflict over the radio waves marked a shift over control of the dynamics of musical progressivism, in which corporate forces and federal regulators attempted to bar local access to transmission space and curb the people's ability to negotiate and craft the sounds of democratic culture. No civic group representing musical progressive ideals gained a powerful enough voice on the radio to offset the intervention of network interests and federal regulators advocating "respectable" musical consumerism in the public interest. These outsiders appropriated the reform discourse with its concerns for democracy and the public interest and created a business model that willfully distorted its purpose. These "progressives" were no longer borrowing from the commercial model to win patronage and popular support; they were the architects of a centralized and market-driven concept of reform. The fight over local control of radio in Chicago would be a harbinger of increased federal and market authority over the contours of public culture and musical life in the decades to come.

EIGHT

SOUND AMERICANS
ECHOES OF REFORM FROM THE 1930S TO THE PRESENT

The era of musical progressivism left important legacies that affected the ways that Americans imagined, produced, and communicated their civic ideals in the twentieth century. The questions that Progressive Era activists posed about music and American identity, the answers that their outreach programs reflected, and the redefinition of democratic ideals that resulted due to struggles involving various musical publics informed subsequent local and national music initiatives. Various changes in American music, society, and governmental institutions also exerted an influential effect on the way that Americans conceptualized the interplay of musical forms, aesthetics, and democratic ideals. Questions about public support of the musical arts and the negotiation of group participation in the cultural displays representing civic values, especially among minority groups, remained recurring, at times controversial issues in cultural reform initiatives. Finally, the increasing power and influence of the federal government both domestically and internationally and the penetration of the marketplace into everyday life raised new questions about the relationship between commerce, the public realm, and the possibilities of civic engagement through cultural reform.

This chapter sketches the trajectory of musical progressive ideas since the 1930s and their continuing impact on the politics of everyday life, popular culture, and democracy. Though it brackets the explosive growth of American consumerism and its impact on music and the culture industries, the chapter surveys major trends in Chicago and the nation to show how musical progressive ideals surfaced repeatedly throughout the twentieth century to legitimate official representations of democracy in action and to express reform sensibilities and American values at home and abroad. Music continued to be a contested domain in which elites, activists, and the "people," variously construed, strove to define their civic ties. As the struggle for control of local radio hinted, the nature of music reform in the name of the public interest changed significantly as the nation became more economically and technologically advanced. As America's horizons grew more global, and as the modern welfare state and corporate capitalism grew up alongside one another, musical outreach extended increasingly beyond the nation's boundaries toward new populations of perceived outsiders.[1]

As late as the eve of the 1929 market crash, the local manifestations of progressive music reform remained abundantly evident in the urban landscape. The community music school model pioneered at Hull House continued to spread nationally. There was a national federation of settlements with a music division, whose board included Eleanor Smith. The field house music reform program expanded into other neighborhoods of Chicago, and the park commissioners were investing more money in concerts than ever before. Tens of thousands of citizens patronized indoor and outdoor park-sponsored concerts, and thousands of children took affordable music and dance lessons. The Civic Music Association continued its teaching and performance work in area schools and field houses. Commercial dancing continued to attract youthful dancers, but under more consistent and regulated conditions.

The collapse of the stock market in 1929 and the onset of the depression challenged the vigorous culture of civic musical outreach in Chicago. The Lincoln Park Commission, whose annual budget for field house park concerts swelled to an average of $4,500 in the mid- to late 1920s, slashed its outlays for music to nil by 1932. The West Chicago Park Commission, which had reported more than 1,000 persons receiving musical instruction annually in its parks by 1927, also drastically reduced its budget.[2] In response to cutbacks in job opportunities for professional musicians, whether in parks or in hotels, cabarets, dance halls, and clubs, James C. Petrillo, president of Chicago Federation of Musicians, Local 10, used union savings to put musicians to work. He organized a variety of free public concerts in city parks. These events featured the specially consolidated Chicago Federation Band, a 100-man unit, and the Chicago Concert Band Association.[3]

By the spring of 1934, between 10 and 15 percent of Cook County residents remained on relief, including an estimated 600 to 800 of Chicago's professional musicians.[4] Even the stalwart Chicago Symphony Orchestra needed an emergency bank loan to stay afloat.[5] In the summer of 1935, Petrillo launched free summer concerts in Chicago's Grant Park, located adjacent to the site of the old Exhibition Building downtown. The union paid for the bulk of an entire summer season of concerts consisting of sixty-six outdoor evening performances—twenty-six symphonic and forty band concerts. The Chicago Symphony Orchestra and the Woman's Symphony Orchestra of Chicago also performed. The summer concerts proved so popular that they became a city institution and continued into the twenty-first century.

Petrillo's creativity brought free music to Chicago during hard times and conveyed a new variant of music reform in the public interest.[6] Though the Grant Park events were open to all, the performers were drawn exclusively from the ranks of Petrillo's whites-only Local 10. Refused participatory privileges on the basis of race, African American musicians missed playing a part in these important civic events. The lengthy history of segregated unionism among musicians in Chicago relegated the African American members of the Musicians' Protective Union, Local 208, to ad hoc fundraisers and benefit concerts in the Black Belt. These events kept African American musicians active, fostered solidarity, and served the depression-wracked Black Belt, but it failed to send a message that the condition of African Americans mattered, especially in civic responses to the crisis held downtown.[7]

NATIONALIZING MUSICAL PROGRESSIVE IDEOLOGY
The Federal Music Project

Amid the Great Depression, public initiatives in music reform shifted away from control by local authorities toward an increasingly centralized federal government apparatus and powerful private interests committed to shaping a role for music and the arts in the nation's public culture. Launched as part of Franklin D. Roosevelt's Works Progress Administration (WPA) in 1935, the Federal Music Project (FMP) catapulted musical progressivism to an unprecedented level. The Federal Art Projects, also known as Federal Project One, also supported art, theater, and writing and began an era of federal commitment to funding culture in the public interest. Rationalized as an emergency measure to temporarily assist the nation's professional musicians, the FMP provided music-related employment of various kinds. The FMP sponsored jobs for musicians as performers in symphonies, bands, and smaller groups, as music teachers, and as transcribers and arrangers for schools and music libraries. At its peak in 1936 the FMP employed more individuals—15,000—than any other federal arts project. Between October 1935 and August 1939, the FMP spent $50 million dollars, sponsored 36,000 musical performances across the country, and reached audiences estimated, in the aggregate, at 36 million people.[8]

Despite clear differences in justification and scope, the FMP's subsidiary aim of promoting the musical arts to strengthen democratic life evoked antecedent concerns of musical progressivism. The FMP resoundingly answered ongoing pleas for federal support of the musical arts made by the National Recreation Association, which had promoted patriotic community sings during World War I. The stated goals of the FMP included promoting high standards of musicianship, stimulating community interest in various forms of music, uplifting and educating the American people, and promoting "constructive ways of using leisure time." These ambitions continued a civic enterprise of aesthetic and social transformation hearkening back to the era of musical progressivism.[9]

As they had in the past, reform activists and musical publics jockeyed to reconcile the aesthetic qualities of outreach content. Nikolai Sokoloff, head of the FMP, subscribed to a narrow interpretation of the nation's musical needs. Formerly the conductor of the Cleveland Symphony Orchestra, Sokoloff argued that the federal government must dedicate the bulk of its aid to promoting the European cultivated tradition of symphonic, choral, opera, and chamber musics to the broadest audiences possible.[10] In Sokoloff's view, not all unemployed musicians were equally deserving of federal largesse. "It is up to us," he declared, "to determine whether a musician who is on relief should be saved as a musician or should be helped without delay to another livelihood." In public remarks, Sokoloff and some other FMP officials indicated that they believed that the marketplace would eventually take care of professional jazz and swing musicians without federal support. These men argued that the depression had created a unique opportunity for a twentieth-century cultured generation to harness the means of government in order to reshape the American musical landscape from one dominated by commercialized forms of popular music (such as swing) to one in which cultivated musical excellence prevailed.[11]

Despite Sokoloff's biases and an FMP state advisory committee in Illinois whose membership comprised individuals drawn exclusively from the Chicago Symphony, professional music schools, and cultivated music clubs, the FMP did not function as Sokoloff's handmaiden. Organized labor successfully defended the entitlement of many rank-and-file musicians to FMP jobs in Chicago.[12] The FMP sponsored an Illinois Symphony Orchestra along with twenty-three other major bands and orchestras, including military and jazz bands and a women's symphony orchestra.[13] Notwithstanding Sokoloff's dream of Euroclassical hegemony, a study in 1935–36 of FMP performances nationwide revealed that John Philip Sousa and George Gershwin ranked second and third behind Victor Herbert as the most commonly heard composers.[14] By the late 1930s on any given month, tens of thousands of Chicago listeners heard the American Federal Orchestra, the Chicago Federal Band, the Columbia Federal Band, the Dearborn Federal Orchestra, the Federal Philharmonic Choir, the Federal Jubilee Singers, and the Federal String Quartet perform.[15]

To an extent that local civic projects during the early years of the depression had not, the FMP made forward strides in including African Americans within civic musical outreach. Countering the Jim Crow exclusions of Local 10–sponsored concerts, the FMP awarded jobs to white and African American musicians alike.[16] In addition to James A. Mundy's acclaimed Jubilee Singers, FMP-sponsored African American units in Chicago included the Columbia Concert Band; the Dixie Orchestra, a swing band; the Colored Concert Band, conducted by Norman L. Black; the Colored Concert Orchestra, conducted by Charles Elgar, a popular local swing orchestra leader; and the Colored Jazz Orchestra, conducted by Zilner Randolph, a talented trumpet player, composer, and arranger, who had worked with Earl "Fatha" Hines, Fletcher Henderson, and Louis Armstrong.[17]

Norman L. Black's Colored Concert Band poster.
Library of Congress.

Although federal support of African American artists helped to
diversify the nature of civic music culture to some extent, reform
outreach again collided with everyday practices of segregation in Chicago. Symphonic and classical concert units of white musicians appeared in public venues on the North Side, in the city's predomi-
nately white suburbs, and in Hyde Park, a white enclave on the South
Side.[18] By contrast, the African American bands, with the exception
of Mundy's Jubilee Singers, performed principally in outdoor settings
at field house and South Side ceremonial parks or in segregated African American public schools on the South and Southwest Sides. Outdoor settings accommodated interracial audiences, but the geograph-

ical clustering of performers and audiences reinforced the color line. African American bands did not get scheduled in lakefront civic showcases, such as Grant or Lincoln Park.[19]

The appearance of African American bands in some Chicago parks by the mid- to late 1930s revealed signs of greater community success in obtaining municipal services for African American neighborhoods. Anna L. Walker, an African American supervisor, taught a generation of African American children music and drama at Union Park. Located about a mile and a half from Hull House, the park served as a recreational center for area youth excluded by skin color from benefiting from the settlement's programs.[20] In the late 1930s under Walker's stewardship, Union Park began hosting the West Chicagoland Music Festival.[21] The gala event incorporated music and drama and, most notably, increased African American participation in shaping the civic character of musical outreach. By the early 1940s, the festival attracted nationally known African American performers, including Keen Fleming's Orchestra, the Dungill Family Orchestra, and the Chicago gospel legend Thomas A. Dorsey. Walker's contributions helped to attract thousands of African American spectators to public parks by expanding the musical repertoire of concerts to embrace the sounds of gospel blues choirs and orchestras that were influential in dozens of Chicago's African American churches.[22]

Also during the 1930s, many African American jazz and swing artists and entertainers, including Lena Horne, Billie Holiday, and Duke Ellington, publicly supported antiracist campaigns on a national level, such as those led by the laborite Popular Front. When the Hitler-Stalin nonaggression pact fatally damaged the movement, African American musicians continued to use their celebrity to fight racism and class exploitation. Their actions combined an appeal to longstanding civic ideals of democratic public culture with an undertone of radicalism that linked African American jazz and swing to an ongoing project to obtain more widespread economic and racial justice.[23]

SWINGING PATRIOTISM
Musical Civics in World War II and After

America's entry into World War II saw a continuation of the federal government's activist role in utilizing music in service of reform at home as well as abroad.[24] The staff of the U.S. secretary of war included an expert consultant on music, and the army and navy maintained special committees to oversee appropriate musical entertainment at the nation's military installations and training facilities.[25] The government also produced so-called Victory Discs (or V-Discs) featuring swing music for international distribution, including use in English- and German-language propaganda radio broadcasts coordinated through the Armed Services Network and the Office of Wartime Information.[26]

As Lewis Erenberg notes, explicitly patriotic songs did not serve as the principal medium of communicating national unity after Pearl Harbor as they had in World War I. Instead the federal government and the commercial music industry collaborated to make big-band swing the official soundtrack of American patriotism. Ragtime and African American jazz had subverted the civic model of many music reformers for decades, as had Popular Front–era jazz and swing. But swing's association with mass audiences and the ethnic and racial pluralism of its bands, its glorification of youth culture, and its ties to therapeutic consumerism made it popular with the troops and a potent ideological weapon for the American government seeking to express the essence of American democratic identity. Swing performed important symbolic work in the government's cultural campaign to emphasize its difference from the avowedly ethnocentric and racist cultures of the Third Reich and empire of Japan.[27]

As in World War I, however, Jim Crow social realities complicated the public image of patriotic harmony that federal music reform hoped to effect. The Glen Miller Orchestra, the government's favored "sweet swing" emissary, was a whites-only unit, undercutting the message of interracial solidarity in the U.S.[28] Miller's music and the squeaky-clean image of the band represented the sanitized, mass-marketed version of a form that African American artists had largely pioneered. Miller's orchestra could not adequately reflect the diversity of the American fighting forces. Nor could Miller's style or sound co-opt swing's symbolic power as an "oppositional style" that lay deeply rooted in African American forms of public expression. During the war, many African Americans expressed their dissatisfaction with Jim Crow by endorsing a "Double V" campaign for victory abroad and a victorious end to racism at home. While supporting the war, they challenged the racial double standard that prohibited full rights and protections of citizenship for African Americans.[29]

During the Cold War, the U.S. government continued its use of music as a tool of persuasion and outreach through a range of activities coordinated by the U.S. Information Agency. These included the expansion of the Voice of America radio network created in 1942 and the State Department's International Educational Exchange and Cultural Presentations programs, which underwrote international goodwill tours by American musicians and cultural performers.[30] As it had in World War II, the reforming power of music served as an ideological weapon. Outreach programs enjoyed an international horizon of operations that attempted to promote American values abroad via selected musics. Whether to convince allies (and foes) that Americans were not commercial philistines, but "cared" about symphonic music; or to demonstrate the creativity of homegrown ethnic and African American musicians, such as Benny Goodman and Louis Armstrong; or even to promote Marian Anderson, an African American singer, whose remarkable talents spanned the cultivated/vernacular divide— such federally funded initiatives skillfully manipulated the complex symbols of American music and democratic culture in order to impress non-Western nations of the cultural power of the United States.[31]

GRANTING MUSIC REFORM
Private Philanthropies and Public Needs

Back in the United States, postwar prosperity and a combination of public and philanthropic support produced a dramatic expansion of institutions dedicated to promoting arts and music as integral to democratic vitality. By the mid-1950s, Americans supported more than 1,000 symphonies, an estimated 600 community orchestras, almost 250 college orchestras, and almost three dozen youth orchestras. The vast majority of these institutions benefited from the generosity of 7,500 philanthropic foundations active in the U.S.[32] The Ford Foundation supported music education in public schools and a Young Composers Project, established in 1959, also endowed residencies for young composers in schools. In the mid-1960s, the Ford Foundation also made a series of major grants to symphonies across the nation to inspire Americans to embrace Euroclassical music as part of the nation's democratic cultural tradition.[33] While such support empowered certain institutions, it had the unintended administrative and political consequence of undermining local control over cultural reforms that had predominated during the Progressive Era. To a degree exceeding attempts by activists to mediate nineteenth- and early-twentieth-century local music production, national foundation work and corporate philanthropy centralized resource allocation and placed authoritative decision making with executives, boards, and peer-review bodies that were structurally removed from residents of the nation's cities as well as from many local arts activists.

The dynamic between local and national reform authority shifted yet again after Congress passed the National Foundation on the Arts and Humanities Act of 1965. Inspired during the Kennedy administration and promulgated as part of Lyndon Johnson's "Great Society," the legislation created a set of independent federal agencies to support the arts and culture, including the National Endowment for the Arts (NEA), the National Endowment for the Humanities (NEH), and the Federal Council on the Arts and the Humanities.[34] Without an economic crisis, a major war, or global strategic concerns to justify its expenditures, the initiative proudly declared the public arts as a permanent institutional concern of American democratic life.

Prior to 1965 the government had supported arts and culture in the United States through so-called indirect mechanisms, such as tax deductions for contributors to educational and philanthropic activities, but no federal body attempted to oversee the fate of public arts.[35] By design, not only would the NEA, NEH, and Federal Council on the Arts and the Humanities help sustain established cultivated institutions, such as operas and symphonies; they would also fund state arts councils assigned to promote experimental and nontraditional artistic and cultural production and underwrite democratic cultural outreach at the grassroots level. In its commitment to eclecticism and decentralization, the Arts and Humanities Act federalized the inclusive spirit of Eleanor Smith's work at Hull House and the early efforts of the Civic Music Association to embrace excellence in local producers and, through diverse cultural forms and perspectives, conferring authority onto them.

In Chicago, the NEA transferred funds to support civic music and culture via the Illinois State Arts Council, created in 1965. Federal money helped underwrite high-profile cultivated performing groups and institutions, such as the Chicago Symphony as well as the Lyric Opera. Funds supported musical outreach in parks and schools, as well as grants-in-aid to nonprofit, tax-exempt organizations and individuals.[36] Between 1974 and 1979, total NEA budget increases averaged 15 percent a year, and spending by state and local arts agencies increased steadily as well, although state budget shortfalls meant that Illinois did not necessarily fund the arts as generously as many states chose to do.[37]

The lucrative broadcast spectrum received federal attention as well, as activists successfully won regulatory support for both quality and diversity on airwaves dominated for decades by commercial networks since the "reform" of the late 1920s. In 1967 Congress created the Corporation for Public Broadcasting (CPB) to restore a civic sensibility to the airwaves. The CPB supported not-for-profit cultural and educational radio initiatives. In addition to funding musical programs of many different types, the CPB helped launch in 1971 National Public Radio (NPR), a network of educational stations that bloomed into a hugely successful and influential news, information, and cultural programming alternative to the commercial broadcast networks.[38]

POSTINDUSTRIALIZATION AND CIVIC CORROSION IN CHICAGO

Although the late 1960s and 1970s marked dramatic real-dollar growth of federal support for the public arts, Chicago, along with large, industrial cities of the Northeast, struggled to contend with a daunting set of economic, social, and cultural challenges that threatened its civic vitality. Strategic reorganization in American industry, whose planning extended almost as far back as the end of World War II, caused a drastic erosion of the urban base of skilled and unskilled labor and manufacturing jobs, and prompted an accelerating decline in Chicago's population.[39] Despite high hopes for President Johnson's war on poverty, the complexity of deindustrialization, the financial demands and divisive political fallout of the Vietnam War and the civil rights era, and disagreements among federal, state, and local activists over how to fix Chicago's ills drained energy and precious resources from urban reform. Continued frustration among African Americans over the discrimination that deprived them of jobs, adequate housing, and municipal services led to uprisings in the late 1960s. Upwardly mobile workers of all classes, ethnicities, and races continued to leave the city in droves, headed for jobs in the burgeoning Chicago suburbs or in the expanding economies of the Sunbelt and the West. In the 1970s, a national recession and high inflation further wracked Chicago's beleaguered urban infrastructure.[40]

Economic constriction and out-migration of industries and urban middle-class residents destabilized the municipal tax base, deferring attention to the aging municipal infrastructure of public parks and institutions that had supported neighborhood life and democratic engagement via music.[41] Sociologists reported alarming concentrations of poverty among a disproportionately female and African American "underclass" living in neighborhoods with failing public schools; understaffed, decrepit, and dangerous municipal parks; dilapidated public housing; and limited local employment prospects. Buffeted by drug violence, disproportionately high rates of incarceration among young African American males, and high rates of infant mortality and AIDS, Chicago's poorest neighborhoods became a political symbol of economic distress, failed postwar liberalism, ill-advised federal policies, and diminished civic expectations.[42]

THE "REAGAN REVOLUTION," THE ARTS, AND THE CIVIC REALM

In the early 1980s, the "Reagan revolution" announced an end to the model of a federally committed public realm of social welfare and cultural enrichment developed by a succession of progressives, New Dealers, and Great Society activists. President Ronald Reagan and his advisers called for economic deregulation, privatization, and deep cuts in urban social spending. The activist state bade farewell to the cities that had given birth to it, but were now in drastic decline and heavily dependent on its pocketbook and centralized services. The Office of Management and Budget (OMB) under David Stockman attempted to slash federal funding of the arts by over 50 percent in the name of returning to what the OMB termed the "historic role of private individual and corporate philanthropic support" for the arts.[43] A counteroffensive led by arts advocates and Congress refuted the OMB's claims about a correlation between increased federal funding and declining private sector support for the arts. The counterinsurgency limited NEA budget cuts in 1982 to about 10 percent, but a new era of austerity for the public arts had begun.

The cutbacks at the NEA were a shock to Chicago and the state of Illinois, removing an important source of support for the city's beleaguered civic outreach sector. With the recession lingering in the Midwest, Governor James R. Thompson added to the stress by cutting off state funding to the Illinois Arts Council entirely. In 1983 the National Assembly of Community Arts Councils reported that Illinois ranked a mediocre thirty-ninth out of the fifty states in arts funding per capita. Chicago fared even worse in the study, languishing at a woeful thirty-eighth out of forty major urban centers in terms of per capita support for the arts.[44] Thompson's cuts proved temporary, but for the rest of the decade, the real-dollar level of federal support for the arts drifted sideways before heading downward in the 1990s.[45] The web of fraternal and benevolent organizations, social clubs, and musical societies of Chicago's late-nineteenth-century neighborhoods no longer existed and thus could not sustain musical civics.[46] Nor were reform-minded musical progressives, Roosevelt New Dealers, or Great Society liberals around to come to the rescue of a unifying vision of civic music culture. By the 1990s studies showed a pattern of mutual reinforcement between community arts organizations, economic revitalization, and civic engagement in cities. But such findings could not offset the bleak conditions facing civic life in urban centers such as Chicago.[47] Nor would corporate philanthropists and private foundations necessarily aid the neediest grassroots outreach organizations or artists who made a point of challenging establishment views in their work.

PISSING CONTESTS
Culture Wars and the NEA

Beginning in 1989 and continuing into the early 1990s, arguments in favor of restoring extensive federal support for arts and culture faced further attack in the form of a partisan backlash against the NEA. Shrill calls for reform or even the dissolution of the NEA came from Republican politicians, New Right pundits, and the Christian conservative lobby. Grants from the NEA supporting two controversial artists, Andrés Serrano and Robert Mapplethorpe, touched off an angry public debate about the function of public art and freedom of expression. Serrano's "Piss Christ," depicting a crucifix suspended in urine, and Mapplethorpe's homoerotic photography prompted a bilious attack by Republican senator Jesse Helms of North Carolina.[48] Congress hurriedly passed legislation banning NEA funding of works "that might be considered obscene, and that do not have serious literary, artistic, political or scientific value."[49] But lawmakers rejected a proposed amendment to the bill by Senator Helms enumerating specific content that should be restricted, such as the sadomasochistic themes that Mapplethorpe, an openly gay man afflicted with AIDS, had explored in his art. Although the NEA requested an "anti-obscenity pledge" from grant recipients, it continued to take political heat from the right. Meanwhile, an outraged constituency made up of political artists, free speech advocates, and gay and lesbian rights activists savaged the NEA for not defending their right to produce democratic public culture, however challenging such work might be to conventional taste.[50]

The NEA controversies reflected the turbulence of the nation's political order, the continued weakening of the welfare state, and profound disagreement over post-1960s social and sexual mores. It also offered certain commonalities and contrasts with struggles over public cultural outreach in the era of musical progressives. The battles over ragtime in Chicago's ceremonial parks or over the city's black-and-tan cabarets in the 1920s were passionate, politicized, and even hateful at times. They also used the media as an organ of amplification and manipulation. But the NEA debate was centered in Washington, where politicians and special-interest groups pitted idealized notions of "artistic freedom" and "government accountability" against each other. The provocative art of Serrano and Mapplethorpe and the heated words on Capitol Hill distracted many ostensibly civic-minded Democrats and Republicans from the evisceration of federal support for urban social welfare and the resulting privatization of public life in America's great cities.

In retrospect, the NEA debacle can be seen as rich in irony when juxtaposed with attempts to define the role of the arts in reforming public culture among musical progressives. The Christian moralists who attacked controversial NEA-funded artists demanded to know why American tax dollars were used to support such work and championed privatization instead. By contrast, the JPA activists of the 1910s and 1920s, shocked by challenges to bourgeois propriety, argued that greater control be given to governmental bodies in order to curtail the debauched excess of the marketplace.

The struggle to control the aesthetic and moral tenor of civic life produced odd allies in both eras, too. Dance reformers and commercial dance hall operators teamed up out of mutual self-interest, but with considerable inner tension. Similarly, the defenders of the NEA's autonomy and public identity, many of them tied to "high" culture institutions supported by public and private philanthropy, found themselves in a sensitive position: that of championing the rights of a proudly combative subculture whose demands for inclusion had potentially dire consequences for the typically mainstream community of grant recipients and institutions, who had tended to marginalize such voices in the past.

When his repeated attempts to quell the controversies failed, NEA chairman John Frohnmayer resigned in February 1992.[51] Though grant funding controversies would recur, the contentious and highly politicized debates receded from the public eye. The media's spotlight shifted to Bill Clinton, the first Democratic president in a decade and a half, leaving the NEA to tiptoe uncertainly into the twenty-first century. Meanwhile, the ongoing privatization of public culture and civic life surged forcefully ahead.[52]

PERFECT PITCH
Music, Consumerism, and Postindustrial Public Culture

After several punishing decades and with a rejuvenated economy, Chicago gradually resuscitated itself and its civic arts and musical life through a pact with the private sector. Beginning in the late 1980s and accelerating through the 1990s, the "let's make a deal" ethos of the Richard M. Daley administration attracted deep-pocketed sponsors to civic events in a way that reoriented the meaning of public space, cultural outreach, and urban reform. While new partnerships burnished Chicago's civic reputation, they also generated a qualitatively different kind of public culture, in which corporate sponsors were increasingly producing the sounds of the city.[53]

In the late nineteenth and early twentieth centuries, Chicago's cultural heterogeneity and the lure of commercial amusements preoccupied civic officials as "problems" to be addressed by reform-minded activists. Today, these attributes are Chicago's bread and butter. They represent cherished assets that are integral to the civic rebirth of the midwestern metropolis led by urban officials and the private sector. The boundaries of a metropolis once hailed as a "city of [ethnic] neighborhoods" are being redrawn as immigration and migration patterns and new technologies of communication connect

Chicago with unprecedented immediacy to eastern Europe, Mexico, Central and South America, the Near and Far East, and the African continent. The 2000 census revealed that for the first time since 1950 Chicago experienced an overall increase in its population. Principles of American cultural citizenship dating at least to the era of Israel Zangwill's play *The Melting Pot* now include the celebration of multicultural diversity, global entrepreneurship, and the municipal embrace of the mass market to consolidate the citizenry.[54]

One symbol of Chicago's postindustrial civic culture is the revival of the nineteenth-century ceremonial park landscape for the twenty-first century. It consists of sparkling streets and sidewalks, a heavy police presence, trees and flowers in profusion, and well-managed, functioning facilities in the downtown area, especially along the lakefront and at Grant Park, where music festivals cater to tourists, conventioneers, suburbanites, and residents (frequently in that order). At the city's celebrated summer music festivals, visitors enter a public realm constituted not as a delivery system for uplifting entertainment, so much as an open-air laboratory devoted to direct marketing and market research on a mass scale. The Grant Park Symphony is a stalwart provider of symphonic music in the summer, and electric blues, gospel, and jazz draw huge crowds as African American music is enshrined at last on the main civic stage. "World music," a marketing category created by the music industry, encompasses the Atlantic and American diasporic sounds from Celtic to reggae to salsa heard annually in the park. The performances are superb, but they are often subordinate to the delivery of the musical publics by the city to the corporate giants who have paid top dollar to capture the assembled throng with their perfect sales pitches.

The multiple musics of park festivals celebrate the abstract concepts of civic engagement and cultural pluralism envisioned by Jane Addams, Ellen Gates Starr, Eleanor Smith, and others, but they are valued for their utility as sales appeals. A major consumer electronics chain sponsors the Chicago Blues Festival and offers a raffle for a home entertainment center in exchange for each contestant's name, address, and answers to questions about household income and spending habits. A *Fortune* 500 company doles out packages of artificially sweetened oatmeal and instant hominy grits to spectators at the Chicago Gospel Festival, who add them to the presupplied goody bags. Nearby, a representative of an Illinois H.M.O. offers complimentary blood pressure screening and dispenses refrigerator magnets. Concert patrons queue up for frozen cheesecake samples, to enter quotidian sweepstakes in which more personal information is required for entrance, or to switch (again) their telephone service.[55]

If corporate pitches dominate the downtown park music experience, a different dynamic prevails outside the glare of the major festivals. Chicago's neighborhood parks continue to manage as best they can, many still providing recognizable forms of musical outreach instituted a century ago. It is a mixed story, however. During the 1980s a number of field house parks in poor areas of the West and South Sides turned into outposts for gangs trafficking in drugs and weapons. In a few instances, courageous supervisors succeeded in reclaiming the parks, but, as was the case in the 1910s, parents and children reported they feared using their own neighborhood parks. Repairing the damage to the integrity of these public areas proved a daunting proposition, and the quality of service remained uneven. A 1990 study of forty parks reported fewer than half attracted "significant participation" from their surrounding neighborhoods. The *Chicago Tribune* observed similar trends in thirty parks that its reporters visited that year.[56]

Nonetheless, in dozens of Chicago's multiethnic industrial neighborhoods ambitious and frugal immigrants, migrants, and laborers, many speaking languages other than English, continue to take advantage of what the field houses have to offer. Anyone may sign up for an opportunity for their children to take affordable music lessons or to participate in music clubs and associations of various kinds. Adults subscribe to park night classes in ballroom, contra, and salsa dancing. Concerts and festivals still sometimes draw on neighborhood talent to provide entertainment for events that are underwritten by local arts organizations, foundations, and, unavoidably, corporate funders. On summer evenings singles, couples, and families with young children continue to heed Henry G. Foreman's advice by coming on over to the park with blankets, picnics, and coolers to hear concerts where the price is always right, and the band playing under the trees may be positively tuneful.

"WALTZ OF HANDS"
The Ballad of Jane and Tupac

Walking in the city reveals that the ghosts of musical progressivism haunt even Chicago's newer public spaces. Back in the 1990s, after years of wrangling, the city of Chicago unveiled a sculpture memorial and small garden park to honor the life of Jane Addams. The park is neither easy to find nor easy to get to, but, once found, it is an oasis of tranquility. It stands north of the Loop overlooking the Ohio Street Beach, between the elevated lip of Lake Shore Drive, where unseen traffic whizzes past, and the Lake Michigan shoreline.[57] Paid for by a private foundation, the choice of location disappointed some who associate Addams with the Near West Side. "Why do we have to have another jewel down there?" complained one community organizer referring to the lakefront. "We could use some jewels on the West Side, too."[58]

As officials explained, the Addams garden park needed to be on the lake as part of its dual purpose of honoring Addams and providing a northerly gateway to the redeveloped municipal navy pier. During the early 1990s, the city spent millions to give the dilapidated municipal waterfront area a dramatic makeover. The pier that once hosted patriotic community singing is now a destination for tourists, school groups, and shoppers, with gorgeous views of the water and the downtown skyline. So-called Navy Pier ("municipal," a term redolent of the old way of imagining civic culture has been dropped) accommodates a chain of shops and restaurants; a convention hall and office complex; and commercial amusements and tourist attractions ranging from lake cruises on high-speed boats to a for-profit children's museum and a massive, illuminated Ferris wheel.

The location of the Addams memorial prompted a newspaper columnist to wax rhapsodic over the decision to situate the garden park "on a picturesque dollop of beachfront in the shadow of the Navy Pier Ferris wheel."[59] Placing a tribute to Addams adjacent to a Ferris wheel, the veritable icon of commerce trumping uplift at the 1893 Columbian Exposition, illustrates yet another of history's minor ironies. Whisking Addams in from the West Side to enhance lakefront urban redevelopment suggests a seamless synthesis of history, civic reform, and marketing, but appearances can also be deceiving. Public urban space remains a site of surprising intersections and revelations, as a walk to the Addams memorial shows.

The sculpture in the garden built to honor Jane Addams is an abstract installation by the renowned artist Louise Bourgeois, inspired in part by Addams early writings. "The final impression was . . . of myriads of hands, empty pathetic, nerveless and workworn," Addams noted after visiting London's East End in 1883. "Perhaps nothing is so fraught with significance as the human hand."[60] Addams words prompted Bourgeois to design an installation consisting of six pedestals situated at the bottom of a circular depression in the middle of the garden. Resting atop each pedestal are representations of individual human hands of men, women, and children hewn from black granite. Bourgeois has described the work as a "waltz of hands," constituting, in her words, "a plea for friendship, of kindness, compassion, tolerance because Jane Addams had this as an ideal."[61]

The installation stunningly captures both the idealism and the self-sacrifice of the progressive "waltz of hands," as well as its human failings, ideological limits, exclusions, and disjunctures. The metaphor of a waltz aptly evokes the genteel surface of progressive reform as it tried to effect a disciplined and harmonious transformation of urban society. For the historian, it also evokes the controlling aspects of this "dance" and the rebellious energies of resistant dancers with whom JPA reformers struggled in the 1910s and 1920s. The individual sculpted hands suggest the fragility of the reform enterprise, if not of its human subjects. These disembodied hands, eerily severed near the wrists, are mostly alone. While some of the hands are touching, they are disconnected from names, faces, or bodies. The effect is decidedly somber and humbling. It leads the viewer to reflect less on Addams herself than on the immensity of her humanitarian task and the extent of the human suffering that she dedicated her life to alleviate and that continues to exist despite her extraordinary life's labors.

On a cold, but sunny autumnal morning during the writing of this book, the park was being put to surprising uses. One slope of the memorial garden showed signs of having recently sheltered a member of Chicago's homeless population. A patch of the tall prairie grasses cultivated within the fenced-off area had been tamped down, with an abandoned mattress placed strategically away from the wind off the lake. No one was in sight. Surrounding the fence that protects the garden and the sculpture installation, metal tablets provided textual information about Addams's life. In keeping with the minimalist quality of Bourgeois's art, a metal placard spelled Addams's name in large block letters. Next to it was added the single word "PACIFIST." A visitor to the park had left a symbolic calling card at the memorial to the Nobel Peace Prize laureate. The visitor had carefully scratched the patina off of the letters in such a way as to brightly highlight the P-A-C in "PACIFIST" Next to that, he or she had scratched the numeral "2," producing a cryptic overlying message: "2PAC."

Jane Addams Memorial, Louise Bourgeois, detail. Chicago
Park District, B. F. Ferguson Monument Fund.

That morning, Jane Addams shared her public memorial with a
citizen's tribute to the slain African American "gangsta" rap musician
Tupac Shakur. Shakur was a commercial rap/hip-hop entertainer/
entrepreneur who got very rich in the early 1990s producing music
and videos that reached millions of urban and suburban kids of all
classes, races, and ethnicities.[62] Like Addams, he gained an international reputation. Unlike Addams, Shakur grew up hard, serving
time in prison along the way. His songs addressed themes of urban
street culture and gangs and expressed personal reflections on street
violence, including the requisite misogynistic sexual bravado typical
of the genre.[63] In his lyrics, Shakur portrayed a street-smart urban
survivor testifying to the spirit of youth and the city streets.

Shakur might well have faded into anonymity, eclipsed by another young, ambitious rapper drawn to the "gangsta" style. But in
1996, at the apex of his career, the twenty-five-year-old Shakur died
in a drive-by shooting in Las Vegas. The unsolved murder prompted
a stream of speculation about his death inside the hip-hop and rap

music industry and in the larger media culture as well. Some cultural critics, fans, and pop sociologists suggested that Shakur's pugnacious attitude and popularity in gang circles hastened his demise. Others linked the celebrity shooting to the shocking frequency of death among young African American males in urban areas. These interpreters insisted that Shakur had the misfortune of being an African American man in the wrong place at the wrong time. A popular movement spread to claim Shakur as a black Everyman, a martyr to the urban violence that was in part a consequence of the pervasive racism in America. Scores of memorial sites on the World Wide Web described the rapper as a sensitive soul and a poet. Academics produced scholarly papers and books devoted to Shakur, while posthumous musical releases flooded the market. His murder even prompted calls for reconciliation among warring gangs in America's cities, most notably by Chuck D., arguably the progenitor of the "gangsta" rap mystique as a member of Public Enemy, who warned young fans about music that appeared to "blur the line between fantasy and reality."[64]

Public space by its nature allows for the possibility of intersections of all kinds, but the linkage of Jane Addams and Tupac Shakur by an unknown hand contextualizes the musical progressive legacy in unexpected ways. How could two persons be any more different—a Nobel Peace Prize winner and a commercial gangsta rap entertainer? Yet each waged a struggle through music to comment on and influence the ways that Americans perceived themselves and the strengths and ills of their culture. Shakur sang of those affected by racism in America and black-on-black violence. On occasion he also called on the victimized to show dignity and compassion. The outpouring of grief from his fans suggested that beneath Shakur's often angry words and posturing he expressed a desperate hope for a redeemed world among a disaffected and alienated population. Jane Addams's settlement outreach attempted to speak to fractious populations as well. Musical progressivism sought to provide artistic outlets for those in industrial occupations. It promoted music as a tool to fight exploitation and indirectly to curb urban violence, offering means for self- and community growth. Addams would have despised Shakur's music and its associated imagery, but she might well have found his message compelling. Shakur would likely have found choice adjectives to mock Victorian pretenses and hypocrisies. As the visitor who connected these two musical activists seemed to imply, however, Addams and Shakur might also have had an extraordinarily interesting discussion about American youth, music, cultural politics, and the pursuit of justice and peace.

Musical progressivism challenged the city of Chicago to redefine the relationship between music, citizenship, and democratic public culture. Activists combined reform dreams of metropolitan unity with aesthetic and moral convictions about the power of music. Unimpressed by the rhetoric of Americanism and democracy that characterized the prolix "cultured generation," musical progressives extended human, technical, and financial resources to implement democratic change directly. They left their comfortable parlors, paneled libraries, and private offices to take to the streets, parks, and neighborhoods. Here they found a world unknown to them, but one that they attempted to engage through the medium of music. While not always successful, and sometimes deeply misguided, these activists achieved their ambition to make music one of the arts of citizenship.

Musical progressivism could not have taken hold as it did without urban residents themselves. On a journey without maps, activists encountered populations dramatically different from themselves, and some in those populations were understandably skeptical about grand schemes associated with a system that too often exploited or ignored the urban industrial populace. To their credit, musical progressives came to listen as well as to speak. Together, these historical actors sought to carry music across social divides, and in doing so they reoriented the way that citizens historically claimed a sense of shared space, place, and American identity through music.

NOTES

ABBREVIATIONS OF ARCHIVAL SOURCES

BLP   Bessie Louise Pierce Papers
CFLPS   Chicago Foreign Language Press Survey Records, University of
           Chicago
CMA   Civic Music Association Reports, Newberry Library
CHS   Chicago Historical Society
CPD   Chicago Park District Special Collections
CPL   Chicago Public Library, Harold Washington Library Center
CSOA   Chicago Symphony Orchestra Archives
EWBP   Ernest Watson Burgess Papers, University of Chicago
GC   Frederick Grant Gleason Collection, Newberry Library
JAP   Bryan, *Jane Addams Papers on Microfilm*
JPAR   Juvenile Protective Association Records, University of Illinois
           at Chicago
MMCS   "Making Music Chicago Style" Collection, Chicago Historical
           Society
RFCC   Records of the Federal Communications Commission (RG
           173), National Archives and Records Administration
UC   University of Chicago
UIC   University of Illinois at Chicago
WPA/FMP   Records of the Work Projects Administration, Federal Music
           Project (RG 69), National Archives and Records Administration
WSNC   West Side Newspaper Collection, Chicago Public Library

INTRODUCTION

1. Jane Addams and Eleanor Smith, "A House Stands on a Busy Street,"
n.d., reel 51, JAP. According to Bryan and Davis, *100 Years at Hull-House*, 108,
the song appeared in 1905.

2. With some regret, I leave aside the vast and important subject of public school music, nor do I directly address church music, both of which are important influences on the tenor of music in public.

3. Musicologist H. Wiley Hitchcock delimits two stylistic categories of American music that serve as a useful, though somewhat problematic shorthand. Forms seen by contemporaries as entertaining and utilitarian he dubbed "vernacular"; music taught and learned for its technical virtuosity, grace, or edifying qualities was "cultivated." See Hitchcock, *Music in the United States*, 44. The argument made in this book draws attention to the production and codification of such a neat dichotomy, as well as to the manner in which aesthetic and utilitarian distinctions reveal contemporary struggles over power and authority waged through such classification systems. For a cogent elaboration of this point, see Broyles, *Music of the Highest Class*, 1–4.

4. Mussulman, *Music in the Cultured Generation*, 77–185, 193. See also Broyles, *Music of the Highest Class*; Ahlquist, *Democracy at the Opera*; Moore, *Yankee Blues*; and M. A. J. Feldman, "George P. Upton." On the struggle between Eurocentrism and views of exceptionalism operating in American music, see Chase, *America's Music*. On debate about trends in American composing and national identity in the Progressive Era, see Tischler, *An American Music*, and Hamm, "Dvořák in America," 344–53.

5. On the sacralization thesis, see DiMaggio, "Cultural Entrepreneurship in Nineteenth-Century Boston," and DiMaggio, "Cultural Entrepreneurship in Nineteenth-Century Boston, Part II"; Levine, *Highbrow/Lowbrow*; and Kasson, *Rudeness and Civility*. An influential critique of the mechanistic quality of the "sacralization" hypothesis that calls for historical attention to social and aesthetic variation within this analytic framework is Locke, "Music Lovers, Patrons, and the 'Sacralization" of Nineteenth-Century Music." See also C. P. Smith, "Symphony and Opera in Progressive-Era Los Angeles." In examining musical progressivism I seek to offer insights into the role of other musical publics in influencing debates about the ultimate purpose of music and social transformation, sometimes, but hardly exclusively, waged through explicit or implied categories of "high" versus "low" or "cultivated" versus "vernacular."

6. On the important contributions of female patrons on late-nineteenth- and early-twentieth-century American musical life, see especially Locke and Barr, *Cultivating Music in America*, and Blair, *The Torchbearers*. On attitudes of art philanthropy to cast a wide social net, see K. D. McCarthy, *Noblesse Oblige*.

7. Kenney, in *Chicago Jazz*, makes a notable effort to connect progressive reform associated with the Juvenile Protective Association to the regulation of jazz in Chicago. See also the analysis of reform ideology and the dramatic pageant in Glassberg, *American Historical Pageantry*.

8. On the vexed/indispensable point, see Rodgers, "In Search of Progressivism"; Crunden, "Thick Description in the Progressive Era"; and

C. Gordon, "Still Searching for Progressivism." For an important argument for resituating the locus of power in the Progressive Era with the urban population, see Ethington, *The Public City*. The Progressive Era defies precise chronological boundaries. I do not rigidly differentiate "Progressive reformers" (1900–1930) from their "nineteenth-century predecessors" as some scholars prefer to do. See L. Gordon, *Heroes of Their Own Lives*, 21–22. I do use a temporal frame of 1870–1930 when speaking of the "Progressive Era." Scholars typically have in mind the years 1890–1920 when discussing ideologies of progressivism. One leading study dates the "Progressive Era" from 1870 to 1940; see Rodgers, *Atlantic Crossings*, 70.

9. In the annals of music education, "progressive" has technical connotations that bear only passing resemblance to the issues that are the focus of this book. See Tellstrom, *Music in American Education*, and Labuta and Smith, *Music Education*.

10. Rodgers, *Atlantic Crossings*, 161. On environmentalism, uplift, and progressive reform, see Rothman, *The Discovery of the Asylum*; Wright, *Moralism and the Model Home*; W. H. Wilson, *The City Beautiful Movement*.

11. Thompson, *The Soundscape of Modernity*, is a path-breaking study on broader issues of technologized sound and progressive ideology. For a provocative treatment of sound's place in abolitionist reform culture, see Cruz, *Culture on the Margins*, 43–66.

12. A few of the important case studies on this subject include Jones, "Class Expression versus Social Control?"; Lears, "From Salvation to Self-Realization"; Kasson, *Amusing the Million*; Peiss, *Cheap Amusements*; Cohen, *Making a New Deal*; Denning, "The End of Mass Culture"; Lears, "Making Fun of Popular Culture."

13. Years ago, Bender called for historical analysis of the processes through which social and cultural behaviors and values emerge and are deemed normative and justifiable as "public" ideals and civic standards in a democratic society; see Bender, "Wholes and Parts." He pointed specifically to Bourdieu, *Distinction*, as a potential model.

14. Bender argued that historical analysis of extrapolitical processes could reveal the undercurrents of struggle in the formation of a democratic polity. As he defined it: "The public culture of a society is a forum where power in its various forms, including meaning and aesthetics, is elaborated and made authoritative. Because of its contested quality, the public is an inherently political collectivity, and this distinguishes it from mere social collectivities or cultural pastiches." Bender, "Wholes and Parts," 126.

15. Historians have faulted Habermas's "public sphere" for a variety of reasons, most notably for its narrow definition of the "political" and its historically problematic account of the rise of "bourgeois" and democratic ideology, not to mention its partitioning of the domains of "public" and "private" social, cultural, and political expression. As Nancy Fraser has argued, the

model structurally and conceptually privileges male members of a dominant class. It remains unable to account for the complex ways in which women, racial minorities, and other political subcultures and collectives have acted to influence public opinion or to catalyze political and social change. Fraser suggests "counterpublics" as an alternative model to account for the status differentials among groups that retain an ability to influence opinion. Fraser, "Rethinking the Public Sphere."

16. As Michel de Certeau has argued, one of the important aspects of "public" spaces in cities is their intrinsic ungovernability. Despite their extensive organization and rationalization, public areas have historically retained their potential as staging grounds for resistance to dominant social systems, or as powerful tools of equalization for a minority or subculture prepared to adapt these spaces for their own purposes. See de Certeau, "Walking in the City."

17. On reform, its architects, and its impact, see Hofstadter, *The Age of Reform*; Wiebe, *The Search for Order*; P. Boyer, *Urban Masses and Moral Order*; L. Gordon, *Heroes of Their Own Lives*; and Rodgers, *Atlantic Crossings*.

18. It is important to stress that "women in public" as a subject for discussion typically assumed a normative ideal of women being white and of a "respectable"—that is, middle-class—socioeconomic status. See Ryan, *Women in Public*.

19. As the republic grew between 1825 and 1850, women participated in the nation's active ceremonial public culture, but in constrained contexts. They typically used voices aligning them with the domestic, private realm of the so-called women's sphere. Civic celebrations often centered on the ubiquitous parade in which women's visible representation often came in the gendered form of idealized symbols of purity, virtue, and nationhood, such as *Justice* or *Liberty*. In short, the permissible role for middle-class women in public in antebellum America remained typically confined to the "public celebration of the virtues of private life." See Ryan, *Women in Public*, 37. The poor, non-native-born, and African American populations of the nation suffered marginalization in these ceremonies, too. See S. G. Davis, *Parades and Power*, and Kerber, *Women of the Republic*. On poor women's experiences, see especially Stansell, *City of Women*.

20. On the radical transformation of American nightlife and its gendered implications, see especially, Erenberg, *Steppin' Out*, and Peiss, *Cheap Amusements*.

21. Progressive activism in the areas of women's protection, juvenile delinquency, and legal reform are surveyed in Odem, *Delinquent Daughters*. On Chicago, see Meyerowitz, *Women Adrift*.

22. U.S. Bureau of the Census, *Eleventh Census*, 1:704.

23. Important overviews of music in American life by historical musicologists include Chase, *America's Music*; Crawford, *The American Musical Landscape*; and Hamm, *Putting Popular Music in Its Place*.

24. One scholar who has raised important questions about the history of audience formation in American music is Nicholas Tawa; see his *Serenading the Reluctant Eagle* and *High-Minded and Low-Down*. For two useful overviews of efforts to engage questions about music's social status by combining elements of historical musicology, ethnomusicology, and social and cultural history methods, see Levy and Tischler, "Into the Cultural Mainstream," and Radano and Bohlman, "Music and Race."

25. See Stokes, "Introduction." On music, experience, and the politics of everyday life, see Small, *Musicking*, and Finnegan, *The Hidden Musicians*. On ethnomusicology and urban musics, see Nettl, *Eight Urban Musical Cultures*, and Reyes-Schramm, "Ethnic Music." On the importance of history to assessing oppositional practices, see Lipsitz, "Against the Wind."

26. For a sampling of notable studies that address issues of music within the bounds of ethnicity, race, and class, see Kusmer, *A Ghetto Takes Shape*; C. Keil, *Urban Blues*; Baraka, *Blues People*; DeVeaux, *The Birth of Bebop*; Glasser, *My Music Is My Flag*; Peña, *The Texas-Mexican Conjunto*; S. E. Smith, *Dancing in the Street*; Greene, *A Passion for Polka*; Stowe, *Swing Changes*; and Aparicio, *Listening to Salsa*. For a review of studies working across these divides, see Peretti, "Chief Amusements." On "Americanism" and music as a compositional and discursive question, see especially Tischler, *An American Music*.

CHAPTER ONE

1. *Chicago Tribune*, May 31, 1873.

2. Sawislak, *Smoldering City*, 163. See also Cronon, *Nature's Metropolis*, 345–47. The 1870 census lists 298,977 residents. Over 100,000 lost their homes during the Great Fire. The financial panic of 1873 and ensuing recession would not hit until the fall.

3. *The Jubilee*, 3; *Chicago Tribune*, June 3, 1873.

4. M. A. J. Feldman, "George P. Upton," 104. Upton joined the *Tribune* in 1861 and served as principal music critic at the *Tribune* from 1863 to 1881.

5. The term "public" refers descriptively to the general body of men and women formed in association at such events. "Publics" refers to the theories of a public sphere constituted by multiple groups seeking resources and acknowledgment as relevant constituents within a larger public body. See discussion in the Introduction.

6. Upton, *Musical Memories*, 250. At the opening of his book, Upton writes: "I dedicate these memories to the ghosts." Upton also coauthored *The Great Conflagration: Its Past, Present, and Future*, described in M. A. J. Feldman, "George P. Upton."

7. On the destruction of the Crosby Opera House, see Upton, *Musical Memories*, 249–51.

8. Thomas's bold reputation stretched back to his decision to found his own symphony orchestra in New York in 1866. He first visited Chicago in

1869 and returned often. The best scholarly account of Thomas's life is Schabas, *Theodore Thomas*. See also the classic accounts in Upton, *Theodore Thomas*, and R. F. Thomas, *Memoirs of Theodore Thomas*. Important analyses of Thomas's impact on American music can be found in Tischler, *An American Music*; Levine, *Highbrow/Lowbrow*; and J. Horowitz, *Wagner Nights*.

9. The first documented opera production of Vincenzo Bellini's *La Sonnambula* in 1850 established a precedent for regular stops in Chicago by opera troupes and touring companies. Fern et al., "Chicago," 418. Andreas, in *History of Chicago*, 3:643–44, makes a similar observation about Chicago's reliance on traveling musical entertainments, rather than on permanent, local institutions presenting classical music.

10. On subsequent activities of the philanthropic elite in Chicago in the late nineteenth and early twentieth centuries, see H. L. Horowitz, *Culture and the City*, and K. D. McCarthy, *Noblesse Oblige*.

11. The description of the tours comes from *The Jubilee*, 3. See also *Chicago Tribune*, June 3, 1873.

12. On the spirited competition between Chicago and Cincinnati, and Chicago's tendency to co-opt innovations, as in the case of meatpacking, see Cronon, *Nature's Metropolis*, 228–30. On the first Cincinnati festival, see Schabas, *Theodore Thomas*, 57–8.

13. The Cincinnati Festivals were biennial events until 1904. The first festival featured selections from Handel, Gluck, Beethoven, Schumann, Mendelssohn, and Schubert. See Upton, *Theodore Thomas*, 2:156. In an ironic twist, Louis Jullien, the French conductor and composer famed for his "Fireman's Quadrille" in which hustling firemen, broken glass, and squirting water accompanied the music, briefly trained Theodore Thomas in the early 1850s. On other critical assessments favoring Thomas, see Schabas, *Theodore Thomas*, 9–10, 53.

14. *Illinois Staats-Zeitung*, May 20, 1871, German, box 14, CFLPS. Throughout this book I rely on the WPA-sponsored translations of the foreign-language press of Chicago and Illinois. These provide an informative window into the imagined communities of Chicago's multilingual and non-English speakers.

15. *Chicago Tribune*, May 10, 1873.

16. Cady organized the Chicago Musical Union on January 31, 1857. See Upton, *Theodore Thomas*, 1:320. On the history of the firm, see Epstein, *Music Publishing in Chicago*.

17. On Jubilee organizing personnel, see Andreas, *History of Chicago*, vol. 3. On the desire to emulate Boston's jubilees, see *The Jubilee*, 27. Dena Epstein, the authoritative scholar of Chauncy Marvin Cady's career believes that, while Upton and Cady may have met, there is no evidence of a close bond or of a sign that Cady felt deeply invested in the fate of European classical music in Chicago. Telephone interview, June 30, 2002.

18. For a well-documented account of the organization and critical reception of the two festivals, see Nicholson, "Gilmore's Boston Peace Jubilees."

19. On the eclectic nature of "popular" music in America at this time, see Crawford, *The American Musical Landscape*; Hamm, *Yesterdays*; Tawa, *The Way to Tin Pan Alley*; and J. Horowitz, *Wagner Nights*.

20. Darlington, *Irish Orpheus*, 51.

21. Nicholson, "Gilmore's Boston Peace Jubilees," 40. Darlington, *Irish Orpheus*, 39–58.

22. John Sullivan Dwight, "The Second Gilmore Jubilee," *Dwight's Journal of Music* 32, no. 8 (July 1872): 270, quoted in Tischler, *An American Music*, 47. On Gilmore's jubilees, see also Levine, *Highbrow/Lowbrow*, 104–7.

23. Upton, *Musical Memories*, 202.

24. Quoted in Darlington, *Irish Orpheus*, 56. On Gilmore as a force in expanding the definition of music education, see Labuta and Smith, *Music Education*, 24–25.

25. "Jubilee" suggests anything from an occasion for general rejoicing to a fiftieth anniversary celebration, to a period of remission from sin, to a time described in Hebrew scripture when slaves were to be emancipated and property restored. See *Oxford English Dictionary*, 2d ed., s.v. "jubilee." On the "divine art of music," see plate 2 in Nicholson, "Gilmore's Boston Peace Jubilees," 243.

26. See program reproduced in Nicholson, "Gilmore's Boston Peace Jubilees," 166.

27. On issues of ethnicity, class, and political conflict challenging the cooperative ethos of the rebuilding effort, see Sawislak, *Smoldering City*, especially 163–216. On the discourse of boosterism and Chicago's destiny both prior to and after the Great Fire, see C. S. Smith, *Urban Disorder*, and Cronon, *Nature's Metropolis*, 23–54.

28. My special thanks to David Scobey for suggesting that I consider the oddly constrained concept of "jubilee" used by its organizers.

29. *Chicago Tribune*, June 6, 1873; Upton, *Musical Memories*, 200.

30. *Chicago Tribune*, June 6, 1873. Even Gilmore's generally upbeat biographer conceded that the Chicago concerts "were inferior not only in volume, but in quality." See Darlington, *Irish Orpheus*, 76. Alfred T. Andreas labeled the Jubilee "buncombe." H. W. Schwartz declared bluntly that "the musical results [in Chicago] were appalling." See Andreas, *History of Chicago*, 3:648, and Schwartz, *Bands of America*, 74.

31. *Chicago Tribune*, June 7, 1873, 2. Because Upton was the principal cultivated music critic of the *Tribune*, it is possible that he authored, or influenced the tone of, unsigned items on major music events in Chicago.

32. *New York World*, June 6, 1873, cited in "What They Say" column of *Chicago Tribune*, June 8, 1873, 2.

33. Ibid.

34. *Cincinnati Gazette*, cited in ibid.

35. On aesthetic refinement as a modality for class in an ideologically "classless" society, see especially Bushman, *The Refinement of America*.

36. "German" for the purposes of this discussion refers to persons whose origins were in territories encompassed by imperial Germany after 1871 and the boundaries subsequently modified by the Treaty of Versailles. On the analytic challenges of relying on state and national membership in speaking of unifying processes of identity construction among "Germans," see K. N. Conzen, "Germans," and K. N. Conzen, *Immigrant Milwaukee*. For further discussion of German-American culture in Chicago, see H. Keil and John Jentz, *German Workers in Chicago*, and H. Keil, *German Workers' Culture*.

37. Although there were Germans and other Slavic groups residing in Bohemia, Moravia, and Silesia, throughout this discussion I will be using "Bohemian" to describe the predecessor cultural and linguistic population that reorganized under the national heading of "Czech" following World War I. For background, see Freeze, "Czechs," 261–72. On Jews in Chicago, see especially Meites, *History of the Jews of Chicago*, and Cutler, *The Jews of Chicago*.

38. Helpful general studies of Chicago's migrant, immigrant, and ethnic populations and life experiences include Pierce, *A History of Chicago*, vol. 3; Cohen, *Making a New Deal*; and Holli and Jones, *Ethnic Chicago*. For specific studies, see, for example, Pacyga, *Polish Immigrants and Industrial Chicago*; Barrett, *Work and Community in the Jungle*; Hofmeister, *The Germans of Chicago*; Keil and Jentz, *German Workers in Chicago*; and Nelli, *The Italians in Chicago*. On the challenges facing African Americans seeking work and housing nearby because of racial bias, see Spear, *Black Chicago*; Drake and Cayton, *Black Metropolis*; and Grossman, *Land of Hope*.

39. The power of neighborhood provincialism in Chicago is a recurring motif in Cohen, *Making a New Deal*. For an overview of music in the labor movement, see P. Foner, *American Labor Songs in the Nineteenth Century*, and Lieberman, *"My Song Is My Weapon"*.

40. On music in everyday life and its associated meanings, see Chase, *America's Music*; Tawa, *The Way to Tin Pan Alley*; Small, *Musicking*; and Finnegan, *The Hidden Musicians*. On the later contributions of ethnic music stores to neighborhood life in the 1920s and 1930s, see Greene, *A Passion for Polka*, and Cohen, *Making a New Deal*. For a national perspective, see Spottswood, *Ethnic Music on Records*.

41. On hybridity, music, and identity formation, see Peña, *The Texas-Mexican Conjunto*, and Gilroy, *The Black Atlantic*.

42. Care is warranted in tracing ethnic, social, and cultural allegiances among late-nineteenth and early-twentieth-century populations of "Germans," "Bohemians," "Poles," and so forth. Even as these designations became codified by newspapers, census reports, and other sources available to

historians, superficial linguistic or national affiliations concealed patterns of trans-European migration, dislocations, civil, ethnocultural, and religious conflicts, and political upheavals that belie stable classification. The multicultural Hapsburg empire supplied Chicago with "Bohemians," "Czechs," and "Czechoslovaks," but such designations fluctuated in the public record. Without reifying these categories, this chapter sets out a range of activities found in the universe of neighborhood music in Chicago, noting where appropriate their significance to the lives of participants linked to various cultural traditions identified with particular immigrant and ethnic subgroups.

43. In the years following Chicago's founding, singing societies and choral groups provided a significant portion of musical entertainment in the downtown area. Among the earliest documented groups were the Old Settler's Society (1835–36), the Chicago Choral Union (1846), the Musical Union (1858–66), and the Oratorio Society (1868–71). Andreas, *History of Chicago*, 1:651. The North American Sängerbund, an association of German singing societies, held a festival in Chicago in 1857, see Devick, "Orlando Blackman," 31.

44. "Foreign stock" was a census designation used in this period to designate a non-native-born individual or the offspring of one or more non-native-born parents.

45. Statistic reported in Andreas, *History of Chicago*, 3:651.

46. Anthony Mallek, an organist, composer, and teacher, headed the organization, while also leading musical services at Holy Trinity Church from 1893 to 1916. Another luminary, Dr. Felix Borowski, won acclaim as a faculty member and later as president of the Chicago Musical College. See also Zglenicki, *Poles of Chicago*, 55–65, 177.

47. *Svornost*, October 4, 1879, Choral Information, Bohemian Singing Societies, box 2, MMCS.

48. *Zgoda*, December 23, 1897, Polish, box 34, CFLPS.

49. Ibid.

50. *Svornost*, February 11, 1884, photocopy from BLP located in Choral Information, Bohemian Singing Societies, box 2, MMCS. On competing claims for wage earners off-hours placing commercial amusements, self-conscious ethnic particularism, class consciousness, and claims to "Americanism in tension," see especially Gerstle, *Working-Class Americanism*; Rosenzweig, *Eight Hours for What We Will*; and Couvares, *The Remaking of Pittsburgh*.

51. For an informative overview of the social world of the *Männerchöre* in another city at this time, see Morrow, "Singing and Drinking in New Orleans," 5–24.

52. Nelson, *Beyond the Martyrs*, 128–29. See also Kiesewetter, "German-American Labor Press," and Petra Lehmann, "Songs of the German-American Labor Movement: Workers' Culture in Late-Nineteenth-Century Chicago" (MS in author's possession). On European patterns, see Dowe, "The

Workingmen's Choral Movement." Numerous immigrant and ethnic groups sponsored workingmen's singing societies and music academies. See Choral Information, box 2, MMCS.

53. See E. R. McCarthy, "The Bohemians in Chicago"; Capek, *The Cechs (Bohemians) in America*, 10, 14, 17, 228; *Svornost*, April 26, 1881, photocopy from BLP located in Choral Information, Bohemian Singing Societies, box 2, MMCS.

54. See *Chicago Tribune*, June 30, 1881, photocopy from BLP located in Festivals, box 38, MMCS. The *Chicago Times*, July 2, 1881, reported that 7,000 were in attendance, but "[t]he singers had some difficulty in competing with the nearby railroad switching yards." See also *Illinois Staats-Zeitung*, July 1, 1881, German, CFLPS; *Marquis' Hand-book of Chicago*, 258–59. Hans Balatka headed the Third Philharmonic Society between 1860 and 1868. The orchestra comprised members of the Great Western Band and a string section. This orchestra was notable for its time because it gave audiences complete symphonies, with Beethoven often on the program. See "Orchestras," unsigned MS in box 49, MMCS. The MS cites the *Chicago Tribune*, February 11, 1861; April 11, 1861; April 28, 1862; and November 14, 1863. It also cites Philharmonic Society Programs 1860–66; and Upton, *Theodore Thomas*, 1:71–162. On Hans Balatka's distinguished career, see Reagan, "Art Music in Milwaukee in the Late Nineteenth Century"; Schleis, "Opera in Milwaukee"; Upton, *Musical Memories*, 262–67.

55. Andreas, *History of Chicago*, 3:649; Nicholson, "Gilmore's Boston Peace Jubilees," 127.

56. Prior to Theodore Thomas's rise to prominence in Chicago, Hans Balatka reigned as the leading area conductor of European classical music. He remained a revered figure in cultivated music circles and continued to be active in the music arena for many years. See, for example, "The Germans of Chicago Honor Bismarck," *Die Abendpost*, August 16, 1898, German, box 13, CFLPS.

57. Andreas, *History of Chicago*, 3:649.

58. *Chicago Tribune*, May 23, 1882, photocopy of transcribed clipping from BLP located in Festivals, box 38, MMCS.

59. *Chicago Tribune*, June 30, 1881, ibid. See also *Chicago Tribune*, May 23, 1882.

60. On the neighborhood role of the Bohemian *Sokol* (literally, falcon), see *Denní Hlasatel*, December 12, 1905, and December 5, 1910, photocopies from BLP located in Choral Information, Bohemian Singing Societies, box 2, MMCS. On the Turners' influence, see, for example, Chambers, "Chicago's Turners."

61. *Illinois Staats-Zeitung*, January 25, 1889, German, box 13, CFLPS. The history of the Philharmonic Society extended back to 1850, and it existed in various incarnations as an important orchestra in the city prior to

the establishment of the Chicago Symphony. See Devick, "Orlando Black-man," 28.

62. Correspondence, Frances L. Roberts, March 18, 1873, Frances Roberts Collection, Chicago Historical Society, Chicago, Ill., quoted in Sawislak, *Smoldering City*, 220.

63. *Illinois Staats-Zeitung*, October 18, 1876, German, box 13, CFLPS.

64. On print media's power to construct such discursive publics, see B. Anderson, *Imagined Communities*.

65. According to one report, the call for reform was at least partially heeded. An experiment with a smoke- and alcohol-free Turner concert in January 1879 attracted a mixed audience of German and American women. "Many a fashionably dressed lady appeared, who, on any other Sunday afternoon, would have scorned the idea of being seen in the Turnhalle [*sic*], or perhaps anywhere except in her home or at church." *Illinois Staats-Zeitung*, January 6, 1879, German, box 13, CFLPS.

66. *Illinois Staats-Zeitung*, January 25, 1889, ibid.

67. Schabas, *Theodore Thomas*, 82.

68. The quotation from Thomas is from a statement made in 1873 during his concerts in New York's Central Park Garden. See ibid., 59.

69. Centennial organizers only committed to paying Thomas's orchestra for the inauguration concert. Subsequent concerts failed to draw crowds, resulting in a truncated schedule and a $20,000 debt in Thomas's name. See Schabas, *Theodore Thomas*, 70–78.

70. The first half-century of Chicago's musical history is littered with failed attempts by conductors to consistently attract audiences to classical European music. See Upton, *Musical Memories*.

71. On practices at European pleasure gardens, see Hamm, *Yesterdays*, 5.

72. Upton, *Theodore Thomas*, 1:69.

73. R. F. Thomas, *Memoirs of Theodore Thomas*, 123–24.

74. Programs, Theodore Thomas Summer Garden Concerts, 1881. These are bound volumes located in the manuscript collections of the Newberry Library, Chicago, Ill.

75. Upton, *Musical Memories*, 183. On the context of the strike, see Schneirov, *Labor and Urban Politics*, 69–76.

76. *Chicago Tribune*, July 11, 1886.

77. Upton, *Theodore Thomas*, 1:171.

78. Quote from a letter to Thomas reproduced in part in Upton, *Theodore Thomas*, 1:70. The signatories of the letter included Wirt Dexter, Edward S. Isham, E. B. McCagg, Henry W. King, J. D. Harvey, and Marshall Field, among others.

79. R. F. Thomas, *Memoirs of Theodore Thomas*, 132.

80. *Chicago Tribune*, August 5, 1877.

81. Upton, *Theodore Thomas*, 2:197–98. He also performed at two fes-

tivals in Chicago in 1882 and 1884 that were well received. See Schabas, *Theodore Thomas*, 119–20, 128.

82. *Chicago Herald*, July 18, 1886, vol. 5, 168, GC.

83. The Chicago "summer nights" concert programs are compiled in Upton, *Theodore Thomas*, 2:197–226.

84. See Fifth Concert, August 18, 1881, Upton, *Theodore Thomas*, 2:200; *Chicago Tribune*, July 3, 1888, vol. 7, GC.

85. On Wagner's impact on American concert-going and audiences of the period, see J. Horowitz, *Wagner Nights*.

86. In *Wagner Nights*, Joseph Horowitz offers an interpretive reading of Teller's novel as an illustration of the spread of Wagnerism. By coincident interest, I use the novel somewhat differently: to capture the unique social dynamics internal to the Thomas concerts and the important democratic social crossings that they engendered.

87. Teller, *The Cage*, 113.

88. Ibid., 95.

89. Ibid., 99. Thomas is credited as the first conductor to present the "Ride of the Valkyries" in the United States in 1870. See Tischler, *An American Music*, 51.

90. On the social construction of middle-class concert listening and the implications of this practice, see Kasson, *Rudeness and Civility*; Levine, *Highbrow/Lowbrow*; and, for comparative data, Johnson, *Listening in Paris*.

91. *Chicago Herald*, July 18, 1886, vol. 5, GC.

92. On apprehensions about unaccompanied women in public, see Ryan, *Women in Public*, and Meyerowitz, *Women Adrift*. On issues of managing sexual activity, see, for example, Odem, *Delinquent Daughters*.

93. *Chicago Tribune*, July 3, 1888, vol. 7, GC.

94. *Chicago Tribune*, August 5, 1888, vol. 7, GC.

95. *Chicago Tribune*, July 10, 1886, vol. 5, GC.

96. *Arbeiter Zeitung*, July, 29, 1882, German, box 13, CFLPS. I have taken the liberty of correcting the translator's use of the word "fair" to "expo" to avoid confusion with the 1893 event.

97. *Chicago News*, August 7, 1890, vol. 10, GC.

98. On the career of Seidl, see J. Horowitz, *Wagner Nights*. On the changing social composition of audiences attracted to Coney Island prior to the 1890s, see Kasson, *Amusing the Million*, 30–34.

99. Upton *Theodore Thomas*, 1:104. His scholarly biographer hints that melancholia and health concerns consumed Thomas between about 1895 and 1905, the year of his death; see Schabas, *Theodore Thomas*, 210–11, 246.

100. For a useful geographic orientation, see the reproduction of "Hills' Guide Map" to the fairgrounds and the Midway included in Badger, *The Great American Fair*.

101. The phrase reworks Warren Susman's "culture of abundance" thesis; it appears in Rydell, *All the World's a Fair*.

102. Classic elaborations of this point include Susman, *Culture as History*, and Trachtenberg and Foner, *The Incorporation of America*. A concise but useful overview of the fair is in Kasson, *Amusing the Million*, 17–28. See also Badger, *The Great American Fair*; Cronon, *Nature's Metropolis*, 341–69; N. Harris and Chicago Historical Society, *Grand Illusions*. For a critique of the celebration of racist forms of Western cultural imperialism at major fairs and expositions of the era, see Rydell, *All the World's a Fair*.

103. The history of musical performances at the Columbian Exposition has garnered considerable scholarly attention. See especially Tischler, *An American Music*, 42–67, and M. McCarthy, "American Music Education." See also N. Harris, "John Philip Sousa." Harris describes Sousa's quest for a singular mass, commercial audience as "cultural meliorism." I distinguish the market-driven premise of this quest from the kinds of sustained civic and place-specific reforms that constituted musical progressivism.

104. On the power relations reflected in the encyclopedic and imperial taxonomies of the fair, see especially Rydell, *All the World's a Fair*. For key statements on artistic selection and hierarchy at the fair, see Guion, "From Yankee Doodle thro' to Handel's Largo," and A. Feldman, "Being Heard."

105. Schabas, *Theodore Thomas*, 197. William Tomlins represented an important link to musical progressivism through his work at Hull House and in developing public opportunities for children's music. See chapter 3.

106. Statement of Music Bureau, June 30, 1892, quoted in Upton, *Theodore Thomas*, 1:194–95.

107. Devick, "Orlando Blackman," 247; Upton, "Musical Societies," 79. As it happened, however, many of these groups declined the invitation. See Guion, "From Yankee Doodle thro' to Handel's Largo," and Schabas, *Theodore Thomas*.

108. See Upton, "Musical Societies," 82, and M. McCarthy, "American Music Education," 124.

109. Thomas's 1905 autobiography includes a detailed discussion of what he considered to be proper etiquette at symphony concerts. On rules at the Exposition concerts, see *Chicago Herald*, September 2, 1893.

110. *Artistic Guide to Chicago and the World's Columbian Exposition and American Culture* (Chicago: R. S. Peale, 1891), 300, quoted in Badger, *The Great American Fair*, 93. As Marie McCarthy observes of the Thomas/Sousa juxtaposition: "This combination of ensembles representing art and popular music was later to symbolize the clash of music cultures during the fair." M. McCarthy, "American Music Education," 123.

111. In order of frequency of appearances at the "Popular Concerts" came Wagner, Dvořák, Johann Strauss Jr., Weber, Tchaikovsky, and Saint-Saëns. See Guion, "From Yankee Doodle thro' to Handel's Largo," 83–92.

112. A work by Amy Beach, specially commissioned by Bertha Honoré Palmer for the dedication of the Exposition, got pulled from the program after William Tomlins and others objected to the "ruffles" in the piece, how-

ever Beach's *Jubilate* did get performed at the opening ceremonies of the Women's Building in the spring of 1893. For a critique of gender bias at the fair, see A. Feldman, "Being Heard," and Whitesitt, "Women as 'Keepers of Culture.'"

113. The pan-American theme of the fair included buildings devoted to a number of Central and South American nations, too.

114. "World's Fair Concert," *Illinois Staats-Zeitung*, June 4, 1893, German, box 14, CFLPS.

115. *New Grove Dictionary of Music and Musicians*, 2nd ed. (2001), s.v. "Dvořák, Antonín"; ⟨http://www.grovemusic.com/shared/views/article.html ?section=music.51222.6⟩ ; Scholes and Kennedy, *The Concise Oxford Dictionary of Music*, 604.

116. Barnes, *Years of Grace*, 137.

117. In the planning stages, Thomas's caginess about who would be invited to participate, combined with poor planning, irritated both would-be participants and potential boosters in the music press. For a detailed recounting of the circumstances leading to the "Debacle at White City," see Schabas, *Theodore Thomas*, 195–212.

118. Ibid., 203–7.

119. Upton, *Musical Memories*, 189.

120. The *Chicago Record-Herald* excoriated Thomas's preachiness to the masses. The paper claimed the public considered it "almost a punishment to hear classical music, while all their senses rejoice at listening to a simple and familiar melody." *Chicago Record-Herald*, June 28, 1893, quoted in N. Harris, "John Philip Sousa," 213. See also Guion, "From Yankee Doodle thro' to Handel's Largo." Thomas had incurred the wrath of organized labor at the founding of the Chicago Orchestra when he refused to favor local musicians over competitors from elsewhere. See Schabas, *Theodore Thomas*, 185–86.

121. George Upton, "Musical Societies," 82.

122. Quoted in Schabas, *Theodore Thomas*, 189.

123. See Kasson, *Amusing the Million*, 22–23, and Badger, *The Great American Fair*, 107.

124. Badger, *The Great American Fair*, 107–8.

125. Badger argues that entertainment and commercial imperatives overdetermined the scientific character of the ethnological displays of the Midway and that Native Americans and African Americans voiced their outrage. See ibid., 105–7.

126. Sabbatarian controversies fought at the federal and local levels meant that the fair did not at first open on Sunday, when most laborers would be able to attend. On the issue of Sunday opening, see ibid., 93–97.

127. N. Harris, "John Philip Sousa."

128. *Illinois Staats-Zeitung*, January 28, 1892, German, box 13, CFLPS.

129. *Illinois Staats-Zeitung*, November 12, 1892, German, box 13, CFLPS.

130. Almost two million copies of "After the Ball" were sold in a two-year span. See Finson, *The Voices That Are Gone*, 71–72, 154.

CHAPTER TWO

1. *Chicago American*, September 9, 1902, CPD.

2. Ibid.

3. *Chicago News*, September 4, 1902, CPD.

4. Breen, *Historical Register*, 505–6.

5. Speaking generally of open-air concerts in American life, historian S. Frederick Starr writes: "From the Civil War through World War I, bandstands were America's great social condensers, architectural embodiments of the national motto, *E pluribus unum.*" See Starr, *Oberlin Book of Bandstands*, 10.

6. Prior to the Civil War, the city of Chicago presented public outdoor concerts with underwriting from local businessmen in downtown Dearborn Park. *Chicago Daily Democrat*, July 29, 1851, May 26, 1852, "Bands" Folder, Information, box 10, MMCS; Pierce, *A History of Chicago*, 3:492.

7. *Chicago American*, August 13, 1901, CPD.

8. See Bluestone, *Constructing Chicago*; Rosenzweig and Blackmar, *The Park and the People*; Cranz, *The Politics of Park Design*. Music gets touched on in Rosenzweig and Blackmar, *The Park and the People*, 226–29, 309–12.

9. I employ the term "ceremonial" to describe the flagship parks of the three systems: Jackson and Washington to the south, Garfield and Douglas to the west, and Lincoln to the north. Due to their founding histories, great size (from one hundred to several hundred acres), and patterns of use, these parks were focal sites of music reform activity.

10. Among the several helpful texts on the social history of middle-class refinement, see Haltunnen, *Confidence Men and Painted Ladies*, and Ryan, *Cradle of the Middle Class*.

11. *Chicago News*, September 4, 1902, CPD.

12. *Chicago Tribune*, September 5, 1902; *Chicago News*, September 4, 1902, CPD.

13. *Chicago News*, September 4, 1902, CPD.

14. *Chicago Tribune*, September 5, 1902, CPD.

15. West Chicago Park Commissioners, "The Municipal Code of the West Chicago Park Commissioners," in "Thirty-fifth Annual Report of the West Chicago Park Commissioners, 1903," 25. As part of the research for this chapter, I systematically surveyed the "Laws and Ordinances" for each park commission as well as published arrest statistics between its founding and 1910.

16. West Park police were reportedly seeking greater powers to deter individuals from "rushing the can" (bringing alcohol into the parks) and to discourage the commonly accepted practice of permitting citizens to sleep

in the park during the hottest nights of the summer. *Chicago News*, July 14, 1902, CPD.

17. Ibid. *Chicago Chronicle*, September 3, 1902, CPD.

18. The definitive history of these semipublic and private parks has yet to be written. On the history of Sharpshooters' Park, an important private park for ethnic Germans, see Palmer, *Social Backgrounds of Chicago's Local Communities*, 26–27. On the impact of commercial amusement parks on public ideals, see especially Kasson, *Amusing the Million*, and Nasaw, *Going Out*.

19. Lincoln Park, formerly Lake Park, was a ceremonial park in form and function prior to the passage of the 1869 legislation. The South and West Park districts were created under the Park Acts, and their identities as public spaces proceeded in a linked, but distinct manner from Lincoln Park. The three independent park bodies were charged with serving North Chicago, South Chicago (encompassing the towns of South Chicago, Hyde Park, and Lake), and West Chicago (the town of West Chicago), respectively. See "Park Acts," reprinted as an appendix to Rauch, *Chicago Public Parks*. Following conventions of the time, I sometimes speak of "South Park(s)" and "West Park(s)."

20. See also Rosenzweig, *Eight Hours for What We Will*, and Baldwin, *Domesticating the Street*.

21. The Commissioners of Lincoln Park would oversee approximately 250 acres comprising Lincoln Park north of the downtown along the Lake Michigan shoreline. The West Chicago Park Commissioners controlled approximately 500 acres, including Douglas Park (established in 1878), Central (renamed Garfield Park in 1881), and Humboldt Park (established in 1877). The South Park Commissioners alone controlled approximately 1,000 acres of parks, including Jackson, Washington, and Lake Front (renamed Grant Park). See "Park Acts," i–xiv. Acreage measures from Pierce, *A History of Chicago*, 3:317. Of the South Parks, Jackson was 593 acres, and Washington was 372 acres. Among the West Parks, Columbus was 154 acres; Humboldt, 206; Garfield, 188; and Douglas, 182. See Bluestone, *Constructing Chicago*, 39, for South Park measures. For the West Parks, see West Chicago Park Commissioners, "Playgrounds and Recreation Centers of the West Chicago Park Commissions," 5.

22. Frederick Law Olmsted and Theodora Kimball, *Frederick Law Olmsted, Landscape Architect, 1822–1903*, 252, quoted in Starr, *Oberlin Book of Bandstands*, 15. Olmsted also fancied music as a medium to cheer the dour crowds at the 1893 Columbian Exposition's White City exhibits; see Kasson, *Amusing the Million*, 23.

23. Horace William Shaler Cleveland executed the South Park Plan on behalf of Olmsted and Vaux. Bluestone, *Constructing Chicago*, 42, 44, 49, 51–52.

24. The best discussion of the bandstand in American architecture re-

mains Starr, *Oberlin Book of Bandstands*. On the City Beautiful Movement, see C. Boyer, *Dreaming the Rational City*, and W. H. Wilson, *The City Beautiful Movement*.

25. In Olmsted's words: "We want . . . to completely shut out the city from the landscape." Olmsted, *Civilizing American Cities*, 80. On Olmsted's discomfort with plebeian commercial recreation, see Rosenzweig and Blackmar, *The Park and the People*.

26. South Park Commissioners, "Rules for the Guidance of Policemen Appointed by the South Park Commissioners," CHS.

27. West Chicago Park Commissioners, "The Municipal Code of the West Chicago Park Commissioners," in "Thirty-fifth Annual Report of the West Chicago Park Commissioners, 1917," 25; Commissioners of Lincoln Park, "Laws and Ordinances Relating to Lincoln Park, 1903," 224.

28. Olmsted and Vaux also designed some of the nineteenth-century's leading asylums for the mentally ill where landscapes sheltered and soothed the frayed nerves of inmates. See Beveridge and Schuyler, "Creating Central Park." For an important argument about industrialization, technology, and turn-of-the-century attitudes about "noise" during the Progressive Era in New York City, see Thompson, *The Soundscape of Modernity*.

29. On status codes of dress and promenading in New York's Central Park, see Scobey, "Anatomy of the Promenade." On sound and noise as politicized cultural measures, see Bailey, "Breaking the Sound Barrier." For further discussion of gender anxieties, the dancing body, and musical progressivism, see chapter 6.

30. As noted above, the tradition of private citizens supporting public concerts preceded the establishment of the major park commissions. West Park officials mentioned the "generous public spirit which has prompted the liberal contributions to sustain these concerts." West Chicago Park Commissioners, "Sixteenth Annual Report," 5.

31. South Park Commissioners, "Report of the South Park Commissioners to the Board of County Commissioners of Cook County from December 1, 1874, to December 1, 1875," 8. A program from Washington Park speaks of "third season" of South Park Concerts. Souvenir Program/ Washington Park, July 1, 1876, CPD.

32. "The first concert given under the auspices of the Commissioners was furnished by the Great Western Light Guard Band in August 1873." Commissioners of Lincoln Park, "Report of the Commissioners of Lincoln Park, 1899," 44, CPD.

33. Hamm, *Yesterdays*, 3–5.

34. For an incomplete, but useful illustration of the range of these musics, see the park music programs at the CPD.

35. South Park Commissioners, "Report of the South Park Commissioners to the Board of County Commissioners of Cook County from Decem-

ber 1, 1874, to December 1, 1875," 7–8; Andreas, *History of Chicago*, 3:169. On the competition between Balatka and Thomas, see Upton, *Musical Memories*, 267–68.

36. Commissioners of Lincoln Park, "Report of the Commissioners of Lincoln Park, 1899," 48, CPD.

37. Correspondence, Johnny Hand to Board of Commissioners of Lincoln Park, May 21, 1886, CPD. Mrs. Palmer quoted in Sengstock, "Chicago's Dance Bands and Orchestras," 25.

38. Suggesting the potential hazards of carriage traffic, one park concert program from 1876 posted a notice on its cover that "[t]he rules governing the movement and positions of carriages . . . will be strictly enforced for the protection and comfort of visitors."

39. Correspondence, Hans Balatka to Lincoln Park Commissioners, June 8, 1875, CPD. Upton, *Musical Memories*, 263–65.

40. Souvenir Program/Washington Park, July 1, 1876, CPD. On parks as promenading spaces and the use of carriages to maintain social insulation from pedestrians, see Scobey, "Anatomy of the Promenade," and Rosenzweig and Blackmar, *The Park and the People*. For an insightful theoretical examination of how inhabiting and moving through urban space can also be read as resistance to its orderings, see de Certeau, "Walking in the City."

41. On the associated transformations of commercial leisure and social respectability in public, see Erenberg, *Steppin' Out*.

42. On the economic and musical history of subscription concerts, see R. L. Davis, *A History of Music in American Life*. On shifts in audience comportment at American concerts see Levine, *Highbrow/Lowbrow*.

43. Some contemporaries challenged the premise that the SPC and WPC served the public interest. "The park system of Chicago has as yet less interest in an artistic or aesthetic point of view than a business point of view." See Chamberlin, *Chicago and its Suburbs*, 1.

44. Chicago South Park Commission, *Report Accompanying Plan for Laying Out the South Park*, 5.

45. Ibid., 4, 6. Emphasis added.

46. There is some indication that the West Chicago Park Commissioners also envisioned their ceremonial parks as magnets for refined citizens from other parts of the city. The parks would "attract hither thousands of people of leisure and culture, whose presence among us must add much to the material as well as social wealth of the city." Quoted in Bluestone, *Constructing Chicago*, 29.

47. Chamberlin, *Chicago and its Suburbs*, 322.

48. As late as 1880, the SPC permitted several private subscription music concerts in the district, suggesting that a semiprivatized character lingered well after the ceremonial parks were officially opened to the public. South Park Commissioners, "Report of the South Park Commissioners to the Board

of County Commissioners of Cook County from December 1, 1880, to December 1, 1881," 18.

49. South Park Commissioners, "Report of the South Park Commissioners to the Board of County Commissioners of Cook County from December 1, 1874, to December 1, 1875," 8.

50. On phaetons, see the following reports from the South Park Commissioners, "Report of the South Park Commissioners to the Board of County Commissioners, December 1, 1878, to December 1, 1879," 11; "Report of the South Park Commissioners to the Board of County Commissioners of Cook County from December 1, 1879, to December 1, 1880," 9; "Report of the South Park Commissioners to the Board of County Commissioners of Cook County from December 1, 1880, to December 1, 1881," 18; "Report of the South Park Commissioners to the Board of County Commissioners of Cook County from December 1, 1881, to December 1, 1882," 19; Marian Osborn, "The Development of Recreation in the South Park System of Chicago," 27.

51. Andreas Simon, *Chicago, the Garden City: Its Magnificent Parks, Boulevards, and Cemeteries* (Chicago: Franz Gindele, 1895), 48, quoted in Bluestone, *Constructing Chicago*, 57.

52. South Park Commissioners, "Report of the South Park Commissioners to the Board of County Commissioners of Cook County from December 1, 1879, to December 1, 1880," 9.

53. On horse and cable-line development to the South Side, see Lind, *Chicago Surface Lines*, 9–11. According to Osborn, "The Development of Recreation," 34, in 1893 the SPC canceled its phaeton service.

54. Bluestone, *Constructing Chicago*, 32.

55. Chamberlin, *Chicago and its Suburbs*, 337.

56. *Chicago Tribune*, August 2, 1868, and August 23, 1868, Information, Bands, box 10, MMCS.

57. Chamberlin, *Chicago and its Suburbs*, 339.

58. Speaking of an upcoming concert in Lincoln Park, one editorial commented that the event would not be occurring were it "not for the Germans of Chicago who on November 4 defended their right to arrange such entertainments on Sunday." *Illinois Staats-Zeitung*, June 5, 1874, German, box 13, CFLPS.

59. Editorial, *Illinois Staats-Zeitung*, June 18, 1875, Information, Concert Halls, photocopy of Bessie Louise Pierce Research Notes for a *History of Chicago*, box 37, MMCS.

60. Breen, *Historical Register*, 135.

61. *Chicago Tribune*, August 7, 1887.

62. Aided by the availability of inexpensive mass-produced valved brass instruments that could reproduce a chromatic scale and were interchangeable and easy to play, brass bands began appearing in American cities, towns, and villages after the Civil War. See Hazen and Hazen, *The Music Men*;

N. Harris, "John Philip Sousa." *Harper's Weekly* estimated 10,000 bands in the late 1880s; see Chase, *America's Music*, 328–9.

63. Chase, *America's Music*, 323–30 (quotation on 329). "Military band" was a term that also embraced civilian groups who performed using combinations of wood, wind, and brass instruments. A military band should not be confused with a brass band, since the former could be more instrumentally varied than the latter. See Kreitner, *Discoursing Sweet Music*, and Hazen and Hazen, *The Music Men*.

64. *Chicago Tribune*, July 11, 1886, 15. Special Park Commission, *Report on Sites and Needs* (Chicago: City of Chicago, 1902). "Foreign population" may allude to immigrants though it could also refer to "foreign stock," those persons who were either non-native-born or the offspring of one or more non-native-born parents. Note that the percentage of foreign-born Chicagoans actually dropped between 1870 and 1880 from 48 to 41 percent. Changes in public behavior patterns may have been driven less by "foreignness" than by an embrace of new modes of public sociability that were "American," yet antithetical to residual mores of Chicago's Victorian elites.

65. The WPC faced particularly strong demands from users due to the population density of the West Side. By 1905, the West Park district had 1,038 persons per acre versus 393 persons per acre in the South Parks and 1,058 per acre in the Lincoln Park district. See "Cities of the United States of over 100,000 Population," in *Annual Report of the Commissioners of Lincoln Park for the Year 1908*, 6, CPD.

66. Schick, *Chicago and its Environs*, 163.

67. Ibid., 162.

68. Ibid.

69. The "respectable" reputation of large parks would not last indefinitely. By 1911 the Chicago Vice Commission, a public morals task force, condemned them as vice-ridden spaces. Another park reformer described a "perfectly appalling record of immorality in the large park areas." See Vice Commission of Chicago, *The Social Evil in Chicago*; DeGroot, "Are the Parks for the People . . . ?," 218.

70. For descriptions of these behaviors, see Schick, *Chicago and Its Environs*. A useful overview of the social shifts described here can be found in Kasson, *Rudeness and Civility*, and Erenberg, *Steppin' Out*. On patterns of female resistance, see especially Peiss, *Cheap Amusements*.

71. Schick, *Chicago and its Environs*, 163.

72. Ibid.

73. *Chicago Tribune*, August 18, 1896, Ethnic Music Information, box 23, MMCS.

74. *Dziennik Chicagoski*, August 27, 1903, Polish, box 34, CFLPS.

75. "Sunday afternoons were set aside for these concerts which were liberally patronized, often by the entire families of residents of these districts." West Chicago Park Commissioners, "Thirty-second Annual Report," 16.

76. West Chicago Park Commissioners, *Proceedings*, July 9, 1901.

77. On the impact of ragtime on American music, see Blesh and Janis, *They All Played Ragtime*; Berlin, *Ragtime*; and Hasse, *Ragtime*. On the racist lyrical content of "coon songs," see Finson, *The Voices That Are Gone*, 200–239.

78. The "ragging" of dance forms referred to the manner in which performers transformed popular dance forms such that "ragtime marches, two steps, and cakewalks coexisted with unsyncopated versions of the same step." Berlin, *Ragtime*, 13. On dance styles, see Perry, " 'The General Motherhood of the Commonwealth,' " 727–28.

79. Leonard, "Reactions to Ragtime," 112; Radano, "Hot Fantasies."

80. Stratton, "Music and Crime," 141.

81. Program list published in *Chicago Tribune*, September 1, 1901, CPD. On the ambivalent response to ragtime among popular conductors, see N. Harris, "John Philip Sousa."

82. *Chicago Tribune*, August 24, 1898. "Take Your Clothes and Go—A Genuine 'Rag time' Coon Oddity" was a popular hit published by Irving Jones in 1897.

83. Concert Program, "Concert in Washington Park, July 16, 1898," Exhibition Materials, Bands, box 10, MMCS. Other bandleaders shared Hand's dislike of ragtime, but adopted a pragmatic perspective in their communications with park officials. Frederick Finney explained that while he did not personally like ragtime, he was no elitist and was prepared "to play music such as the popular tastes of the present age demand." Correspondence, Frederick Finney to Commissioners of Lincoln Park, March 9, 1899, CPD.

84. Despite Hand's unhappiness, the LPC retained the conductor for future concerts. See Commissioners of Lincoln Park, "Expenditures for the Fiscal Year Ending December 31, 1900," CPD.

85. *Chicago Tribune*, August 26, 1898.

86. The reaction of the South Park Commissioners to the controversy is not known. Examination of extant concert programs, including those performed by Johnny Hand, suggest that the SPC remained at least in the late 1890s a civic musical sphere still overseen by supporters of traditional European and American musics.

87. *Chicago Tribune*, July 12, 1901, CPD. The *Tribune* reported that concert expenditures for the 1901 summer season totaled $1,800 for Lincoln Park; $2,000 for the SPC; and $3,500 for the WPC's concerts. Area railways supplied money for the extra business they received. The major parks received $400–500 from the street railway for Lincoln Park concerts, and Union Traction supplied $1,000 to the WPC, while the Metropolitan elevated train gave $800.

88. *Chicago Inter-Ocean*, August 11, 1901, CPD.

89. *Chicago American*, August 13, 1901, CPD. The previous summer, William Randolph Hearst had established the newspaper as a voice for the Democratic Party in Chicago. Hearst already controlled the *Chicago Examiner*,

a morning paper. On Hearst's involvement with Chicago newspapers and party politics, see Nasaw, *The Chief*, 152–53, 159. On print media as a driving force of "progressive" ideology among laborers, see Ethington, *The Public City*.

90. *Chicago American*, August 13, 1901, CPD.

91. *Chicago American*, August 16, 1901, CPD.

92. *Chicago American*, August 13, 1901, CPD.

93. "Just Because He Made Dem Goo Goo Eyes" by Silas Leachman was a hit Victor recording in 1901.

94. *Chicago Tribune*, August 13, 1901, CPD.

95. *Chicago Post*, May 10, 1902, CPD. The *Tribune* ran a spoof "Ach! Dot String Band!" in which it printed what appeared to be a fabricated interview with "the deposed musical authority of Lincoln Park," Johnny Hand, warning the Thomas musicians of what lay in store for them with ragtime audiences. *Chicago Tribune*, May 11, 1902.

96. *Chicago Tribune*, May 10, May 18, 1902, CPD.

97. *Chicago Journal*, May 10, 1902, CPD.

98. *Chicago Journal*, October 5, 1902, CPD.

99. *Chicago Tribune*, May 18, 1902, CPD.

100. Ibid.

101. Municipal officials in nearby Oak Park, Illinois, made a similar decision, shifting from classical to popular music since "[t]he people of Oak Park and vicinity will not come out to be educated." See *Chicago Tribune*, July 11, 1902.

102. *Chicago Inter-Ocean*, July 10, 1902, CPD.

103. *Chicago Inter-Ocean*, July 9, 1902, CPD.

104. Another sign of progressive rededication to uplift can be found in 1910 in New York City, where, after years in which the Tammany administration supplied ragtime in Central Park, the new park commissioner under Mayor William Gaynor declared that classical music would return to the city's parks. See *Chicago Record-Herald*, February 25, 1910.

105. *Chicago Tribune*, July 28, 1906.

CHAPTER THREE

1. Polacheck [Hilda Satt Polacheck], *I Came a Stranger*, 51.

2. Ibid., 51–52.

3. Amalie Hannig, "Christmas at Hull House," 31, quoted in A. F. Davis and McCree, *Eighty Years at Hull-House*, 93. Hull House was nonsectarian, but Jane Addams and others ardently supported the Christmas concerts as an appropriate activity for everyone in the neighborhood. Writing on the prevailing tenor of secular humanism of Hull House, one scholar concludes that Hull House was "[i]n but not of, the social gospel movement." See Sklar,

"Hull House in the 1890s," 663. The concert of Christmas music on December 23, 1894, featured works by Carl Reinecke, Peter Cornelius, Niels Gade, and Adolf Jensen. See reel 51, JAP.

4. Polacheck, *I Came a Stranger*, 52. The year of the Christmas party that Polacheck attended may have been either 1895 or 1896; see ibid., 205 n. 1.

5. Satt went on to become a lifelong friend of Addams and to work for various progressive women's social and political causes. She collected her recollections of Hull House in the 1950s. See Polacheck, *I Came a Stranger*. For less glowing evaluations of progressive reform from the anecdotal perspective of settlement users, see Ets, "Rosa and the Chicago Commons," and Yezierska, "The Free Vacation House."

6. One group that Satt did *not* see were African Americans, who were not invited to participate at Hull House, or at most Chicago-area settlements. Her experience represented incorporation into an American nation implicitly understood as for whites only. For more on segregation in northern industrial settlements, see Crocker, *Social Work and Social Order*, and Lasch-Quinn, *Black Neighbors*.

7. Early histories include A. F. Davis, *Spearheads for Reform*, and A. F. Davis and McCree, *Eighty Years at Hull-House*. On feminism and Hull House, see Sklar, "Hull House in the 1890s." Lippmann, *A Preface to Politics*, 150–55, offers an important early observation about the exceptionalism of Hull House within the settlement movement. Key revisionist works include Trolander, *Professionalism and Social Change*, and Carson, *Settlement Folk*, which also mentions musical activity. For a fine assessment of feminist ideology in the reform community, see Muncy, *Creating a Female Dominion*. L. Gordon, *Heroes of Their Own Lives*, is an outstanding study and influential critique of maternal and middle-class biases in Progressive Era welfare work. For an overview of trends in historiography, see Spratt, "Beyond Hull House."

8. On the bourgeois tendencies of reformers, see Crocker, *Social Work and Social Order*.

9. Lears, *No Place of Grace*, 79–83. On reform and social control, see Jones, "Class Expression versus Social Control?," and Karger, *The Sentinels of Order*.

10. On the "myth" of Hull House, see Lissak, *Pluralism and Progressives*. On the problem of racial exclusion and the importance of African American settlements, see Lasch-Quinn, *Black Neighbors*.

11. Hundreds of women's amateur musical societies imitated forms of musical outreach at Hull House by providing instruction at settlements, community music schools, hospitals, schools, and prisons. On their activity and impact, see Blair, *The Torchbearers*, 44–75. On community music schools, see Cords, "Music in Social Settlement and Community Music Schools," and Evans, Klein, and Delgado, "Too Intrinsic for Renown."

12. For a useful discussion of the distinction between "assimilation" and

"Americanization" in U.S. ethnic historiography, see Kazal, "Revisiting Assimilation." I do not agree that music at Hull House produced syncretism or fusion of forms so much as a negotiation and redefinition of multiple musical expressions in which settlement personnel and users enjoyed different levels of control in different contexts. See Crocker, *Social Work and Social Order*, 58.

13. This follows Linda Gordon's insightful analysis of power and agency in *Heroes of Their Own Lives*. For a cultural studies approach to "performance" history (excluding music) at Hull House, see Jackson, *Lines of Activity*.

14. For the impact that the admixture of Platonic ideals, romanticism, and transcendentalism had on "the melioristic potential of musical beauty," see Mussulman, *Music in the Cultured Generation*, 23, 42–44. On "musical idealism" in antebellum Boston, particularly the versions propagated by John S. Dwight and Lowell Mason, see Broyles, *Music of the Highest Class*, 215–34. On the search for a usable past among reform advocates of historical pageantry as a tool of civic reform, see Glassberg, *American Historical Pageantry*.

15. Anthropologists, ethnomusicologists, and historians have variously documented the ubiquity of belief across the cultural spectrum in the power of music to determine social stability and express power. African tribal societies relied on music and aural communication to consolidate authority. Cultures in Asia, the Middle East, and India subscribed to the links between music, social behavior, and natural forces. For a selective overview of the roots of Western aesthetic thought about music, see Lippman, *A History of Western Musical Aesthetics*, 3–16.

16. On Addams's early life, see A. F. Davis, *American Heroine*, 3–37. See also Tims, *Jane Addams*, 17–24. Addams's academic transcript and various course notebooks from Rockford are included in the JAP.

17. See "Essays of Class of 1881, Rockford Seminary," reel 27, JAP. Plato's works introduced key arguments in the metaphysical and ethical properties of the lyric. He posited the laws of musical harmony as proof of balance and order in the universe. See Plato, *The Republic*, 86–87.

18. On Addams's registration status, see *Twenty-Seventh Annual Catalogue of the Officers and Students of Rockford Seminary, Rockford, IL, 1877–78*, reel 27, JAP; Linn, *Jane Addams*, 60. Addams's older stepbrother, Henry W. Haldeman, to whom she was close, studied music at the Conservatorium in Leipzig and according to his business card briefly taught violin and voice. Misc. Papers, reel 37, JAP.

19. Linn, *Jane Addams*, 31–47.

20. A. F. Davis, *American Heroine*, 32–33.

21. Quoted in Linn, *Jane Addams*, 85.

22. Toynbee Hall offered no music programs. The quoted excerpt from the charter appears on the masthead of the *Hull House Bulletin*.

23. On domestication as a reform principle, see especially Sklar, *Catharine Beecher*; Sklar, *Florence Kelley and the Nation's Work*; Muncy, *Creating a*

Female Dominion; and Baldwin, *Domesticating the Street*. On ideologies of home-life and virtue, see Wright, *Moralism and the Model Home*, 5–12.

24. Through temperance work, tenement rehabilitation, public health reform, municipal service reform (water, building code improvements, ventilation, and light), and child welfare work, progressive women, such as Florence Kelley, and tenement reform activists, such as Edith Abbott and Sophonisba Breckenridge, transformed the urban environment of Chicago and politicized aspects of everyday life that had been virtually ignored before. Wright, *Moralism and the Model Home*, 104–15.

25. On music as a domesticating force and symbol in nineteenth-century bourgeois settings, see Tawa, *High-Minded and Low-Down*; Leppert, *The Sight of Sound*; and Locke and Barr, *Cultivating Music in America*.

26. On Addams's life-long identification with the work of Ruskin, see Linn, *Jane Addams*, 75, 89, 106.

27. On the difficulties of transplanting the politics behind the "craft ideal" to the United States, see Lears, *No Place of Grace*, 60–65, and Boris, *Art and Labor*, 189–93.

28. *Hull-House Maps and Papers*, 170.

29. Ibid., 178.

30. Hull House also maintained a dramatic association. Shirley Burns, "The Drama a Sociological Force," *Green Book*, November 1909, 945, reel 57, JAP; "Should Teach Child to Act," *Chicago Tribune*, December 9, 1909, reel 57, JAP.

31. Munsterberg, "Music," 181.

32. "A Function of the Social Settlement," in Addams, *The Social Thought of Jane Addams*, 188.

33. "Sunday Concerts [1891–1892]," reel 50, JAP. The quotation is from "Weekly Programme of Lectures, Clubs, Classes, March 1, 1892," ibid. See also Eleanor Smith, "Fundamentals and Ideals with Which the Music School Was Established," speech delivered at "The Music School and the Community," Staff Dinner—Hull House, June 10, 1938, folder 2, box 5, Alma Birmingham Papers, UIC (hereafter cited as Smith, "Fundamentals and Ideals.")

34. Hull House offered piano lessons three days a week by three different teachers, and eventually expanded classes to four days by 1894. "Weekly Programme of Lectures, Clubs, Classes, 1891"; "Weekly Program of Lectures, Clubs, Classes, Winter/Spring 1894," 769, reel 50, JAP.

35. Addams, *Twenty Years at Hull-House*, 378–80.

36. "Hull-House, Sunday Afternoon, Nov. 27th, 1892," reel 51, JAP.

37. Concert Programs, Sunday, March 4, 1894; Sunday, October 7, 1894; February 3, 1895, reel 51, JAP.

38. "Sunday Afternoon Concerts," *Hull-House Bulletin*, May 1896, 4, reel 51, JAP.

39. Ibid.

40. "Sunday Afternoon Concerts," *Hull-House Bulletin*, January 1, 1897, 1, reel 51, JAP.

41. "Sunday Afternoon Concerts," *Hull-House Bulletin*, May 1896, 4, reel 51, JAP.

42. Munsterberg, "Editorial Bric-a-brac."

43. Smith, "Fundamentals and Ideals." Smith gives Mary Rozet Smith particular credit for endowing and promoting the music school.

44. Using the case of historical pageants in the 1910s and 1920s designed to bind immigrants and multiethnic constituents, David Glassberg argues that aesthetic pragmatism guided musical selections toward "light classical . . . familiar themes from Bach, Dvořák, and Tchaikovsky." See Glassberg, *American Historical Pageantry*, 83.

45. *Hull-House Bulletin*, Midwinter 1900, n.p., Louise Dekoven Bowen Scrapbooks, CHS.

46. Smith, "Fundamentals and Ideals."

47. Extant correspondence between Addams and Smith focuses on health concerns. The resignation letter is not known to have survived. See M. L. M. Bryan, Slote, and De Angury, *The Jane Addams Papers*, 526.

48. Correspondence, Jane Addams to Eleanor Smith, August 6, 1901, reel 4, JAP.

49. Addams, *Twenty Years at Hull-House*, 378.

50. While the first documented vocal instruction in Chicago schools occurred in the early 1840s, it took more than fifty years to appoint a supervisor of music in the high schools, and evidence suggests that instrumental music teaching was still not accredited at this time. Music programs were treated as a frill and often threatened with budget cuts or outright elimination. See Mistak, "A General History of Instrumental Music in the Chicago Public Schools," 22. On individual struggles to improve Chicago's public musical education, see Devick, "Orlando Blackman."

51. Fees for lessons at the Hull House Music School in 1900 totaled "one dollar for a term of ten lessons"; *Hull-House Bulletin*, Midwinter 1900, n.p., reel 51, JAP. Eleanor Smith recalled that many teachers (herself included) taught students for free since many could simply not afford to pay even the modest fees. See E. Smith, "Fundamentals and Ideals."

52. On professionals trained at the music school, see Addams, *Twenty Years at Hull-House*, 380.

53. M. L. M. Bryan and A. F. Davis, *100 Years at Hull House*, 94; *Hull-House Yearbook*, September 1, 1906–September 1, 1907, n.p., Hull-House Association Records, Eleanor Smith Papers, UIC.

54. Addams, *Twenty Years at Hull-House*, 380–81.

55. Ibid.

56. The use of children and young women in commercial entertainment represented one of the areas that stimulated early-twentieth-century morals reformers associated with juvenile protection and child labor reform. Addams decried the custom in her book, *The Spirit of Youth and the City Streets*. On the activity of the Juvenile Protective Association, see P. G. Anderson, "The Good to Be Done."

57. "[We] had made the plan for the Music School in Germany some years before we returned and put it into effect," Smith recalled. Schenck, *Music Schools and Settlement Music Departments*, 18.

58. Schumann's *Music and Musicians*, published in English in 1880 and reissued in 1891, contained "Rules and Maxims for Young Musicians," which took a holistic approach to musicianship by stressing training in voice and piano. Schumann and Ritter, *Music and Musicians*, 409–18. See also Smith, "Fundamentals and Ideals," 1–2; Mussulman, *Music in the Cultured Generation*, 44; and M. A. J. Feldman, "George P. Upton," 22–25.

59. Eleanor Smith obituary, *Chicago Sun*, July 1, 1942, Eleanor and Gertrude Smith Papers, UIC.

60. On Cady's influence on music education, see Shiraishi, "Calvin Brainerd Cady," and Birge, *History of Public School Music*, 206.

61. Another stalwart instructor at Hull House was Eleanor's sister Gertrude, also trained in classical music.

62. A traditionalist when it came to technical matters, Smith did not use the Tonic Sol-Fa system, a simplified scale notation designed for novice singers that was favored by innovative musical educators, such as William L. Tomlins. The Tonic Sol-Fa system generated heated debate among music educators in the Chicago press during the late 1880s as a result of Tomlins's experiments with youth choruses in the public schools. See Devick, "Orlando Blackman," 192–200.

63. "Recital of the Hull House Music School, April 20th, 1897," reel 51, JAP.

64. Smith specified these groups as the predominant early users of the music school. See E. Smith, "Fundamentals and Ideals," 2.

65. The collaboration of Smith and Monroe, a singularly influential literary figure who went on to edit *Poetry: A Magazine of Verse*, reinforces the inappropriateness of describing the aesthetic project of Hull House as, strictly speaking, anti-modern.

66. Smith, "Fundamentals and Ideals," 3.

67. "The Troll's Holiday," playbill, reel 51, JAP; E. Smith, *The Eleanor Smith Music Course, Book 4*, 4. Smith's teaching texts, such as the *Modern Music Series* and the *Eleanor Smith Series*, won widespread distribution in public schools across the United States.

68. Smith eventually published these as *Hull-House Songs* in a commem-

orative edition to benefit the settlement in 1915. Obituary, *Chicago Sun*, July 1, 1942; "Service to Honor the Memory of Eleanor Smith, Founder of Hull House Music School, October 3, 1942," folder 8, Eleanor Smith Papers, UIC.

69. *Hull-House Yearbook*, September 1, 1906–September 1, 1907, Hull-House Association Records, UIC; Addams, *Twenty Years at Hull-House*, 377–8.

70. Tomlins served in the employ of the Chicago Public Schools at various points in the early 1890s. Devick, "Orlando Blackman."

71. The Tonic Sol-Fa method combined singing and breathing exercises with physical exercises drawing on Delsartian methods of dramatic expression. François Delsarte, a French singer and drama educator, pioneered a method of applied aesthetic movements brought to the United States and popularized by Steele Mackaye. For an account of the controversial method and the struggle to incorporate it into the Chicago Public Schools, see Devick, "Orlando Blackman."

72. Reagan, "Art Music in Milwaukee," 179.

73. Tomlins, "Moral Forces in Music," 626.

74. The distinguished music critic W. S. B. Mathews wrote: "Everything turned upon the true sentiment and spiritual interpretation of the song expressed through the awakened individuality of the child." See Mathews, "Mr. Tomlins' Work with Children," 62; Devick, "Orlando Blackman," 149; "Prizes Offered for Ballads," *Chicago Record*, ca. May 2, 1895, reel 55, JAP. Theodore Thomas, by contrast, opposed children's participation in serious musical festivals. See Schabas, *Theodore Thomas*, 57.

75. Tomlins, "Moral Forces in Music," 625–26.

76. Quoted in Devick, "Orlando Blackman," 237. There is insufficient available evidence to determine if Tomlins ever worked with African American children or children of other racial minority groups.

77. Nash, under the direction of Tomlins, also ran the Hull-House Choral Society, open to "[m]embers of the Hull-House Clubs and classes who are over 16 years of age." See *Hull-House Bulletin* 1, no. 2 (February 1896): n.p., reel 53, JAP. In 1899 Nash was also involved in coordinating youth concerts in the neighborhood near the Illinois Steel Works. See *Musical Record* 452 (September 1899): 401–2.

78. *Hull-House Bulletin* 2 (June 1897): n.p., reel 53, JAP.

79. "Prizes Offered for Ballads," *Chicago Record*, ca. May 2, 1895, reel 55, JAP.

80. Ibid. Tomlins invoked major and bloody skirmishes at Andrew Carnegie's Homestead Works steel mills in Pennsylvania in 1892 and at George M. Pullman's railway car manufacturing plant south of Chicago in 1894. Montgomery, *The Fall of the House of Labor*, 36–43, 128–29.

81. Ibid.

82. Addams, *Twenty Years at Hull-House*, 377.

83. On the subject of control problems at settlements, see Lasch-Quinn, "Progressives and the Pursuit of Agency," 258–63.

84. On the impact of the *Little Red Songbook* and the songs of Joe Hill, see, for example, Kornbluh, *Rebel Voices*, 127–57.

85. Addams, *Twenty Years at Hull-House*, 380.

86. Selective and romantic claims on folk essences in popular music are engaged in important ways by Filene, " 'Our Singing Country,' " and Gilroy, " 'Jewels Brought from Bondage.' "

87. Addams, *Twenty Years at Hull-House*, 378.

88. Ibid.

89. Ibid., 231–32.

90. Ibid., 233.

91. Ibid., 235.

92. Dewey, "The School as Social Center."

93. *Hull-House Bulletin* 5, no. 2 (1902): n.p., Hull-House Association Records, UIC.

94. Niecks, "The Ethical Aspects of Music, Second Lecture," 15–16.

95. Gilder, "Art Brought into the Lives of Wage-Earners," 417–20. New York City was another center for settlement music schools, most famously at the Music School Settlement of New York.

96. Riley, "A Study of the Higher Life of Chicago," 60.

97. Seligman, "Music for and by the Many," 420 (emphasis added).

98. Hull House permitted registered clubs to sponsor social dances at the settlement beginning in the 1890s.

99. Addams, *The Spirit of Youth and the City Streets*, 98. Between 1902 and 1905 Hull House also shifted its education courses from a collegiate, liberal arts emphasis to one focused on manual craft skills. See Lissak, *Pluralism and Progressives*, 47.

100. The reported membership in the Boys' Club was 1,000. *Hull-House Yearbook*, September 1, 1906–September 1, 1907, Hull-House Association Records, UIC.

101. *Hull-House Yearbook*, January 1, 1913, 22, Hull-House Association Records, UIC; Gertrude Howe Britton, "The Boy Problem in the Nineteenth Ward," n.p., reel 50, JAP.

102. "Why the Dance Halls Flourish," *Spokane Spokesman Review*, March 8, 1909; L. B. Jones, "Music as a Social Force," 61.

103. On alternative approaches to engaging commercial music recreation, see the discussion of the Juvenile Protective Association in chapter 6.

104. Roosevelt to Zangwill, October 15, 1908, quoted in Gleason, "The Melting Pot," 24; Addams quoted in Mann, *The One and the Many*, 110.

105. Several important characters in the play are musicians or music educators, and conflict and consensus over music's aesthetic and social pur-

pose drives the story ahead. See Sollors, *Beyond Ethnicity*, 67–69, 172–73, 182–83. Michael Rogin argues that Zangwill errs in not making the sound-track of *The Melting Pot* either vaudeville or Tin Pan Alley music, which he contends was the more accurate space in which a generation of European Jews found the key to self-integration into American popular culture. In Rogin's view, casting Quixano as a kind of American Dvořák rather than a proto-Gershwin, as well as using a symphony to sound the notes of the people, reveals that Zangwill was spinning the tale in a more palatable "culti-vated" direction for its progressive audiences. Rogin's gloss suggests the importance of more extensively considering this history. See Rogin, *Blackface, White Noise*, 64–66.

106. Transcript of Art Hodes Interview, 2, Jazz Institute of Chicago Oral History Interviews, UC.

107. Hodes and Hansen, *Hot Man*, 7.

108. Transcript of Art Hodes Interview, 2, Jazz Institute of Chicago Oral History Interviews, UC.

109. Ibid., 3.

110. Ibid., 8; Collier, *Benny Goodman*, 20. Collier reports that Hodes played with the Marionettes at Hull House in 1920–21, citing the *Hull-House Yearbook* for 1921.

111. Transcript of Art Hodes Interview, 2, Jazz Institute of Chicago Oral History Interviews, UC.

112. Hodes and Hansen, *Hot Man*, 7.

113. Goodman and Kolodin, *The Kingdom of Swing*, 15.

114. Transcript of Art Hodes Interview, 3, Jazz Institute of Chicago Oral History Interviews, UC.

115. Jimmy McPartland of the Austin High Gang, a leading white Chi-cago jazz combo, connected with Goodman at the Columbus Park Refectory at a "tea dance." Collier, *Benny Goodman*, 20–22, 32.

116. On Petrillo and his impact of music and labor in the United States, see Leiter, *The Musicians and Petrillo*.

CHAPTER FOUR

1. For a description of the opening gala, see Breen, *Historical Register*, 323. This dedication opened the first field house park in the area that fea-tured indoor recreational space. McKinley Park, a large playground, opened in the spring of 1903. The University of Chicago Settlement also operated a small private park in the area, see G. Taylor, "Public Recreation Facilities," 306. On Foreman's credentials, see Marquis, *The Book of Chicagoans*, 242. On McDowell's support of musical uplift, see McDowell, "Sung with Neighbors Back-of-the-Yards."

2. Details on the neighborhood described in Special Park Commission,

"Report on Sites and Needs," 1. See also *Chicago Record Herald,* July 27, 1904, quoted in Chicago Public Library, *"A Breath of Fresh Air,"* 19.

3. Foreman's remarks appeared in the *Chicago Tribune,* May 14, 1905, quoted in Dominic Pacyga, "Parks for the People," in Chicago Public Library, *"A Breath of Fresh Air,"* 18.

4. According to A. F. Davis, *Spearheads for Reform,* 81, "Foreman studied settlements and hired former settlement house workers to supervise in recreation centers." To track the changes in music programs and policies in ceremonial and neighborhood parks, this study relies on the author's analysis of the official records, annual reports, and minutes of the three major park commissions between 1869 and 1929.

5. The Lincoln Park district supported the development of small parks in the town of North Chicago and in Lake View in the 1910s, and field house parks gradually appeared there. However, the earliest as well as the most innovative and sustained work in musical progressivism prior to World War I took place on the West and South Sides, and that is the focus of this chapter.

6. On "whiteness" as a socially constructed form of group privilege, see Roediger, *The Wages of Whiteness,* and Fishkin, "Interrogating 'Whiteness' Complicating 'Blackness.' "

7. For a trenchant overview of national attitudes toward urban parks and progressive ideals at this time, see Jon Teaford, *The Unheralded Triumph,* 252–58. On ideological tensions during the Progressive Era among city planners concerning the relationship between beauty and practicality in their work, see W. H. Wilson, *The City Beautiful Movement,* and P. Boyer, *Urban Masses and Moral Order.* Quotation in G. Taylor, "Public Recreation Facilities," 304.

8. On parks recreation reform, see Cavallo, *Muscles and Morals,* and Cranz, *The Politics of Park Design.* I disagree with the assertion of a rigid dichotomy between a "reform park" and an "authentic" immigrant, ethnic, or laboring park area because it misses the extent to which field houses were under multiple claims as "ethnic" and "American" spaces. See Cranz, *The Politics of Park Design,* 221.

9. G. Taylor, "Public Recreation Facilities," 306, credits the Municipal Science Club, "a group of men who included several social settlement residents" with sponsoring the resolution that spurred the investigation.

10. One exception in the South Park area to the freeze on new park construction was McKinley Park, at the intersection of Archer and Western Avenues, which served the stockyards and steel factories. South Park Commissioners, "Annual Report of the South Park Commissioners for Fiscal Year Ending 1904," 7. See also Chicago Public Library, *"A Breath of Fresh Air,"* 16; *New York Tribune,* June 1, 1902, Hull House Scrapbooks, June 1902, reel 55, JAP.

11. By 1904, the city had slipped to an undistinguished seventh in met-

ropolitan park acres per citizen. See Todd, Byron, and Vierow, *The Chicago Recreation Survey*, 18–19. G. Taylor, "Public Recreation Facilities," 305, reported that between 1880 and 1903 Chicago's population had increased over 272 percent, while its park acreage had only grown about 59 percent.

12. Special Park Commission, "Report on Sites and Needs," 1–2. See Grossman, *Land of Hope*, 127.

13. South Park Commissioners, "Annual Report of the South Park Commissioners for Fiscal Year Ending 1904," 7.

14. Ibid., 6, and Breen, *Historical Register*, 317.

15. Additional funds were directed toward the completion of Grant Park in downtown Chicago and toward reclamation of 215 acres of Lake Michigan shoreline for an expansion of Lincoln Park. In all, Illinois agreed to appropriate $4 million for neighborhood park and playground development, and passed along $2.5 million more over the next five years. O'Neill, "Chicago Playgrounds and Park Extension," 798. On appropriations to districts, see Mero, "The South Park System," 213–16. The West Park neighborhood parks opened between 1905 and 1917. On the referendum, see G. Taylor, "Public Recreation Facilities," 308.

16. G. Taylor, "Public Recreation Facilities," 310.

17. Todd, Byron, and Vierow, *Chicago Recreation Survey*, 22–23. "The Clubhouses for the people," as the field houses were called, also received a brief, but glowing mention in the text of *The Chicago Plan of 1908*. Armour Square stood at the intersection of Thirty-third and Thirty-fourth Streets, Fifth, and Shields in the heart of an Irish American neighborhood. See McDowell, "The Field Houses of Chicago," 537.

18. Since the late nineteenth century, Lincoln Park officials had distinguished their park as different from the other ceremonial parks because of a tradition of welcoming members of all classes, and its proximity to the central business district, which made it a popular destination of all segments of the North and West Side population. Bluestone, *Constructing Chicago*, 32, 35.

19. According to Osborn, "The Development of Recreation," 34, "The parks in Chicago before 1900 were not planned for these groups [working-class immigrants] and were not within the reach of them."

20. The petition is mentioned in West Chicago Park Commissioners, "Fifty-seventh Annual Report," 1926, 40.

21. Foreman's speeches were published in pamphlet form. See, for example, his address on Labor Day 1904 at Morgan Park: Foreman, "Recreation Needs of Chicago," 6, 10 (emphasis in original). The city of Chicago, not the major park commissions, opened Morgan Park while progressive activists lobbied state legislators to amend the 1869 Park Act, allowing the majors to proceed with new construction. See also Foreman's remarks in the *Chicago Daily News*, April 22, 1904, and the *Chicago Record-Herald*, April 23, 1904. Foreman's phraseology is echoed virtually word for word in Special Park Commission, "Annual Report for Fiscal Year 1904."

22. B. Smith, "City Playgrounds."

23. *Chicago Record-Herald*, June 1, 1902, Hull House Scrapbooks, June 1902, reel 55, JAP.

24. Chicago Public Library, *"A Breath of Fresh Air,"* 9.

25. *Chicago Record-Herald*, July 27, 1904, quoted in Chicago Public Library, *"A Breath of Fresh Air,"* 19.

26. Foreman, "Recreation Needs of Chicago," 10.

27. Petitioning the commissioners proved a common way to draw the South and West Chicago Park Commissioners to certain neighborhoods. See Breen, *Historical Register*, 321, 482, for the cases described there.

28. The opening ceremonies at neighborhood parks typified the ethnic flavor of park reception and anticipated future patterns of use. Small Park no. 1 (later Eckhart Park) on the West Side opened in August 1908 with performances by the Polish Singing Society, Chor Filaretow, the Central Turn-verein, the St. Boniface Church Chorus, dances from groups associated with Chicago Commons settlement, and members of the Paderewski Club performing Polish songs. See West Chicago Park Commissioners, "West Chicago Park Commissioners, Forty-fourth Annual Report, 1912," 20. On the power of occasional community opposition and park development, see Breen, *Historical Register*, 326.

29. Among the considerations that it ranked in determining where to situate field house parks on the West Side, the Special Park Commission used the "[d]ensity of population under twenty-one years of age" as an indicator. Interestingly, "Juvenile Delinquency" ranked seventh in importance. See Special Park Commission, "Report of the Committee to Study Sites," 6362.

30. On gender constraints on professional women and bias toward men as supervisors of instrumental (thought not vocal) instruction, see Macleod, " 'Whence Comes the Lady Tympanist?,' " 299–300.

31. The phrase was used in the *Chicago Record-Herald*, July 27, 1904, reprinted in Chicago Public Library, *"A Breath of Fresh Air,"* 19. The assertion that "the reform park segregated the ages and the sexes" is inaccurate given that families attended concerts together as they had always done at the ceremonial parks, and couples dances were soon to be added. Cranz, *The Politics of Park Design*, 63.

32. McDowell, "The Field Houses of Chicago," 538.

33. Patten, "Education through Activity," 790–91.

34. South Park Commissioners, "Annual Report of the South Park Commissioners, for a Period of Twelve Months from March 1, 1909, to February 28, 1910, Inclusive," 55.

35. Named to honor Bernard Eckhart, a West Park commissioner, Small Park no. 1 was "situated in the Polish section of the Seventeenth Ward on the North West Side, in one of the congested districts of the city." West Chicago Park Commissioners, "West Chicago Park Commissioners, Forty-fourth Annual Report, 1912" 104.

36. West Chicago Park Commissioners, "Fortieth Annual Report of the West Chicago Park Commissioners," 23, 36, 38, 40.

37. West Chicago Park Commissioners, "Proceedings," January 10, 1911. The progressive journal *The Playground* is dotted with ads for phonograph records in the service of reform via music. See *The Playground* 7, no. 3 (June 1913); 7, no. 10 (January 1914); 12, no. 1 (April 1918).

38. West Chicago Park Commissioners, "Proceedings," January 9, 1912.

39. Most neighborhood parks employed fewer than five policemen, in contrast to the hundreds of officers salaried by the major parks. See statistics in "Annual Reports" for Lincoln, South, and West Chicago Park Commissioners.

40. South Park Commissioners, "Annual Report of the South Park Commissioners for Fiscal Year Ending 1904," 44.

41. "I have carefully inquired into the comparative merits of the different bands named," wrote Foster in 1907, "and believe the six best bands to be: the First Regiment Band, the Second Regiment Band, John A. Hand's Band, The Seventh Regiment Band, Rosenbecker's Band, T. A. Feiman's Band. . . . [S]hould the bands at any time fail to furnish satisfactory music, then their assignment will be discontinued." Concerts ran from the Saturday after the Fourth of July and continued through the end of August. South Park Commissioners, "Proceedings," 10:149–50, CPD. On Foster's forty-five years of service to Chicago parks, see Various, "Tributes to J. Frank Foster," CPD.

42. South Park Commissioners, "Annual Report of the South Park Commissioners for Fiscal Year 1906," and South Park Commissioners, "Report of the South Park Commissioners for a Period of Fifteen Months from December 1, 1906, to February 29, 1908, Inclusive," 48–49, CPD.

43. "The People and the Parks" table in South Park Commissioners, "Annual Report of the South Park Commissioners for the Year Ended February 28, 1913," 46, CPD.

44. "Auditor's Report" in West Chicago Park Commissioners, "Forty-fourth Annual Report, 1912," 164–72. On a bitter winter day, Bredfield's Band drew a crowd to the opening of Stanford Park on the West Side. *Chicago Examiner*, February 23, 1910, reel 57, JAP.

45. West Chicago Park Commissioners, "Fortieth Annual Report of the West Chicago Park Commissioners," 76.

46. On the scope of "popular" song in this era, see Tawa, *The Way to Tin Pan Alley*, 8–12.

47. "Forty-first Annual Report of the West Chicago Park Commissioners, 1909," 43, 45.

48. *Die Abendpost*, August 2, 1908, German, box 11, CFLPS.

49. In this case, getting to know the people's leisure needs marked a crucial first step: "Knowledge of the customs, traditions, and mode of life

among such people, gained by intelligent study, gave the field house director points of contact between the people and the park service which resulted in most gratifying response." South Park Commissioners, "Annual Report of the South Park Commissioners for Fiscal Year Ended February 28, 1909," 39.

50. Some years earlier, West Park officials had faced criticism for implementing Sunday concerts. See West Chicago Park Commissioners, "Thirty-second Annual Report of the West Chicago Park Commissioners for the Year Ending December 31, 1900," 16. See also "Minutes," August 5, 1907, in South Park Commissioners, "Proceedings," 10:243, CPD. In August 1907, the SPC agreed to curtail Sunday band concerts (along with baseball) at Ogden Park, at Sixty-fifth Street and Racine, when several pastors complained in a petition.

51. On public drinking in Chicago, see Duis, *The Saloon*. On reform struggles to temper plebeian Sunday culture in another industrial context, see Rosenzweig, *Eight Hours for What We Will*, 128–55.

52. South Park Commissioners, "Annual Report of the South Park Commissioners, for a Period of Twelve Months from March 1, 1909, to February 28, 1910, Inclusive," 10, 38.

53. Although spontaneous dancing broke out at outdoor concerts in the major park districts, there is no evidence of outdoor dance events in field house parks. The West Chicago Park Commissioners had a specific history of banning dances in outdoor pavilions, for example. See West Chicago Park Commissioners, "Proceedings of the Board of West Chicago Park Commissioners," May 28, 1901.

54. Speaking of the "dry" dance scene at Hull House, Jane Addams wrote: "We tried experiments with every known 'soft drink,' from those extracted from an expensive soda water fountain to slender glasses of grape juice, but so far as drinks were concerned we never became a rival to the saloon, nor indeed did anyone imagine that we were trying to do so." Addams, *Twenty Years at Hull-House*, 131–32.

55. *Chicago Evening American*, January 12, 1909, Louise Dekoven Bowen Scrapbooks, vol. 1, CHS.

56. On the call for municipal dance alternatives, see *Chicago Record-Herald*, June 21, 1911, and Vice Commission of Chicago, *The Social Evil in Chicago*.

57. *Chicago Record-Herald*, June 21, 1911. Nor were all reformers necessarily content to merely offer alternatives to the commercial hall. As chapter 6 will show, the Juvenile Protective Association took a more interventionist approach by launching an extraordinary effort to bring public dancing under bourgeois social control through direct investigation and other forms of political pressure.

58. For an assessment of progressive attempts at co-opting dancing for purposes of regulation elsewhere, see Lambin, "Report of the Advisory

Dance Hall Committee of the Women's City Club and the City Recreation Committee." See also Perry, " 'The General Motherhood of the Commonwealth.' "

59. South Park Commissioners, "Proceedings," 16:256, CPD.

60. Eckhart Park hosted 118 dances that year; Stanford Park, 48; Dvorak, 45, and Holstein Park, 96. Data drawn from "Showing Summary of the Uses of the Different Small Park Facilities for the Year of 1913," in West Chicago Park Commissioners, "Forty-fifth Annual Report, 1913," 143.

61. West Chicago Park Commissioners, "Forty-fourth Annual Report, 1912," 22.

62. "After the small parks had been operating for two years, the South Side alone showed a decrease in delinquency of seventeen percent relative to the delinquency of the whole city." Allen T. Burns, "Relation of Playgrounds to Juvenile Delinquency," quoted in South Park Commissioners, "Annual Report of the South Park Commissioners for Fiscal Year Ended February 28, 1909," 11.

63. Borosini, "Public Recreation Facilities," 147.

64. Mero, "The South Park System," 217.

65. South Park Commissioners, "Annual Report of the South Park Commissioners for 1912," 45.

66. Juvenile Protective Association, "Annual Report, 1911–12," reel 52, JAP.

67. Smergalski, "Social Dancing in West Park Recreation Centers," 544.

68. Smergalski recalled that the diverse nature of the crowds made them "somewhat hard to direct in behavior." Ibid. WPC officials expressed concerns about crime in areas near field house parks, and the police ranks swelled from 76 in 1906 to 120 patrolmen by the end of 1913. See South Park Commissioners, "Annual Report of the South Park Commissioners for Fiscal Year 1906," 95, CPD, and West Chicago Park Commissioners, "West Chicago Park Commissioners, Forty-sixth Annual Report," 166.

69. On ragtime-era dance styles, see Dillon, *From Dance Hall to White Slavery*, and Perry, " 'The General Motherhood of the Commonwealth.' "

70. The Lincoln Park Commissioners, by contrast, had reluctantly succumbed to popular pressure by voting to allow "modern dances" at the park's South Refectory. See "Minutes," October 21, 1914, in Commissioners of Lincoln Park, "Official Proceedings of the Lincoln Park Commissioners, Vol. 9," CPD.

71. Smergalski, "Social Dancing in West Park Recreation Centers," 547.

72. Goodman and Kolodin, *The Kingdom of Swing*, 32.

73. Smergalski, "Social Dancing in West Park Recreation Centers," 544–45.

74. "South Park Commissioners, Application for Use of Halls and Club Rooms, Conditions," reprinted in South Park Commissioners, "Annual Re-

port of the South Park Commissioners for the Period March 1, 1911, to February 29, 1912, Inclusive," 45, CPD.

75. Ibid., 44.

76. Ibid.

77. Ibid. (emphasis added).

CHAPTER FIVE

1. DeGroot, "Are the Parks for the People or the People for the Parks?," 219.

2. Here DeGroot distorted the facts to make his point. A glance at their annual reports would have reminded DeGroot that the West Chicago and South Park Commissioners invested thousands of dollars to employ competent professional musicians. Ibid.

3. Ibid., 220. "Drink to Me Only with Thine Eyes" was a popular ballad using the lyrics of the poet Ben Jonson's "To Celia" (1616).

4. Zanzig, *Music in American Life*, 236. Communication from Civic Music Association, August 26, 1913, in West Chicago Park Commissioners, "Proceedings," 1913, 8658; Correspondence, Amalie Hofer Jerome of CMA to LPC, August 8, 1913, in Commissioners of Lincoln Park, "Minutes of Meeting of August 18, 1913," 253, CPD.

5. West Chicago Park Commissioners, "Proceedings," 1913, 8658.

6. Correspondence, CMA of Chicago to President and Board of South Park Commissioners, April 22, 1914, in South Park Commissioners, "Proceedings," 21:145, CPD; Civic Music Association of Chicago, "First Annual Report," CMA.

7. The Lincoln Park Commissioners were feeling the progressive heat themselves and invoked the policy of Illinois governor Edward F. Dunne as an incentive to "throw off the cloak of special privileges which had kept from the people numerous advantages to which they were entitled." See Lincoln Park Commissioners, "Report of the Commissioners of Lincoln Park: Summary of Work Accomplished during the Period July 31st 1913–July 31st, 1915," 12, CPD.

8. K. D. McCarthy, *Noblesse Oblige*, 111–12. McCarthy singles out Hutchinson as "the only member of the Gilded Age elite to make the transition to the progressive view."

9. Civic Music Association of Chicago, "First Annual Report," 12, CMA (emphasis in original).

10. Ibid.

11. The CSO gave seven such concerts in 1914–15 and ten in 1915–16. See Civic Music Association, "Report of Board of Directors for the Season 1914–1915," and Civic Music Association, "Condensed Report for the Season 1915–1916," CHS.

12. Trustee Minutes, December 19, 1916, CSOA. On the name change of the group, see CSO 30th Season Program, February 11–12, 1921, box 1, folder "2nd Season 1920–21 Misc.," CSOA. Leaders of the Chicago Symphony Orchestra were casting their glances beyond the circle of elite patrons of the musical arts to other Chicago residents who might become more active supporters of cultivated music under the right circumstances. As recently as 1900, the CSO had almost turned control of their organization over to the University of Chicago in hopes of sustaining its existence. See clipping 1925 n.d., Philo Otis Scrapbook, Newberry Library. *Chicago Herald and Examiner*, January, 28 1920, box 1, 1919–1978, Civic Orchestra file, CSOA. "Civic Orchestra/Training Orchestra of the Chicago Symphony Orchestra/Fact Sheet" at ⟨http://www.webcom.com/icsom/news97/news1197/120597civicfaq.html⟩; Correspondence "To the members of the Civic Music Association, October, 1916," Civic Music Association folder, CSOA.

13. Civic Music Association, "List of Members and Contributors, Reports of Teachers, Comments by Press and Musicians, etc., July, 1915," 14, CMA.

14. The organization organized children's and adult's choruses and produced events at Seward and Hamlin in the Lincoln Park district; Dvorak and Eckhart in the West Parks; and Hamlin, Holstein, Sherman, Hamilton, Palmer, Mark White Square, Seward, and Armour Square in the South Parks. As further evidence of its democratic perspective, concerts were also held for African American audiences at the First Baptist Church, Thirty-first Street and South Park Avenue, and the La Salle Extension University, 2550 S. Michigan Avenue, since no field house parks existed in the Black Belt. See Commissioners of Lincoln Park, "Minutes of Meeting of October 13, 1915," 38, CPD, and South Park Commissioners, "Proceedings," 21:145–46, CPD.

15. Correspondence, March 2, 1914, and November 12, 1914, Civic Music Association, "List of Members and Contributors . . . ," 12, CMA. Zeisler sat on the CMA's Board of Directors. See CMA letterhead in Civic Music Association, Miscellaneous pamphlets, James Forgan Papers, CHS.

16. The *Boston Transcript* wrote approvingly: "The artists in music who play before these people of the field-houses and the school halls are receiving something in return from their audiences which they cannot get from wealthier Americans, and that is frankly hearty appreciation of their genius." Civic Music Association, "List of Members and Contributors . . . ," 14, CMA.

17. Civic Music Association Concert Program, May 23, 1915, "Orchestra Hall, Civic Music Association, Annual Festivals, 1915–1942," Playbills and Programs, 1843–1979, series 4, box 102, UC.

18. By the end of 1916 the CMA boasted of offering "549 children's classes in small parks and schools, 28 children's classes at the municipal pier . . . 307 choral rehearsals in small parks and schools, 9 community sings at the municipal pier, 25 programs by local talent, [and] 2 spring festivals by

Civic Music Clubs." See CMA Program, "Fall Festival of the Civic Music Association of Chicago at Orchestra Hall, Tues Evening, November 14, 1916, 8:15 o'clock," Playbills and Programs, 1843–1979, series 4, box 102, UC.

19. Pacyga, "Chicago's Pilsen Park," 117–18. Local citizens had fought hard to obtain a field house park in Pilsen by collecting two thousand signatures, which they presented to the WPC; see Breen, *Historical Register*, 482.

20. The park officially opened on June 25, 1908. See West Chicago Park Commissioners, "West Chicago Park Commissioners, Forty-fourth Annual Report, 1912," 24.

21. *Denní Hlasatel*, November 19, 1914, Czech, box 1, CFLPS.

22. West Chicago Park Commissioners, "West Chicago Park Commissioners, Forty-fifth Annual Report," 91. Dvořák famously celebrated America's underappreciated folk music heritage in Antonín Dvořák, "Music in America."

23. *Denní Hlasatel*, December 12, 1905, box 2, Choral Information, Bohemian Singing Societies, MMCS; *Denní Hlasatel*, September 21, 1913, Czech, box 4, CFLPS; Bekken, "Working-Class Newspapers, Community and Consciousness," 254.

24. For more on the history of ethnic presses as booster institutions and the business ties of their editorial board composition, see Janowitz, *The Community Press in an Urban Setting*, 1–58. On Cesky Dum, see *Denní Hlasatel*, April 28, 1913, Czech, box 4, CFLPS.

25. *Denní Hlasatel*, November 28, 1914, Czech, box 4, CFLPS.

26. Census information collected by Joanne Meyerowitz as part of her study of women and work in the Progressive Era indicates that Bohemian women constituted a modest, but significant percentage of independent female wage workers in Chicago by 1910. See Meyerowitz, *Women Adrift*, 11, 23.

27. "Extracts from Teachers' Reports," Albie Sladek, June 24, 1915, in Civic Music Association, "List of Members and Contributors . . . ," 9, CMA.

28. Concert Program to Accompany Bohemian Arts Club Exhibit, December 17–31, 1916, box 22, Ethnic, Bohemian Information, MMCS.

29. Albie Sladek, June 24, 1915, in Civic Music Association, "List of Members and Contributors . . . ," 9, CMA; Civic Music Association, "Fifth Annual Report."

30. "Extracts from Teachers' Reports," *Deutsche Frauen Voklslieder Verein*/Mark White Square, Marie Ruef Hofer, June 25, 1915, in Civic Music Association, "List of Members and Contributors . . . ," 8, CMA (emphasis in original).

31. Ibid.

32. Civic Music Association of Chicago, "First Annual Report," 7, CMA.

33. "Extracts from Teachers' Reports," Lily Wadhams Moline, June 10, 1915, in Civic Music Association, "List of Members and Contributors . . . ," 9, CMA.

34. "Extracts from Teachers' Reports," Anna McPherson, June 10, 1915, in Civic Music Association, "List of Members and Contributors . . . ," 9, CMA.

35. On these dynamics see Higham, *Strangers in the Land*, and Kennedy, *Over Here*.

36. Items culled from *Narod Polski*, May 19, 1915; *Dziennik Zwiazkowy*, March 7, 1917; *Dziennik Zwiazkowy*, February 28, 1918; *Dziennik Zwiazkowy*, April 22, 1918, Polish, box 34, CFLPS.

37. In the fall of 1914, the German American Club of Chicago and Cook County sponsored "a movement for promoting Germanism." The group declared that "the object is a local political one, but non-partisan," supporting candidates of German descent for office. See *Illinois Staats-Zeitung*, September 26, 1914, German, box 16, CFLPS; K. N. Conzen, "Germans." For an overview, see Luebke, *Bonds of Loyalty*.

38. Holli, "The Great War Sinks Chicago's German *Kultur*," 260–311.

39. For an account of the summer concert, see ibid., 272. On the Rhine as a signifier in German Romantic music, see Porter, *The Rhine as Musical Metaphor*.

40. *Chicago Tribune*, January 28, 1915; *Die Abendpost*, January 28, 1915, German, box 15, CFLPS. During the Franco-Prussian War, German soldiers often rallied their spirits with renditions of "Die Wacht am Rhein" ("The Watch over the Rhine"). Tappan, *The World's Story*, 7:249–50; see also Porter, *The Rhine as Musical Metaphor*.

41. Freidel and Brinkley, *America in the Twentieth Century*, 124.

42. Trustee Minutes, December 21, 1917; December 30, 1917; February 14, 1919, February 19, 1919, CSOA.

43. After the war ended, Stock quietly returned to the CSO effective February 28, 1919, and by October the orchestra had discontinued the policy of playing the national anthem. See Trustee Minutes, February 14, 1919, and February 14, 1919, CSOA. On a similar crisis in Boston, see Tischler, *An American Music*.

44. Woods, *The Settlement Horizon*, 153–54; Spalding, "The Work of the Music School Settlement in Americanizing Its Patrons," 533.

45. Tischler, *An American Music*, notes the impact of the war on the manner that composers and elite critics also leaned (or were propelled) toward "musical Americanism." See also Zuck, *A History of Musical Americanism*. Hundreds of amateur women's musical societies across the country also focused their "reform" attentions on patriotic musical duty. See Blair, *The Torchbearers*, 65–75.

46. On the contested theme of "Americanism" in organized labor during this era, see Gerstle, *Working-Class Americanism*. On the civic and racial dimensions of the discourse, see Gerstle, *American Crucible*.

47. In Lincoln Park in 1918, the Illinois War Recreation Committee

covered 30 percent of the costs of the community sings. See Commissioners of Lincoln Park, "Minutes of Meeting, June 12, 1918," CPD. The National Recreation Association, founded in 1906 to promote municipal public recreation, helped promote singing festivals nationally via its War Camp Community Service for servicemen. The NRA also mass-produced booklets for community sings. See Knapp, "Play for America," 104–7; "Community Songs," n.d., CPD.

48. On lantern slides, see Commissioners of Lincoln Park, "Minutes of Meeting, August 16, 1916," 7, CPD.

49. Spalding, "The Work of the Music School Settlement in Americanizing Its Patrons," 533.

50. Civic Music Association, "Officers for 1916–17," n.p., CHS.

51. Civic Music Association, "Annual Festival of the Civic Music Association of Chicago at Orchestra Hall, Weds. eve, January 8, 1918," n.p., CHS.

52. Civic Music Association, "Fifth Annual Report," 11; Commissioners of Lincoln Park, "Minutes of Meeting, February 12, 1918," 4, CPD. On the role of Four Minute Men on the home front, see Creel, *How We Advertised America*.

53. Civic Music Association, "Officers for 1916–17," n.p., CHS.

54. Juvenile Protective Association, "Seventeenth Annual Report," 18, reel 52, JAP.

55. "Community Singing under the Auspices of the Civic Music Association of Chicago," pamphlet, East Garfield Park, box 3, folder 1, Special Collections, CPL.

56. For a comparative statement on the cultural work of gender mobilization on the home front during World War II, see Westbrook, "Fighting for the American Family." On women, gender, and war exigencies, see Kerber, *Women of the Republic*.

57. On popular music and affect, see Finson, *The Voices That Are Gone*, and Dror, "Creating the Emotional Body." On racialization of European immigrants, see Jacobson, *Whiteness of a Different Color*.

58. See Drake and Cayton, *Black Metropolis*, and Grossman, *Land of Hope*.

59. The interpretive approach to these songs emphasizes their "preferred meanings" rather than the oppositional or alternative readings that listeners may have ascribed to them. See Hall, "Encoding/Decoding."

60. On racial masquerades, ethnicity, and white Americanism in American history, see Huggins, "Personae"; Lott, *Love and Theft*; Roediger, *The Wages of Whiteness*; and Rogin, *Blackface, White Noise*. See also Dennison, *Scandalize My Name*, and Finson, *The Voices That Are Gone*.

61. E. Smith, *The Eleanor Smith Music Course, Book 4*, 4.

62. Orchestra Hall, Civic Music Association, Annual Festivals, 1915–1942, Playbills and Programs, 1843–1979, series 4, box 102, UC.

63. South Park Commissioners, "Annual Report of the South Park Commissioners for Fiscal Year Ended February 28, 1909," 10–11.

64. Woodward, *The Strange Career of Jim Crow*, 19–20; Grossman, *Land of Hope*, 127, 164.

65. Jordan, *White over Black*, 542–69; Williamson, *A Rage for Order*, 281–87; Woodward, *The Strange Career of Jim Crow*.

66. Drake and Cayton, *Black Metropolis*, 61. On housing discrimination, see Alzada P. Comstock, "Chicago Housing Conditions, 6: The Problem of the Negro," 253–54, referenced in Pacyga, *Polish Immigrants and Industrial Chicago*, 213.

67. The dimensions of the Black Belt are described in Grossman, *Land of Hope*, 123–27. Census information is in Spear, *Black Chicago*.

68. On the history of labor tension, race, and urban culture, see Drake and Cayton, *Black Metropolis*, and Grossman, *Land of Hope*. On the geography and cultural anxieties surrounding spaces of interracial contact in Chicago and New York in this period, see Mumford, *Interzones*.

69. On the politics of race, class, and property on the South Side, see especially Spear, *Black Chicago*, for the period 1890–1920, and Hirsch, *Making the Second Ghetto*, for 1940–1960.

70. "The Colored People of Chicago, An Investigation Made for the JPA by A. P. Drucker, Sophia Boaz, A. L. Harris, Miriam Schaffner, Text by Louise de Koven Bowen, 1913," folder 128, JPAR, UIC.

71. Special Park Commissioners, "Annual Report, 1908," 6.

72. Drake and Cayton, *Black Metropolis*, 64, 293. Careful examination of the official minutes and annual reports of the South and West Park Commissioners between 1900 and 1919 shows these documents to be mostly silent about the social changes affecting Chicago and the subject of race tensions on park grounds.

73. Correspondence, M. P. Boynton, Secretary Woodlawn Ministerial Association to SPC, February 26, 1914, in South Park Commissioners, "Proceedings," 21:107, CPD.

74. African American children and adults frequented a number of municipal and Special Park Commission playgrounds constructed in the 1900s within the Black Belt. These adjoined public schools and were available for public use on weekends and late afternoons and evenings. There were fourteen such playgrounds in the Black Belt by 1919, but they were spartan and lacked the indoor space and amenities of the field house parks. During the 1900s and 1910s, the SPC built seven field house parks on the periphery of the Black Belt, with the unstated implication that these were reasonably accessible to the African American population. Chicago Commission on Race Relations [hereafter Commission], *The Negro in Chicago*, 272.

75. Sociologist Frederic Thrasher, described the formation of one South

Side gang "merely as the result of a dozen or more fellows (from sixteen to twenty-two years of age) meeting casually on a street corner at the entrance of one of Chicago's parks and later on in 'Mike's' poolroom a short distance away." Thrasher and Short, *The Gang*, 37.

76. Hughes, *The Big Sea*, 33, quoted in Grossman, *Land of Hope*, 118.

77. Commission, *The Negro in Chicago*, 288–89.

78. Ibid., 115, 248.

79. Ibid., 289.

80. Ibid., 250.

81. The large parks were only marginally better. As mentioned above, Washington Park had 10 percent annually, while Jackson Park, on the other side of the segregated white enclave of Hyde Park, had but 2 percent annually. Ibid., 275–76.

82. Ibid., 292. A Carnegie Corporation researcher echoed the observation about Chicago parks that "if they are in mixed districts, the tendency is for the race which is in the majority to identify itself with the park, while the others use it comparatively little." Daniels, *America via the Neighborhood*, 272.

83. Commission, *The Negro in Chicago*, 272.

84. Ibid., 279. *The Negro in Chicago* suggests that park swimming pools were integrated, but it is not known whether swimming lessons were readily available or affordable to most African American children.

85. Robert Abbott, "Ruffianism in the Parks," *Chicago Defender*, July 12, 1919.

86. Ibid. (emphasis added). Several summers previously a white man had tried to rape an African American girl in Washington Park, leading to calls for action from the *Defender*. See *Chicago Defender*, July 25, 1914.

87. Tuttle, *Race Riot*, 3–7. The JPA criticized the conduct of the Chicago Police, calling the death of Eugene Williams "the most serious and momentous lapse in juvenile protection ever known in Chicago." Juvenile Protective Association, "Eighteenth Annual Report," 23, reel 52, JAP. Ironically, this very stretch of beach had generated interest by the Special Park Commission in 1902 as the potential "nucleus of an ideal resort" in an underserved neighborhood. See Special Park Commission, "Report on Sites and Needs," n.p.

88. Detailed accounts of the riot can be found in Commission, *The Negro in Chicago*, and Tuttle, *Race Riot*. On disproportionate injuries and fatalities, see Tuttle, *Race Riot*, 64–65.

89. "Public Opinion in Race Relations," in Commission, *The Negro in Chicago*, 520–94.

90. For a description of such a case, see Thrasher, *The Gang*, 328. See also Robert S. Abbott, "Ruffianism in the Parks," *Chicago Defender*, July 12, 1919.

91. Grossman, *Land of Hope*, 178–9.

92. Commission, *The Negro in Chicago*, 278, 280. Perhaps the supervisor

spoke only for his park since park police in Washington Park were known to break up interracial fracases on a semiregular basis by spring 1919. See South Park Commissioners, "Proceedings," 26:203, CPD.

93. Commission, *The Negro in Chicago*, 290.

94. An incident of Polish harassment of Jews is reported in Bukowski, *Big Bill Thompson*, 96. As described earlier, Hilda Satt had recollections of Jewish fear of Christian Poles. See Polacheck, *I Came a Stranger*, 8–9.

95. Commission, *The Negro in Chicago*, 281.

96. West Chicago Park Commissioners, "Recreation Centers, Playgrounds, and Swimming Pools of the West Chicago Park Commissioners," 6.

CHAPTER SIX

1. Sinaiko, *Reclaiming the Canon*, 113–15. As Sinaiko notes, Yeats served as a member of the Irish Senate. He worked on a committee devoted to monitoring progressive innovation in primary education. The "sixty-year-old smiling public man" described in the poem may allude to the poet himself, who visited a girls school during an official tour of duty in the period preceding the composition of this poem.

2. Key studies on commercial dancing and identity formation include Erenberg, *Steppin' Out*; Peiss, *Cheap Amusements*; Cohen, *Making a New Deal*; and Greene, *A Passion for Polka*. Scholars emphasize the importance of the urban dance hall as a site of popular resistance and identity formation among American women. The urban dancing phenomenon marked a shift from nineteenth-century homosocial worlds of "respectable" bourgeois recreation in which men gathered in public settings to socialize, while women forged bonds in the privacy of domestic settings.

3. On gay sexual identity and the Jazz Age, see Garber, " 'T'aint Nobody's Business,' " and Chauncey, *Gay New York*. On issues of segregation and public recreation at this time, see Nasaw, *Going Out*, and Mumford, *Interzones*. The gender, racial, and sexual subcultures springing up around commercial music and dancing, most notably jazz, reflected the sheltering powers of commercial public space, as well as the concomitant flexing of class and race privileges, not uncommonly at the expense of marginalized groups.

4. Many cities mounted campaigns to investigate commercial dance in the early twentieth century, including Baltimore, Cleveland, Kansas City, Milwaukee, New York, and San Francisco. See Wagner, *Adversaries of Dance*, 296–97. On New York's efforts, see Elisabeth I. Perry, " 'The General Motherhood of the Commonwealth.' "

5. Kenney, *Chicago Jazz*. Kenney's point about the importance of differentiating as much as possible between "jazz" music and the "Jazz Age" is crucial. The former embraces a compositional and aesthetic movement in modern music, while the latter encompasses the contested realm of ideas and

social and cultural practices shaping its meanings and popular reception. For an excellent assessment of race, popular music, and the discursive construction of the nation in the 1930s, see Stowe, *Swing Changes*.

6. Innumerable reform organizations such as the Hyde Park Protective League, the Chicago Law and Order League, and, in the 1920s, the Committee of Fifteen found reasons to be concerned about youth dancing in public and investigated aspects of it as part of their work.

7. See "History and Survey of Work," in "Annual Report of the JPA, 1910," 11–13, reel 52, JAP.

8. P. G. Anderson, "The Good to Be Done," 241.

9. See annual reports of the JPA from the early 1910s in reel 53, JAP. Harriet Vittum organized public dances at Small Park no. 1 (Eckhart Park); see "Annual Report of the JPA, 1911–12."

10. One of the JPA's subsidiary interests included the use of youth performers in vaudeville and music theater, a practice that they found objectionable and attempted to quash. See "Juvenile Occupations Department, Report for 1924," folder 12, JPAR.

11. On the lengthy history of reform movements in the United States dedicated to policing working-class female sexuality, see especially Stansell, *City of Women*; Odem, *Delinquent Daughters*; Barron, "Sex and Single Girls," 838–47.

12. Kenney, *Chicago Jazz*. Key studies on social responses include Peretti, *The Creation of Jazz*, and Ogren, *The Jazz Revolution*.

13. Southern, *The Music of Black Americans*; Baraka, *Blues People*; Leonard, *Jazz and the White Americans*. Scholars link negative social and aesthetic assessment of jazz and other forms of African American music and its creators and fans to ingrained patterns of economic exploitation and animus stretching at least as far back as the arrival of the first enslaved Africans in the Americas. Concomitant with such racialized denigration came celebrations of jazz as a soundtrack of African American "primitive" or authentic genius among intellectuals, impresarios, and musicians of both races. On the historical power of the music to animate resistance and rebut denigration of African Americans, see Levine, *Black Culture and Black Consciousness*. For a prime collection that addresses the theoretical challenge of black musics to conventional divisions of aesthetic, sociological, and historical analysis, see Radano and Bohlman, *Music and the Racial Imagination*.

14. In the 1920s the commercial music industry appropriated the form and improvisational character of African American jazz, circulating it widely via phonographs and radio, even as many African American artists confronted exploitation and outright theft of their work by forces ranging from white competitors to manipulative producers and music executives. See Baraka, *Blues People*. On the impact of race recordings, see Lieb, *Mother of the Blues*, and Carby, "It Just Be's Dat Way Sometime," 9–22.

15. For theoretical issues pertaining to the sociology of dance, see especially H. Thomas, *Dance, Modernity, and Culture*. A well-documented historical survey of dance and social regulation in the United States, to which my discussion is indebted, is Wagner, *Adversaries of Dance*.

16. The Great Awakening–era itinerant preacher George Whitefield noted that in North Carolina in the late 1730s there were "several dancing-masters, but scarcely one regular settled minister." Whitefield, *George Whitefield's Journals*, Wednesday, January 9, 1740, n.p.

17. Kraus, *History of the Dance*, 100–101.

18. Quoted in Marks, *America Learns to Dance*, 20–21; see also Kraus, *History of the Dance*, 97–118.

19. On the rupture in hegemonic Protestant asceticism that paralleled the phenomenon of dancing in Chicago discussed here, see Lears, *No Place of Grace*. On dancing as counterproductive to the ennobling activity of work, see Broyles, *Music of the Highest Class*, 95.

20. On the emergence of the American middle class in this era and their social and recreational habits, see especially Bushman, *The Refinement of America*; Blumin, *The Emergence of the Middle Class*; and Ryan, *Cradle of the Middle Class*. On the preponderance of etiquette and advice literature as an instrument of discrimination in a democratic culture, see Haltunnen, *Confidence Men and Painted Ladies*.

21. "Dance," in W. H. Harris and Levey, *The New Columbia Encyclopedia*, 716–17; Wagner, *Adversaries of Dance*, 144.

22. Bournique Scrapbook Collection, CHS.

23. Pamphlet, Bournique Scrapbook Collection, CHS.

24. See "Chicago Balls Invitation" folder, Bournique Scrapbook Collection, CHS. After the turn of the century, organizations in Chicago's African American neighborhoods, such as the Manasseh Club, are known to have held regular balls. See Drake and Cayton, *Black Metropolis*, 145.

25. Wagner, *Adversaries of Dance*; Marks, *America Learns to Dance*; Zorbaugh, *The Gold Coast and the Slum*, 56, 64.

26. On the transition to mainstream respectability for commercial public dancing, see Erenberg, *Steppin Out*.

27. Faulkner, *From the Ball-room to Hell*, 154.

28. Ibid., 8–9.

29. For a comparative case history of vice in New York City, see Gilfoyle, *City of Eros*.

30. On the social construction of masculinity and public amusement culture where currents of race and whiteness also operated, see Bederman, *Manliness and Civilization*; Gorn, *The Manly Art*; Hine and Jenkins, *A Question of Manhood*.

31. S. L. Johnson, "Bulls, Bears, and Dancing Boys," and Gilfoyle, *City of Eros*. On the bright lights district of Chicago, see Asbury, *Gem of the Prairie*.

On the problematic class assumptions supporting the bourgeois reform tendency of shunning women in public occupational settings such as these, see Stansell, *City of Women*.

32. "History of Chicago's Sexual Underground," unpublished, undated manuscript, Gregory Sprague Collection, folder 1, box 13, CHS.

33. See Andrews, *Chicago after Dark*; Reckless, *Vice in Chicago*; Keyes, "The Forgotten Fire," 52–65; and Green and Holli, *The Mayors*, 16–32. References to the "Levee" can be found as early as 1892; see for example "Raiding the Levee," *Chicago Inter-Ocean*, July 16, 1892, 3. On the ritual practices of sporting men in antebellum America and the rise of the music hall as a site of commercialized vice in New York, see Gilfoyle, *City of Eros*, 92–116, 224–50.

34. Harland, *The Vice Bondage of a Great City*, 192. The style of such reform literature had important antecedents in the urban penny press of the 1840s and its coverage of high-profile murders, sex crimes, and intrigues. See Tucher, *Froth and Scum*; H. L. Horowitz, *Rereading Sex*; and Pittenger, "A World of Difference."

35. S. P. Wilson, *Cesspools of Infamy*, 95.

36. Ibid., 197.

37. Ibid., 222.

38. S. P. Wilson, *Chicago by Gaslight*, 78. For a nuanced series of readings of popular fiction and moral exposés on single women as victims in urban settings at this time, see Meyerowitz, *Women Adrift*.

39. S. P. Wilson, *Chicago by Gaslight*, 78 (emphasis added). "Axminster" refers to a machine-woven carpet mass-produced in the English town of the same name.

40. Ibid.

41. For a related argument concerning the role of the Jacksonian-era penny press, see Tucher, *Froth and Scum*.

42. On the significance of the Chicago saloon, see Duis, *The Saloon*. Rosenzweig, *Eight Hours for What We Will*, is a key study of alcohol's place and recreational reform policy in Worcester, Massachusetts.

43. Marks, *America Learns to Dance*. For embodiments of this phenomenon, see, for example, Pacyga, *Polish Immigrants and Industrial Chicago*; Barrett, *Work and Community in the Jungle*; and Cohen, *Making a New Deal*. On the links between political patronage and commercial nightlife in New York City, see Czitrom, "Underworlds and Underdogs."

44. By the turn of the century, some saloons welcomed women and girls into the public world of drinking through special "family" or "ladies'" back room entrances and annexes, known as "wine rooms" where women gathered proximate to, but spatially segregated from, men. See "Family Entrance Closed in Chicago Saloons," *The Survey* 32 (May 1914): 170.

45. "Study of Prohibition by National Federation of Settlements Prior

to Publication of 'Does Prohibition Work?,'" Lee Demarest Taylor Papers, folder 76, UIC. See also *Chicago Record Herald*, January 11, 1905.

46. As Peiss argues in *Cheap Amusements*, 56–76, the seductive allure of anonymity in public and a chance to "put on style" through the use of fashions, finery, and attitudes that might have been ridiculed or not permitted at home exerted a powerful appeal on wage-earning women who patronized dance halls in New York City.

47. *Chicago Record-Herald*, January 16, 1905. Although laws barred the sale of liquor to minors, the Chicago Police Department did not consistently enforce the rules, particularly if unscrupulous proprietors were willing to reward them for their discretion and "protection" from police harassment.

48. *Chicago Record-Herald*, January 9, 1905; January 16, 1905; February 26, 1905; *Chicago Tribune*, January 23, 1905.

49. *Chicago Record-Herald*, January 23, 1905 (emphasis added).

50. Using JPA-generated evidence, Cohen, *Making a New Deal*, 146–47, argues that reformers failed to acknowledge the "ethnic clusters" that cleaved together despite what to an outsider appeared to be a mass event comprised of individuals randomly distributed.

51. *Narod Polski*, January 17, 1900, Polish, box 32, CFLPS.

52. *Narod Polski*, April 24, 1907, Polish, box 35, CFLPS.

53. *Dziennik Zwiazkowy*, November 30, 1914, Polish, box 32, CFLPS.

54. *Narod Polski*, July 6, 1904, Polish, box 32, CFLPS. On commercial culture serving as an escape valve for women, see Peiss, *Cheap Amusements*.

55. Harrison served from 1897 to 1905 and again from 1911 to 1915. The characterization of him as a "reform boss" appears in Green and Holli, eds., *The Mayors*, 21. On the rampant corruption and graft within the police department in protecting red-light-district activity during these years, see G. Taylor, "The Police and Vice in Chicago," 160–65.

56. Harrison issued orders to close the West Side Levee in 1903. See "Plague Spot of Chicago Must Go," *New York World*, November 6, 1903, reel 55, JAP; Green and Holli, *The Mayors*, 22–23.

57. *Chicago Record-Herald*, January 25, 1905.

58. In the late nineteenth century, regulators in New York City noted a similar migration of prostitutes out of brothels into music halls and other mixed-use public settings. See Gilfoyle, *City of Eros*, 295–97.

59. Riley, "A Study of the Higher Life of Chicago," 54.

60. Vice Commission of Chicago, *The Social Evil in Chicago*.

61. Ibid., 261–62.

62. Similar investigations conducted in these years in Cleveland, Kansas City, Milwaukee, New York, and other cities led the Playground and Recreation Association of America to propose standardized dance hall ordinances. See Schoenfeld, "Commercial Recreation Legislation."

63. Moving-picture shows represented the distant runner-up among

youth. Their nightly estimated attendance numbered 32,000. Bowen, "Dance Halls," 383–87. On the number of halls (some licensed, others not), see Bowen, "Our Most Popular Recreation Controlled by the Liquor Interests, a Study of the Public Dance Halls by the JPA, 1911," 1–8, folder 135, JPAR. The calculation of 14.5 percent of Chicago youths (six to twenty years of age) was derived from "Composition and Characteristics of the Population for Wards of Cities of 50,000 or More," in U.S. Bureau of the Census, *Thirteenth Census of the United States*, 2:191.

64. Gertrude Howe Britton, "The Public Dance Hall and Its Relation to Vice, January 26, 1912," n.p., folder 104, JPAR. See also, Bowen, *Growing Up with a City*, 120–24.

65. Meyerowitz, *Women Adrift*, 61. On the presence of lodging houses, see Louise De Koven Bowen, "Some Legislative Needs in Illinois," 1914, 19, folder 133, JPAR.

66. Juvenile Protective Association, "Annual Report of the JPA, 1911–12"; Juvenile Protective Association, "Annual Report of the JPA, 1913–14," reel 52, JAP.

67. Bowen, "Our Most Popular Recreation Controlled by the Liquor Interests, a Study of the Public Dance Halls by the JPA, 1911," folder 135, JPAR.

68. See Green and Holli, *The Mayors*. Days before the closure of the Levee, an estimated 10,000 demonstrators marched through downtown Chicago, singing hymns and calling for a "clean Chicago." See Committee of Fifteen Newsletter, January 1936, folder 9, box 6, EWBP.

69. Juvenile Protective Association, "Seventeenth Annual Report," 18, reel 52, JAP.

70. Zorbaugh, *The Gold Coast*, 116.

71. "Boost by Making City Safe for Youth, Plea," *Chicago News*, May 15, 1920, Louise Dekoven Bowen Scrapbooks, vol. 2, CHS.

72. Binford, "On with the Dance," 98–99.

73. Bowen, "The Public Dance Halls of Chicago"; "Mrs. Bowen in Exposé of Vice among Young," *Chicago American*, April 24, 1916, Louise Dekoven Bowen Scrapbooks, vol. 2, CHS. As David Nasaw and others have demonstrated, the vast majority of early-twentieth-century commercial amusements, including cabarets, with the exception of the black and tans discussed below, systematically excluded African Americans. See Nasaw, *Going Out*.

74. Erenberg, *Steppin' Out*.

75. On related entertainment traditions in which barriers between audiences and entertainers tended to be porous, see Allen, *Horrible Prettiness*, and Snyder, *The Voice of the City*. Cabaret work supported many white jazz musicians who performed for segregated audiences on the North and West Sides.

76. Edwards, *Popular Amusements*, 68, and Erenberg, *Steppin' Out*. Morals investigators quoted in Bowen, *Fighting to Make Chicago Safe for Children*, 12.

77. Zorbaugh, *The Gold Coast and the Slum*, 120.

78. It is important to note that reformers thought of white women when they made these pronouncements. The figure of an African American woman in such a setting might not have invited the same degree of sympathy from reformers. See, for example, Carby, "Policing the Black Woman's Body." On the issue of policing women's sexuality through the overdetermined term "prostitute," see Odem, *Delinquent Daughters*, and Barron, "Sex and Single Girls."

79. Less reliably documented are rules governing the restrictions of cabaret singers. JPA records suggest that on occasion African American female vocalists appeared outside the Black Belt. There are also hints that African American musicians appeared outside the Black Belt, but such appearances would have been infrequent since they risked punishment from the union. On the two unions' roles in segregating performance venues, see Spivey, *Union and the Black Musician*; Dance, *The World of Earl Hines*; Travis, *An Autobiography of Black Jazz*; Vaillant, "Staying in the Black."

80. Bowen, *Fighting to Make Chicago Safe for Children*, 13.

81. Ibid.

82. Bowen, "The Public Dance Halls of Chicago, revised edition, 1917," 4–5, folder 135, JPAR.

83. Bowen, *Fighting to Make Chicago Safe for Children*, 12.

84. "Mrs. Bowen in Exposé of Vice among Young," *Chicago American*, April 24, 1916, Louise Dekoven Bowen Scrapbooks, vol. 2, CHS.

85. As Kenney argues in the case of black-and-tan dance clubs, "Instead of 'vice' itself, the Dreamland, Sunset, and Royal Gardens specialized in presenting unprecedented spectacles of interracial contacts in social dancing." See Kenney, *Chicago Jazz*, 24.

86. The precise origins of the black and tan in Chicago are unknown, but there is little evidence prior to the 1920s of organized interracial institutions in Chicago outside of the red-light interracial sex trade. The conspicuous exception was the Manasseh Club, a turn-of-the-century fraternal organization for laboring interracial couples in Chicago. See Drake and Cayton, *Black Metropolis*, 145–47.

87. See Travis, *An Autobiography of Chicago Jazz*.

88. As white jazz pianist Art Hodes recalled of many cabarets outside the Black Belt, "The band was strictly for background and a little dancing. . . . [T]he entertainers were the most important people in the place, the band was at the bottom of the ladder." Hodes and Hansen, *Hot Man*, 14 (quotation in text on 1).

89. Sunset Cabaret report, November 21, 1922, folder 93, JPAR. On white participants in the jazz subculture, both musicians and audience mem-

bers, see Leonard, *Jazz and the White Americans*; Condon, *We Called It Music*; and Mezzrow, *Really the Blues*. For a critical assessment of Mezzrow's recollections, in *Really the Blues*, of "passing" in the racialized jazz subculture, see Wald, *Crossing the Line*, 67–68.

90. A few larger halls catered to African Americans in the 1920s, such as the Savoy. Exclusion of African Americans and most Asians were reported in the large dance halls of New York City in the early 1920s, too. See Mason, "Satan in the Dance-Hall," 175–82, and Todd, Byron, and Vierow, *The Chicago Recreation Survey*, vol. 1.

91. On the homosexual subculture at Chicago black and tans, see Mumford, *Interzones*.

92. This statement is based on a complete examination of the known surviving records of the JPA in Special Collections at the University of Illinois at Chicago.

93. Affidavit of Theodore Schulze and Grace Powell, March 15, 1922, Records of the Circuit Court of Cook County, 22C B84828: *The People of the State of Illinois on Relation of Edward J. Brundage, Attorney General of the State of Illinois, and Robert E. Crowe, State's Attorney of Cook County, IL vs. Edward Fox and Samuel Rifas*.

94. Affidavit of Benjamin Blinstrub, April 27, 1922, Records of the Circuit Court of Cook County, 22C B84828: *The People of the State of Illinois on Relation of Edward J. Brundage, Attorney General of the State of Illinois, and Robert E. Crowe, State's Attorney of Cook County, IL vs. Edward Fox and Samuel Rifas*.

95. "Pioneer Cabaret, December 16, 1923," folder 93, JPAR.

96. "Report on Visits to Old Houses of Prostitution on the South Side and a Statement of Conditions Found, April 15, 1923, Nels Anderson," Commercialized Prostitution in Chicago, IL, 1922–23, folder 92, JPAR.

97. JPA investigators reported frequent conversations with waiters about which women were working the clubs as prostitutes. A complaint lodged against one black and tan revealed that an investigator drinking whiskey high-balls "was solicited for sex by female performers in the show for $5 and that he was later provided with a 'hootchie-kootchie' dance; that while this affiant was there he was solicited to prostitution by two white women and one colored woman." See Records of the Circuit Court of Cook County, 22C B84828, *The People of the State of Illinois on Relation of Edward J. Brundage, Attorney General of the State of Illinois, and Robert E. Crowe, State's Attorney of Cook County, IL vs. Edward Fox and Samuel Rifas*.

98. "Schiller Cabaret, November 25, 1922," folder 93, JPAR. Street solicitations outside of black and tans were also reported, see "Summary, April 30, 1923," Commercialized Prostitution in Chicago, IL, 1922–23, folder 92, JPAR.

99. Jessie Binford, "Testimony in the Criminal Court of Cook County,

January Term 1923," Commercialized Prostitution in Chicago, IL, 1922–23, folder 92, JPAR.

100. Affidavit of Benjamin Blinstrub, April 27, 1922. On masquerades of this sort in Harlem, most notably the phenomenon of interracial drag events such as the Hamilton Lodge balls of the 1920s and early 1930s, see Chauncey, *Gay New York*, 257–64.

101. Evidence of male performers in drag at North Side cabarets appears occasionally. See Derby Cabaret, December 12, 1922, folder 92, JPAR; Kenney, *Chicago Jazz*, 3–34.

102. The sociologist and taxi-dance researcher Paul Cressey claimed that the originary site of the taxi-dance to be the "Barbary Coast dance hall" in San Francisco, which thrived until morals activists closed the city's red-light district in 1913. See Cressey, *The Taxi-Dance Hall*, 179–80.

103. DeFilippis Paper, folder 6, box 129, EWBP. Initially, taxi-dance halls masqueraded as "educational" establishments avoiding licensing rules applying to city amusement statutes. The JPA succeeded in inducing the halls to register as licensed city amusements, thus subjecting them to tighter scrutiny and regulation. See Cressey, *The Taxi-Dance Hall*, 276.

104. Cressey, *The Taxi-Dance Hall*, 186.

105. See Hodes and Hansen, *Hot Man*, 1; "Athenian," Public Dance Halls, folder 103, JPAR.

106. Hodes and Hansen, *Hot Man*, 1, 32. Hodes performed at the Rainbow Gardens Café on Madison and Lafflin and at the Capitol Dancing School nearby.

107. On social and cultural aspects of geography and urban space, see especially de Certeau, "Walking in the City," and K. J. Anderson, "Cultural Hegemony."

108. Cressey, *The Taxi-Dance Hall*, 186. The age of the female employees of the halls ranged from late teens to early twenties, and it follows that there may have been minors (as well as older women) who took jobs in these halls. As the sarcasm of the report indicates, JPA reformers assumed these "so-called instructors" to be sex workers.

109. Ibid., 211.

110. Ibid., 9. As noted, African Americans were excluded.

111. It should be noted that taxi-dances welcomed many different kinds of men. Caucasian men included about 20 percent of the total. See ibid., 110.

112. All evidence suggests that African American, Filipino, Pacific Island, and Mexican women did not work at these halls.

113. This applied to the Mexican *solos*, men who worked in heavy industry and sent their wages back to family members in the southern United States or in Mexico. See the informative study of P. S. Taylor, *Mexican Labor in the United States*.

114. On the popularity of black and tans among Filipinos in Los Angeles, see España-Maram, "Brown 'Hordes' in McIntosh Suits."

115. Cressey, *The Taxi-Dance Hall*, 4, 256.

116. [Howard Gold?], "An Evening in the New American Dance Hall," folder 6, box 129, EWBP.

117. Cressey, *The Taxi-Dance Hall*, 8.

118. Ibid.

119. Ibid., 6.

120. Hodes and Hanson, *Hot Man*, 32.

121. Cressey, *The Taxi-Dance Hall*, 132.

122. Ibid., 10–11.

123. The Trianon required "proper attire" and it bedecked its floor managers in tuxedos. Neither it nor the Aragon, built in 1926, permitted African American patrons; indeed they did not support swing in the mid-1930s, either. See Banks, "The World's Most Beautiful Ballrooms."

124. Jessie Binford recalled that the hall operators "soon saw the value of association," but only after investigations and demands coaxed them to the negotiating table. Binford, "On with the Dance," 99. Halls affiliated with the National Association of Ballroom Proprietors and Managers included Guyon's Paradise, Harmon's Dreamland, the Trianon Ballroom, and Merry Gardens. See also Cressey, *The Taxi-Dance Hall*, 204–6.

125. Paul Cressey Notes, folder 5, box 129, EWBP; Paul Cressey, "Autobiographical of S. A. [name withheld], Dancing Master," folder 92, JPAR.

126. Cressey, *The Taxi-Dance Hall*, 199–205. Binford, "On with the Dance," 98–99.

127. Building on the pioneering urban sociology of Ernest W. Burgess and Robert Park, professors at the University of Chicago, Cressey set out "to trace the natural history of the taxi-dance hall as an urban institution . . . and to analyze its function in terms of the basic wishes and needs of its male patrons." Cressey, *The Taxi-Dance Hall*, xi.

128. "The patrons of the taxi-dance hall constitute a variegated assortment. The brown-skinned Filipino rubs elbows with the stolid European Slav. The Chinese chop-suey waiter comes into his own alongside the Greek from the Mediterranean. The newly industrialized Mexican peon finds his place in the same crowd with the 'bad boys' of some of Chicago's first families." Cressey, *The Taxi-Dance Hall*, 9. Mumford offers a critique of the ethnocentric and racialized assumptions of construing urban men of color as "marginal men." See Mumford, *Interzones*.

129. On the importance of a "cover story" for multicultural and multiracial populations, see Hall, "Ethnicity."

130. Mumford, *Interzones*, 66–70.

131. The argument of "sexual racism" does not engage the racial varia-

tion among the male clientele, such as the fact that the relative percentages of Caucasian and Filipino male patrons at taxi-dances were the same, suggesting that recuperating masculine privilege across racial barriers marked an important dimension of the taxi-dance's cultural work.

132. In effect, there transpired a "resignifying" of these identities that proved transgressive. See Butler, *Gender Trouble*, 124.

133. Cressey, *The Taxi-Dance Hall*, 12, 58, 256.

134. Ibid., 5. A similar finding about the physical attributes of taxi-dance girls emerged in a study of taxi-dancing in New York. See Mason, "Satan in the Dance-Hall," 179. On a somewhat different reading of the chorus girl typology in terms of respectfully desexualized "healthy, coy playmates," see Erenberg, *Steppin' Out*. On the emergence of an "American" female image and identity, see especially the discussion of Hollywood star Mary Pickford in May, *Screening Out the Past*. Investigators observed that ethnic representation among the female workers leaned toward Polish girls and women, with a few Italian or Jewish women reported. On blacking up to perform rituals of Otherness, see Huggins, "Personae," and Rogin, *Blackface, White Noise*.

135. In keeping with the conventions of his ethnographic research, Cressey used pseudonyms for his female subjects. He provided a table of these ethnic subjects and their "American" aliases as illustrative of the glamorization the dancers affected through their name choices. See Cressey, *The Taxi-Dance Hall*, 97.

136. On the influence that Filipino dancers had on representations of the sexualized masculine body of color in the presence of white women, see España-Maram, "Brown 'Hordes' in McIntosh Suits."

137. Cressey, *The Taxi-Dance Hall*, 44.

138. Ibid., 12. One informant discounted the theory that taxi-dancing encouraged prostitution by pointing out that patrons of a taxi-dance could merely visit a prostitute if what they truly wanted was sex. Untitled report, folder 6, box 129, EWBP.

139. Walter Reckless manuscript, n.p., Papers Relating to Walter Reckless' *Natural History of Vice Areas*, folder 8, box 134, EWBP.

140. On the anonymity and intimacy that commercial culture afforded relative to the policed environs of neighborhood sociability, see, for example, Kasson, *Amusing the Million*, and Peiss, *Cheap Amusements*.

141. "June Frazee alias Frazier," Cases from Dance Hall Study, folder 4, box 135, EWBP.

142. See Cressey, *The Taxi-Dance Hall*, 12.

143. Constance Weinberger paper on Dreamland Ballroom, 8, folder 10, box 126, EWBP.

144. Cressey, *The Taxi-Dance Hall*, 100.

145. Ibid., 51.

146. Ibid., 44, 51, 93.

147. Ibid., 100.

148. Ibid., 113.

149. Ibid., 113–14.

150. Ibid., 244, 247.

151. Ibid., 244.

152. Chicago Dancing Academy, folder 6, box 129, EWBP.

153. On this point, see also España-Maram, "Brown 'Hordes' in Mc-Intosh Suits," 129. On historical and discursive issues explaining such race and sexual anxiety, see Bederman, *Manliness and Civilization*; Williamson, *A Rage for Order*; Jacobson, *Whiteness of a Different Color*; and Hine and Jenkins, *A Question of Manhood*.

154. *Chicago Tribune* January 3, 1926; *Chicago Journal*, September 8, 1928; Paul Cressey material, folder 8, box 129, EWBP; Cressey, *The Taxi-Dance Hall*, 219 ("Pinoys" was a slang term for Filipinos).

155. Paul Cressey material, folder 8, box 129, EWBP.

156. Correspondence, July 7, 1934, folder 90, JPAR.

157. After visiting over one hundred dance halls, dance academies, and taxi-dance halls, investigators from the Committee of Fifteen, a morals policing organization with ties to Jessie Binford's JPA, concluded that "there was no immediate securing of competent evidence of commercial prostitution." Memorandum to Directors, May 27, 1930, folder 6, box 6, Committee of Fifteen Papers, UC; Reckless, *Vice in Chicago*, 160–61.

158. "Brief Report on Work of Committee of Fifteen for Five Weeks Period Ending with June 2nd, June 11, 1934," 3, folder 8, box 6, Committee of Fifteen Papers, UC. On presence of vice elsewhere, see "Century of Progress, 1934, Conditions in Chicago" in "General Summary, July 7, 1934," folder 89, JPAR.

159. Binford, "Taxi-Dance Halls," 502–9. The quoted lyrics are from Richard Rodgers and Lorenz Hart, "Ten Cents a Dance."

160. One survey suggested that widespread acceptance of unescorted women in taverns removed the need for the taxi-dance as a public institution. See Todd, Byron, and Vierow, *The Chicago Recreation Survey*, 141–2.

161. Erenberg, *Swingin' the Dream*; Stowe, *Swing Changes*.

CHAPTER SEVEN

1. "Chain" stations did not produce all of their own programs. In proto-network fashion, they made arrangements to carry outside programs, such as concerts, sporting events, and comedy/dramas in association with other stations. See the first two volumes of Barnouw's history of broadcasting in the United States, *A Tower in Babel* and *The Golden Web*. A list of "Stations Now Licensed in the Chicago Area" as of November 1928 showed sixty-seven licensed stations. Docket 285, RFCC.

2. On the "invention" of traditions of ethnicity and the problematic nature of assimilation theory as a linear construct, see K. N. Conzen, "Ethnicity as Festive Culture"; Gerstle, "Liberty, Coercion, and the Making of Americans"; H. Keil, *German Workers' Culture in the United States*; K. N. Conzen, Walker, and Nagler, *Making Their Own America*; and Kazal, "Revisiting Assimilation."

3. See B. Anderson, *Imagined Communities*, and Hilmes, *Radio Voices*. Barbara Savage writes of the importance in the late 1930s of a "new aural public sphere, a discursive political forum for a community of millions of listeners spanning the boundaries of region, class, race, and ethnicity"; Savage, *Broadcasting Freedom*, 1. For a contemporary example of the importance of African American broadcasting in Chicago using public sphere theory, see Squires, "Black Talk Radio."

4. There is some conceptual utility to considering the extent to which local broadcasters constituted an approximation of Nancy Fraser's "counterpublic" model of democratic communication. See Fraser, "Rethinking the Public Sphere."

5. There is a substantial literature on cultural geography and power that suggests a need for further research into broadcasting's symbolic reconfiguring of urban space. See, for example, K. J. Anderson, "Cultural Hegemony," and the essays in Fyfe, *Images of the Street*.

6. A 1922 presentation at Hull House by University of Chicago physics professor F. M. Kanestine, "Newest Inventions in Radio," was "illustrated by Apparatus." See "Course of Lectures at Hull House, 1922," 842, reel 50, JAP. Park commissioners used phonographs as part of field house recreation as previously noted, but they did not systematically purchase radios.

7. The Gads Hill Settlement appeared on WMAQ in 1925, and a combined chorus of children from a dozen settlements appeared on WGN in 1927 as part of the third in an annual series of intersettlement music festivals. See "Club Leaders Report/Orchestra and Violin," folder 11, box 2, Gad's Hill Center Records, UIC; *Chicago Daily News*, April 8, 1927, in Chicago Federation of Settlements, January 1927–September 1934, folder 1, box 9, Lea Demarest Taylor Papers, CHS. While the South Park Commissioners allowed the Mayor's Radio Commission to hold a special convention in Soldier Field, it blocked a request for a "Radio Fans" picnic in Jackson Park in 1924. See South Park Commissioners, "Proceedings," 31:232, 356.

8. The manner in which groups use technology and the commercial music industry to sustain and consolidate elements of an ethnic heritage is an important insight in Greene, *A Passion for Polka*.

9. Stone, "Radio Has Gripped Chicago," quoted in Barnouw, *A Tower in Babel*, 88.

10. The 1923 Radio Survey results are reported by E. A. Beane, supervisor of radio in Chicago, in a letter to the commissioner of navigation in

Washington, December 21, 1923, FCC General Records, File 1179 #6, box 105, RFCC. For analysis of the importance of national radio to 1920s listeners, see Smulyan, *Selling Radio*, 20–36.

11. See Stone, "Radio Has Gripped Chicago," and Weinrott, "Chicago Radio."

12. McChesney, *Telecommunications, Mass Media, and Democracy*, 18.

13. Accounts of the events and political economy of regulation include Rosen, *The Modern Stentors*; McChesney, *Telecommunications, Mass Media, and Democracy*; and Streeter, *Selling the Air*.

14. See Rosen, *Modern Stentors*; McChesney, *Telecommunications, Mass Media, and Democracy*; and Smulyan, *Selling Radio*. For background profiles of members of the FRC, see Flannery, *Commissioners of the FCC*, 1–32.

15. This insight follows a tradition of inquiry into the history of radio from the bottom up, with a focus on the pioneers in the prenetwork era. See Douglas, *Inventing American Broadcasting*; Smulyan, *Selling Radio*; Butsch, "Crystal Sets and Scarf-Pin Radios"; and others. For a perspective on gender and rural radio culture in the 1920s, see Vaillant, " 'Your Voice Came in Last Night but It Sounded a Little Scared,' " 63–88.

16. Further research is needed to determine the extent to which systematic discrimination may have existed among commerce officials who were assigning licenses. There is cause for suspicion here, since most radio historians have suggested that it was "easy" to obtain a broadcast license.

17. On the racialized notion of "whiteness," see especially Roediger, *The Wages of Whiteness*; Saxton, *The Rise and Fall of the White Republic*; and the overview in Fishkin, "Interrogating 'Whiteness' Complicating 'Blackness.' "

18. "Whiteness" is a marker of an elusive historical process of racial formation. On the theoretical challenge of addressing race, specifically "blackness" without essentializing it, see Gilroy, *The Black Atlantic*, and Gilroy, *Against Race*. On the importance of retaining a concept of race and African American difference, see especially Holt, *The Problem of Race in the Twenty-first Century*, and Omi and Winant, *Racial Formation in the United States*.

19. Lipsitz, "The Possessive Investment in Whiteness," 369. On race and listening, see Barlow, *Voice Over*.

20. Ibid.; Newman, *Entrepreneurs of Profit and Pride*; Savage, *Broadcasting Freedom*; and Cantor, *Wheelin' on Beale*. A classic study that includes an important early treatment of racism and negative portrayals of African Americans on radio is MacDonald, *Don't Touch that Dial!* The efforts of white disc jockeys to "pass" as "black" and gain street credibility and the ear of youthful fans of rock 'n' roll are discussed in Douglas, *Listening In*, 238–45.

21. Cohen, *Making a New Deal*, 138. WCFL was a subsidiary of the American Federation of Labor, the only station in the country owned and operated by organized labor. WCFL received funding from listeners, but, unlike the vast majority of independents, WCFL had a national horizon in its

operational mandate—to promote pro-farmer and pro-laborer sympathies and consciousness via radio. See Godfried, *WCFL*. Relevant information appears in dockets pertaining to WCFL before the Federal Radio Commission in author's possession.

22. Cohen, *Making a New Deal*, 325.

23. Cohen emphasizes that the different spatial relations between work and home altered the social and cultural tenor of African American community formation and undermined the possibility of class-based solidarity. See ibid., 33–38. Godfried *WCFL*, 115. confirms the problem of race when he notes that "WCFL responded well to the perceived special needs of Chicago's ethnic communities, but its record with African Americans proved far less exemplary." As Hilmes, *Radio Voices*, 5–6, has wondered: "If radio unified the shop floor, leveled the cultural experiences of diverse races, ethnicities, and regions, and spread a sense of national awareness, what were the lines and parameters, the desired and the excluded, the fiercely contested hierarchies, of this common radio imaginary?"

24. Information gleaned from program guides in author's possession.

25. According to popular accounts, one could build a radio set with a Quaker Oats box, copper wire, and a three-dollar crystal. Crystal sets did not require batteries, but they did require headsets. Tube radios had speakers powered by batteries or electricity. Generally, the more tubes in a set, the better the sound quality. By 1928, an estimated 63 percent of radio owners owned manufactured sets. It was noted, however, that crystal and single-tube models were still "in wide use on farms and rural sections." U.S. Federal Radio Commission, *Second Annual Report*, 221–22. Poorer urban residents may have pursued this homemade solution to access the airwaves. A 1928 nationwide study published by a Chicago advertising firm estimated that for every radio set in use in America there were an average of five listeners gathered at any given time. See Erwin, Wasy, and Company, "A Study of Radio as an Advertising Medium," 12. Census data from 1930 reveal that black Chicago residents were less likely to own a radio than whites, although this is not an entirely reliable indicator of radio's popularity since listening habits appear to have varied among different groups. Rural patterns of early radio consumption reveal similar group listening tendencies. See Wik, "The USDA and the Development of Radio," 178.

26. See Carby, "It Just Be's Dat Way Sometime," 9–22, and Kenney, *Recorded Music in American Life*.

27. WIBO Transcript, Docket 1104, RFCC.

28. List of remote programs gleaned from program guides in author's possession. See also Godfried, *WCFL*, 116, and Cohen, *Making a New Deal*, 155. I speak of a "remapped" Chicago in the manner of cultural geographers who argue that urban space represents culturally constructed and contested social and discursive domains. See, for example, Meinig and Jackson, *The*

Interpretation of Ordinary Landscapes; K. J. Anderson, "Cultural Hegemony"; and M. P. Conzen, *The Making of the American Landscape*.

29. The Austin High Gang comes to mind as a group of white musicians inspired by phonographs and radio to head for the South Side. See Leonard, *Jazz and the White Americans*.

30. On the phonograph's role, see Kenney, *Recorded Music in American Life*.

31. On the contested cultural history and politics of "blackness," see especially Gilroy, " 'Jewels Brought from Bondage,' " and Gray, *Watching Race*.

32. None of the program information I examined mentions African Americans producing their own shows, or even appearing physically in the studios as performers, until *The Negro Hour* was broadcast on WSBC in 1928. WCFL was a notable exception; it gave several African American teen groups studio time in the 1920s. See Godfried, *WCFL*, 116. Protections that labor unions might have afforded African American musicians in hurdling these barriers were limited due to the Jim Crow union structure dividing the city's professional musicians by race.

33. Issues of "blacking up" in commercial entertainment contexts from vaudeville and minstrelsy to Hollywood and broadcasting are crucial here. See especially "Racial Masquerade and Ethnic Assimilation in the Transition to Talking Pictures," in Rogin, *Blackface, White Noise*, 121–56.

34. WGN Clipping, July 13, 1928, Docket 892, RFCC. WGES offerings mentioned in *West Town News*, October 7, 1927, WSNC. The WENR minstrels are described in WENR Docket 478, RFCC. Godfried, *WCFL*, 115. On the extraeconomic implications for the non–African American artists who appropriated and inhabited "black" music forms, see Lipsitz, *Dangerous Crossroads*, 53–54. McFadden, " 'America's Boyfriend Who Can't Get a Date'," analyzes gender and racial subjectivity, cultural hegemony, and radio programs in the network era.

35. Ely, *The Adventures of Amos 'n' Andy*, 4. The author documents the popular reception of *Amos 'n' Andy* on Chicago's South Side. Hall, "Encoding/Decoding."

36. WSBC Program List, Docket 3021, RFCC; Cohen, *Making a New Deal*, 135.

37. Silverstein quoted by Jack L. Cooper in Jack L. Cooper Testimony, 32, Docket 3021, RFCC.

38. Ibid. Cooper was asked by federal regulators in 1935: "Is there any other station in Chicago, and if so what one is it, that is rendering the same service to the colored race that Station WSBC is rendering?" Cooper replied that "WSBC for four years, or five and a half years, was the only station in the United States that maintained its own colored studios, colored announcers, and all colored talent." Cooper noted that WEAF in New York ran a program called the *Negro Improvement Hour*, but with white announcers introducing

black talent; ibid., 35–36. While African American musicians performed in studios, and may have been interviewed, there is no evidence that any other Chicago radio station featured an African American announcer.

39. On the history of such cultivation ambitions among African Americans, see Gaines, *Uplifting the Race*. For a sociological perspective on class and cultural interplay in the Black Belt, see Drake and Cayton, *Black Metropolis*.

40. In *Voice Over*, 96, Barlow notes: "In effect, these black radio pioneers were middle-class reformers who took an entrepreneurial and assimilationist approach to racial progress."

41. On themes of gender and sexuality that troubled middle-class African Americans and whites alike, see especially Carby, " 'It Just Be's Dat Way Sometime.' "

42. Cooper Testimony, 34, Docket 3021, RFCC.

43. J. Louis Guyon Testimony, WGES Docket 5A, 24, RFCC; *West Town News*, November 11, 1927, WSNC.

44. Guyon Testimony, WGES Docket 5A, 24, RFCC.

45. Ibid., 26.

46. The importance of folksy connectivity was a key theme in early broadcasting beyond the urban fringes. See Smulyan, "Radio Advertising to Women in Twenties America, and Vaillant, " 'Your Voice Came in Last Night.' "

47. *West Town News*, March 18, 1927, folder 4, box 5, WSNC.

48. *West Town News*, September 3, 1926, folder 3, box 5, WSNC.

49. *Die Abendpost*, December 12, 1930, Germans, box 13, CFLPS.

50. Guyon Testimony, WGES Docket 5A, 25, RFCC.

51. Ibid.; "An Evening Gathering at Guyon's Paradise Garden, Chicago," De Vincent Sheet Music Collection, National Museum of American History. Ethnic composition information comes from Chicago Fact Book Consortium, *Local Community Fact Book*, 70.

52. Guyon Testimony, WGES Docket 5A, 30, RFCC.

53. Guyon's early experiences are described in Cressey, *The Taxi-Dance Hall*, 193. The description of the neighborhood comes from Hodes and Hansen, *Hot Man*, 1. See also S. P. Wilson, *Cesspools of Infamy*.

54. JPA report on Victoria Hall quoted in Cressey, *The Taxi-Dance Hall*, 193.

55. Handbill in the possession of a family member, Jean Guyon, described in a telephone interview with the author in Chicago, June 15, 1996.

56. On national trends to reform dance halls, see Perry, " 'The General Motherhood of the Commonwealth.' " On race tension, see Chicago Commission on Race Relations, *The Negro in Chicago*.

57. *Chicago Tribune*, December 10, 1913, 5.

58. Charter for National Association of Ballroom Proprietors and Man-

agers, National Association of Ballroom Proprietors and Managers, folder 102, JPAR. The organization was formed on April 20, 1921, and incorporated in Illinois on June 23, 1921. Its objectives were spelled out in the charter: "To unite proprietors and managers of public dance halls for mutual protection; to promote the exchange of ideas beneficial to the profession; to provide for uniform methods in dancing and the perfection of ball room dancing in general; and to place the profession on a higher plane of respectability and morality. Not for pecuniary profit."

59. *Chicago Defender*, July 17, 1920. Guyon later broke from the watchdog organization since it seemed to have too liberal an attitude toward certain modern dances.

60. On the opening date, see Cressey, *The Taxi-Dance Hall*, 193. According to the file of a bankruptcy case involving Guyon from the late 1930s, the Paradise was built in December 1915. See Illinois State Bankruptcy from Case File, 430, box B764, National Archives and Records Administration, Great Lakes, Chicago, Ill.

61. Cressey, *The Taxi-Dance Hall*, 193–94.

62. Correspondence, October 1, 1928, Docket 1104, RFCC.

63. Not all frequencies were equally audible to listeners, owing to the nature of radio-wave forms and the mounting congestion on the air, including interference from stations outside Chicago.

64. Correspondence, October 3, 1928, Docket 307, RFCC.

65. Correspondence, September 25, 1927, Docket 307, RFCC.

66. On ethnic responses to assimilation pressures in other "public" arenas besides the airwaves, see especially Keil, *German Workers' Culture*, and Orsi, *The Madonna of 115th Street*.

67. Correspondence, September 30, 1928, Docket 307, RFCC.

68. Northshore Congregational Church Pamphlet, c. 1928, Docket 1147, RFCC.

69. Rev. J. C. O'Hair Testimony, 132, Docket 1147, RFCC.

70. See Walter Reckless report on lodging houses, n.p., folder 8, box 134, EWBP.

71. On Bohemianism in Chicago, see Zorbaugh, *The Gold Coast and the Slum*. On the role of the "New Woman" in influencing bohemian culture in New York City, see Stansell, *American Moderns*. See also Peiss, *Cheap Amusements*, and Meyerowitz, *Women Adrift*.

72. Rev. J. C. O'Hair Testimony, Docket 1147, RFCC.

73. Ibid. "Chain arrangements" referred to proto-network alliances among stations to carry the same program.

74. Miss U. Bryant, January 27, 1931, Docket 1147, RFCC (emphasis added). Written by Charles Tindley, "Nothing Between" celebrated the renunciation of "all sinful pleasure."

75. Mr. and Mrs. W. H. Smith, January 20, 1931, Docket 1147, RFCC.

76. Hedges, "Broadcasting in the Chicago Metropolitan Area," program, *Chicago Broadcaster's Association Annual Benefit*, 1927, 47, Radiophone Station KYW, book 2, WENR-KYW Scrapbook Collection, Library of American Broadcasting, College Park, Md.

77. A court decision upheld WJAZ's challenge to federal authority of the airwaves in 1926 and contributed to the restive radio climate in Chicago and across the nation. Stations boldly strayed from their frequency assignments and allotted power outputs to escape interference from their neighbors.

78. See Hennessey, *From Jazz to Swing*, and Erenberg, *Swingin' the Dream*, 3–31.

79. Broadcast Remote List, April 25, 1934, Docket 2143, RFCC.

80. "Description of WENR Studios," Docket 881, RFCC. Quoted in Mitchell, *Radio's Beautiful Day*, 12.

81. For a description of the upscale transformation of radio studios, see Barnouw, *Tower in Babel*, 85–88.

82. Joseph Cavadore Testimony, Docket 2994, 62, RFCC.

83. *West Town News*, October 27, 1927, WSNC.

84. U.S. Federal Radio Commission, *Sixth Annual Report*, 25.

85. Flannery, *Commissioners of the FCC*, 1. Eugene Sykes went on to become chairman of the FCC in 1934.

86. Stations such as WMAQ and WGN stressed that they provided a full range of musical services, which in essence obviated the need for independents of any kind.

87. Eugene Sykes quoted in the *New York Times*, March 18, 1927, excerpt reprinted in Flannery, *Commissioners of the FCC*, 2.

88. On Robinson's credentials see Flannery, *Commissioners of the FCC*, 28–29.

89. Testimony, WQJ, Docket 581, RFCC. On Robinson's opposition to General Order No. 40, see McChesney, *Telecommunications, Mass Media, and Democracy*, 35–37.

90. Flannery, *Commissioners of the FCC*, 29. On the tensions between WCFL and federal regulators, see Godfried, *WCFL*, 79–105, and McChesney, *Telecommunications, Mass Media, and Democracy*, 65–69.

91. Hedges Testimony, Docket 581, RFCC.

92. The statement derives from my having read several hundred docketed case files and transcripts pertaining to radio regulation in Chicago and other regional areas between 1924 and 1935.

93. Miscellaneous testimony, Dockets 868, 2143, 1174, RFCC.

94. Joseph Cavadore Testimony, Docket 2994, 60–64, RFCC.

95. Correspondence. Docket 307, RFCC.

96. Testimony, Chicago Broadcast Association, Docket 3101, RFCC.

97. Quoted in correspondence, John Fitzpatrick, President of Chicago

Federation of Labor, to Hon. Joseph D. Beck, House of Representatives, January 5, 1929, Docket 342, RFCC.

98. Miscellaneous Correspondence, Docket 307, RFCC.

99. Ibid.

100. Ibid.

101. Ibid.

CHAPTER EIGHT

1. As Warren Susman has argued in *Culture as History*, the Depression stirred a range of cultural self-examinations. One example was the folk music revival of the 1930s and early 1940s, embraced especially by intellectuals and the Left. See Whisnant, *All That Is Native and Fine*; Lieberman, *"My Song is My Weapon"*; and Filene, *Romancing the Folk*.

2. West Chicago Park Commissioners, "Fifty-ninth Annual Report, 1927–28," 63–64. LPC average from annual reports.

3. The Chicago Concert Band Association performed in Grant Park. The two bands presented a series of public concerts in August and September 1931. See Rode, "The Concert Band in Chicago," 93, 104.

4. Cook County figures published in Works Progress Administration, "Achievements of W.P.A. Workers in Illinois, July 1st 1935–June 30th 1938," 3. Statistic on musicians reported by Joel Lay, regional director of Federal Music Project in *Chicago Daily News*, October 23, 1935, Press Clippings, 1936–40, FL-IL, box 40, WPA/FMP. The replacement of pit orchestras by the proliferation of sound-movie projection systems was already putting a strain on working musicians by the early 1930s; see Barbash, *Unions and Union Leadership*, 307. See also Albert Goldberg, "IL Music Project, Narrative Report for July 1939," Monthly Narrative Reports, GA-NH, 1939, entry 805, box 7, WPA/FMP.

5. In a five-year period from 1929 to 1934, national membership in the American Federation of Musicians dropped from 146,000 to 100,000. See Seltzer, *Music Matters*, 27. As early as fall 1934, private investors approached the CSO to discuss a low-price public concert series to be held in Soldier's Field. See CSO Minutes of the Trustees, November 18, 1932; April 12, 1933; October 24, 1933; and October 30, 1934, CSOA.

6. Mayor Edward J. Kelly, who had served as head of the South Park district, praised Petrillo for the morale-boosting summer concerts, which Kelly called "the most popular series of musical events ever held in Chicago." "First Annual Report, 1935, Chicago Park District, May 1, 1934 to December 31, 1935," 8, 24, CHS. The Chicago Park District marked the consolidation of the major park commissions—Lincoln, South, and West—along with nineteen other smaller districts. For a list of performers at the Grant Park concerts, see *The Grant Park Music Festival*.

7. Spivey, *Union and the Black Musician*, 50.

8. On the institutional history of the FMP, see Bindas, *All of This Music*, xiii, 9–10.

9. Ibid., xv. See Zanzig, *Music in American Life*. On the National Recreation Association, see Knapp, "Play for America."

10. Bindas, *All of This Music*. Under the FMP's folk arts project, WPA employees at the state level researched and collected folk music, compiling important historical material for public access and use. See William F. McDonald, *Federal Relief Administration and the Arts*, 637–42.

11. *Chicago Daily News*, December 17, 1935, Press Clippings 1936–1940, FL-IL, box 40, WPA/FMP. On jazz, swing, and the FMP, see *Chicago Daily News*, April 20, 1937, ibid.

12. Sokoloff's implication that symphonic music and art song merited greater support from the government than commercial forms, such as swing, antagonized Joseph Weber, president of the American Federation of Musicians. On labor and the FMP, see Bindas, *All of This Music*, 8.

13. Works Progress Administration, "Achievements of W.P.A. Workers in Illinois, July 1st 1935–June 30th 1938," 22. From July 1937 to July 1938, an estimated 700 FMP musicians performed across the state. By the late 1930s the FMP supported between ninety and 100 performances per month in Chicago in concert halls, public schools, parks, and other public settings. See, for example, Albert Goldberg, "IL Music Project, Narrative Report for February, March, July 1939," Monthly Narrative Reports, GA-NH, 1939, entry 805, box 7, Entry 805, WPA/FMP.

14. See Ewen, *Music Comes to America*, 235–36.

15. In July 1939 these groups gave a total of eighty-seven concerts, with an estimated attendance of 77,981. Works Progress Administration, "Achievements of W.P.A. Workers in Illinois, July 1st 1935–June 30th 1938," 22.

16. Ewen, *Music Comes to America*, 233; Spivey, *Union and the Black Musician*; Erenberg, *Swingin' the Dream*, 24–25. In these same years, African American civic leaders, intellectuals, and radio artists, in cooperation with New Deal officials produced nationally distributed series such as "Americans All, Immigrants All," "Freedom's People," "Heroes in Bronze," "New World a Comin'," and "Destination Freedom." While they did not emphasize music per se, these programs attempted to reclaim airwaves dominated by the sounds of whiteness described in the preceding chapter. See Savage, *Broadcasting Freedom*.

17. *Chicago Bee*, July 26, 1936; *Chicago Times*, August 15, 1937, *Chicago Times*, November 8, 1938, Press Clippings 1936–1940, Illinois–Chicago, box 40, WPA/FMP.

18. Census figures report that Hyde Park was 98 percent white in 1930. The area assumed a more racially integrated character in subsequent decades. See Chicago Fact Book Consortium, *Local Community Fact Book*, 111–13.

19. Published calendars and schedules of FMP performances appeared regularly in Chicago newspapers. See Press Clippings 1936–1940, Illinois–Chicago, box 40, WPA/FMP.

20. The area was almost 17 percent African American in 1930—the largest concentration of blacks on the West Side. By 1950, that percentage more than doubled. It was Union Park that the Chicago Commission on Race Relations singled out as having relatively good usage statistics among African Americans in 1920 relative to the South Side. To estimate the racial composition of the area around Union Park, the community area boundaries of the Near West Side and accompanying census data are used. See "Community Area—Near West Side, Population and Housing Characteristics, 1930–1980," in Chicago Fact Book Consortium, *Local Community Fact Book*, 76.

21. The practice of staging a West Chicago Park festival originated in the 1920s when it was held at the municipal navy pier.

22. One festival attracted an estimated 8,500 people. Scrapbook of Mrs. Barbara Griffin, courtesy of CPD. "Interview with Gwen O'Connor Griffin," transcribed at ⟨http://streetlevel.iit.edu/youthprojects/chs/nws/gweno.html⟩. On Dorsey and Chicago's church music scene, see M. W. Harris, *The Rise of Gospel Blues*, 105–9.

23. On the more radical political associations of jazz and swing, see Stowe, *Swing Changes*, and Denning, *The Cultural Front*. Lena Horne and Duke Ellington most notably protested racial double standards. See Erenberg, *Swingin' the Dream*, 204–5.

24. For the context of visual culture in the war effort, and its self-conscious domestic and international manipulation by the Office of Wartime Information, see Roeder, *The Censored War*. On Hollywood's involvement with federal authority, see Koppes and Black, "What to Show the World."

25. Shaffer, "Music in America," 856.

26. Erenberg, *Swingin' the Dream*, 182, 185; Shulman, *The Voice of America*.

27. Erenberg, *Swingin' the Dream*, 182; Stowe, *Swing Changes*.

28. Erenberg, ibid., 202, concludes that the Glenn Miller Orchestra was "all-white rather than all-American."

29. Ibid., 181–210. For a careful assessment of themes of resistance, race, cultural history, and the distinction between politics waged via "style" and via Cold War–era emphasis on racial equality and American exceptionalism, see Stowe, *Swing Changes*, 230–39.

30. See Matthews, "Art and Politics," and Von Eschen, "'Satchmo Blows Up the World.'"

31. As Von Eschen argues after Wagnleitner, the cultural status of African American music and the vexed racial history of American nationalism challenged government hegemony over the meaning of these tours and their decoding among foreign audiences. See Von Eschen, "'Satchmo Blows Up the World,'" and Wagnleitner, "The Empire of Fun."

32. Shaffer, "Music in America," 850–51; Allen F. Davis, "Philanthropy," in Foner and Garraty, *The Reader's Companion to American History*, 833–34. Not all of these philanthropic grants were new, of course. The Carnegie Corporation began supporting settlement and community music schools back in the 1920s. Cords, "Music in Social Settlement and Community Music Schools."

33. Labuta and Smith, *Music Education*, 34. See also Cobb, "Looking Ahead—Private Sector Giving to the Arts and Humanities." On the influential nature of the Ford Foundations's support for the Chicago Symphony, for example, see U.S. Congress, House Committee on Government Operations, *Interrelationship of Federal And State Funding for the Arts in Illinois*, 123.

34. There are, of course, numerous federal cultural agencies, some of which have an important impact on exposing Americans to music. The Smithsonian Institution historically received annual appropriations that exceeded those given to the NEA and NEH. See Mulcahy, "Government and the Arts," 313, table 1 ("Appropriations for Major Federal Cultural Agencies, 1983–85").

35. DiMaggio, "Can Culture Survive the Marketplace?," 65.

36. Library of Congress, *"Millions for the Arts,"* 24–25, 39. See also Mulcahy, "Government and the Arts," 317; DiMaggio, "Decentralization of Arts Funding."

37. Between 1975 and 1990, spending by state arts agencies more than doubled in real dollars. In 1980 the United States boasted more than 3,000 local arts councils, about one quarter of which had direct ties to local government and constituted the final link on the federal-state chain. Policy Research and Planning Department, *International Data on Public Spending on the Arts*, 143–44.

38. In 1945 the FCC took an important first step in agreeing to set aside FM bandwidth space for special use by educational and nonprofit broadcasters. See Vaillant, "Radio."

39. Between 1950 and 1960, Chicago lost about 2 percent of its population; between 1960 and 1970, an additional 5 percent; and between 1970 and 1980, an additional 11 percent. Chicago Fact Book Consortium, *Local Community Fact Book*, xvi.

40. On the kind of socioeconomic conditions that adversely affected Chicago after World War II, albeit less dramatically perhaps than Detroit, see Sugrue, *The Origins of the Urban Crisis*, 3–14, 127–28.

41. Vander Weele, *Reclaiming Our Schools*, 130. After years of borrowing against expected revenues, the Chicago Public School system collapsed in 1979, undermining the futures of thousands of young residents. As of 1990, a third of Chicago's public schools had been built prior to 1930.

42. For a summary overview assessing what historical conditions differentiated this moment from other eras of hard times in inner cities, see Sugrue, "The Structures of Urban Poverty." See also Katz, *The Undeserving*

Poor. For a provocative analysis of Chicago's particular challenges, see W. J. Wilson, *The Truly Disadvantaged*, 49–55.

43. OMB working paper on the NEA, quoted in Mulcahy, "Government and the Arts," 323.

44. U.S. Congress, House Committee on Government Operations, *Interrelationship of Federal and State Funding for the Arts in Illinois*, 2. An NEA survey of arts participation reported that exposure to music lessons declined from 47 percent to 40 percent between 1982 and 1992, and the fraction of households in which someone played an instrument declined from 51 percent in 1978 to 38 percent in 1997. Putnam, *Bowling Alone*, 114–15, 462 n. 61.

45. Mulcahy, "Government and the Arts," 321.

46. On the importance of fraternal and benevolent associations in Chicago neighborhoods prior to the New Deal, see Cohen, *Making a New Deal*, and Drake and Cayton, *Black Metropolis*. On the rise of corporate welfare capitalism that substituted itself for ethnocentric and neighborhood-controlled institutions, see Montgomery, *The Fall of the House of Labor*.

47. One 1988 NEA report declared that "basic arts education does not exist in the United States today." See "Toward Civilization: A Report on Arts Education," quoted in Evans, Klein, and Delgado, *Too Intrinsic for Renown*, 85; Mulcahy, "Government and the Arts," 321. Relative to Philadelphia, San Francisco, and Atlanta, Chicago suffered from a shortage of nonprofit institutions in the 1990s. It ranked last in the per capita number of arts and culture organizations with 2.2 for every 10,000 Chicagoans in the mid-1990s. Stern, "Working Paper #9," 15. By the mid-1990s Chicago supported only 3.2 social organizations (churches, social clubs, unions, neighborhood groups) per 1,000 residents, making it a laggard among peer urban centers. See Stern, "Working Paper #9," 18.

48. Few Americans were made aware that the Serrano piece received NEA funding through a grant application in which specific artists and works were not enumerated. Reverend Donald Wildmon of the American Family Association, televangelist Pat Robertson, and New York senator Alphonse D'Amato were among those who condemned Serrano's work. Representative Richard Armey (R.-Texas) joined over 100 members of Congress in protesting NEA funding of an exhibit of Mapplethorpe's work. See Wyszomirski, "From Accord to Discord," 2. There were also calls for decentralization to the state level. See DiMaggio, "Decentralization of Arts Funding."

49. *Congressional Quarterly Weekly*, September 30, 1989, 2550, referenced in Wyszomirski, "From Accord to Discord," 4.

50. On the NEA funding controversies, see Bolton, *Culture Wars*, and Frohnmayer, *Leaving Town Alive*.

51. During the New Hampshire Republican primary campaign preceding the 1992 presidential election, incumbent challenger Patrick Buchanan ran ads linking George H. W. Bush to controversial artworks funded by the

NEA. A. H. Levy, *Government and the Arts*, 116–24. For a thoughtful critique of "myths" surrounding the NEA and the exceptionalism of the 1989–92 controversies, see ibid., 1–46.

52. The Enola Gay controversy at the Smithsonian in the early 1990s marked another occasion when federally funded cultural work that engaged sensitive subjects, such as America's role in nuclear weapons proliferation and the suffering of hundreds of thousands of Japanese civilians, would not be stomached by influential citizens' groups or defended by a vocal outcry.

53. For a critique anticipating some of the dangers of the privatization of public space that occurred during this time, see Sennett, *The Fall of Public Man*. On the impact of late-twentieth-century economic trends on the arts, see Zukin, *Loft Living*. For a trenchant critique of the limited imaginings of urban revitalization efforts in Baltimore, see Harvey, *Spaces of Hope*, 137–81. On problems of privatization and the absence of vital civic space in Los Angeles, see M. Davis, *City of Quartz*. For a more optimistic survey of the vitality of urban public space as a civic realm, see Lees, "Urban Public Space."

54. The literature on postindustrial urban culture formation is extensive, and both utopian and dystopian visions are expressed. The issues of postmodernity and the play of surface authenticities is part of the story of mortgaging history in Chicago. See Harvey, *The Condition of Postmodernity*, and Baudrillard, "The Precession of Simulacra." Census report noted in "The Nation: Mexican-Americans Forging a New Vision of America's Melting Pot," *New York Times*, April 30, 2001.

55. These observations are derived from visits to summer concert performances at various ceremonial and neighborhood Chicago parks on the North, West, and South Sides between 1992 and 1998.

56. See "City Parks Are No Place to Play: First in a Series about Why Kids Don't Use Chicago's Parks," *Chicago Tribune*, November 11, 1990, and "Kids Flock to Parks Where Employees Care: Second in a Series about Why Kids Don't Use Chicago's Parks," *Chicago Tribune*, November 12, 1990. The articles cited findings from a separate 1990 study by Friends of the Parks.

57. *Chicago Tribune*, October 30, 1994, and November 4, 1994.

58. *Chicago Sun-Times*, October 27, 1994.

59. Mary Schmich, "Memorial Park Honors a Woman Nearly Forgotten," *Chicago Tribune*, August 16, 1996.

60. Addams, *Twenty Years at Hull-House*. Ellen Gates Starr invoked a variation on the significance of hands to the co-founders of Hull House when she wrote: "It is a feeble and narrow imagination which holds out to chained hands fair things which they cannot grasp,—things which they could fashion for themselves were they but free." See *Hull-House Maps and Papers*, 178.

61. *Chicago Tribune*, March 24, 1995.

62. "It's something to see videos connect white kids in Utah to black kids in South Chicago to Croats and Brazilians," wrote Chuck D. of the group

Public Enemy. See Chuck D., "The Sound of Our Young World," *Time*.com, May 16, 2001, 1.

63. On the cultural politics of rap and hip-hop, see Rose, *Black Noise*; Baker, *Black Studies, Rap, and the Academy*; and Kelley, "Kickin' Reality, Kickin' Ballistics."

64. Dyson, *Holler If You Hear Me*; Chuck D., "The Sound of Our Young World," 2.

BIBLIOGRAPHY

ARCHIVAL MATERIALS

Chicago Historical Society, Chicago, Illinois
    Special Collections
        Bournique Scrapbook Collection
        Louise Dekoven Bowen Scrapbooks
        James Forgan Papers
        "Making Music Chicago Style" Collection
        Gregory Sprague Collection
        Lee Demarest Taylor Papers
Chicago Park District, Chicago, Illinois
    Special Collections
Chicago Public Library, Harold Washington Library Center, Chicago, Illinois
    Municipal Reference Collection
        Special Collections
    West Side Newspaper Collection
Chicago Symphony Orchestra Archives, Chicago, Illinois
Circuit Court of Cook County, Illinois
    Records
Library of American Broadcasting, College Park, Maryland
    Broadcast Pioneers Library of American Broadcasting
    WENR-KYW Scrapbook Collection
National Archives and Records Administration, College Park, Maryland
    Records of the Federal Communications Commission (RG 173)
National Archives and Records Administration, Washington, D.C.
    Records of the Work Projects Administration, Federal Music Project
        (RG 69)
National Museum of American History, Smithsonian Institution,
    Washington, D.C.
    De Vincent Sheet Music Collection

Newberry Library, Chicago, Illinois
    Civic Music Association Reports, 1913–38
    Frederick Grant Gleason Collection
    Philo Otis Scrapbook
University of Chicago, Chicago, Illinois
    Special Collections, Joseph Regenstein Library
        Ernest Watson Burgess Papers
        Chicago Foreign Language Press Survey Records
        Committee of Fifteen Papers
        Bessie Louise Pierce Papers, 1839–1974
        Playbills and Programs, 1843–1979
    Chicago Jazz Archive
        Jazz Institute of Chicago Don DeMicheal Archives Collection
University of Illinois at Chicago, Chicago, Illinois
    Richard J. Daley Library, Special Collections
        Alma Birmingham Papers
        Gad's Hill Center Records
        Hull-House Association Records
        Juvenile Protective Association Records
        Eleanor Smith Papers
        Lee Taylor Papers

PERIODICALS

Die Abendpost
Arbeiter Zeitung
Chicago Chronicle
Chicago Daily News
Chicago Defender
Chicago Evening Post
Chicago Herald
Chicago Inter-Ocean
Chicago Record-Herald
Chicago Tribune
Cincinnati Gazette
Commissioners of Lincoln Park. *Annual Reports.* 1873–1933.
Denní Hlasatel
Dziennik Chicagoski
Dziennik Zwiazkowy
Hull-House Bulletin
Illinois Staats-Zeitung
Narod Polski
New York World
The Playground

South Park Commissioners. *Annual Reports.* 1873–1933.
Svornost
West Chicago Park Commissioners. *Annual Reports.* 1873–1933.
——. *Proceedings.* 1873–1933.
Zgoda

PUBLISHED SOURCES

Addams, Jane. *The Social Thought of Jane Addams.* Edited by Christopher Lasch. New York: Irvington, 1982.
——. *The Spirit of Youth and the City Streets.* New York: Macmillan, 1909.
——. *Twenty Years at Hull-House.* New York: Macmillan, 1910.
Ahlquist, Karen. *Democracy at the Opera: Music, Theater, and Culture in New York City, 1815–60.* Urbana: University of Illinois Press, 1997.
Allen, Robert Clyde. *Horrible Prettiness: Burlesque and American Culture.* Chapel Hill: University of North Carolina Press, 1991.
Anderson, Benedict. *Imagined Communities.* New York: Verso, 1991.
Anderson, Kay J. "Cultural Hegemony and the Race-Definition Process in Chinatown, Vancouver." *Environment and Planning, D: Society and Space* 6 (1988): 127–49.
Andreas, Alfred T. *History of Chicago from the Earliest Period to the Present Time.* 3 vols. Chicago: A. T. Andreas, 1885–86.
Andrews, Shang. *Chicago after Dark.* Chicago: C. J. Heck, 1882.
Aparicio, Frances R. *Listening to Salsa: Gender, Latin Popular Music, and Puerto Rican Cultures.* Hanover, N.H.: Wesleyan University Press, 1998.
Asbury, Herbert. *Gem of the Prairie: An Informal History of the Chicago Underworld.* New York: Knopf, 1940.
Badger, Reid. *The Great American Fair: The World's Columbian Exposition and American Culture.* Chicago: N. Hall, 1979.
Bailey, Peter. "Breaking the Sound Barrier: A Historian Listens to Noise." *Body and Society* 2, no. 2 (1996): 49–66.
Baker, Houston A., Jr. *Black Studies, Rap, and the Academy.* Chicago: University of Chicago Press, 1993.
Baldwin, Peter C. *Domesticating the Street: The Reform of Public Space in Hartford, 1850–1930.* Columbus: Ohio State University Press, 1999.
Banks, Nancy. "The World's Most Beautiful Ballrooms." *Chicago History* 2, no. 4 (1973): 206–15.
Baraka, Imamu Amiri. *Blues People: Negro Music in White America.* New York: William Morrow, 1963.
Barbash, Jack, ed. *Unions and Union Leadership.* New York: Harper and Brothers, 1959.
Barlow, William. *Voice Over: The Making of Black Radio.* Philadelphia: Temple University Press, 1999.

Barnes, Margaret Ayer. *Years of Grace*. Dunwoody, Ga.: Norman S. Berg, 1930.

Barnouw, Erik. *The Golden Web: A History of Broadcasting in the United States, 1933–1953*. New York: Oxford University Press, 1968.

——. *A Tower in Babel: A History of Broadcasting in the United States to 1933*. New York: Oxford University Press, 1966.

Barrett, James R. *Work and Community in the Jungle: Chicago's Packinghouse Workers, 1894–1922*. Urbana: University of Illinois Press, 1987.

Barron, Dana L. "Sex and Single Girls in the Twentieth Century." *Journal of Urban History* 25, no. 6 (1999): 838–47.

Baudrillard, Jean. "The Precession of Simulacra." In *Media and Cultural Studies: Keyworks*, edited by Meenakshi Gigi Durham and Douglas M. Kellner, 521–49. Oxford: Blackwell, 2001.

Bederman, Gail. *Manliness and Civilization: A Cultural History of Gender and Race in the United States, 1880–1917*. Chicago: University of Chicago Press, 1995.

Bender, Thomas. "Wholes and Parts: The Need for Synthesis in American History." *Journal of American History* 73 (June 1986): 120–36.

Berlin, Edward. *Ragtime: A Musical and Cultural History*. Berkeley: University of California Press, 1980.

Beveridge, Charles, and David Schuyler. *The Papers of Frederick Law Olmsted*. Vol. 3, *Creating Central Park, 1857–1861*. Baltimore: Johns Hopkins University Press, 1983.

Bindas, Kenneth J. *All of This Music Belongs to the Nation: The WPA's Federal Music Project and American Society*. Knoxville: University of Tennessee Press, 1995.

Binford, Jessie. "On with the Dance." *The Survey* 54 (1925): 98–99.

——. "Taxi-Dance Halls." *Journal of Social Hygiene* 19, no. 9 (1933): 502–9.

Birge, Edward B. *History of Public School Music in the United States*. Philadelphia: Oliver Ditson, 1937.

Blair, Karen J. *The Torchbearers: Women and Their Amateur Arts Associations in America, 1890–1930*. Bloomington: Indiana University Press, 1994.

Blesh, Rudi, and Harriet Janis. *They All Played Ragtime: The True Story of an American Music*. New York: Knopf, 1950.

Bluestone, Daniel. *Constructing Chicago*. New Haven: Yale University Press, 1991.

Blumin, Stuart M. *The Emergence of the Middle Class: Social Experience in the American City, 1760–1900*. New York: Cambridge University Press, 1989.

Bolton, Richard, ed. *Culture Wars: Documents from the Recent Controversies in the Arts*. New York: New Press, 1992.

Boris, Eileen. *Art and Labor: Ruskin, Morris, and the Craftsman Ideal in America*. Philadelphia: Temple University Press, 1986.

Borosini, Victor Von. "Public Recreation Facilities: Our Recreation Facilities and the Immigrant." *Annals of the American Academy of Political Science and Social Science* 25 (March 1910): 141–51.

Bourdieu, Pierre. *Distinction: A Social Critique of the Judgment of Taste.* Translated by Richard Nice. Cambridge, Mass.: Harvard University Press, 1984.

Bowen, Louise Dekoven. "Dance Halls." *The Survey* 26 (1911): 383–87.

——. *Fighting to Make Chicago Safe for Children.* Chicago: Juvenile Protective Association, 1920.

——. *Growing Up with a City.* New York: Macmillan, 1926.

Boyer, Christine. *Dreaming the Rational City: The Myth of American City Planning.* Cambridge, Mass.: MIT Press, 1983.

Boyer, Paul. *Urban Masses and Moral Order in America, 1820–1920.* New York: Oxford University Press, 1978.

Breen, Daniel, ed. *Historical Register of the Twenty-two Superseded Park Districts, Chicago Park District.* Vol. 1. Washington, D.C.: Works Progress Administration, 1941.

Broyles, Michael. *Music of the Highest Class: Elitism and Populism in Antebellum Boston.* New Haven: Yale University Press, 1992.

Bryan, Mary Lynn McCree, ed. *Jane Addams Papers on Microfilm.* Ann Arbor: University Microfilms International, 1985.

Bryan, Mary Lynn McCree, and Allen Freeman Davis. *100 Years at Hull-House.* Bloomington: Indiana University Press, 1990.

Bryan, Mary Lynn McCree, Nancy Slote, and Maree De Angury, eds. *The Jane Addams Papers: A Comprehensive Guide.* Bloomington: Indiana University Press, 1996.

Bukowski, Douglas. *Big Bill Thompson, Chicago, and the Politics of Image.* Urbana: University of Illinois Press, 1998.

Bushman, Richard L. *The Refinement of America: Persons, Houses, Cities.* New York: Knopf, 1992.

Butler, Judith P. *Gender Trouble: Feminism and the Subversion of Identity.* New York: Routledge, 1990.

Butsch, Richard. "Crystal Sets and Scarf-Pin Radios: Gender, Technology and the Construction of American Radio Listening in the 1920s." *Media, Culture and Society* 20 (1998): 557–72.

Cantor, Louis. *Wheelin' on Beale: How WDIA-Memphis Became the Nation's First All-Black Radio Station and Created the Sound that Changed America.* New York: Pharos Books, 1992.

Capek, Thomas. *The Cechs (Bohemians) in America: A Study of Their National, Cultural, Political, Social, Economic, and Religious Life.* Boston: Houghton Mifflin, 1920.

Carby, Hazel. "It Just Be's Dat Way Sometime: The Sexual Politics of Women's Blues." *Radical America* 20, no. 4 (June/July 1986): 9–22.

——. "Policing the Black Woman's Body in an Urban Context." *Critical Inquiry*, no. 18 (Summer 1992): 738–55.

Carson, Mina. *Settlement Folk: Social Thought and the American Settlement Movement, 1885–1930.* Chicago: University of Chicago Press, 1990.

Cavallo, Dominick. *Muscles and Morals*. Philadelphia: University of Pennsylvania Press, 1981.

Chamberlin, Everett. *Chicago and Its Suburbs*. Chicago: T. A. Hungerford, 1874.

Chambers, Robin L. "Chicago's Turners: Inspired Leadership in the Promotion of Public Physical Education." *Yearbook of German-American Studies* 24 (1989): 105–14.

Chase, Gilbert. *America's Music: From the Pilgrims to the Present*. Rev. 3d ed. Urbana: University of Illinois Press, 1987.

Chauncey, George. *Gay New York: Gender, Urban Culture, and the Making of the Gay Male World, 1890–1940*. New York: Basic Books, 1994.

Chicago Commission on Race Relations. *The Negro in Chicago: A Study of Race Relations and a Race Riot*. Chicago: University of Chicago Press, 1922.

Chicago Fact Book Consortium. *Local Community Fact Book, 1980*. Chicago: Chicago Review Press, 1984.

Chicago Public Library, Department of Special Collections. *"A Breath of Fresh Air": Chicago's Neighborhood Parks of the Progressive Reform Era, 1900–1925*. Chicago: Special Collections Department of the Chicago Public Library and the Chicago Park District, 1989.

Chicago South Park Commission. *Report Accompanying Plan for Laying Out the South Park, Olmsted, Vaux, and Co. Landscape Architects*. Chicago: Evening Journal, 1871.

Chuck D. "The Sound of Our Young World." *Time*.com, May 16, 2001, 1–2.

Cobb, Nina Kressner. *Looking Ahead—Private Sector Giving to the Arts and Humanities*. Washington, D.C.: President's Committee on the Arts and Museums, 1996.

Cohen, Lizabeth. *Making a New Deal: Industrial Workers in Chicago, 1919–1939*. New York: Cambridge University Press, 1990.

Collier, James Lincoln. *Benny Goodman and the Swing Era*. New York: Oxford University Press, 1989.

Commissioners of Lincoln Park. *Report of the Commissioners of Lincoln Park*. Chicago: Commissioners of Lincoln Park, 1899.

Comstock, Alzada P. "Chicago Housing Conditions, 6: The Problem of the Negro." *American Journal of Sociology* 28 (September 1928).

Condon, Eddie. *We Called It Music*. 1947. Reprint, Westport, Conn.: Greenwood Press, 1970.

Conzen, Kathleen Neils. "Ethnicity as Festive Culture: Nineteenth-Century German America on Parade." In *The Invention of Ethnicity*, edited by Werner Sollors, 44–76. New York: Oxford University Press, 1989.

——. "Germans." In *Harvard Encyclopedia of American Ethnic Groups*, edited by Stephan Thernstrom, 406–25. Cambridge, Mass.: Harvard University Press, 1980.

——. *Immigrant Milwaukee*. Cambridge, Mass.: Harvard University Press, 1976.

Conzen, Kathleen Neils, Mack Walker, and Jörg Nagler. *Making Their Own America: Assimilation Theory and the German Peasant Pioneer.* New York: Berg, 1990.

Conzen, Michael P. *The Making of the American Landscape.* Boston: Unwin Hyman, 1990.

Couvares, Francis G. *The Remaking of Pittsburgh: Class and Culture in an Industrializing City, 1877–1919.* Albany: State University of New York Press, 1984.

Cranz, Galen. *The Politics of Park Design: A History of Urban Parks in America.* Cambridge, Mass.: MIT Press, 1982.

Crawford, Richard. *The American Musical Landscape.* Berkeley: University of California Press, 1993.

Creel, George. *How We Advertised America: The First Telling of the Amazing Story of the Committee on Public Information That Carried the Gospel of Americanism to Every Corner of the Globe.* New York: Harper and Brothers, 1920.

Cressey, Paul. *The Taxi-Dance Hall.* Chicago: University of Chicago Press, 1932.

Crocker, Ruth H. *Social Work and Social Order: The Settlement Movement in Two Industrial Cities, 1889–1930.* Urbana: University of Illinois Press, 1992.

Cronon, William. *Nature's Metropolis: Chicago and the Great West.* New York: Norton, 1991.

Crunden, Robert M. "Thick Description in the Progressive Era." *Reviews in American History* 19, no. 4 (1991): 463–67.

Cruz, Jon. *Culture on the Margins: The Black Spiritual and the Rise of American Cultural Interpretation.* Princeton: Princeton University Press, 1999.

Cutler, Irving. *The Jews of Chicago: From Shtetl to Suburb.* Urbana: University of Illinois Press, 1996.

Czitrom, Daniel. "Underworlds and Underdogs: Big Tim Sullivan and Metropolitan Politics in New York, 1889–1913." *Journal of American History* 78, no. 2 (1991): 536–58.

Dance, Stanley. *The World of Earl Hines.* New York: Scribner, 1977.

Daniels, John. *America via the Neighborhood.* New York: Harper and Brothers, 1920.

Darlington, Marwood. *Irish Orpheus: The Life of Patrick S. Gilmore, Bandmaster Extraordinary.* Philadelphia: Olivier-Maney-Klein, 1959.

Davis, Allen Freeman. *American Heroine: The Life and Legend of Jane Addams.* New York: Oxford University Press, 1973.

——. *Spearheads for Reform: The Social Settlements and the Progressives, 1890–1914.* New York: Oxford University Press, 1967.

Davis, Allen F., and Mary Lynn McCree, eds. *Eighty Years at Hull-House.* Chicago: Quadrangle Books, 1969.

Davis, Mike. *City of Quartz: Excavating the Future in Los Angeles.* London: Verso, 1990.

Davis, Ronald L. *A History of Music in American Life*. Vol. 2, *The Gilded Years, 1885–1920*. Huntington, N.Y.: Robert Krieger, 1980.

Davis, Susan G. *Parades and Power: Street Theatre in Nineteenth-Century Philadelphia*. Philadelphia: Temple University Press, 1986.

de Certeau, Michel. "Walking in the City." In *The Practice of Everyday Life*, translated by Steven F. Rendall, 91–110. Berkeley: University of California Press, 1984.

DeGroot, Edward B. "Are the Parks for the People or the People for the Parks?" *The Playground* 7, no. 6 (1913): 217–20.

Denning, Michael. *The Cultural Front: The Laboring of American Culture in the Twentieth-Century*. New York: Verso, 1996.

——. "The End of Mass Culture." *International Labor and Working-Class History* 37 (1990): 4–17.

Dennison, Sam. *Scandalize My Name: Black Imagery in American Popular Music*. New York: Garland, 1982.

DeVeaux, Scott Knowles. *The Birth of Bebop: A Social and Musical History*. Berkeley: University of California Press, 1997.

Dewey, John. "The School as Social Center." *National Educational Association Proceedings* 41 (1902): 373–83.

Dillon, John. *From Dance Hall to White Slavery*. Chicago: C. C. Thompson, 1912.

DiMaggio, Paul. "Can Culture Survive the Marketplace?" In *Nonprofit Enterprise and the Arts: Studies in Mission and Constraint*, edited by Paul DiMaggio, 65–92. New York: Oxford University Press, 1986.

——. "Cultural Entrepreneurship in Nineteenth-Century Boston: The Creation of an Organization Base for High Culture in America." *Media, Culture, and Society* 4 (1982): 33–50.

——. "Cultural Entrepreneurship in Nineteenth-Century Boston, Part II: The Classification and Framing of American Art." *Media, Culture and Society* 4 (1982): 303–22.

——. "Decentralization of Arts Funding from the Federal Government to the States." In *Public Money and the Muse*, edited by Stephen Benedict, 216–52. New York: Norton, 1991.

Douglas, Susan. *Inventing American Broadcasting, 1899–1922*. Baltimore: Johns Hopkins University Press, 1987.

——. *Listening In: Radio and the American Imagination*. New York: Times Books, 1999.

Dowe, Dieter. "The Workingmen's Choral Movement in Germany before the First World War." *Journal of Contemporary History* 13, no. 2 (1978): 269–96.

Drake, St. Clair, and Horace R. Cayton. *Black Metropolis: A Study of Negro Life in a Northern City*. 1945. Rev. and enl. ed. Vol. 1. New York: Harper and Row, 1962.

Dror, Otniel E. "Creating the Emotional Body: Confusion, Possibilities, and Knowledge." In *An Emotional History of the United States*, edited by Peter N. Stearns and Jan Lewis, 172–94. New York: New York University Press, 1998.

Duis, Perry. *The Saloon: Public Drinking in Chicago and Boston, 1880–1920.* Urbana: University of Illinois Press, 1983.

Dvořák, Antonín. "Music in America." *Harpers Magazine* 90 (1895): 428–34.

Dyson, Michael Eric. *Holler If You Hear Me: Searching for Tupac Shakur.* New York: Basic Civitas Books, 2001.

Edwards, Richard Henry. *Popular Amusements.* New York: Association Press, 1915.

Eley, Geoff. "Nations, Publics, and Political Cultures: Placing Habermas." In *Culture/Power/History*, edited by Nicholas Dirks and Geoff Eley, 297–335. Princeton: Princeton University Press, 1994.

Ely, Melvin Patrick. *The Adventures of Amos 'n' Andy: A Social History of an American Phenomenon.* New York: Free Press, 1991.

Epstein, Dena J. Polacheck. *Music Publishing in Chicago before 1871: The Firm of Root and Cady, 1858–1871.* Detroit: Information Coordinators, 1969.

Erenberg, Lewis. *Steppin' Out: New York Nightlife and the Transformation of American Culture, 1890–1930.* Westport, Conn.: Greenwood Press, 1981.

——. *Swingin' the Dream: Big Band Jazz and the Rebirth of American Culture.* Chicago: University of Chicago Press, 1998.

Erwin, Wasy, and Company. *A Study of Radio as an Advertising Medium.* Chicago: Erwin, Wasy, and Company, 1928.

España-Maram, Linda N. "Brown 'Hordes' in McIntosh Suits: Filipinos, Taxi Dance Halls, and Performing the Immigrant Body in Los Angeles, 1930s–1940s." In *Generations of Youth: Youth Cultures and History in Twentieth-Century America*, edited by Joe Austin and Michael Nevin Willard, 118–35. New York: New York University Press, 1998.

Ethington, Philip J. *The Public City: The Political Construction of Urban Life in San Francisco, 1850–1900.* New York: Cambridge University Press, 1994.

Ets, Marie Hall. "Rosa and the Chicago Commons: 'How Can I Not Love America?'" In *Immigrant Women*, edited by Maxine Schwartz Seller, 196–99. Albany: State University of New York Press, 1994.

Evans, Richard, Howard Klein, and Jane Delgado. *Too Intrinsic for Renown: A Study of the Members of the National Guild of Community Schools of the Arts.* New York: Lila Wallace–Reader's Digest Fund, 1992.

Ewen, David. *Music Comes to America.* New York: Thomas Y. Crowell, 1942.

"Family Entrance Closed in Saloons." *The Survey* 32 (May 1914): 170.

Faulkner, T. A. *From the Ball-room to Hell: Facts about Dancing, a Dancing Master's Experience.* Chicago: R. F. Henry, 1894.

Feldman, Ann. "Being Heard: Women Composers and Patrons at the 1893 World's Columbian Exposition." *Notes* 47, no. 1 (September 1990): 7–20.

Fern, Annette, Sara Velez, Bruce Carr, and J. Bradford Robinson. "Chicago." In *The New Grove Dictionary of American Music*, edited by H. Wiley Hitchcock and Stanley Sadie, 1:418–24. New York: Grove's Dictionaries of Music, 1986.

Filene, Benjamin. "'Our Singing Country': John and Alan Lomax, Leadbelly, and the Construction of an American Past." *American Quarterly* 43, no. 4 (1991): 602–24.

——. *Romancing the Folk: Public Memory and American Roots Music*. Chapel Hill: University of North Carolina Press, 2000.

Finnegan, Ruth. *The Hidden Musicians: Music-Making in an English Town*. Cambridge: Cambridge University Press, 1989.

Finson, Jon. *The Voices That Are Gone: Themes in Nineteenth-Century American Popular Song*. New York: Oxford University Press, 1994.

Fishkin, Shelley F. "Interrogating 'Whiteness' Complicating 'Blackness': Remapping American Culture." *American Quarterly* 47, no. 3 (1995): 428–66.

Flannery, Gerald V. *Commissioners of the FCC, 1927–1994*. Lanham, Md.: University Press of America, 1995.

Foner, Eric, and John A. Garraty, eds. *The Reader's Companion to American History*. Boston: Houghton Mifflin, 1991.

Foner, Philip. *American Labor Songs in the Nineteenth Century*. Urbana: University of Illinois Press, 1977.

Foreman, Henry G. "Recreation Needs of Chicago." Chicago: Cook County Board, 1904.

Fox, Richard Wightman, and T. J. Jackson Lears, eds. *The Power of Culture: Critical Essays in American History*. Chicago: University of Chicago Press, 1993.

Fraser, Nancy. "Rethinking the Public Sphere: A Contribution to the Critique of Actually Existing Democracy." In *Habermas and the Public Sphere*, edited by Craig Calhoun, 109–42. Cambridge, Mass.: MIT Press, 1992.

Freeze, Karen Johnson. "Czechs." In *Harvard Encyclopedia of American Ethnic Groups*, edited by Stephan Thernstrom, 261–72. Cambridge, Mass.: Harvard University Press, 1980.

Freidel, Frank, and Alan Brinkley. *America in the Twentieth Century*. New York: McGraw-Hill, 1982.

Frohnmayer, John. *Leaving Town Alive: Confessions of an Arts Warrior*. Boston: Houghton Mifflin, 1993.

Fyfe, Nicholas R., ed. *Images of the Street: Planning, Identity, and Control in Public Space*. New York: Routledge, 1998.

Gaines, Kevin Kelly. *Uplifting the Race: Black Leadership, Politics, and Culture in the Twentieth Century*. Chapel Hill: University of North Carolina Press, 1996.

Garber, Eric. "'T'aint Nobody's Business': Homosexuality in 1920s Harlem." In *Gay Roots: Twenty Years of Gay Sunshine: An Anthology of Gay History, Sex, Politics, and Culture*, edited by Winston Leyland, Clark Taylor, and John Mitzel, 141–47. San Francisco: Gay Sunshine Press, 1991.

Gerstle, Gary. *American Crucible: Race and Nation in the Twentieth Century*. Princeton: Princeton University Press, 2001.

———. "Liberty, Coercion, and the Making of Americans." *Journal of American History* 84, no. 2 (1997): 524–75.

———. *Working-Class Americanism: The Politics of Labor in a Textile City, 1914–1960*. New York: Cambridge University Press, 1989.

Gilder, Richard Watson. "Art Brought into the Lives of Wage-Earners." *Charities* 13, no. 19 (1905): 417–20.

Gilfoyle, Timothy J. *City of Eros: New York City, Prostitution, and the Commercialization of Sex, 1790–1920*. New York: Norton, 1992.

Gilroy, Paul. *Against Race: Imagining Political Culture beyond the Color Line*. Cambridge, Mass.: Harvard University Press, 2000.

———. *The Black Atlantic: Modernity and Double Consciousness*. Cambridge, Mass.: Harvard University Press, 1993.

———. "'Jewels Brought from Bondage': Black Music and the Politics of Authenticity." In *The Black Atlantic: Modernity and Double Consciousness*, 72–110. Cambridge, Mass.: Harvard University Press, 1993.

Glassberg, David. *American Historical Pageantry: The Uses of Tradition in the Early Twentieth Century*. Chapel Hill: University of North Carolina, 1990.

Glasser, Ruth. *My Music Is My Flag: Puerto Rican Musicians and Their New York Communities, 1917–1940*. Berkeley: University of California Press, 1995.

Gleason, Philip. "The Melting Pot: Symbol of Fusion or Confusion?" *American Quarterly* 16, no. 1 (1964): 20–46.

Godfried, Nathan. *WCFL, Chicago's Voice of Labor, 1926–78*. Urbana: University of Illinois Press, 1997.

Goodman, Benny, and Irving Kolodin. *The Kingdom of Swing*. New York: Frederick Ungar, 1939.

Gordon, Colin. "Still Searching for Progressivism." *Reviews in American History* 23, no. 4 (1995): 669–74.

Gordon, Linda. *Heroes of Their Own Lives: The Politics and History of Family Violence*. New York: Viking, 1988.

Gorn, Elliott J. *The Manly Art: Bare-Knuckle Prize Fighting in America*. Ithaca: Cornell University Press, 1986.

The Grant Park Music Festival: A 60-Year Record, 1935–1994. Chicago: Grant Park Concerts Society, 1995.

Gray, Herman. *Watching Race: Television and the Struggle for "Blackness."* Minneapolis: University of Minnesota Press, 1995.

Green, Paul M., and Melvin G. Holli, eds. *The Mayors: The Chicago Political Tradition*. Carbondale: Southern Illinois University Press, 1987.

Greene, Victor. *A Passion for Polka: Old-Time Ethnic Music in America.* Berkeley: University of California Press, 1992.

Grossman, James R. *Land of Hope: Chicago, Black Southerners, and the Great Migration.* Chicago: University of Chicago Press, 1989.

Guion, David. "From Yankee Doodle thro' to Handel's Largo: Music at the World's Columbian Exposition." *College Music Symposium* 24, no. 1 (1984): 81–96.

Habermas, Jürgen. *The Structural Transformation of the Public Sphere: An Inquiry into the Category of Bourgeois Society.* Translated by Thomas Burger. Cambridge, Mass.: MIT Press, 1992.

Hall, Stuart. "Encoding/Decoding." In *Culture, Media, Language*, edited by Stuart Hall, Dorothy Hobson, Andrew Lowe, and Paul Willis, 128–38. London: Hutchinson, 1980.

——. "Ethnicity: Identity and Difference." *Radical America* 23 (1989): 9–20.

Haltunnen, Karen. *Confidence Men and Painted Ladies: A Study of Middle-Class Culture in America, 1830–1870.* New Haven: Yale University Press, 1982.

Hamm, Charles. "Dvořák in America: Nationalism, Racism, and National Race." In *Putting Popular Music in Its Place*, 344–53. New York: Cambridge University Press, 1995.

——. *Putting Popular Music in Its Place.* New York: Cambridge University Press, 1995.

——. *Yesterdays: Popular Song in America.* New York: Norton, 1979.

Hannig, Amalie. "Christmas at Hull House." *Ladies Home Journal*, December 1911, 31.

Harland, Robert. *The Vice Bondage of a Great City.* Chicago: Young People's Civic League, 1912.

Harris, Michael W. *The Rise of Gospel Blues: The Music of Thomas Andrew Dorsey in the Urban Church.* New York: Oxford University Press, 1992.

Harris, Neil. "John Philip Sousa and the Culture of Reassurance." In *Cultural Excursions: Marketing Appetites and Cultural Tastes in Modern America*, 198–232. Chicago: University of Chicago Press, 1990.

Harris, Neil, and Chicago Historical Society. *Grand Illusions: Chicago's World's Fair of 1893.* Chicago: Chicago Historical Society, 1993.

Harris, William H., and Judith S. Levey, eds. *The New Columbia Encyclopedia.* New York: J. B. Lippincott, 1975.

Harvey, David. *The Condition of Postmodernity: An Inquiry into the Origins of Cultural Change.* Cambridge, Mass.: Blackwell, 1990.

——. *Spaces of Hope.* Berkeley: University of California Press, 2000.

Hasse, John Edward, ed. *Ragtime: Its History, Composers, and Music.* New York: Schirmer, 1985.

Hazen, Margaret Hindle. "The Brass Band Movement." In *The Oberlin Book of Bandstands*, edited by S. Frederick Starr, 30–36. Washington, D.C.: Preservation Press, 1987.

Hazen, Margaret Hindle, and Robert M. Hazen. *The Music Men: An Illustrated History of Brass Bands in America, 1800–1920*. Washington, D.C.: Smithsonian Institute Press, 1987.

Hennessey, Thomas J. *From Jazz to Swing: African-American Jazz Musicians and Their Music, 1890–1935*. Detroit: Wayne State University Press, 1994.

Higham, John. *Strangers in the Land*. New Brunswick, N.J.: Rutgers University Press, 1955.

Hilmes, Michele. *Radio Voices: American Broadcasting, 1922–1952*. Minneapolis: University of Minnesota Press, 1997.

Hine, Darlene Clark, and Earnestine Jenkins. *A Question of Manhood: A Reader in U.S. Black Men's History and Masculinity*. Bloomington: Indiana University Press, 1999.

Hirsch, Arnold R. *Making the Second Ghetto: Race and Housing in Chicago, 1940–1960*. New York: Cambridge University Press, 1983.

Hitchcock, H. Wiley. *Music in the United States*. Englewood Cliffs, N.J.: Prentice-Hall, 1969.

Hodes, Art, and Chadwick Hansen. *Hot Man: The Life of Art Hodes*. Urbana: University of Illinois Press, 1992.

Hofmeister, Rudolf. *The Germans of Chicago*. Champaign, Ill.: Stipes, 1976.

Hofstadter, Richard. *The Age of Reform*. New York: Knopf, 1955.

Holli, Melvin. "The Great War Sinks Chicago's German *Kultur*." In *Ethnic Chicago*, edited by Peter d'A. Jones and Melvin G. Holli, 260–311. Grand Rapids, Mich.: Eerdmans, 1981.

Holli, Melvin, and Peter d'A. Jones. *Ethnic Chicago: A Multicultural Portrait*. 4th ed. Grand Rapids, Mich.: Eerdmans, 1995.

Holt, Thomas C. *The Problem of Race in the Twenty-first Century*. Cambridge, Mass.: Harvard University Press, 2000.

Horowitz, Helen Lefkowitz. *Culture and the City: Cultural Philanthropy in Chicago from the 1880s to 1917*. Lexington: University Press of Kentucky, 1976.

———. *Rereading Sex: Battles over Sexual Knowledge and Suppression in Nineteenth-Century America*. New York: Knopf, 2002.

Horowitz, Joseph. *Wagner Nights: An American History*. Berkeley: University of California Press, 1994.

Huggins, Nathan. "Personae: White/Black Faces—Black Masks." In *Harlem Renaissance*, 244–301. New York: Oxford University Press, 1971.

Hughes, Langston. *The Big Sea: An Autobiography*. New York: Knopf, 1945.

Hull-House Maps and Papers: A Presentation of Nationalities and Wages in a Congested District of Chicago, Together with Comments and Essays on Problems Growing Out of the Social Conditions. New York: T. Y. Crowell, 1895.

Jackson, Shannon. *Lines of Activity: Performance, Historiography, Hull-House Domesticity*. Ann Arbor: University of Michigan Press, 2000.

Jacobson, Matthew Frye. *Whiteness of a Different Color: European Immigrants and the Alchemy of Race.* Cambridge, Mass.: Harvard University Press, 1998.

Janowitz, Morris. *The Community Press in an Urban Setting.* Glencoe, Ill.: Free Press, 1952.

Johnson, James H. *Listening in Paris: A Cultural History.* Berkeley: University of California Press, 1995.

Johnson, Susan Lee. "Bulls, Bears, and Dancing Boys: Race, Gender, and Leisure in the California Gold Rush." *Radical History Review*, no. 60 (1994): 4–37.

Jones, Gareth Stedman. "Class Expression versus Social Control? A Critique of Recent Trends in the Social History of 'Leisure.' " *History Workshop*, no. 4 (1977): 163–70.

Jones, Lester B. "Music as a Social Force." *World Today*, January 1910, 60–63.

Jordan, Winthrop. *White over Black: American Attitudes toward the Negro, 1550–1812.* New York: Norton, 1977.

The Jubilee: A Magazine Devoted to the Interests of the Mammoth Chicago Jubilee, conducted by P. S. Gilmore, commencing Thursday, June 5th, 1873, in the Michigan Southern and Rock Island Passenger Depot. Chicago: Carpenter and Sheldon, 1873.

Karger, Howard Jacob. *The Sentinels of Order: A Study of Social Control and the Minneapolis Settlement House Movement, 1915–1950.* Lanham, Md.: University Press of America, 1987.

Kasson, John F. *Amusing the Million: Coney Island at the Turn of the Century.* New York: Hill and Wang, 1978.

——. *Rudeness and Civility: Manners in Nineteenth-Century Urban America.* New York: Hill and Wang, 1990.

Katz, Michael B. *The Undeserving Poor: From the War on Poverty to the War on Welfare.* New York: Pantheon, 1989.

Kazal, Russell A. "Revisiting Assimilation: The Rise, Fall, and Reappraisal of a Concept in American Ethnic History." *American Historical Review* 100, no. 2 (1995): 437–71.

Keil, Charles. *Urban Blues.* Chicago: University of Chicago Press, 1990.

Keil, Hartmut, ed. *German Workers' Culture in the United States, 1850–1920.* Washington, D.C.: Smithsonian Institution Press, 1988.

Keil, Hartmut, and John Jentz, eds. *German Workers in Chicago: A Documentary History of Working-Class Culture from 1850 to World War I.* Urbana: University of Illinois Press, 1988.

Kelley, Robin. "Kickin' Reality, Kickin' Ballistics: Gangsta Rap and Postindustrial Los Angeles." In *Race Rebels: Culture, Politics, and the Black Working Class*, 183–227. New York: Free Press, 1994.

Kennedy, David M. *Over Here: The First World War and American Society.* New York: Oxford University Press, 1980.

Kenney, William Howland. *Chicago Jazz: A Cultural History, 1904–1930*. New York: Oxford University Press, 1993.

———. *Recorded Music in American Life: The Phonograph and Popular Memory, 1890–1945*. New York: Oxford University Press, 1999.

Kerber, Linda. *Women of the Republic*. New York: Norton, 1986.

Keyes, Jonathan J. "The Forgotten Fire." *Chicago History* 26 (Fall 1997): 52–65.

Kiesewetter, Renate. "German-American Labor Press: The *Verbote* and the *Chicagoer Arbeiter-Zeitung*." In *German Workers' Culture in the United States, 1850–1920*, edited by Charles Keil, 137–55. Washington, D.C.: Smithsonian Institution Press, 1988.

Koppes, Clayton, and Gregory Black. "What to Show the World: The Office of Wartime Information and Hollywood, 1942–1945." *Journal of American History* 64, no. 1 (June 1977): 87–105.

Kornbluh, Joyce, ed. *Rebel Voices: An I.W.W. Anthology*. Ann Arbor: University of Michigan Press, 1964.

Kraus, Richard. *History of the Dance in Art and Education*. Englewood Cliffs, N.J.: Prentice-Hall, 1969.

Kreitner, Kenneth. *Discoursing Sweet Music: Town Bands and Community Life in Turn-of-the-Century Pennsylvania*. Urbana: University of Illinois Press, 1990.

Kusmer, Kenneth. *A Ghetto Takes Shape: Black Cleveland, 1870–1930*. Urbana: University of Illinois Press, 1976.

Labuta, Joseph A., and Deborah A. Smith. *Music Education: Historical Contexts and Perspectives*. Upper Saddle River, N.J.: Prentice Hall, 1997.

Lambin, Maria Ward. *Report of the Advisory Dance Hall Committee of the Women's City Club and the City Recreation Committee*. New York: n.p., 1924.

Lasch-Quinn, Elisabeth. *Black Neighbors: Race and the Limits of Reform in the American Settlement House Movement, 1890–1945*. Chapel Hill: University of North Carolina Press, 1993.

———. "Progressives and the Pursuit of Agency." *Reviews in American History* 25, no. 2 (1997): 258–63.

Lears, T. J. Jackson. "From Salvation to Self-Realization: Advertising and the Therapeutic Roots of the Consumer Culture, 1880–1930." In *The Culture of Consumption: Critical Essays in American History, 1880–1980*, edited by Richard Wightman Fox and T. J. Jackson Lears, 3–38. New York: Pantheon, 1983.

———. "Making Fun of Popular Culture." *American Historical Review* 97, no. 5 (1992): 1417–30.

———. *No Place of Grace: Antimodernism and the Transformation of American Culture, 1880–1920*. New York: Pantheon, 1981.

Lees, Lynn Hollen. "Urban Public Space and Imagined Communities in the 1980s and 1990s." *Journal of Urban History* 20, no. 4 (1994): 443–65.

Leiter, Robert. *The Musicians and Petrillo*. New York: Bookman Associates, 1953.

Leonard, Neil. *Jazz and the White Americans*. Chicago: University of Chicago Press, 1962.

——. "The Reactions to Ragtime." In *Ragtime: Its History, Composers, and Music*, edited by John Edward Hasse, 102–13. New York: Schirmer, 1985.

Leppert, Richard D. *The Sight of Sound: Music, Representation, and the History of the Body*. Berkeley: University of California Press, 1993.

Levine, Lawrence. *Black Culture and Black Consciousness: Afro-American Folk Thought from Slavery to Freedom*. New York: Oxford University Press, 1977.

——. *Highbrow/Lowbrow: The Emergence of Cultural Hierarchy in America*. Cambridge, Mass.: Harvard University Press, 1988.

Levy, Alan, and Barbara L. Tischler. "Into the Cultural Mainstream: The Growth of American Music Scholarship." *American Quarterly* 42, no. 1 (March 1990): 57–73.

Levy, Alan Howard. *Government and the Arts: Debates over Federal Support of the Artist in America from George Washington to Jesse Helms*. Lanham, Md.: University Press of America, 1997.

Library of Congress. Education and Public Welfare Division. *"Millions for the Arts": Federal and State Cultural Programs, an Exhaustive Senate Report*. Washington, D.C.: Washington International Arts Letter, 1972.

Lieb, Sandra R. *Mother of the Blues: A Study of Ma Rainey*. Amherst: University of Massachusetts Press, 1981.

Lieberman, Robbie. *"My Song Is My Weapon": People's Songs, American Communism, and the Politics of Culture, 1930–1950*. Urbana: University of Illinois, 1989.

Lincoln Park, Commissioners of. "Laws and Ordinances Relating to Lincoln Park." 1903.

Lind, Alan R. *Chicago Surface Lines: An Illustrated History*. 3d ed. Park Forest, Ill.: Transport History Press, 1979.

Linn, James Weber. *Jane Addams: A Biography*. New York: Appleton-Century, 1935.

Lippman, Edward. *A History of Western Musical Aesthetics*. Lincoln: University of Nebraska Press, 1992.

Lippmann, Walter. *A Preface to Politics*. New York, 1913.

Lipsitz, George. "Against the Wind: Dialogic Aspects of Rock and Roll." In *Dangerous Crossroads: Popular Music, Postmodernism, and the Poetics of Place*, 99–132. Minneapolis: University of Minnesota Press, 1990.

——. "The Possessive Investment in Whiteness: Racialized Social Democracy and the 'White' Problem in American Studies." *American Quarterly* 47, no. 3 (1995): 369–87.

Lissak, Riva. *Pluralism and Progressives: Hull House and the New Immigrants, 1890–1919*. Chicago: University of Chicago Press, 1989.

Locke, Ralph P. "Music Lovers, Patrons, and the 'Sacralization" of

Nineteenth-Century Music." *Nineteenth-Century Music* 17, no. 2 (1993): 149–73.

Locke, Ralph P., and Cyrilla Barr, eds. *Cultivating Music in America: Women Patrons and Activists since 1860*. Berkeley: University of California Press, 1997.

Lott, Eric. *Love and Theft: Blackface Minstrelsy and the American Working Class*. New York: Oxford University Press, 1993.

Luebke, Frederick C. *Bonds of Loyalty: German-Americans and World War I*. De Kalb: Northern Illinois University Press, 1974.

MacDonald, J. Fred. *Don't Touch That Dial!: Radio Programming in American Life, 1920–1960*. Chicago: Nelson-Hall, 1979.

Macleod, Beth Abelson. " 'Whence Comes the Lady Tympanist?': Gender and Instrumental Musicians in America, 1853–1990." *Journal of Social History* 27, no. 2 (1993): 291–308.

Mann, Arthur. *The One and the Many: Reflections on the American Identity*. Chicago: University of Chicago Press, 1979.

Marks, Joseph E. *America Learns to Dance: A Historical Study of Dance Education in America before 1900*. New York: Dance Horizons, 1957.

Marquis, Albert Nelson, ed. *The Book of Chicagoans*. Chicago: A. N. Marquis, 1911.

Marquis' Hand-Book of Chicago. Chicago: A. N. Marquis, 1885.

Mason, Gregory. "Satan in the Dance-Hall." *American Mercury* 2, no. 5 (1924): 175–82.

Mathews, W. S. B. "Mr. Tomlins' Work with Children." *Music* 2 (May 1892): 60–67.

Matthews, Jane de Hart. "Art and Politics in Cold War America." *American Historical Review* 81, no. 4 (1976): 762–87.

May, Lary. *Screening Out the Past: The Birth of Mass Culture and the Motion Picture Industry*. New York: Oxford University Press, 1980.

McCarthy, Kathleen D. *Noblesse Oblige: Charity and Cultural Philanthropy in Chicago, 1849–1929*. Chicago: University of Chicago Press, 1982.

McCarthy, Marie. "American Music Education as Reflected in the World's Columbian Exposition in Chicago, 1892–93." *Bulletin of Historical Research in Music Education* 15 (1994): 111–42.

McChesney, Robert W. *Telecommunications, Mass Media, and Democracy*. New York: Oxford University Press, 1993.

McDonald, William F. *Federal Relief Administration and the Arts*. Columbus: Ohio State University Press, 1968.

McDowell, Mary. "The Field Houses of Chicago and Their Possibilities." *Charities* 18 (1907): 535–38.

——. "Sung with Neighbors Back-of-the-Yards." *The Survey* 31, (January 3, 1914): 406–8.

McFadden, Margaret. " 'America's Boyfriend Who Can't Get a Date': Gender, Race, and the Cultural Work of the Jack Benny Program, 1932–1946." *Journal of American History* 80, no. 1 (1993): 113–34.

Meinig, D. W., and John Brinckerhoff Jackson. *The Interpretation of Ordinary Landscapes: Geographical Essays*. New York: Oxford University Press, 1979.

Meites, Hyman L., ed. *History of the Jews of Chicago*. 1924. Reprint, Chicago: Chicago Jewish Historical Society and Wellington Publishing, 1990.

Mero, Everett B., ed. *American Playgrounds*. New York: Baker and Taylor, 1909.

Meyerowitz, Joanne J. *Women Adrift: Independent Wage Earners in Chicago, 1880–1930*. Chicago: University of Chicago Press, 1988.

Mezzrow, Mezz, and Bernard Wolfe. *Really the Blues*. Garden City, N.Y.: Doubleday, 1972.

Mitchell, Everett. *Radio's Beautiful Day*. Aberdeen, S.D.: North Plains Press, 1983.

Montgomery, David. *The Fall of the House of Labor*. New York: Cambridge University Press, 1987.

Moore, MacDonald Smith. *Yankee Blues: Musical Culture and American Identity*. Bloomington: Indiana University Press, 1985.

Morrow, Mary Sue. "Singing and Drinking in New Orleans: The Social and Musical Functions of Nineteenth-Century German *Männerchöre*." *Southern Quarterly* 27, no. 2 (1989): 5–24.

Mulcahy, Kevin V. "Government and the Arts in the United States." In *The Patron State: Government and the Arts in Europe, North America, and Japan*, edited by Milton C. Cummings Jr. and Richard S. Katz, 311–82. New York: Oxford University Press, 1987.

Mumford, Kevin J. *Interzones: Black/White Sex Districts in Chicago and New York in the Early Twentieth Century*. New York: Columbia University Press, 1997.

Muncy, Robyn. *Creating a Female Dominion in American Reform, 1890–1935*. New York: Oxford University Press, 1991.

Munsterberg, Emil. "Editorial Bric-a-brac." *Music* 17 (December 1899): 179–82.

Mussulman, Joseph A. *Music in the Cultured Generation: A Social History of Music*. Evanston, Il.: Northwestern University Press, 1971.

Nasaw, David. *The Chief: The Life of William Randolph Hearst*. Boston: Houghton Mifflin, 2000.

———. *Going Out: The Rise and Fall of Public Amusements*. New York: Basic Books, 1993.

Nelli, Humbert. *The Italians in Chicago, 1880–1930*. New York: Oxford Press, 1970.

Nelson, Bruce. *Beyond the Martyrs: A Social History of Chicago's Anarchists, 1870–1900*. New Brunswick, N.J.: Rutgers University Press, 1988.

Nettl, Bruno, ed. *Eight Urban Musical Cultures: Tradition and Change*. Urbana: University of Illinois Press, 1978.

Newman, Mark. *Entrepreneurs of Profit and Pride: From Black-Appeal to Radio Soul*. New York: Praeger, 1988.

Niecks, Frederick. "The Ethical Aspects of Music, Second Lecture." *Music* 22, no. 1 (September 1902): 1–16.

Odem, Mary E. *Delinquent Daughters: Protecting and Policing Adolescent Female Sexuality in the United States, 1885–1920.* Chapel Hill: University of North Carolina Press, 1995.

Ogren, Kathy. *The Jazz Revolution.* New York: Oxford University Press, 1989.

Olmsted, Frederick Law. *Civilizing American Cities: A Selection of Frederick Law Olmsted's Writings on City Landscapes.* Edited by S. B. Sutton. Cambridge, Mass.: MIT Press, 1971.

Olmsted, Frederick Law, and Theodora Kimball. *Frederick Law Olmsted, Landscape Architect, 1822–1903.* New York: G. P. Putnam's Sons, 1922.

Omi, Michael, and Howard Winant. *Racial Formation in the United States: From the 1960s to the 1980s.* New York: Routledge and Kegan Paul, 1986.

O'Neill, A. W. "Chicago Playgrounds and Park Extension." *Charities* 12, no. 32 (1904): 798–99.

Orsi, Robert. *The Madonna of 115th Street: Faith and Community in Italian Harlem, 1880–1950.* New Haven: Yale University Press, 1985.

Pacyga, Dominic A. "Chicago's Pilsen Park and the Struggle for Czechoslovak Independence during World War One." In *Essays in Russian and East European History: Festschrift in Honor of Edward C. Thaden,* edited by Leo Schelbert and Nick Ceh, 117–29. Boulder, Colo.: East European Monographs, 1995.

———. *Polish Immigrants and Industrial Chicago: Workers on the South Side, 1880–1922.* Columbus: Ohio State University Press, 1991.

Patten, Simon N. "Education through Activity: The Philosophy of the Public Park." *Charities* 12, no. 32 (1904): 790–93.

Peiss, Kathy. *Cheap Amusements: Working Women and Leisure in Turn-of-the-Century New York.* Philadelphia: Temple University Press, 1986.

Peña, Manuel H. *The Texas-Mexican Conjunto: History of a Working-Class Music.* Austin: University of Texas Press, 1985.

Peretti, Burton. "Chief Amusements: New Work on the Centrality of Music and Leisure in City Culture." *Journal of Urban History* 24, no. 4 (1998): 534–41.

———. *The Creation of Jazz: Music, Race, and Culture in Urban America.* Urbana: University of Illinois Press, 1992.

Perry, Elisabeth I. "'The General Motherhood of the Commonwealth': Dance Hall Reform in the Progressive Era." *American Quarterly* 37, no. 5 (1985): 719–33.

Pierce, Bessie Louise. *A History of Chicago.* Vol. 2, *From Town to City.* New York: Knopf, 1940.

———. *A History of Chicago.* Vol. 3, *The Rise of a Modern City.* New York: Knopf, 1957.

Pittenger, Mark. "A World of Difference: Constructing the 'Underclass' in Progressive America." *American Quarterly* 49, no. 1 (1997): 26–65.

Plato. *The Republic of Plato*. Edited by Francis MacDonald Cornford. London: Oxford University Press, 1941.

Polacheck, Hilda Satt. *I Came a Stranger: The Story of a Hull-House Girl*. Urbana: University of Illinois Press, 1989.

Policy Research and Planning Department. *International Data on Public Spending on the Arts in Eleven Countries*. London: Arts Council of England, 1998.

Porter, Cecelia Hopkins. *The Rhine as Musical Metaphor: Cultural Identity in German Romantic Music*. Boston: Northeastern University Press, 1996.

Putnam, Robert. *Bowling Alone: The Collapse and Revival of American Community*. New York: Simon and Schuster, 2000.

Radano, Ronald. "Hot Fantasies: American Modernism and the Idea of Black Rhythm." In *Music and the Racial Imagination*, edited by Ronald Radano and Philip V. Bohlman, 459–80. Chicago: University of Chicago Press, 2000.

Radano, Ronald, and Philip V. Bohlman. "Music and Race, Their Past, Their Presence." In *Music and the Racial Imagination*, edited by Ronald Radano and Philip V. Bohlman, 1–53. Chicago: University of Chicago Press, 2000.

——, eds. *Music and the Racial Imagination*. Chicago: University of Chicago Press, 2000.

Rauch, John H. *Chicago Public Parks: Their Effects upon the Moral, Physical, and Sanitary Conditions of the Inhabitants of Large Cities with Special Reference to the City of Chicago*. Chicago: S. C. Griggs, 1869.

Reckless, Walter Cade. *Vice in Chicago*. Chicago: University of Chicago Press, 1933.

Reyes-Schramm, Adelaida. "Ethnic Music, the Urban Area, and Ethnomusicology." *Sociologus* 29 (1979): 1–17.

Rodgers, Daniel T. *Atlantic Crossings: Social Politics in a Progressive Age*. Cambridge, Mass.: Harvard University Press, 1998.

——. "In Search of Progressivism." *Reviews in American History* 10, no. 4 (1982): 113–32.

Roeder, George H. *The Censored War: American Visual Experience during World War Two*. New Haven: Yale University Press, 1993.

Roediger, David R. *The Wages of Whiteness*. London: Verso, 1991.

Rogin, Michael Paul. *Blackface, White Noise: Jewish Immigrants in the Hollywood Melting Pot*. Berkeley: University of California Press, 1996.

Roosevelt, Theodore. *Letters*. Cambridge, Mass.: Harvard University Press, 1951.

Rose, Tricia. *Black Noise: Rap Music and Black Culture in Contemporary America*. Hanover, N.H.: Wesleyan University Press, 1994.

Rosen, Philip T. *The Modern Stentors: Radio Broadcasting and the Federal Government, 1920–1934.* Westport, Conn.: Greenwood Press, 1980.

Rosenzweig, Roy. *Eight Hours for What We Will: Workers and Leisure in an Industrial City, 1870–1920.* New York: Cambridge University Press, 1983.

Rosenzweig, Roy, and Elizabeth Blackmar. *The Park and the People: A History of Central Park.* Ithaca: Cornell University Press, 1992.

Rothman, David J. *The Discovery of the Asylum: Social Order and Disorder in the New Republic.* Rev. ed. Boston: Little, Brown, 1990.

Ryan, Mary P. *Cradle of the Middle Class: The Family in Oneida County, New York, 1790–1865.* Cambridge: Cambridge University Press, 1990.

———. *Women in Public: Between Banners and Ballots, 1825–1880.* Baltimore: Johns Hopkins University Press, 1990.

Rydell, Robert W. *All the World's a Fair: Visions of Empire at American International Expositions, 1876–1916.* Chicago: University of Chicago Press, 1984.

Savage, Barbara Dianne. *Broadcasting Freedom: Radio, War, and the Politics of Race, 1938–1948.* Chapel Hill: University of North Carolina Press, 1999.

Sawislak, Karen. *Smoldering City: Chicagoans and the Great Fire, 1871–1874.* Chicago: University of Chicago Press, 1995.

Saxton, Alexander. *The Rise and Fall of the White Republic: Class Politics and Mass Culture in Nineteenth-Century America.* London: Verso, 1990.

Schabas, Ezra. *Theodore Thomas.* Urbana: University of Illinois Press, 1989.

Schenck, Janet. *Music Schools and Settlement Music Departments.* Boston: National Federation of Settlements, 1923.

Schick, Louis. *Chicago and its Environs.* Chicago: L. Schick, 1891.

Schneirov, Richard. *Labor and Urban Politics: Class Conflict and the Origins of Modern Liberalism in Chicago, 1864–97.* Urbana: University of Illinois Press, 1998.

Schoenfeld, Julia. "Commercial Recreation Legislation." *The Playground* 7, no. 12 (March 1914): 461–81.

Scholes, Percy Alfred, and Michael Kennedy. *The Concise Oxford Dictionary of Music.* 3d ed. New York: Oxford University Press, 1980.

Schumann, Robert, and Frances Malone Ritter. *Music and Musicians: Essays and Criticisms.* London: W. Reeves, 1891.

Schwartz, H. W. *Bands of America.* New York: Da Capo Press, 1975.

Scobey, David. "Anatomy of the Promenade: The Politics of Bourgeois Sociability in Nineteenth-Century New York." *Social History* 17, no. 2 (1992): 203–27.

Seligman, Alfred Lincoln. "Music for and by the Many." *Charities* 13, no. 19 (1905): 420–23.

Seltzer, George. *Music Matters.* Metuchen, N.J.: Scarecrow Press, 1989.

Sengstock, Charles, Jr. "Chicago's Dance Bands and Orchestras." *Chicago History* 16, no. 1 (1987): 25–37.

Sennett, Richard. *The Fall of Public Man*. New York: Norton, 1974.

Shaffer, Helen B. "Music in America." *Editorial Research Reports* 2, no. 22 (1956): 849–65.

Shiraishi, Fumiko. "Calvin Brainerd Cady: Thought and Feeling in the Study of Music." *Journal of Research in Music Education* 47, no. 2 (1999): 150–62.

Shulman, Holly Cowan. *The Voice of America: Propaganda and Democracy, 1941–1945*. Madison: University of Wisconsin Press, 1990.

Sinaiko, Herman. *Reclaiming the Canon: Essays in Philosophy, Poetry, and History*. New Haven: Yale University Press, 1998.

Sklar, Kathryn Kish. *Catharine Beecher: A Study in American Domesticity*. New Haven: Yale University Press, 1973.

———. *Florence Kelley and the Nation's Work: The Rise of Women's Political Culture, 1830–1900*. New Haven: Yale University Press, 1995.

———. "Hull House in the 1890s: A Community of Women Reformers." *Signs* 10 (Summer 1985): 658–77.

Small, Christopher. *Musicking: The Meanings of Performing and Listening*. Hanover: University Press of New England, 1998.

Smergalski, F. J. "Social Dancing in West Park Recreation Centers of Chicago, Illinois." *The Playground* 17 (January 1924): 544–47.

Smith, Bertha. "City Playgrounds." *Munsey's Magazine* 31, no. 2 (1904): 287–94.

Smith, Carl S. *Urban Disorder and the Shape of Belief: The Great Chicago Fire, the Haymarket Bomb, and the Model Town of Pullman*. Chicago: University of Chicago Press, 1995.

Smith, Catherine Parsons. "Symphony and Opera in Progressive-Era Los Angeles." In *Music and Culture in America, 1861–1914*, edited by Michael Saffle, 299–321. New York: Garland, 1998.

Smith, Eleanor. *The Eleanor Smith Music Course, Book 4*. New York: American Book Company, 1908.

Smith, Suzanne E. *Dancing in the Street: Motown and the Cultural Politics of Detroit*. Cambridge, Mass.: Harvard University Press, 1999.

Smulyan, Susan. "Radio Advertising to Women in Twenties America: 'A Latchkey to Every Home.'" *Historical Journal of Film, Radio, and Television* 13, no. 3 (1993): 299–314.

———. *Selling Radio: The Commercialization of American Broadcasting 1920–1934*. Washington, D.C.: Smithsonian Institution Press, 1994.

Snyder, Robert W. *The Voice of the City: Vaudeville and Popular Culture in New York*. New York: Oxford University Press, 1989.

Sollors, Werner. *Beyond Ethnicity: Consent and Descent in American Culture*. New York: Oxford University Press, 1986.

Southern, Eileen. *The Music of Black Americans: A History*. 3d ed. New York: Norton, 1997.

South Park Commissioners. "Proceedings." Vol. 10. 1907.

———. "Proceedings." Vol. 16. 1911.

———. "Proceedings." Vol. 21. 1914.

———. "Proceedings." Vol. 26. 1919.

———. "Proceedings." Vol. 31. 1924.

Spalding, W. R. "The Work of the Music School Settlement in Americanizing Its Patrons." *The Musician* 23 (August 1918): 533.

Spear, Allan H. *Black Chicago: The Making of a Negro Ghetto, 1890–1920*. Chicago: University of Chicago Press, 1967.

Special Park Commission of the City of Chicago. "Annual Report for Fiscal Year 1904." Chicago, 1905.

———. "Annual Report, 1908." Chicago, 1908.

———. "Report on Sites and Needs." Chicago: City of Chicago, 1902.

Spivey, Donald. *Union and the Black Musician: The Narrative of William Everett Samuels and Chicago Local 208*. Lanham, Md.: University Press of America, 1984.

Spottswood, Richard K. *Ethnic Music on Records: A Discography of Ethnic Recordings Produced in the United States, 1893 to 1942*. Urbana: University of Illinois Press, 1990.

Spratt, Margaret. "Beyond Hull House: New Interpretations of the Settlement Movement in America." *Journal of Urban History* 23, no. 6 (1997): 770–76.

Squires, Catherine. "Black Talk Radio: Defining Community Needs and Identity." *Harvard International Journal of Press/Politics* 5, no. 2 (2000): 73–96.

Stansell, Christine. *American Moderns: Bohemian New York and the Creation of a New Century*. New York: Metropolitan Books, 2000.

———. *City of Women: Sex and Class in New York, 1789–1860*. Urbana: University of Illinois Press, 1987.

Starr, S. Frederick, ed. *The Oberlin Book of Bandstands*. Washington, D.C.: Preservation Press, 1987.

Stokes, Martin. "Introduction: Ethnicity, Identity and Music." In *Ethnicity, Identity and Music*, edited by Martin Stokes, 1–27. Oxford: Berg, 1994.

Stowe, David W. *Swing Changes: Big-Band Jazz in New Deal America*. Cambridge, Mass.: Harvard University Press, 1994.

Stratton, Henry. "Music and Crime." *The Arena* 27 (January 1902): 137–49.

Streeter, Thomas. *Selling the Air: A Critique of the Policy of Commercial Broadcasting in the United States*. Chicago: University of Chicago Press, 1996.

Sugrue, Thomas. *The Origins of the Urban Crisis*. Princeton: Princeton University Press, 1996.

———. "The Structures of Urban Poverty: The Reorganization of Space and Work in Three Periods of American History." In *The "Underclass" De-*

bate: Views from History, edited by Michael B. Katz, 85–117. Princeton: Princeton University Press, 1993.

"Sunday Afternoon Concerts." *Hull-House Bulletin* 1, no. 5 (1896): 4.

Susman, Warren. *Culture as History: The Transformation of American Society in the Twentieth Century*. New York: Pantheon, 1984.

Tappan, Eva March, ed. *The World's Story: A History of the World in Story, Song and Art*. Vol. 7, *Germany, The Netherlands, and Switzerland*. Boston: Houghton Mifflin, 1914.

Tawa, Nicholas. *High-Minded and Low-Down: Music in the Lives of Americans, 1800–1861*. Boston: Northeastern University Press, 2000.

———. *Serenading the Reluctant Eagle*. New York: Schirmer, 1984.

———. *The Way to Tin Pan Alley: American Popular Song, 1866–1910*. New York: Schirmer, 1990.

Taylor, Graham. "The Police and Vice in Chicago." *The Survey* 23, (November 6, 1909): 160–65.

———. "Public Recreation Facilities: Recreation Developments in Chicago Parks." *Annals of the American Academy of Political and Social Science* 35, no. 2 (March 1910): 88–105.

Taylor, Paul Schuster. *Mexican Labor in the United States*. Vol. 2, no. 7, *Chicago and the Calumet Region*. Berkeley: University of California Press, 1928.

Teaford, Jon. *The Unheralded Triumph: City Government in America, 1870–1900*. Baltimore: Johns Hopkins University Press, 1984.

Teller, Charlotte. *The Cage*. New York: D. Appleton, 1907.

Tellstrom, A. Theodore. *Music in American Education, Past and Present*. New York: Holt, Rinehart and Winston, 1971.

Thomas, Helen. *Dance, Modernity, and Culture: Explorations in the Sociology of the Dance*. New York: Routledge, 1995.

Thomas, Rose Fay. *Memoirs of Theodore Thomas*. New York: Moffat, Yard, and Company, 1911.

Thompson, Emily. *The Soundscape of Modernity*. Cambridge, Mass.: MIT Press, 2002.

Thrasher, Frederic Milton, and James F. Short. *The Gang: A Study of 1,313 Gangs in Chicago*. Chicago: University of Chicago Press, 1963.

Tims, Margaret. *Jane Addams of Hull House, 1860–1935: A Centenary Study*. New York: Macmillan, 1961.

Tischler, Barbara. *An American Music: The Search for an American Musical Identity*. New York: Oxford University Press, 1986.

Todd, Arthur J., William F. Byron, and Howard L. Vierow. *The Chicago Recreation Survey, 1937*. Vol. 1, *Public Recreation*. Chicago: City of Chicago, 1937.

———. *The Chicago Recreation Survey, 1937*. Vol. 2, *Commercial Recreation*. Chicago: City of Chicago, 1937.

Tomlins, William. "Moral Forces in Music." *American Art Journal* 61, no. 14 (October 1893): 625–26.

Trachtenberg, Alan, and Eric Foner. *The Incorporation of America: Culture and Society in the Gilded Age.* New York: Hill and Wang, 1982.

Travis, Dempsey. *An Autobiography of Black Jazz.* Chicago: Urban Institute Press, 1983.

Trolander, Judith Ann. *Professionalism and Social Change: From the Settlement House Movement to Neighborhood Centers, 1886 to the Present.* New York: Columbia University Press, 1987.

Tucher, Andie. *Froth and Scum: Truth, Beauty, Goodness, and the Ax Murder in America's First Mass Medium.* Chapel Hill: University of North Carolina Press, 1994.

Tuttle, William M. *Race Riot: Chicago in the Red Summer of 1919.* New York: Atheneum, 1970.

U.S. Bureau of the Census. *Eleventh Census of the United States: 1890.* Vol. 1. Washington, D.C.: Government Printing Office, 1890.

———. *Thirteenth Census of the United States: 1910.* Vol. 2. Washington, D.C.: Government Printing Office, n.d.

U.S. Congress. House Committee on Government Operations. Government Activities and Transportation Subcommittee. *Interrelationship of Federal and State Funding for the Arts in Illinois: Joint Hearing before Certain Sub-committees of the Committee on Government Operations and the Committee on Education and Labor, House of Representatives.* 98th Cong., 1st sess., June 17, 1983. Washington, D.C.: Government Printing Office, 1983.

U.S. Federal Radio Commission. *Second Annual Report of the Federal Radio Commission.* Washington, D.C.: Government Printing Office, 1928.

———. *Sixth Annual Report of the Federal Radio Commission.* Washington, D.C.: Government Printing Office, 1932.

Upton, George. *Musical Memories.* Chicago: A. C. McClurg, 1908.

———. "Musical Societies of the United States and Their Representation at the World's Fair." *Scribner's,* July 1893, 68–83.

———, ed. *Theodore Thomas: A Musical Autobiography.* 2 vols. Chicago: A. C. McClurg, 1905.

Vaillant, Derek. "Radio." In *Encyclopedia of American Cultural and Intellectual History,* edited by Mary Kupiec Cayton and Peter W. Williams, 515–26. New York: Scribner, 2001.

———. "Sounds of Whiteness: Local Radio, Racial Formation, and Public Culture in Chicago, 1921–1935." *American Quarterly* 54, no. 1 (March 2002): 25–66.

———. " 'Your Voice Came in Last Night but It Sounded a Little Scared': Rural Radio Listening, Progressivism, and 'Talking Back' in Wisconsin, 1920–1932." In *Radio Reader,* edited by Michele Hilmes and Jason Loviglio, 63–88. New York: Routledge, 2001.

Vander Weele, Maribeth. *Reclaiming Our Schools: The Struggle for Chicago School Reform*. Chicago: Loyola University Press, 1994.

Vice Commission of Chicago. *The Social Evil in Chicago: A Study of Existing Conditions with Recommendations by the Vice Commission of Chicago*. 1911; reprint, New York: Arno Press, 1976.

Von Eschen, Penny M. " 'Satchmo Blows Up the World': Jazz, Race, and Empire during the Cold War." In *"Here, There, and Everywhere": The Foreign Politics of American Popular Culture*, edited by Reinhold Wagnleitner and Elaine Tyler May, 163–78. Hanover: University Press of America, 2000.

Wagner, Ann. *Adversaries of Dance: From the Puritans to the Present*. Urbana: University of Illinois Press, 1997.

Wagnleitner, Reinhold. "The Empire of Fun, or Talkin' Soviet Union Blues: The Sound of Freedom and U.S. Cultural Hegemony in Europe." *Diplomatic History* 23, no. 3 (1999): 499–524.

Wald, Gayle Freda. *Crossing the Line: Racial Passing in Twentieth-Century U.S. Literature and Culture*. Durham, N.C.: Duke University Press, 2000.

Weinrott, Lester. "Chicago Radio: The Glory Days." *Chicago History* 3, no. 1 (1974): 14–22.

Westbrook, Robert. "Fighting for the American Family." In *The Power of Culture: Critical Essays in American History*, edited by Richard Wightman Fox and T. J. Jackson Lears, 195–221. Chicago: University of Chicago Press, 1993.

West Chicago Park Commissioners. "Playgrounds and Recreation Centers of the West Chicago Park Commissioners." 1917.

——. "Recreation Centres, Playgrounds, and Swimming Pools of the West Chicago Park Commissioners." 1919.

——. "Report of the Committee to Study Sites for Additional Small Parks and Pleasure Grounds in the West Park District." In *Proceedings of the Board of West Park Commissioners*. Chicago: West Chicago Park Commissioners, 1911.

Whisnant, David E. *All That Is Native and Fine: The Politics of Culture in an American Region*. Chapel Hill: University of North Carolina Press, 1983.

Whitefield, George. *George Whitefield's Journals, 1737–1741*. New York: William Wale, 1905.

Whitesitt, Linda. "Women as 'Keepers of Culture': Music Clubs, Community Concert Series, and Symphony Orchestras." In *Cultivating Music in America: Women Patrons and Activists since 1860*, edited by Ralph Locke and Cyrilla Barr, 65–86. Berkeley: University of California Press, 1997.

Wiebe, Robert H. *The Search for Order, 1877–1920*. New York: Hill and Wang, 1967.

Wik, Reynold. "The USDA and the Development of Radio." *Agricultural History* 62 (Summer 1988).

Williamson, Joel. *A Rage for Order: Black/White Relations in the American South since Emancipation*. New York: Oxford University Press, 1986.

Wilson, Samuel Paynter. *Chicago and Its Cess-pools of Infamy*. Chicago: n.p., [1910–15].

——. *Chicago by Gaslight*. Chicago, [1910].

Wilson, William H. *The City Beautiful Movement*. Baltimore: Johns Hopkins University Press, 1989.

Wilson, William J. *The Truly Disadvantaged*. Chicago: University of Chicago Press, 1987.

Woods, Robert A., and Albert J. Kennedy. *The Settlement Horizon: A National Estimate*. New York: Russell Sage Foundation, 1922.

Woodward, C. Vann. *The Strange Career of Jim Crow*. 3d rev. ed. New York: Oxford University Press, 1974.

Works Progress Administration. "Achievements of W.P.A. Workers in Illinois, July 1st 1935–June 30th 1938." Information Service, WPA, Illinois, 1938.

Wright, Gwendolyn. *Moralism and the Model Home: Domestic Architecture and Cultural Conflict in Chicago, 1873–1913*. Chicago: University of Chicago Press, 1980.

Wyszomirski, Margaret Jane. "From Accord to Discord: Arts Policy during and after the Culture Wars." In *America's Commitment to Culture: Government and the Arts*, edited by Kevin V. Mulcahy and Margaret Jane Wyszomirski, 1–46. Boulder, Colo.: Westview Press, 1995.

Yezierska, Anzia. "The Free Vacation House." In *Immigrant Women*, edited by Maxine Schwartz Seller, 199–205. Albany: State University of New York Press, 1994.

Zanzig, Augustus D. *Music in American Life, Present and Future*. New York: Oxford University Press, 1932.

Zglenicki, Leon Thaddeus. *Poles of Chicago, 1837–1937: A History of One Century of Polish Contribution to the City of Chicago, Illinois*. Chicago: Polish Pageant, 1937.

Zorbaugh, Harvey. *The Gold Coast and the Slum: A Sociological Study of Chicago's Near North Side*. 1929. Reprint, Chicago: University of Chicago Press, 1983.

Zuck, Barbara A. *A History of Musical Americanism*. Ann Arbor, Mich.: University Microfilms International, 1980, 1978.

Zukin, Sharon. *Loft Living: Culture and Capital in Urban Change*. New Brunswick, N.J.: Rutgers University Press, 1989.

UNPUBLISHED SOURCES

Anderson, Paul G. "The Good to Be Done." Ph.D. diss., University of Chicago, 1988.

Bekken, Jon Everett. "Working-Class Newspapers, Community and Consciousness in Chicago, 1880–1930." Ph.D. diss., University of Illinois, 1992.

Cords, Nicholas John. "Music in Social Settlement and Community Music Schools, 1893–1939: A Democratic-Esthetic Approach to Music Culture." Ph.D. diss., University of Minnesota, 1970.

Devick, Royce Devon. "Orlando Blackman: A Study of His Contribution to Music Education in the Chicago Public Schools (1863–1899)." Ph.D. diss., University of Iowa, 1972.

Feldman, Mary Ann J. "George P. Upton: Journalist, Music Critic and Mentor to Early Chicago." Ph.D. diss., University of Minnesota, 1983.

Green, Shannon. " 'Art for Life's Sake': Music Schools and Activities in U.S. Social Settlement Houses, 1892–1942." Ph.D. diss., University of Wisconsin, 1990.

Knapp, Richard F. "Play for America: The National Recreation Association, 1906–1950." Ph.D. diss., Duke University, 1971.

Lichty, Lawrence. "A Study of the Careers and Qualifications of Members of the Federal Radio Commission." M.A. thesis, Ohio State University, 1961.

McCarthy, Eugene Ray. "The Bohemians in Chicago and Their Benevolent Societies, 1875–1946." M.A. thesis, University of Chicago, 1950.

Mistak, Alvin Frank. "A General History of Instrumental Music in the Chicago Public Schools, 1900–1950." Ph.D. diss., University of Iowa, 1969.

Nicholson, Jon Seymour. "Patrick Gilmore's Boston Peace Jubilees." Ph.D. diss., University of Michigan, 1971.

Osborn, Marian. "The Development of Recreation in the South Park System of Chicago." M.A. thesis, University of Chicago, 1928.

Reagan, Ann B. "Art Music in Milwaukee in the Late Nineteenth Century, 1850–1900." Ph.D. diss., University of Wisconsin, 1980.

Riley, Thomas James. "A Study of the Higher Life of Chicago." Ph.D. diss., University of Chicago, 1905.

Rode, Glenn G. "The Concert Band in Chicago from 1893 to 1985." M.A. thesis, Northeastern Illinois University, 1985.

Schleis, Thomas Henry. "Opera in Milwaukee: 1850–1900." M.A. thesis, University of Wisconsin, 1974.

Stern, Mark J. "Working Paper #9: Is All the World Philadelphia?: A Multicity Study of Arts and Cultural Organizations, Diversity, and Urban Revitalization." Social Impact of the Arts Project, School of Social Work, University of Pennsylvania, 1999.

Vaillant, Derek. "Staying in the Black: Music, Identity, and the Merger of Local 208." M.A. thesis, University of Chicago, 1993.

INDEX